Foundation Flash Applications for Mobile Devices

Richard Leggett
Weyert de Boer
Scott Janousek

friendsof
DESIGNER TO DESIGNER™
an Apress® company

Foundation Flash Applications
for Mobile Devices

ISBN-13: 978-1-59059-558-9

ISBN-10: 1-59059-558-0

Printed and bound in the United States of America 9 8 7 6 5 4 3 2 1

Trademarked names may appear in this book. Rather than use a trademark symbol with every occurrence of a trademarked name, we use the names only in an editorial fashion and to the benefit of the trademark owner, with no intention of infringement of the trademark.

Java™ and all Java-based marks are trademarks or registered trademarks of Sun Microsystems, Inc., in the United States and other countries.

Apress, Inc., is not affiliated with Sun Microsystems, Inc., and this book was written without endorsement from Sun Microsystems, Inc.

Distributed to the book trade worldwide by Springer-Verlag New York, Inc., 233 Spring Street, 6th Floor, New York, NY 10013. Phone 1-800-SPRINGER, fax 201-348-4505, e-mail orders-ny@springer-sbm.com, or visit www.springeronline.com.

For information on translations, please contact Apress directly at 2560 Ninth Street, Suite 219, Berkeley, CA 94710.

Phone 510-549-5930, fax 510-549-5939, e-mail info@apress.com, or visit www.apress.com.

The information in this book is distributed on an "as is" basis, without warranty. Although every precaution has been taken in the preparation of this work, neither the author(s) nor Apress shall have any liability to any person or entity with respect to any loss or damage caused or alleged to be caused directly or indirectly by the information contained in this work.

The source code for this book is freely available to readers at www.friendsofed.com in the Downloads section.

Credits

Lead Editor
Chris Mills

Technical Reviewers
Marco Casario
Cesar Tardaguila

Editorial Board
Steve Anglin, Ewan Buckingham,
Gary Cornell, Jason Gilmore,
Jonathan Gennick, Jonathan Hassell,
James Huddleston, Chris Mills,
Matthew Moodie, Dominic Shakeshaft,
Jim Sumser, Matt Wade

Project Manager | Production Director
Grace Wong

Copy Edit Manager
Nicole Flores

Copy Editors
Heather Lang
Damon Larson

Assistant Production Director
Kari Brooks-Copony

Production Editor
Laura Esterman

Compositor
Diana Van Winkle

Artist
April Milne

Proofreaders
Liz Welch
Lori Bring

Indexer
Toma Mulligan

Cover Image Designer
Corné van Dooren

Interior and Cover Designer
Kurt Krames

Manufacturing Director
Tom Debolski

CONTENTS AT A GLANCE

CONTENTS

Chapter 6 **Mobile Gaming** **185**

ABOUT THE AUTHORS

Richard Leggett has over six years experience with Flash and currently holds the position of senior creative developer at AKQA, London. His passion for everything new is the very thing that led him to Flash Lite in the first place, as Leggett believes mobile technology is the next frontier and the next step in the logical progression of the Web's expansion into every aspect of our lives. He has spoken at several industry conferences including Spark, Flashforward, and the very first Flash on the Beach, as well as being interviewed in magazine articles on the subject of Flash and occasionally speaking at user groups in his native country, the United Kingdom. Leggett tries to remain heavily involved in the Flash community, and you can find him online in the Flash Lite Yahoo Group as well as at his personal web sites: www.richardleggett.co.uk and www.flashmobileforum.org.

Weyert de Boer is a New Media designer and developer, currently working as a freelancer in the Netherlands. He has a wide range of skills, including over six years of experience with Flash and several years of .NET and Delphi programming under his belt. He has been working in the field of mobile application development for two years and enjoys it particularly because of his interest in the limitations of mobile devices and how to solve the problems associated with mobile content delivery. He has been a Borland Technology Partner for five years.

Aside from his freelance work, he is also currently studying for his bachelor degree in interaction design and cultural anthropology. He will speak at WebDU in 2007 and likes to share his passion for development with other people around the world on his blog, found at www.innerfuse.biz/blog.

Scott Janousek is a Flash and Flash Mobile developer currently working in the Boston area of the United States. In addition to his experience with mobile development, Scott has an accumulated ten years' of diverse software engineering and Web consulting background, and several of those years were dedicated to the creation of interactive multimedia, including CD-ROMs, DVDs, webcasts, kiosks, RIAs, and web sites.

Today, Scott is an Adobe Certified Flash Designer and Developer, as well as a recognized Flash Lite Subject Matter Expert. In addition, he is also an Adobe Certified Instructor for Flash Lite and Adobe Certified Developer for Mobile Application Development. He holds a bachelor's degree in computer science from the University of Massachusetts, Amherst.

An active and contributing member of the Boston Adobe Mobile and Devices User Group (AMaDUG), Boston Flash Platform User Group (BFPUG), and Mobile Monday Boston (MoMoBoston), Scott is passionate about the Flash platform across mobile devices as well as for the desktop. When he has a chance, he speaks at new media institutes, user groups, and conferences about Flash and Flash Mobile, including most recently the Design & Technology Festival (FITC) 2006, Adobe MAX 2006, and Adobe MAX Asia Pacific 2006. He has also written a number of technical articles on Flash Mobile technologies, such as Flash Lite, including some of which can be found on the Adobe Developer Center web site. Check out his blog at www.scottjanousek.com/blog for more information about his latest Flash and Mobile endeavors, as well as his occasional post about the latest and greatest portable consumer electronic devices.

ABOUT THE MAIN TECHNICAL REVIEWER

Marco Casario is a dynamic developer in the Adobe (formerly Macromedia) world. He's an Adobe Certified Instructor in Flex and Flash Lite (Flash and Dreamweaver certified), and he collaborates extensively with Adobe Italy as a speaker and promoter of several events and road shows.

Marco has recently found Comtaste SRL (www.comtaste.com), a company dedicated to exploring new frontiers in the rich Internet application field, where accessibility and usability have added further importance to the PDF format and the relevant Acrobat application tools.

He's also the founder of the most-populated Flash Lite Group (http://groups.yahoo.com/group/FlashLite), which reaches more than 1200 active users. Learn more about Marco Casario at his blog entitled "hands on Adobe world" (http://casario.blogs.com), which currently receives several thousands of unique visitors every day.

ABOUT THE COVER IMAGE DESIGNER

Corné van Dooren designed the front cover image for this book. Having been given a brief by friends of ED to create a new design for the Foundation series, he was inspired to create this new setup combining technology and organic forms.

With a colorful background as an avid cartoonist, Corné discovered the infinite world of multimedia at the age of 17—a journey of discovery that hasn't stopped since. His mantra has always been "The only limit to multimedia is the imagination," a mantra that is keeping him moving forward constantly.

After enjoying success after success over the past years—working for many international clients, as well as being featured in multimedia magazines, testing software, and working on many other friends of ED books—Corné decided it was time to take another step in his career by launching his own company, Project 79, in March 2005.

You can see more of his work and contact him through www.cornevandooren.com or www.project79.com.

If you like his work, be sure to check out his chapter in *New Masters of Photoshop: Volume 2*, also by friends of ED (2004, ISBN: 1-59059-315-4).

ACKNOWLEDGMENTS

I imagine it is not unusual that there are far too many people to thank. It has been a very long journey, and of course, we didn't want to release the book unless it contained the latest and greatest information on mobile Flash technologies. The only thing is that Adobe developers are far too good at what they do, and they kept releasing newer and better versions of Flash Lite at a pace equal to our writing! In the end all is well, and as a result, hopefully this book is more complete and stands in better stead for the future by covering a broader range of up-to-date topics and technologies than it may have originally.

I'd like to give my gratitude, indeed, to all of the great and patient people at friends of ED: to Chris Mills, Grace Wong, Laura Esterman, and Heather Lang for all their professional help and guidance through the whole process.

Also, my thanks go out to Scott and Weyert, my coauthors, who stepped in with their wealth of knowledge to make sure this book had everything it needed.

Of course, finally, I'd like to thank my girlfriend, friends, and family for being supportive and for understanding why I just didn't have time . . . well, some things never change!

Richard Leggett

INTRODUCTION

It's always great to see people's faces when they copy their first Flash Lite applications or games onto their phones and press Run. The reaction is usually, "Wow!" Even something that would appear trivial when viewed on a web site somehow looks wholly impressive when running on that little color screen in your hand. By picking up this book, you're guaranteed to experience this moment for yourself.

The aims of this book are to build on your current skill level—whether you're a beginner with no experience with Flash or an advanced coder with years of web programming prowess—and to give you the skills you need to create great content for mobile devices. At first, mobile Flash development might seem like a no brainer; you may have heard that you can just throw your Flash at the phone, and it just works—that's only half true. Creating content for devices carries with it a world of new limitations and possibilities, and it may require you to change how you think about users. On top of that, you are given new functionality to play with that can enrich the experience and give users what they really need, wherever they may be at the time.

The chapters in this book will cover how to build and run your first Flash Lite applications, how to structure and optimize them as well as how to employ user interface controls when you have no mouse to rely on, consume web services, and control Apple's iTunes. You'll also see how to program games full of not only graphics and sounds, but math and physics to boot. There's more to Flash than games and applications; you'll also discover mobile-specific genres of wallpapers, screensavers, and animated ring tones. The final chapters discuss how to go about getting your content out there in the real world, how to make money from it, and of course, some important predictions for the future.

Examples

There are many examples throughout this book. Some of the code is for Flash Lite 1.X, some for Flash Lite 2.X. The aim is to give you detailed introductions to programming for both of these platforms, as well as some general Flash knowledge, including a primer on ActionScript 2, which covers classes, inheritance, and (dare I say?) _root assimilation (you'll see!). Fear not; each topic is accompanied by a working example that you can modify piece by piece.

In addition to smaller files containing illustrated examples of specific bits of code, we have also included full examples of several applications and games for you to dig into, as well as any server-side elements they use, written in Java, .NET, ColdFusion, and PHP. Flash Lite works with all these and more. The aim is to give you something concrete to take apart and extend at your leisure, beyond the theory and illustrations contained in the book.

To obtain this book's code examples, please visit http://www.friendsofed.com/downloads.html.

Layout conventions

To keep this book as clear and easy to follow as possible, the following text conventions are used throughout.

Important words or concepts are normally highlighted on the first appearance in **bold type**.

Code is presented in `fixed-width font`.

New or changed code is normally presented in **`bold fixed-width font`**.

Pseudo-code and variable input are written in *`italic fixed-width font`*.

Menu commands are written in the form Menu ➤ Submenu ➤ Submenu.

Where I want to draw your attention to something, I've highlighted it like this:

> *Ahem, don't say I didn't warn you.*

Sometimes code won't fit on a single line in a book. Where this happens, I use an arrow like this: ➥.

```
This is a very long section of code that should be written all on the same ➥
line without a break.
```

Part One

GETTING STARTED

Part One of this book is composed of four chapters: an overview of Flash, an introduction to mobile devices and associated technologies, and in-depth looks at Flash Lite 1.1, Flash Lite 2.0, and ActionScript. These core topics provide a gentle introduction to the subject of Flash for mobile devices and will get you started creating content for your devices in no time at all.

Chapter 1

MACROMEDIA AND ADOBE FLASH: AN OVERVIEW

Let me first explain the vagueness of this title. Throughout the book, I use "Macromedia" when referring to Flash releases prior to 2006, and "Adobe" for those thereafter. The "Macromedia" name has been sitting in front of the word "Flash" for the past six years, but times have changed, and you are about to see just how!

You may already use Flash on a daily basis, or you may have heard of it or played a few Flash games on a web site and are not completely sure what it can be used for or where its strengths lie. Whatever your situation, reevaluating just what *you* think Flash is and where it is heading is always beneficial. Many descriptions have been given to Flash over the years, ranging from "vector animation tool" and "web-design tool" all the way to "rich Internet platform." Well, Flash is all of these things and more. These descriptions vary greatly, because Flash is always changing—being used for new things and going in completely new and interesting directions. This evolutionary nature has never been truer than right now.

Perhaps one of the most interesting areas of Flash's evolution is the mobile sector—after all, that is the main focus of this book. Flash provides one of the most versatile cross-platform development environments available today. Leveraging mobile technology puts Flash in a position of power over rival technologies; your mobile applications can now communicate with desktop clients and server applications with minimal effort and without requiring two teams of developers to cater to the different platforms. Scaling also becomes less of an issue than it was previously. A desktop version of a chat application might include full-motion, face-to-face video, whereas the mobile version might deal solely with the text side of the chat; still, everyone is communicating in the same room, breaking down previous technological barriers. The future of mobile Flash is even brighter when you consider the ever-more-powerful features being added to the Flash Player and the mobile devices themselves, including high-speed networks, video cameras, biometrics, and more powerful processors.

This chapter discusses the following topics:

- A brief history of Flash
- ActionScript
- Rich Internet Applications (RIAs)
- Peripheral Flash technologies (for example, Flash Communication Server)
- Mobile Flash
- The future

A brief history of Flash

Knowing where Flash came from helps in understanding its underlying strengths and how it fits together as a development platform.

Flash started life as just a glint in the eye of Jonathan Gay. Gay spent his high school years programming Apple computers—writing games and drawing tools. He went on to write some very popular titles, including the Dark Castle game series. He later worked on a product named SmartSketch, a drawing package that was later given the ability to add animation to web pages through Netscape's plug-in API. SmartSketch became SmartSketch Animator, then CelAnimator, and just before shipping, FutureSplash. FutureSplash began to get noticed by some very big names. Disney and Microsoft both adopted it for its unrivaled TV-like feel, using it for animation in revolutionary new sites like Disney Online and MSN. It doesn't take a genius to figure out that the name FutureSplash next evolved into Flash, a name we know so well. Macromedia bought into the idea in December 1996, Flash 1.0 was born, and the Web would never be the same again.

Over the next few years Flash progressed through versions 2 and 3, and, eventually, to version 4. Something interesting was happening all over the Web—people were using Flash for more than just animation. Macromedia Flash 2 and 3 introduced basic scripting abilities that meant content could become a little bit more dynamic than other content on the Web at the time. Flash 4 improved greatly upon this scripting with the ability to write expressions, dynamically alter the position and properties of graphical elements at runtime, and even respond to user input while all of this was going on.

The conception of Flash 4 is often seen as the golden age in Flash history. Some very familiar names such as Colin Moock, Manuel Clement (www.mano1.com), Yugo Nakamura (www.yugop.com), and Samuel Wan rose to god status. Some people were even writing 3-D engines in Flash 4 (see Figure 1-1 for an example); some of this content can still be found at sites such as www.FlashKit.com. I don't have enough pages here to list all of the great innovators of the Flash movement, but my thanks go out to all of them.

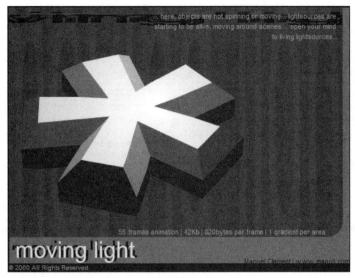

Figure 1-1 Mano1's 3-D experiments in Flash 4

Once the seeds of the Flash flora had been sown, it was just a matter of time before it outgrew its animation roots. Although many still consider it the best technology for displaying animation on the Web, Flash started to take on a new role in the creation of anything from guestbooks to full-blown e-shops. Macromedia coined the term **Rich Internet Application** (RIA) to describe a rich, web-deployed client capable of real-time and asynchronous interaction with a server, providing all manner of possibilities. Flash had the ability to maintain state on the client, which traditional HTML applications envied, but it also had the ability to present to an astonishing (and skyrocketing) number of desktops rich graphics, sounds, dynamic charts, and fully interactive experiences containing a variety of combined information and media.

As Flash's popularity increased, more and more people jumped on the bandwagon, using Flash for personal sites, advertisements, and banners. This upsurge in usage led to a grim era in Flash evolution. Flash's reputation was hit hard by bloated sites with lengthy introductions, perpetual preloaders, and repetitive background music—not to mention the pop-up advertisements that appeared right over the news you were trying to read. People fed up with the few web developers who exploited Flash's power for intrusive and klugdy uses began to employ Flash content blockers and to avoid sites using Flash altogether. But things soon started to improve. Developers realized that, even with super-fast broadband connections, users just wanted to see the content or information they came for with no fanfare, bells, or whistles in most cases. As a result, Flash began to be used as it should be used—to provide a richer experience than what is achievable through traditional web technologies. Later versions of the Flash Integrated Development Environment (IDE) and Flash Player attracted developers from many backgrounds, not just designers but Java, C++, and Visual Basic programmers to name a few. These developers demanded professional tools for large-scale projects, and that is exactly what they got with Flash MX 2004, Flex, and the wealth of third-party tools now available. Figure 1-2 shows the Flash product timeline from FutureSplash to today.

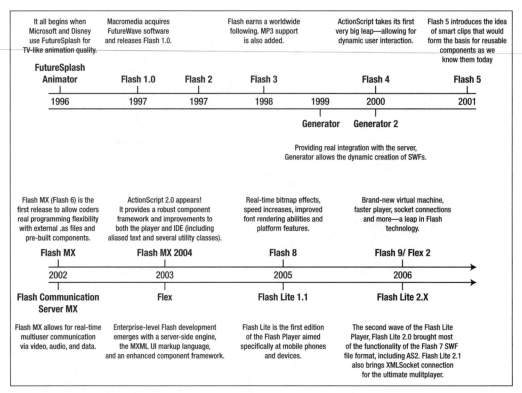

The following text appears within the timeline figure:

It all begins when Microsoft and Disney use FutureSplash for TV-like animation quality.

Macromedia acquires FutureWave software and releases Flash 1.0.

Flash earns a worldwide following. MP3 support is also added.

ActionScript takes its first very big leap—allowing for dynamic user interaction.

Flash 5 introduces the idea of smart clips that would form the basis for reusable components as we know them today

FutureSplash Animator	Flash 1.0	Flash 2	Flash 3		Flash 4	Flash 5
1996	1997	1997	1998	1999	2000	2001

Generator   Generator 2

Providing real integration with the server, Generator allows the dynamic creation of SWFs.

Flash MX (Flash 6) is the first release to allow coders real programming flexibility with external .as files and pre-built components.

ActionScript 2.0 appears! It provides a robust component framework and improvements to both the player and IDE (including aliased text and several utility classes).

Real-time bitmap effects, speed increases, improved font rendering abilities and platform features.

Brand-new virtual machine, faster player, socket connections and more—a leap in Flash technology.

Flash MX	Flash MX 2004	Flash 8	Flash 9/ Flex 2
2002	2003	2005	2006
Flash Communication Server MX	Flex	Flash Lite 1.1	Flash Lite 2.X

Flash MX allows for real-time multiuser communication via video, audio, and data.

Enterprise-level Flash development emerges with a server-side engine, the MXML UI markup language, and an enhanced component framework.

Flash Lite is the first edition of the Flash Player aimed specifically at mobile phones and devices.

The second wave of the Flash Lite Player, Flash Lite 2.0 brought most of the functionality of the Flash 7 SWF file format, including AS2. Flash Lite 2.1 also brings XMLSocket connection for the ultimate mulitplayer.

Figure 1-2 The Flash product timeline

Designers who use Flash are now experiencing what some call a second, or even third, golden age of Flash development. The tools have matured, the enthusiasm is still there, and the community spirit is greater than ever. With Flash, the possibilities are endless—not even Adobe knows everything that the user community has planned for their treasured technology.

ActionScript

ActionScript is at the heart of the Flash Player. It is the language that powers the logic and interaction that takes place on screen. More than just the player and the IDE have been evolving; ActionScript has undergone many transformations and changes itself since it was first introduced with Flash 2 in 2000. Macromedia has added support for new constructs, objects, and properties with every version. The new face of ActionScript is that of a cleaner, faster, and more manageable beast.

With Flash 4, ActionScript scripting came into its own, giving designers the ability to add logic to their sites and to begin experimenting with math and physics. This release was followed shortly by ActionScript 1.0 for Flash 5, a flexible programming language based on ECMA Script Language Specification, Edition 3 (ECMA-262), the language specification also used for JavaScript 1.5. Building on this standard meant developers could quickly acclimatize to the syntax. They soon started developing extensions to the core objects to provide more functionality (commonly known as **prototypes**) and full-blown components to fill almost any need from color pickers to data grids. ActionScript 2.0 took designers even further, allowing true object-oriented programming with class-based inheritance, inter-faces, exceptions, and access levels for methods and member variables, making it more familiar to Java and C# programmers. Design patterns began to find their way into Flash applications, its code base, and even Macromedia's supplied classes, all of which led to coding standards being formed by the Flash community—a true sign of Flash's maturity. With Flash 9 (a new virtual machine) and Adobe's purchase of Macromedia, Flash has been taken to a whole new level, with stricter programming and a runtime debugger. The time to begin a career in this technology has never been better.

Object-oriented programming

You could argue that some form of object-oriented programming was possible with ActionScript in Flash 4. You could mimic objects using movie clips, store methods in frames, and execute the code with the call() function. However, this functionality wasn't really object-oriented programming as we think of it today; it was merely a strange hybrid of structural programming and movie-clip-based hier-archy. With Flash 5, Macromedia gave us the language that resembles the ActionScript we are used to writing today. ActionScript 1.0 was a prototype-based language. This type of language differs from a class-based language in that in a prototype-based language an object can contain both data and behaviors (there's no real distinction between a class and an instance of a class). You can even dynam-ically change the class of an object at runtime. In ActionScript, everything is an object; you can call string methods on a string *literal* simply by wrapping the string literal in parentheses and adding .methodName() to the end, for example, ("hello").indexOf("o"). All sorts of object-oriented tricks can be employed in a prototype-based language, including inheritance, composition, and even some tricks that simply aren't possible in class-based languages like Java, such as adding methods to an already established class. While this prototype-based approach is very well suited for user interface (UI) development and environments with tight memory constraints, it isn't the best for large-scale applications, which might be a reason that ActionScript 2.0 was created.

ActionScript 2.0

ActionScript underwent what, at first, might appear to be a complete overhaul in Flash MX 2004, which heralded the introduction of ActionScript 2.0 (AS2).

AS2 is an ECMA-262 Edition 4 implementation that allows fully object-oriented programming. Most of the code you write in ActionScript 2 looks just like Java, barring a few syntax differences. Many of the practices associated with Java or C# development can also be ported to ActionScript (for more infor-mation, see *Design Patterns: Elements of Reusable Object-Oriented Software* by Erich Gamma, Richard Helm, Ralph Johnson, and John Vlissides [Addison-Wesley, 1995]). In fact, AS2 offers a whole new way of working. You have been able to include code in separate .as files since Flash 5, but with AS2 you can build huge libraries of reusable code that can be shared among many developers and projects, managed with source control systems, and extended without fear of underlying functionality being altered. For a shining example of this just look at the AS2lib project at www.as2lib.org that aims to provide a fully functional, common, standard library on par with the Java class library or the C++ stan-dard template library, providing utility classes, tools for unit testing, reflection, and in the future, GUI components.

ActionScript 3.0

Although this book has little to do with ActionScript 3.0 (AS3), focusing instead on the mobile profiles of the player, I think it's good to include AS3 for posterity. AS3 is the third incarnation of the

ActionScript language and a rung higher up the evolutionary ladder of an ideal programming language. With Flex Builder 2 and Flash 9 on the way, AS3 provides a more logical way of scripting. It provides more powerful programming constructs and a core language structure, with things like event dispatching being built in as core language objects (as opposed to being bolted on as in previous versions). Coupled with a completely rewritten player, Flash Player 8.5, AS3 allows you to do more than ever before including writing low-level protocols, using Sockets and ByteArrays, and visually superior games and applications.

The term "design pattern" is familiar to most developers. Introduced in the 1995 text *Design Patterns*, a **design pattern** can be described as a standard solution for solving a common problem in software design. Although you have always been able to use design patterns in ActionScript 1.0, with ActionScript 2.0 and 3.0, the class-based syntax allows for easy visualization and implementation of these practices in real-world projects. Adobe even includes a few commonly used design patterns in the event listener model present in AS2 components and utility classes, such as mx.utils.Delegate, which allows for a callback function to be run in the scope of another object to help maintain code readability. Other common design patterns used frequently in ActionScript development include the observer pattern, the delegate event model, model-view-controller architecture, and the iterator. Having standard ways of doing things in Flash rapidly speeds up development times; there's no point in reinventing the wheel.

Rich Internet Applications

With the advent of Flash 5 and MX the ability to create truly robust web applications finally became a reality. The stateless nature of the Web didn't lend itself to creating rich user experiences like those found in desktop applications, but Flash came along and provided the mechanism to display text, graphics, and video and to maintain information on the client, dynamically requesting information from a database behind the scenes via a server-side programming language such as ASP.NET, JSP, PHP, or ColdFusion. The player got faster in many ways as it matured, while keeping the critical download size as small as possible. Macromedia started to make drastic improvements to the player to increase its speed and to open opportunities for developers to create inspirational sites (see Figure 1-3 for an example). The XML object was converted to a native data type in Flash Player 6, which meant the new player blazed through data received from a web service, file store, or server-side script.

New possibilities, such as real-time, multiuser chats, began to be exploited across the globe. The XMLSocket class allowed two-way communication with socket servers written in Java, Perl, or even PHP, and third parties began to make tools to interface with a Flash client, providing detailed APIs to aid development. Macromedia also introduced smart clips in Flash 5, which matured into fully functional user interface components in Flash MX. These components included buttons, validated text input fields, pie charts, and data grids. Best of all, you could view the source for a component and extend the functionality to meet any need without having to write your own component from scratch. The version 2 component architecture, introduced in Flash MX 2004, provides a flexible yet powerful base for creating and extending components. This base allows developer communities to discuss common issues and solutions because of the shared, standardized nature of the architecture. Third parties have also created both open source and commercial component frameworks that are compatible with the Macromedia component architecture yet provide extra functionality, speed, and corrections for some of the things found lacking in the original architecture.

The Flash Player has become *the* vessel for all great web experiences, finding its place first in the experimental and then in the commercial. Flash application development is rapid, cross-platform, and, best of all, tried and tested.

Figure 1-3 The RoadRunner broadband portal (www.rr.com), an RIA

Peripheral Flash technologies

Flash also incorporates a whole collection of peripheral technologies designed to add more power to your applications. These technologies usually run on a server, although Flash-based technologies have started to appear on desktops and embedded devices as well. I'd like to go over several of the most common peripherals and examine what they offer for Flash development.

Flash Remoting

Flash Remoting is Adobe's solution for providing fast and efficient data transportation between a server-side source and a Flash client. ActionScript Message Format (AMF) is the binary format used by Flash Remoting; it was created to replace the use of plain text or XML for transferring data between server and client. As the format is binary rather than human readable, it allows for larger amounts of data, such as database record sets, to be transported over HTTP to and from a Flash client in no time at all. The AMF data is converted to server native formats on one end and Flash native data formats on the other end. This conversion is performed transparently by the Flash Remoting gateway and Flash 6+ client. Adobe also provides a set of APIs for using Flash Remoting in your ActionScript; the set includes a set of components and classes that can be downloaded from the Adobe web site.

There are several implementations of Flash Remoting; some (including the official Adobe version) have a cost, and some are available for free:

- **Adobe Flash Remoting MX**: This commercial solution works with ColdFusion, J2EE, .NET, and in stand-alone mode (current cost is $999).
- **AMFPHP**: This is a free, open source PHP gateway to Flash Remoting. Currently at version 1.0, this solution is very fast and robust.
- **PHPObject**: Although strictly speaking not Flash Remoting, this free alternative to Flash Remoting can achieve many of the same goals.
- **OpenAMF**: You can use this free Java port of AMF PHP with J2EE.
- **WebORB**: FlashORB comes in two versions: a free version for Java and a commercial J2EE or .NET version (starting at $799 with support). FlashORB's professional edition offers Flash Remoting and many other features including an XML socket server.

Flash Media Server

Flash Media Server (FMS) allows for real-time video conferencing, voice and text chat, multiplayer games, and streaming video downloads. It also allows data and logic to be stored and executed on the server side to create a more-intelligent multiuser environment. FMS uses Real-Time Messaging Protocol (RTMP) to communicate between server and client. This format is closed and at present there are no alternatives to Adobe's FMS solution. For an excellent of example of FMS in action, check out Adobe Breeze Live on the Adobe web site (www.adobe.com/breeze). Breeze and Breeze Live are technologies that utilize FMS to provide real-time conference, presentation, and whiteboard abilities. It is important to mention, however, that this technology is very expensive, so it won't suit everybody. FMS is currently priced at $4,500 for the professional license, and Breeze Live is available as a software license, annual subscription, or monthly pay-per-use by contacting Adobe. You can also get FMS and Breeze services on a pay-per-use plan, as monthly hosting from third parties, and with several other options available direct from Adobe.

Stand-alone SWF wrappers

Several applications take SWF (exported Flash) files and produce native executables for Windows and Macintosh. A SWF (pronounced "swiff") file can normally be converted to a native executable by the stand-alone Flash Player that comes with the Flash IDE, but these SWF wrappers can also embed extra functionality into these projectors, which allows for functionality including .as local file storage, database access, and many other features that you cannot achieve through ActionScript alone.

Some of the most popular Flash projector applications include the following:

- **mProjector**: Usually preferred for its synchronous command model, it is also able to produce Mac projector files, unlike many of the other projector tools.
- **Jugglor**: Jugglor from FlashJester software is one of several tools offered to enhance a Flash movie with features like DirectX and joystick support.

- **Zinc**: Zinc is favored by many for its incredible ease of use, large feature set, and scriptable engine. It used to be known as FlashStudioPro.
- **Screenweaver**: In September 2005, Screenweaver rose from the dead with an open source attempt; the results look great, and this old dog has some brand-new tricks.

Flex and the Flash platform

Flash has the highest penetration figures of any plug-in; over 97 percent of web users can view Flash content. In fact, it is the most widely deployed software platform in the world. For this reason alone, companies have realized that it's not just content created in the Flash IDE that can benefit from this global audience. In 2004, Macromedia released a server product known as Flex. Flex allows applications to be dynamically generated by a server based on an XML-based user interface markup language (MXML) and ActionScript, for the logic. Flex has matured into a high-end tool for creating large-scale robust business applications, including e-commerce and corporate solutions. The FlexBuilder is a GUI from Adobe that shares much of the Dreamweaver code base and work flow. It enables rapid development and testing of Flex applications and provides a useful suite of tools, including network traffic monitoring and remote debugging.

Flex may offer the best solution for developing high-end applications, but the original Flex 1.0 price tag—$15,000 per CPU—reflected this high-end status. Thankfully, with the release of Flex 2, the pricing strategy changed drastically. A *free* version with very few limitations is now available, with an option for a less-pricey upgraded version that includes server-side data services, charting components, and a reasonably priced (under $1,000) IDE, although the IDE is also optional. There are also other alternatives that cater to small- to medium-sized businesses and beyond, and we look briefly at those next.

Alternatives to Flex and the Flash IDE

You have several alternatives to using Flex or Flash for creating your SWF applications. Laszlo Systems released their OpenLaszlo presentation server as an open source (and therefore free) alternative to Flex in 2004. Laszlo is poised to be an excellent solution going forward into 2007. Laszlo uses a markup language similar to MXML called LZX to create its SWF output; recent versions also permit content to be compiled not just on the server but on the client itself. For more information, you can visit www.openlaszlo.org.

A C# alternative for creating SWFs is Xamlon. Rather than creating a proprietary markup language for the UI definition, Xamlon uses Microsoft's Extensible Application Markup Language (XAML) language to define its interfaces and C# for the coding. This means that you don't have to learn multiple languages (ActionScript, MXML) if you are already confident using C# and XAML, making Xamlon a perfect solution for Windows desktop developers wanting to deploy applications over the Internet. More information is available at www.xamlon.com.

Finally, a host of lower-priced applications can create SWF files, from Swish MAX, which includes *full* scripting ability and is available at www.swishzone.com, to Sothink SWF Quicker, which can be found at www.sothink.com.

Open source Flash

I've mentioned a couple of alternatives to the Flash IDE. While these, most likely, will never live up to Adobe's IDE, they are an option for those who do not require the full functionality of the Flash IDE or those who choose not to use it for other reasons. However, in early 2004, something new began to happen in the Flash community. Nicolas Cannasse of Motion-Twin Technologies created an open source Flash compiler, capable of taking ActionScript 2 and compiling it into a SWF without an IDE at all; this compiler is called Motion-Twin ActionScript 2 Compiler (MTASC). The community quickly responded by creating a set of tools for integrating MTASC with Eclipse, a very popular open source IDE originally used for Java development. These tools include the ActionScript Development Tool (ASDT), a plug-in to incorporate MTASC into Eclipse, and Flashout, another Eclipse plug-in used to display outputted SWF and display any trace output. Another addition to the open source arsenal was swfmill, an application that can build SWFs containing library items from media source files using an XML file structure. With these tools, you can produce Flash projects without any Adobe products at all, but having used these tools extensively, I believe that, although they meet some needs, they are not suited for all Flash projects. Keeping up with the Flash Player's new functionality would take a huge team of open source developers to achieve. Nevertheless, having alternatives available to those with the patience to pursue other routes spurs Adobe on to better the IDE and the player, which can only be good for us, the faithful Flash developers.

Mobile Flash

Now that we've looked at the world of Flash in general, it's time to focus on the main subject of this book—the mobile editions of the Flash Player. Flash for mobile devices comes in three flavors:

- *Flash for Pocket PC*: a personal digital assistant (PDA) version of the desktop profile
- *Flash Lite*: a mobile-specific profile of the Flash Player
- *FlashCast*: a streaming web technology that utilizes the Flash Lite player

Flash for Pocket PC

Flash for Pocket PC is a version of the desktop Flash Player profile that supports all of the functionality of the Flash 6 or Flash 7 player, including XML, UI components, and data loading. Although PDA sales are declining in relation to those of other mobile devices, PDAs still provide a large market for which to develop games and applications. Flash Player for Pocket PC is available as a free download at the Adobe web site. However, creating stand-alone applications that incorporate Flash for Pocket PC requires that you purchase a Flash Player for Pocket PC stand-alone license, which currently costs $499.

The Flash for Pocket PC software development kit (SDK) can also be downloaded from the site and includes tips, code samples, and components to get you started. The progression to developing Flash for Pocket PC from desktop versions of the player is generally painless; the similarities are many, and the community forums are in place to help when you get stuck. Chapter 2 discusses some of the possibilities of Flash for Pocket PC.

Flash Lite

Flash Lite is the mobile phone profile of the Flash Player and is available in two versions: Flash Lite 1.0 and Flash Lite 1.1 are based on the Flash 4 player, and Flash Lite 2 is based on the Flash 7 player. Flash

Lite provides scriptable animation and user interactivity. Mobile will play a huge part in Flash's future; nothing currently rivals Flash for development times and added value in applications and products. Thankfully, you have the chance to catch this wave early on, when the learning curve is most shallow and the opportunities are yet to be taken advantage of.

Figure 1-4 shows a virtual pet experiment I have been working on (source included on this book's web site). Things like virtual pets on mobiles have yet to really take off. Community-based applications like this have previously been held back by limited graphics, limited network speeds, and high costs. Now that the barriers are down, it's time to start producing!

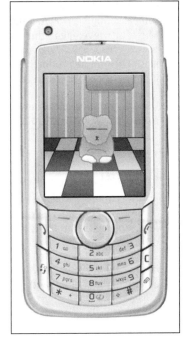

Figure 1-4 Flash Lite content

FlashCast

FlashCast is the latest mobile technology from Adobe. It allows for the distribution of rich media services (news, animation, games, and media) over a dedicated mobile network that is able to deliver content updates over SMS, HTTP, and UDP. FlashCast consists of a server and a client (residing on a phone). The server handles all of the billing information for content subscribers and deals with the delivery of the differential content updates. It also manages what are called **channels**, which are created with the Flash IDE. FlashCast can be seen as a TV-like experience, where these channels can be delivered over General Packet Radio Service (GPRS) and 3G consisting of games, information, applications, and shows. Among FlashCast's key features are the push and pull mechanisms that allow for content update over a variety of the media mentioned previously. These features make FlashCast a complete content and user-management solution for mobile operators, providing channel programming, hosting, scheduling, and server-side logic. Companies like NTT DoCoMo in Japan have leveraged FlashCast to serve a wide variety of content to millions of subscribers over their i-mode infrastructure.

The future

Where are we today? I can safely say most Internet users have experienced or interacted with Flash content, whether or not they knew exactly what technology they utilized. For years, Flash has been tarred with a reputation for being the means to create intrusive, oversized, and noisy banner ads. While it is true that Flash is the perfect candidate for creating those monstrosities, they represent just a tiny percentage of the Flash content created today. Just a few applications of Flash technology currently in use include FlashPaper, Flex, RIAs, web sites, feature animations, e-learning content, broadcast productions, console and PC game UIs, set-top box UIs, cell phone UIs, and of course, mobile content (Flash Player, Flash Lite, and FlashCast). All of these applications leverage the use of the Flash Player to display scalable, interactive content, from graphics and video to sound and music. They represent an enormous range of uses, from high-end business development with the Flex application server, which dynamically compiles server-side ActionScript scripts and flexible UI markup code into extremely lightweight, highly effective user interfaces for cell phones, including phones from Nokia and Samsung.

Flash has secured its place in the future of desktop and mobile development as the perfect platform for delivering rich online and offline experiences. This has been proven time and again, like when Microsoft leveraged the Flash platform for its Innovation web page (www.microsoft.com/mscorp/innovation/yourpotential) and when T-Mobile delivered its flagship News Express service Flash Lite mobile product in 2004 (which bundled an early Flash Lite player; you can read more about it at www.adobe.com/mobile/news_reviews/news).

We will also look at the future of Flash Lite in the final chapter of this book—where Flash Lite seems to be going and what you can expect from the Adobe mother ship in going forward.

Summary

In this chapter, we explained the history of Flash, from its roots as an animation tool to where it has come today. We discussed ActionScript as the driving force behind Flash applications, which enables rich and intuitive user experiences, and finally, Flash as a platform capable of deploying applications on a wide variety of devices from desktops to mobile phones.

In the next chapter, we will look at mobile devices in detail, including what types of device are available, their limitations, and what technologies we can use to create content for them.

Chapter 2

MOBILE DEVICES

Most of the development of mobile applications, of course, takes place not on the device itself but in a specially created development environment on your computer. It's also possible to *test* applications, to a certain extent, on that same computer using emulators and, in the case of Flash, the Flash stand-alone player. Testing applications for mobile devices on desktop computers makes it easy to forget that your *target* platform—the mobile phone, PDA, or other device—may behave very differently. The IDE and emulators may offer little more than a rough approximation of how your application runs in the wild. In a worst-case scenario, your application may even cease to function at all when transferred to the device, leaving you poised for an all-night debugging session immediately before launch. Before opening Flash and before you even plan your application, the target platform should be very clear in your mind, including any features, limitations, and problems that might arise when dealing with that platform.

In this chapter, I go through every stage of device consideration, where mobile devices come from and where they're heading. Some of the topics I discuss follow:

- The wireless revolution—its history and the cultural value of mobile phones
- Types of devices
- Limitations imposed by devices and other factors
- Existing technologies used in mobile devices
- Successful applications
- The future of mobile devices

The wireless revolution

Wireless communication is one of the fastest growing industries in the world, without a shadow of a doubt. The numbers are almost frightening—the current number of mobile users worldwide of more than 1.5 billion is expected to grow to 1.87 billion by 2007, according the Boston-based Yankee Group (www.yankeegroup.com). This huge audience, for the most part, already accepts mobile content as yet another commodity and is not afraid of spending hard-earned cash on calls, text messages, multimedia, and services alike, and this trend shows no signs of slowing any time soon. Indeed, the number of mobile phone users has long since surpassed the number of home Internet users in both the United States and Europe. How has this pocket revolution taken place? In this section, we look at some of the factors and trends that have facilitated this revolution.

Mobile evolution

We have many inventions to thank for the evolution of the mobile phone: Alexander Graham Bell's original telephone in 1876, Lars Magnus Ericsson's original and not-so-portable car phone, the Motorola 8000 handheld portable phone in 1984, and so on. There are simply too many influential people, companies, and conglomerates (such as Nokia and Sony Ericsson) in this rich communicative history to acknowledge everyone. Instead, let's fast forward to the not-so-distant past, where the function of a telephone began to change.

The first cellular or mobile phones were big old bricks with an antenna longer than a CB radio's, without a screen, and with the battery life of a cheap, remote-controlled car. Modern phones, on the other hand, have multimegapixel cameras, gigabytes of storage space, extremely efficient batteries, and high-speed data connections. Figure 2-1 shows this evolution of the mobile phone. The line between the desktop computer and the handheld device is starting to blur. The device capabilities are becoming less important, and the content is once again becoming king. New content is in such high demand, in fact, that brand-new markets open up daily in this fast-paced industry.

Figure 2-1. The evolution of the mobile phone

These remarkable little devices have snuck quietly into our world, becoming more useful every day, adding more functions that we cannot live without. This time it's not geeks or the military leading the way and pushing the envelope of a new technology, as they did with the Internet. It's everyday people—kids, teenagers, and adults—who are spending increasing amounts of time and money making calls; sending text messages; and downloading ring tones, videos, and more. I can say with confidence that few 14- to 25-year-olds in the West (anywhere for that matter) would be caught dead without their mobile phones! (Well, maybe a few, but who's counting?) Indeed, Japan, Italy, and the United Kingdom see frantic adoption rates for mobile technologies and services, which lead to mobile fads spreading like wildfire (big-budget TV advertising for ring tone downloads finally became a reality in early 2004). While the United States is generally slower to adopt these technologies because of its large size and historically fragmented cellular infrastructure (not to mention "mobile party pays" pricing structures), don't be fooled into thinking there's still time to prepare for mobile device fads. Widespread adoption has *already* happened, and the services, the hardware, and the consumers are already in place.

Content and infrastructure

An insatiable appetite for content drives the technology forward. Content can be anything from a one-off stock quote to an annoying video ring tone. People want content *now*, and we, as Flash developers, are here to give it to them. Established mobile content providers are in place to lend us a helping hand, including major global players like Preminet, Jamster, and Handango. For the consumer, finding and purchasing content has never been easier. Finding content often involves watching a TV advertisement, clicking a banner on a web page, or surfing to a mobile operator's portal page on a phone. Paying for content has also been made dangerously easy; by calling a number or sending a text message, you can spend all of the change in your pocket on a 10-second video clip or addictive mobile game. These established content providers make distributing your games, applications, screensavers, or other innovations extremely easy and cost effective. New programs even offer some level of digital rights management (DRM) and guarantee consumer safety with regard to security.

The infrastructure for selling your wares is available; people want to *buy* your wares; and the technology to transport your content also exists—with 3G providing the lightning-fast backbone for the mobile entertainment industry. The only thing left is for you to provide a service!

What is 3G?

3G is the third generation of wireless data communication protocols. It supersedes GPRS, EDGE (Enhanced Data rates for Global Evolution) or 2.5G, the slower yet incredibly popular GSM (Global System for Mobile Communications), and CDMA (Code-Division Multiple Access) or 2G. Typically, 3G speeds are measured in megabits per second, rather than kilobits per second, so 3G is essentially broadband in your pocket. 3G and its successors, such as 4G, allow extremely large amounts of data to be transmitted to and from a phone at the high speeds typically found on desktop connections. Data speeds have been a limiting factor in the development of mobile applications in the past, and although we must always design for the lowest common denominator, the future looks good. You can already see widespread use of video communication and even mobile TV streaming. In addition to the great compression ratios that result in much smaller downloads that Flash gives you, it can make full use of these higher data speeds to offer real-time information, multiplayer games, chats, virtual tours, and even group video conferencing.

Cultural acceptance

The use of mobile devices for everything *in addition to* voice calls has exploded in popularity all over the world. It's not just a case of necessity. You can see these trends beginning in Asia (particularly in Japan); spreading west across Europe, past Nokia's headquarters in Finland and engulfing the United Kingdom; before racing across the Atlantic and Pacific to hit the United States from both east and west.

Mobile devices presently provide a wide variety of features other than interpersonal communication, including music, news, weather, GPS navigation, road maps (trip planners), video, and photography to name a few. What we are beginning to see is the cultural acceptance of mobile devices as necessary utilities as well as portable entertainment centers. Service providers like travel agencies, real estate agents, e-learning schools, and dating services will soon take advantage of mobile technology to provide more people with the information they provide, wherever those people are.

Decreasing cost

One thing that has held the mobile content industry back is the cost of the content itself. In early 2005, a ring tone could cost anything from $1 to $5. Costs were also hidden in the data charges incurred by simply searching for content to buy online. In response to customer dissatisfaction, most service operators allow you to browse their own pages free of charge and pay only for the content you download, and the prices *are* dropping rapidly.

You may currently pay around $2 to download a megabyte of data over a 2.5G network, which equates to about 1,000 plain-text e-mails. However, the high-speed nature of 3G brings with it streaming video and full-track music, which dictate that this price must fall, as a single megabyte may only represent a few minutes of video. Value for money is, after all, still an important factor for consumers. As the price of downloading falls, the number of people downloading rich content rises, and the stigma attached to these premium content services will fade.

Increasing customization

A phone is much more than just a useful piece of plastic that lets you play a few games and make calls. Phones can be customized to suit the individual: the case can be changed; wallpapers and themes can be downloaded for the UI; ring tones and music can be installed; and custom emoticons, images, and sounds can be sent with text messages. You might say individuality is a key aspect of mobile phone well-being, that is, the contentment with a phone through the customization or personalization of it. The outward expression of personal identity through the customization of a mobile phone has been capitalized on by the numerous mobile content suppliers and retailers who sell an almost unlimited number of phone face plates, from neon pink ones to those with a wood-grain effect.

Customization is also an aspect of mobile culture that has led to the mobile phone being much more than just a telephony device; it is a piece of techno-jewelry and is of value not just materially but also sentimentally, as ridiculous as that may sound.

Synchronization and convergence

Hardware manufacturers have promised the convergence of mobile devices with other technology for many years but are only now beginning to make this happen. I don't want separate address books on my PC, my phone, and my PDA. **Convergence** allows me synchronize these devices using established, globally accepted protocols and data exchange formats. In much the same way that XML led the way for a whole variety of web-related technologies, such as web services, to be created, the mobile world is embracing languages like Synchronized Multimedia Integration Language (SMIL) to send information among completely different devices. SMIL is an XML-based markup language that allows, for example, a Nokia phone to send a Multimedia Message Service (MMS) message containing text, video, sound, and images to a Sony Ericsson phone without worrying about compatibility issues—standards to the rescue!

Thinking back to my problem of keeping track of addresses stored on multiple devices, I see that it would be helpful to have a common language to synchronize these address books. Well guess what? There is—Microsoft's Messaging API (MAPI) facilitates the synchronization of address books (including e-mail and postal addresses and phone numbers). I can connect my Symbian handset to my laptop using Bluetooth technology and run the synchronization wizard that comes with the phone. The phone's address book is synchronized with my Outlook address book; any conflicts are automatically resolved; and I am informed of the changes. I can do the same with my PDA, and my contacts can then be uploaded to a central location using software provided by my mobile operator, in case I somehow lose all three devices. I'm happy.

Convergence is at the center of mobile application theory. If I want my messaging or chat application to be successful, I don't want users to have to sign up for an account with someone they don't know; they should be able to use their existing MSN or AIM login, instead of remembering yet another username and password.

In early 2005, Symbian licensed Microsoft's ActiveSync protocol, which can be used to synchronize e-mail, calendar entries, contacts, and more. This sort of synchronization allows mobile devices to become the productivity boosters they are meant to be! Synchronization becomes particularly important when you consider how frequently we use our (what we might call) "personal devices" on a daily basis.

Invasive nature of personal devices

I take my mobile phone everywhere—to work, to the gym, even to the shower. OK, that last example is a slight exaggeration, but it is never more than ten feet away from me. When devices are used as extensively and frequently as mobile phones are, we, the mobile content providers, can tap into people's lives wherever they may go.

It could be argued that mobile phone content reaches more people than TV. While the statistics indicate TV is still more popular per capita, a TV is a passive device. We have learned to ignore advertisements to some degree, and we can simply switch the channel. A cell phone or PDA, on the other hand, draws your attention when it bleeps, bloops, and flashes from atop the coffee table. A ringing phone *must* be answered, which is why cell phones have been accused by some of being anti-social devices. However, this mentality of cell phone users is tremendously useful to those of us trying to sell them things! Let's consider an example scenario: My phone receives an MMS message. I wonder who it might be, so I wake up from my slumbering state on the couch. I *open* the message. It's not from a friend, but it does contain a funny video clip with a link to a SWF file at the end. I enjoyed the video, so I click the link to see if there's more, and it launches a rich user interface where I'm presented with options to browse and purchase DVDs. Though not subtle, it got me to the DVD store, and I didn't even leave the couch. This result is much more productive than a TV ad could be and no doubt costs much less.

A CRM dream

Customer relationship management (CRM) is the term given to the methods and applications that allow the management of customers and customer behavior over time. In an ideal world, we could know where our customers (or our clients' customers) are and what they are up to at all times. Of course, this ideal scenario would border on stalking, but following their spending habits or even tastes in music would still be a plus. Now, if only they would carry a device that could discreetly and legally inform us of this information whenever they checked their e-mail . . .

Without stretching the truth too far, or worse, entering the realm of Big Brother and conspiracy theory, I can say that mobile devices allow the spending habits, interests, and even the *physical location* of consumers to be tracked like nothing else. Most purchases made from a mobile phone are linked to the phone number or International Mobile Equipment Identity (IMEI), the unique identifier, associated with the handset. Better yet, hardly anybody shares a mobile phone, which means every user can be uniquely identified, unlike with a PC. If "Amazon mobile" becomes available for making purchases, who's to say there won't be a little box that reads, "I give permission to receive news of products that may interest me"? Amazon.com has the best CRM in the business; imagine if they could invade your personal space by sending e-mails or text messages directly to your phone (shudder). Traditionally, mobile shopping has been hampered by limited technology; tiny screens; stateless, poor-quality Wireless Application Protocol (WAP) pages; and a lack of understanding on how to use these pages by the end user. With Flash, we can change all of that; in fact, you can already obtain a Flash application that allows you to shop Amazon.com from your Flash Lite–enabled handset or Flash 6–enabled PDA (see Figure 2-2). More information and a download are available at www.macromedia.com/devnet/devices/articles/ishop.html.

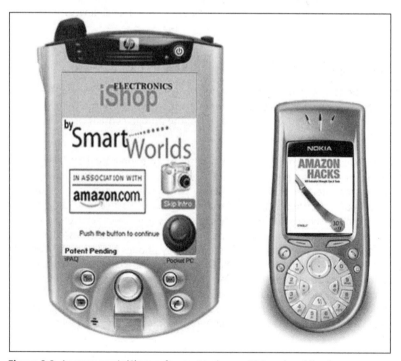

Figure 2-2. Amazon.com's iShop software running on PDA and mobile phone

Types of devices

Some might say the first truly popular mobile device was the Sony Walkman; it provided as much entertainment as a few mixed tapes and a pair of AA batteries could possibly offer. Today, many types of device are found in this rapidly evolving market: phones, PDAs, in-car navigation systems, digital cameras, and more. Manufacturers and developers need a way to standardize the operation of these products. The battle-hardened Flash player is just the thing to provide flexible UIs that can communicate with lower-level APIs yet maintain a consistent look and feel across many types of devices. Have you ever noticed that if you learn to use Microsoft Word, you can transfer those skills directly into pretty much any other successful word-processing application on the market? If someone can't use a product, they'll find another that they *can* use; this is the same for mobile devices. Let's take a look at some of the devices on the market today.

Mobile phones and their operating systems

The mobile phone is, without doubt, the most popular of all mobile devices. Growth in this sector is phenomenal. Nokia has cornered the market for many years; their revolutionary views on usability coupled with excellent construction has earned them this deserved place. Nokia still leads the way with its wide range of phones, from the Series 40 mass-market phones to the Series 60 smart phones, to the more-powerful Series 80 and 90 mobile communicators. They also have a licensing arrangement with Adobe and incorporated the Flash Lite player into new handsets for the UI and as a built-in rich media player in early 2005. Other big players include Siemens (which is also adopting the Series 60), Samsung, Sony Ericsson, Motorola, and LG Electronics, as well as several other smaller manufacturers. Figure 2-3 shows a Nokia Series 60 phone alongside those of several other players.

Figure 2-3. The Nokia 6681, the Samsung SGH-x426, and the Sony Ericsson K600i

The clear market leader in operating systems (OSs) is Symbian OS; shipments of Symbian-based phones doubled in 2004, rising to 14.4 million units. Symbian OS comes in several profiles, each targeted at a specific set of device capabilities. These range from Series 40 for low-end devices, to Series 90 for larger, more powerful devices, and UIQ for touch-screen devices. Nokia has had a hand in the development of Symbian since helping to found it in 1998. However, Symbian is owned by a whole consortium of manufacturers, and both Sony Ericsson and Siemens quickly adopted the OS for some of their smart phone models. Other partners include Samsung, Motorola, and LG. The chart in Figure 2-4 illustrates how popular Symbian is when compared to rival smart phone OSs.

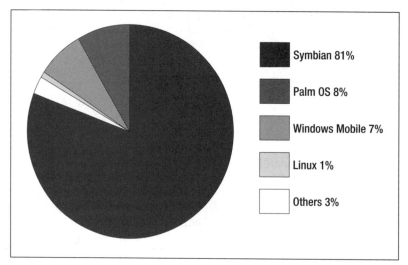

Figure 2-4. Percentage of phones running each available smart phone OS in 2004

When creating the Flash Lite 1.1 player, Macromedia, of course, decided on Symbian as its OS of choice. This ensured the largest market possible could view Flash content. Symbian is also one of the only operating systems to go down-market and cater for utilitarian (non–smart phone) handsets with its Series 40 OS. However, it is important to realize many phones still run on proprietary OSs developed by the phone manufacturers, and Microsoft also has big plans for its Windows Mobile OS. Nevertheless, Flash is being burned into more and more handsets every day, and the capabilities of low-end phones continue to rise. We can now comfortably assume there is a large enough potential market to make Flash and Flash Lite development for mobile phones a very prosperous venture indeed.

PDAs and their operating systems

PDAs provided mobile applications long before mobile phones could. Typically, PDAs are used for personal information management (PIM), which includes organizing contacts, office documents, calendar events, and multimedia files. With more processing power, larger screens, and a variety of input devices, PDAs are well suited to running highly dynamic and powerful applications. Nevertheless, the PDA has seen a big decline in sales since the introduction of the smart phone. Most likely because of PDAs' high costs, the increased capabilities of smart phones, and the lower prices of laptops, PDAs are being pushed into an awkward middle spot. Still popular in the business market, these devices sport more functionality than a phone, including global positioning system (GPS) services (facilitating route planning and road maps), pocket versions of Microsoft Office or equivalent software, and handwriting recognition via a stylus or pen. With offerings from Casio, HP, Sony, Palm, Toshiba, and several other manufacturers, a wide choice is available to the PDA buyer (see Figure 2-5 for an example). Fortunately, the majority of PDAs run the Windows Mobile/Pocket PC OS, which supports the Flash 6 player. More information on running the Flash Player on Pocket PC can be found at www.antmobile.com/.

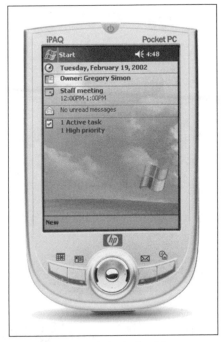

Figure 2-5. The HP iPAQ Pocket PC

As stated previously, Pocket PC (with Windows Mobile Edition) is the most popular OS for PDAs. It provides a lot of the functionality and familiarity of the Windows operating system, including support for .NET application development and, of course, Flash Player. Other OSs include Symbian, Apple, PalmOS, and LinuxOS. At present, only Windows and Symbian OSs support the Adobe Flash player.

Other devices

More devices than just mobile phones and PDAs can run Flash content. A whole host of devices can already run a Flash player or may be able to in the near future. The SWF file format is now open—a brave move by Adobe that led to the creation of a whole generation of tools capable of both creating and displaying Flash content in places Adobe might have never had time to look. You can also license the Flash player SDK (both the regular desktop and Pocket PC versions), which opens up the world of Flash content to almost any device. Although this book's main focus is on mobile phones and PDAs, many of the techniques described in it can be applied to other devices that may or may not be fully portable.

Handheld gaming consoles

The three major players in the handheld gaming scene are Sony with its PlayStation Portable (PSP), Nintendo with the Gameboy, and Tiger Telematics with the Gizmondo. Consoles have been a playground for hackers in the past, from running Linux on an Xbox to enabling the web browser on the PSP. Flash makes for the perfect game UI, and in fact, many games featuring an all-Flash UI have already been created for all types of consoles. Figure 2-6 shows a commercial example of Flash being used in a game.

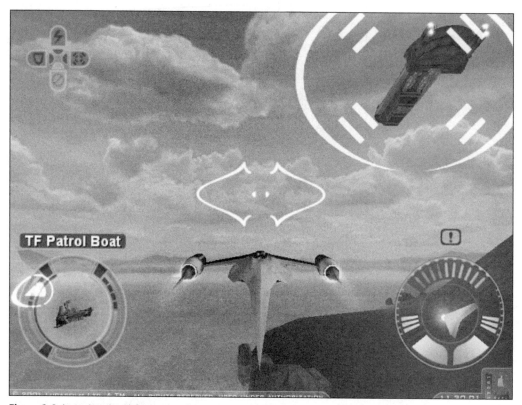

Figure 2-6. LucasArts StarFighter game (image copyright LucasArts Entertainment Company LLC)

Portable music devices

It was only a matter of time before the Flash player reached portable music devices. Apple continues to innovate with its hugely successful iPod range, introducing sleeker models, color screens, and photo-viewing abilities. One company that took things a step further is iRiver with the iRiver U10, a music device that comes with the Flash Lite 1.1 player preinstalled. iRiver is yet another device type to look forward to developing content for as more and more manufacturers take note of it.

GPS navigation systems

We are beginning to find in-car navigation systems in increasing numbers of vehicles, not just in top-of-the-line models. Devices like the TomTom portable GPS navigation system (see Figure 2-7) offer real-time 3-D maps and route planning that can be displayed on car monitors, PDAs, and even mobile phones. Adobe has licensed the Flash Player SDK to world-leading technology platform companies and consumer electronics manufacturers, including Toshiba Information Systems. Flash is being used for various in-car navigation systems UIs all over the world right now.

Figure 2-7. The TomTom GPS navigation system displayed on an in-car monitor, a mobile phone, and a PDA

Device limitations

Among the problems encountered when developing applications for such a wide range of devices are the various limitations imposed by each platform. Flash has proven to be a truly cross-platform solution that might finally allow you to "write once, run anywhere" without dealing with the fragmentation found in other well-known platforms.

In this section, we look at the following hardware limitations and physical and social aspects of mobile devices:

- The speed of the CPU and amount of RAM
- The screen (size, resolution, and colors)
- Input devices
- Ergonomics
- Networks and connectivity
- Data storage
- Security
- Other limitations to consider

CPU and RAM

CPU speeds in current phones are reaching the 300MHz range and are expected to exceed 500MHz in no time at all. PDAs offer even faster speeds, of course, but these speeds are not so startlingly fast when you compare them to a desktop's multigigahertz power. However, they *are* fast enough to run pretty much any application or game you would want to design for these devices, within reason. With lower CPU speeds, you cannot expect millions of instructions to be carried out per second; parsing data is a great example of abusing a phone's processor. When dealing with data in the form of XML returned from a server, for example, Flash struggles to process even a medium-sized document containing just a few lines, which causes a noticeable slowdown. Parsing XML is an extremely processor-unfriendly task, and there are ways to reduce the load on the CPU, such as finding a balance between speed and size.

When it comes to Flash, however, the major limiting factor is RAM. The Flash Lite 1.1 player for the Symbian OS is assigned 750KB of RAM at startup, of which the player itself takes roughly 450KB. This leaves you at most 300KB with which to create movie clips, play sounds, display bitmaps, and execute code.

Screen size and resolution

The screen size is perhaps one of the most obvious limitations found in mobile devices and one that will persist as long as screens are fixed to the device itself. Rugged roll-up and projection screens are still a long way off! We have to consider the current state of affairs, and how we can work with today's devices and the problems that may arise.

The small screen *size* however is not the only thing to consider. The screen *resolution* also plays an important role in usability. The higher the resolution, the more room you have to display your content. You can make the font a little bit larger to aid with legibility; you can provide the user with more options, show more information, display images at full size, and provide a much richer user experience all around. I have spoken briefly about the operating systems used on mobile phones and PDAs. These operating systems tend to impose certain standardized limitations on the phone or PDA they run on; these limitations include screen resolution. Table 2-1 shows a few of the popular screen sizes for mobile phones, listed by OS.

Table 2-1. Screen resolutions for mobile OSs

OS	Screen Dimensions (pixels)	Example Phone Models
Symbian Series 40	128$\times$128	Nokia 6100
Symbian Series 60	176$\times$208	Nokia N91 and 6680, Siemens SX1
Symbian Series 80	640$\times$200	Nokia 9500 Communicator
Symbian Series 90	640$\times$320	Nokia 7710
Symbian UIQ	320$\times$208	Sony Ericsson P900, Motorola A1000
Windows Mobile	320$\times$240 – 640$\times$480	Motorola MPx220, SDA Music Smartphone
PalmOS*	160$\times$160	Treo 600
LinuxOS	240$\times$320	Motorola E6280

New versions of PalmOS support resolutions of 240$\times$5240 and 320$\times$5320.

Drawing a table for PDA screen resolutions would be much more difficult. Certain PDAs, such as the Windows Mobile Edition models, support a whole variety of customizable screen resolutions anywhere from 320×240 to a rather random 1000×1000 and higher in the future. What is relevant, however, is that PDAs generally have screens that run higher resolutions than their mobile phone counterparts. As a Flash designer, it is easier to design for almost any size screen because of the scalable nature of the vector rendering engine. As a general rule of thumb, I test Flash content for PDAs at 320×240 and at 640×480.

While the screen size is increasing, mobile device screens are by no means able to equal desktop resolutions just yet. This means that screen size is still a constraint. In a nutshell, keep the screen simple! Optimizing content for limited screen real estate is covered in Chapter 4 of this book, which discusses application development.

Screen color depth

According to a 2004 report on iSuppli's Market Watch web page, it is estimated that by 2008, the majority of cell phones will feature full color displays, with a 96% penetration rate (`www.isuppli.com/marketwatch`). This figure may vary depending on the country in question, of course; at the present time, it is virtually impossible to purchase a cell without a color screen in the United Kingdom, even in the budget phone market (less than $80). There isn't a single Flash Lite 1.1–capable phone without a color screen, and there is no chance there ever will be. So you can rely on the fact that you have at least a 16-bit color display to work with. That gives you 65,536 colors—not bad. With this many colors, you can display almost any form of information, from text to feature-length animations!

Keypads

Mobile phone keypads have evolved over the years. Most now include the following keys, which can be considered standard:

- Number keys 0 to 9 (also containing three letters on most keys)
- Star and hash/pound symbol keys (generic phone functions)
- A four-directional pad (used in UI navigation)
- Call (green) and cancel call (red) buttons
- Soft keys (usually two keys that have dynamic behaviors)

Nonstandard keys may include volume controls, menu access controls, and keys to access other phone-specific functions (such as camera operation). However, you can usually assume the keys present in the previous list are at your disposal. When developing games and applications, it's often best to provide alternative ways of navigating, such as allowing control via the directional pad or the number keys 2, 4, 6, and 8. In this way, you allow the users to find their own preferred ways of navigating an application, and therefore, become more comfortable with its usage.

Some PDAs feature QWERTY (fully featured) keypads. While these speed up typing and are a lot more flexible than a phone keypad, they don't suit all situations. QWERTY keypads are almost always too large to fit the majority of mobile phones, but are sometimes offered as a plug-in accessory (or via Bluetooth). Phones have solved this problem by accepting a standard form of text input known as **T9 predictive text**, which allows words to be typed by touching the key containing the letter just once, rather than repeatedly hitting the same key to access the second or third letter.

Other input devices

Even though the keypad is the primary input device for most handsets, some phones also offer a joystick in place of a directional keypad or a stylus device (found in UIQ handsets). This variance is always something to consider when creating action games.

> *Although Flash Lite 1.1 supports the use of a stylus/pen device (treated as mouse input), it does not support drag and drop events including* dragOut, *dragOver and* releaseOutside. *The* startDrag() *and* stopDrag() *commands are also unsupported.*

Ergonomics

Most phones are designed for single-handed navigation. To achieve this feat, the buttons must be laid out in a manner that prevents the phone from slipping out of your palm, and the buttons must also be large enough to press with a thumb. The Nokia 7610 has perhaps one of the most awkward keypad layouts, which can cause problems when playing games (see Figure 2-8). Some high-end phones have wide screens and dual-handed navigation to better suit playing games or viewing video content. When developing the early mobile phones, Nokia experimented with single strip keypads, on which all of the keys were arranged horizontally, and quickly decided on the standard 3×4 layout (not including function keys) that we have today.

Figure 2-8. The Nokia 7610 (on the left) alongside the much-improved Nokia 6681

Connectivity and network speeds

Network speeds are generally slow, although 3G is now coming into operation, as discussed previously in the chapter. What is not always certain is whether the application you create will have the ability to go online at all. Users may choose to disallow it, maybe to save money, or they may not have coverage for GPRS or 3G data transmission. Creating applications that can work in two states (online and offline) can help to create a better user experience, and local caching of data saves data costs and means that a user is likely to use the application more often.

Data storage

Substantial data storage space on mobile phones is now commonplace. Series 60 and up devices come with the ability to plug in memory cards to expand the system memory to anything from 64MB to well over a gigabyte. As the amount of storage space increases the amount of resources you use in your applications and games starts to become insignificant. For example, though a fully featured picture gallery was unheard of just a year ago, it is now possible to create an application that downloads and stores a large number of images from the Internet, perhaps tied in with a user's online photo album at Flickr (for more details on Flickr, you can visit www.flickr.com).

Security

The possibilities offered by a mobile device are limited by the security restrictions in place. If you are developing applications in Java for the J2ME platform, you are forced to adhere to the stringent security sandbox restrictions that come with it. The Flash player carries with it even tighter security restrictions, with calls to getURL() being allowed only when a key is physically pressed by the user in certain implementations.

Other limitations to consider

Device limitations aren't just caused by the devices themselves. There are certain social stigmas attached to these devices, especially with mobile phones. It's important to realize these limitations don't just come from the device, but also the people who use them.

User expectations and human-computer interaction (HCI) limitations

Phone users do not generally have the patience of computer users. Why should they? A phone should not take several minutes to boot up before you can do anything, so why should it take more than a few seconds to carry out any task? This mentality keeps the mobile phone and PDA one step ahead of the desktop computer in terms of the availability of functionality. You certainly wouldn't want a phone crashing or showing a blue screen when you're trying to call for help in an emergency! This imposes a limitation on you, the application designer, in that your application must behave in a way that doesn't break with the user experience; a mobile application should be responsive and not made overcomplicated by unnecessary features.

Self-inflicted limitations (by you, the developer)

The only other thing that might limit you is your imagination. There really isn't much that can't be achieved with today's mobile technology. Some might say we, as mobile developers, are even less limited than those working with desktops, as the desktop imposes several constraints on the user, such as the inability to move around. One of the benefits of mobile development is that the user can take the device anywhere and everywhere, adding the surrounding environment into the user experience. The fact that the mobile device is with someone when walking down the street looking for somewhere to eat, or considering going to watch a movie means that we can capitalize on new opportunities.

Other existing technologies for mobile development

The fact that you are reading this book suggests that you are at least interested in Flash as a platform for developing your mobile applications and games, but many other platforms are out there that you might also consider. This section introduces the most popular of these platforms, examines their various pros and cons, and compares them to Flash or Flash Lite.

Java 2 Mobile Edition

Java 2 Mobile Edition (J2ME) is, by far, the most well- established platform for creating applications on a variety of devices. Java was initially created for the mobile market, designed as a language for consumer smart devices, and originally known as the Oak Project. After being renamed Java ("Oak" was already taken by another language), it was ported to various platforms including the Windows and Linux desktops. Java, in the form of J2ME, became the most popular mobile development platform in 1999 for its small form and ease of use.

J2ME is split into two main profiles aimed at both low- and high-end embedded devices. Connected Device Configuration (CDC) is used with set-top boxes and other high-end consumer devices, whereas Connected Limited Device Configuration (CLDC) is used with the mobile handsets and PDAs that this book targets. To add to the abbreviation soup, the Mobile Information Device Profile (MIDP) is a profile that sits on top of the CLDC configuration and provides the developer with a framework and set of APIs to aid in application development with J2ME. Figure 2-9 shows how these various configurations and profiles fit together.

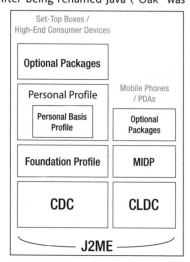

Figure 2-9. The J2ME platform

J2ME pros

J2ME has the following advantages:

- **Fully object-oriented and mature language**: Java is a fully mature, fully object-oriented language that enforces best practices at all times. This makes application development very robust and maintainable.

- **Speed**: Although Java is interpreted, which is never as quick as running native code, the Java virtual machine (JVM) is heavily optimized for low-powered devices and can perform most tasks at speed sufficient to avoid any issues. However, intensive tasks such as graphical manipulation should be kept to a minimum.

- **Security**: Java is inherently secure and runs in a security sandbox on the device. The JVM inspects and verifies all classes to ensure they are not going to perform an illegal operation at runtime.

- **Local storage**: The J2ME libraries provide local storage facilities through what is called the Record Management System (RMS). MIDP 2.0 (found in Series 60 devices) allows for different Java applications to share data through the RMS.

- **Large community of developers**: The Java community is vast, and support is plentiful through numerous forums and superb documentation.

- **MIDP framework**: The MIDP framework includes classes for creating graphical user interfaces (GUIs), responding to user events, handling file access, and dealing with security.

J2ME cons

J2ME has the following disadvantages:

- **Device-dependent behavior**: Java can behave differently on various devices because of the numerous profiles and configurations available, along with the introduction of new functionality found in optional packages (for example, JSR 82,[1] which introduces Bluetooth access). Because of this device dependence, thorough testing is required on all target devices before final deployment. Sun has announced that J2ME/JME will also target CDC devices, which are less limited in terms of processors, RAM, and so on than current mobile phones, which means that coding for desktops (and other profiles) will not be as varied as it currently is.

- **No scalable graphics**: At the present, there is no standard for scalable graphics in J2ME as with the vector graphics found in Flash; progress is under way with JSR 226, but scalable graphics are still a long way off.

J2ME development tool options

The following development tool options can be used with J2ME:

- Sun's J2ME wireless toolkit (free, basic features)
- Eclipse IDE (free, full IDE but requires the J2ME plug-in and wireless toolkit)
- Borland JBuilder Mobile Set (not free, full IDE)
- Sun ONE Studio Mobile Edition (not free, full IDE)

---

1. A Java Specification Request (JSR) is a formal request for a new Java API. You can view all current JSRs at www.jcp.org/en/jsr/all.

Other options that are perhaps not as popular but also worth considering include the free NetBeans IDE (which integrates with the wireless toolkit) and Metrowerks CodeWarrior Wireless Studio. All of the options mentioned include the facilities to compile and test in a device emulator on the desktop.

Symbian native C++

C++ applications can run natively on the device, making the applications less portable, but this usually means you have more speed and more control over the device.

Symbian native C++ pros

Symbian native C++ has the following advantages:

- **Speed**: Nothing compares to the speed of a natively compiled application. C++ for Symbian allows real-time 3-D games with the quality of PlayStation (PSOne) graphics.
- **Vast libraries of C++ code**: C++ is one of the oldest established languages, so there are literally thousands of web sites and books dedicated to writing code in C++. If you can't find the code to perform the task you're trying to achieve, it probably can't be done.
- **Local storage**: Like J2ME, native C++ can create files on the device and read back data at a later date. C++ applications can also work outside of the usual sandbox associated with mobile programming, which could also be seen as a negative.
- **Access to all device capabilities**: With C++, no limits are imposed on which phone features your application can access, including the phonebook, camera, assisted GPS, and Bluetooth.

Symbian native C++ cons

Symbian native C++ has the following disadvantages:

- **Hard to get started**: It's very difficult to get started in Symbian C++ development. You need to have the correct development environment (Visual C++ or CodeWarrior) or be very confident (and patient) with command-line programming. There are plenty of examples, but the learning curve is notoriously steep.
- **Extremely long development cycles**: While it is possible for an individual to develop mobile applications and games in C++, the amount of code required to get a functioning application is far greater than with any of the other platforms discussed.
- **Different for each device**: There are few standards in C++ coding, and you must test on almost every device to be sure functionality is consistent. The downside of unlimited power is unlimited possibilities.
- **Not so secure**: Virus engineers and Bluetooth snarfers favor C++ as their weapon of choice, as it imposes very few limits on what can be achieved through native code. It's also fairly easy to ruin your machine with mischievous code (see the following "Memory management" point).
- **Memory management**: Another negative aspect of using C++ is that the memory is unmanaged. This makes it much easier to create memory leaks or, at the very least, to waste memory. Cleaning up after yourself when using variables and pointers in your code can be a time-consuming process!

Symbian native C++ development tool options

The following development tools can be used with Symbian native C++:

- Symbian C++ SDK (free, requires command compilation)
- Microsoft Visual C++ 6/.NET (not free, full IDE)
- Eclipse IDE (free, full IDE, requires a Symbian C++ plug-in)
- Borland C++ Builder (not free, full IDE)

Another option is the Metrowerks CodeWarrior Wireless Studio (not free). All options require the Symbian C++ SDK from Nokia.

Binary Runtime Environment for Wireless (BREW)

The Binary Runtime Environment for Wireless (BREW) is a programming platform developed by Qualcomm for CDMA-based phones. BREW provides an SDK and emulator for developing and testing applications written in C++ or C.

BREW pros

BREW has the following advantages:

- **Power of C++**: Brew includes all of the functionality of C++.
- **Security**: All BREW applications must be digitally signed to run on a device. Only authenticated BREW developers can obtain the software to sign applications, and once complete, an application must be sent to Qualcomm to undergo testing before it can be sent to a content provider for sale.
- **Virtual marketplace**: BREW also provides a virtual marketplace for the distribution and sale of your applications.

BREW cons

BREW has the following disadvantages:

- **Requires a BREW-enabled handset**: BREW applications can only run on a limited number of handsets, for example, the Nokia 3205.
- **Same cons as C++**: BREW is written in C or C++, so it brings with it all of the problems found with other C++ development for Symbian.

BREW development tool options

The following development tools can be used with BREW:

- BREW SDK (free, no compilation)
- ARM RealView compilation tools (not free, full IDE, requires the BREW SDK)
- Visual C++ (not free, full IDE, requires both the BREW SDK and the ARM RealView compilation tools)

BREW also requires an authentication suite, which must be purchased alongside any of the development tool options listed previously.

Python for Symbian

Python is an endearing language favored by many web developers as a shining example of how a programming language should be written. It is **multiparadigm language**, which means it allows you to write your code however you like—structured, object-oriented, or even functionally.

Python for Symbian pros

Python for Symbian has the following advantages:

- **Can be compiled into a native installer**: Python scripts can be converted to a native Symbian application installer with the use of the py2sis.exe utility that ships with the Python SDK; this solves many distribution and implementation problems. However, it still requires an interpreter (see "Python for Symbian Cons").

- **Supports all of a phone's capabilities**: As with C++, Python supports all of a phone's native capabilities, such as access to a phone's local storage.

Python for Symbian cons

Python for Symbian has the following disadvantages:

- **Requires a Python interpreter**: The biggest drawback is that the Python interpreter needs to be installed on the target device before anything can run on it. The interpreter's file size is fairly large, so including it in the installer file is a bit of a stretch with regards to easy distribution.

- **No graphics API**: At the present time, there is no defined graphical API for programming with Python for Symbian; this means you'll have to define your own graphics routines for the most part, although a subset of the native UI components is accessible.

- **Limited user community**: Nokia has a Python for Symbian forum and the Python development community as a whole is fairly large. However, there aren't many posts in the forum, and the API is specific to the Symbian platform.

Python for Symbian development tool options

The following development tools can be used with Python for Symbian:

- Python for Series 60 SDK (free, command-line compilation)
- Free Python IDEs like IDLE, PythonWin, and MacPythonIDE

The free IDEs may require some custom configuration to work alongside the Python for Series 60 SDK.

It's pretty clear that no single technology can be labeled "the best" for mobile development; they *all* have their good, and not-so-good, points. For the best possible combination, it is perfectly acceptable to use Flash alongside one of these other technologies to boost the power of the Flash player with extra functionality. Flash can be used for the bulk of the application logic, presentation, and connectivity, with a J2ME midlet or a C++ application listening for commands from the Flash player to perform tasks out of its reach, such as accessing GPS or Bluetooth or saving data locally.

What makes a device successful?

Now there are more choices than ever when it comes to choosing a mobile device to suit your needs. You can choose among mass-market consumer phones, smart phones, full-fledged pocket communicators, and PDAs. These devices all have a few things in common, but some are clearly more popular than others. So what makes one device more successful than another, when they all do pretty much the same things?

In this section, we dissect two very different devices, examining their merits and failures.

The Pogo

The Pogo was a PDA and phone device that was way ahead of its time (back in 1996) and unfortunately doomed to fail for this very reason. The Pogo, shown in Figure 2-10, featured an entirely Flash-driven UI. The UI was a touch screen, designed to be operated by a finger or with the supplied stylus pen. The screen was fairly large, and the software fairly intuitive. The software provided e-mail, telephone, games, and music functionalities. So what went wrong?

The Pogo was underpowered; technology at the time just didn't have the processing power to run the Flash player at a decent speed (the Pogo had a 75-MHz processor), and the bundled games illustrated this. The device also looked fairly awkward. Holding a

Figure 2-10. The Pogo

large rectangular screen up to your ear to make a call not only looked strange, it felt awkward in the hand. Also, the front-lit LCD screen wasn't very bright, making the tiny text hard to read in anything but direct sunlight. The Pogo was also very expensive; at £300[2] for the unit and a monthly charge on top of that, there simply wasn't a widespread demand for phones of its caliber. PDAs catered to the more demanding tasks, and the average consumer just had no need for it. The cost of data at the time was very high, even over GSM, and the Pogo had no PC connection; everything had to be downloaded or transferred via memory card. This indicates a distinct lack of infrastructure, which we now have, and convergence was clearly still in the distance.

The Pogo was a device that would have most likely been successful if brought out a few years later. With its high-speed use of the GSM network (using a proprietary compression algorithm), and integrated e-mail, MP3 music, and games, it resembles today's smart phones.

2. This product was available in the United Kingdom but not in the United States, so the cost is provided in pounds.

The Nokia 3210

Nokia rarely gets it wrong. Nokia's user interfaces are consistently easy to navigate and standard across all ranges; the latest Symbian offerings' functionality still resembles some of the functionality of early monochrome handsets (for example, locking a Nokia's keypad has involved the same combination of key presses for years). One of the most popular phones of all time was the Nokia 3210, shown in Figure 2-11. This phone is durable, performs well in most lighting conditions, has great battery life, and has stood the test of time—it's still in wide use today, and it was released in 1999.

The Nokia UI has long included the use of graphical icons and directional pad navigation to cycle between the various options. This functionality has since been adopted by all mobile phone manufacturers as *the* way to present the functions of a mobile phone, and it works very well. The keypad on the Nokia 3210 is also one of the most simple, and the buttons are reasonably large and evenly spaced. The keypad tied into the phone's UI very nicely, as the UI was both fast and responsive. The phone also houses an internal antenna, which adds to the aesthetics and made quite a splash when first introduced—this is something some phones today still don't manage! The 3210 also helped to make the mobile phone the fashion accessory it is today, introducing changeable front *and* back covers, making this one very popular phone among teens and securing it a firm place as one of the most frequently purchased phones of all time.

Figure 2-11. The robust Nokia 3210

As you can see in the Pogo and the Nokia 3210, more than just fancy features make a device successful. There are many factors to consider including ease of use, size, shape, intuitiveness, and even the current state of other technologies—no device is an island; they all require a robust infrastructure to realize their full potential.

Successful applications

Some applications prove to be more successful than others. Those applications that prove *very* successful are often included in a device's OS as standard (such as e-mail, calendar, contacts, and MP3 player features). Business and productivity applications make up a fairly large percentage of all applications sold via content providers, but games for mobile devices are also a growing industry—with more processing power every year, the possibilities are almost endless.

In this section, we look at the types of application that have proven successful over the years and where future possibilities lie.

Business and productivity applications

Business applications, such as Microsoft Excel, tend to be hard to translate to the small screen. However, it has been done very successfully. Where mobile applications really take off is with small applications that perform specific tasks, such as keeping track of your shopping list or allowing you to use your favorite messenger client to talk to your friends when you're on the move. Flash tends to be suited to the latter; while you could, theoretically, write a pocket spreadsheet application in Flash, it wouldn't be very responsive and most likely wouldn't support the standard spreadsheet file formats. A friend once asked me, "Why don't you make an e-mail application in Flash Lite?" Well again, you *could*, but if you think about doing this for a second, you realize that there aren't really any phones that support Flash that don't have a built-in e-mail client already!

Key success factors (other than an actual use, as in the case of our e-mail application) include a familiar navigation system (using the platform's native menu system is always an option in Flash Lite), substantial user feedback (don't punish the user for pressing the wrong button), and a decent help system in case anything goes wrong.

Games

Mobile games are now big business. Global mobile gaming events include Game Developers Conference (GDC) Mobile and the Mobile Entertainment Summit at Cellular Telecommunications Industry Association (CTIA) WIRELESS. With substantial financial backing and some of the big name game producers like Electronic Arts (EA) getting into the mobile scene, is there room for the individual or smaller company? Yes, there is. Fortunately, Flash is perfectly suited for the rapid creation of games with smaller development teams and shorter development cycles. We have already discussed some of the reasons for using Flash instead of existing mobile technologies such as J2ME and native C++, but another key factor in the success of games in the mobile market is purely and simply the fact that people do not want to spend hours playing a role-playing game or a point-and-click adventure on their handsets. Mobile games are at their best when you can simply pick them up and play for a short amount of time when sitting on the train, the

Figure 2-12.
BlueskyNorth's
Presi-Dance

bus, or plane. Flash is very effective for quickly developing simple but addictive games in a matter of days that could otherwise take months to develop. These sorts of games fit nicely into the category of "pick up and play," not to mention games created to correspond to specific events in the news and current affairs, like BlueskyNorth's Presi-Dance game (see Figure 2-12).

One area where mobile games fall short is in playability. Traditional mobile handsets are simply not designed with games in mind. Portrait screens and tiny buttons make for clumsy game playing. When designing games for mobile devices, realize that only a few phones, such as the Nokia N-Gage and LG's 3-D accelerated game phone, can offer really excellent game experiences. But it is possible to design games that are suited to the mobile profile: turn-based, strategy, and puzzle-based games all work very nicely on these limited devices. This is an area that is bound to improve as devices mature and people become accustomed to using them for all of the activities discussed in "The Future of Devices" section of this chapter.

Market opportunities

A great many markets are yet to be saturated in the mobile world. Although slightly controversial, mobile content for the adult and gambling industries generated an estimated $6.5 billion in 2006. A huge slice of this revenue is in video downloads alone. This market is relatively untapped; people are not yet used to gambling using their mobile phone. Flash gives us the technology to create virtual casinos on handsets, with secure online betting facilitated by the same back-end that powers the growing online casinos found on the Web today, including 888.com.

It's not just the adult-oriented industries that have room for growth; the education and entertainment markets are also yet to be cornered. Current technologies allow us to make swift moves into new areas at very little cost. Just as eBay was started by a guy simply wanting to sell Pez dispensers, the mobile world will see its own success stories in the coming years.

The future of devices

It's easy to think that mobiles are heading the way of the PDA—ever more powerful, sporting more features, and, in essence, becoming a portable extension of the desktop. This view of things to come is very shortsighted, however. We have found that one of the key success factors in the growth of the mobile phone is usability. People don't want a full-fledged computer in their pocket that can do anything, but they do want something that does a few jobs very well, very quickly, and requiring as little learning as possible.

Overcomplicating devices can seal their fates. The late Jef Raskin, of Apple fame, was a strong believer in keeping things simple. He was once quoted as saying,

> Imagine if every Thursday your shoes exploded if you tied them the usual way. This happens to us all the time with computers, and nobody thinks of complaining.

I think he hit the nail on the head when it comes to why mobile phones are still not considered computers in many ways. People have bad experiences with computers, because computers always manage to find a way to break, no matter how well you stick to the rules. Mobile phones on the other hand have a great history of usability, and when a phone doesn't work as it should, people reject it, and that particular model is discontinued within weeks.

So where *are* devices heading? Well, increased power is, no doubt, coming. Three-dimensional graphic coprocessors and plenty of RAM mean that the mobile gaming industry will flourish. PDAs are likely to continue to drop in popularity, as consumers are favoring smart phones for all of their non-PC tasks. As mentioned previously in this chapter, convergence is already happening, but I expect it to continue to develop, with cross-platform communication standards being enforced along the way. As for Flash, well, it would be wrong to think the more-powerful desktop Flash player will not be able to run on mobiles in the very near future. In fact, the Nokia 7710 already supports the Flash 6 player, so why not the Flash 7 and then Flash 8 players? One thing you can rely on is that mobile devices are here to stay, and as developers, we play an important role in shaping the future of their use, just as they play an important role in shaping how we live our lives.

Summary

The mobile devices are the core entities with which we work. The devices lead us to pitfalls, setbacks, and limitations, but they also open up a whole new world to us in which we can create and deploy our games and applications, a world where our applications go wherever our clients go, and this concept is very exciting. In the next chapter, we will discuss Flash Lite, one of the technologies that has changed the way we think about mobile applications, especially the way we develop for them.

Chapter 3

FLASH LITE 1.1 AND YOUR FIRST FLASH LITE APPLICATION

Flash Lite is Adobe's flagship application in the mobile world. Like its big brother the desktop Flash player, the Flash Lite player provides a feature-rich platform for delivering multimedia experiences over a range of devices from mobile phones to set-top boxes. Although Flash Lite 1.1 doesn't support *all* of the functionality of the desktop profile, the same underlying features, including vectors, bitmap graphics, MP3 sound, and a flexible scripting engine, provide more than enough power to create versatile and engaging mobile applications. However, Flash Lite 2 (see Chapter 4) does allow for the use of ActionScript 2 and should prove much less alien to those of you already accustomed to creating Flash content for the Web. It's important to note that the Flash Lite player, like the desktop player, always plays content created for a previous version, so content authored for Flash Lite 1.1 can be played without any modifications in the Flash Lite 2 player.

> *If you're interested in working with Flash Lite 2 but have little or no experience in ActionScript, you might find reading* Foundation Flash 8 *(Kristian Besley and Sham Bhangal: friends of ED, 2006) perfect for getting you up to speed on ActionScript and the techniques involved.*

Flash Lite's true potential becomes clear when we compare it to existing, more established technologies such as Sun's J2ME. It is *very* clear that Flash Lite is quickly becoming a formidable force in the rapid creation of games and applications for mobile devices such as cell phones and PDAs. The desktop Flash player is ubiquitous—it reached 98 percent browser penetration back in 2004. In the mobile industry, we don't yet see these sorts of figures, but Adobe is taking every measure to ensure we don't have to wait around too long before we reach a critical mass, so we can be assured of mass market penetration of our Flash Lite applications very soon. This chapter contains Flash setup information and a lot of general Flash and ActionScript theory. If you are already comfortable with a version of ActionScript, you might prefer to skim through and pick out the bits that appear unfamiliar. In this chapter, I cover the following topics:

- Setting up your Flash Lite studio
- Obtaining a Flash Lite player for your device
- Creating a simple test application
- A Flash Lite 1.1 ActionScript primer, including variables, operators, and control structures
- Coding conventions
- FSCommand2 commands
- Useful functions
- Limitations of ActionScript for Flash Lite
- Version inconsistencies and pitfalls
- SWF tools
- The Flash Lite 1.1 Content Development Kit (CDK)

Without further ado, let's head straight into it and create some Flash Lite content.

Setting up your Flash Lite studio

If you are using Flash MX 2004, this section is for you. If you are using Flash 8 Professional or Flash 9 Professional, you can skip the subsequent "Installation" section if you wish, as these are already set up for Flash Lite development. Beginning Flash Lite development has the following prerequisites:

- **Flash MX Professional 2004 or later**: Version 7.0.1 or greater is required; 7.2 or Flash 8 Pro is recommended.
- **The Flash Lite player for the Flash IDE**: FlashLite1_1.dll for PC, or FlashLite1_1.dmg for Mac.
- **Flash Lite 1.1 publish profile configuration file**: FlashLite1_1.xml.
- **The device's configuration file**: *DevicesMsg.cfg*.
- **Device templates**: Flash-based "emulators" for different mobile devices allowing you to easily test your applications.

The Flash Lite player, publish profile configuration file, and device configuration file are included as part of the Flash Lite 1.1 CDK, which is available for download at the following URL:

www.macromedia.com/devnet/devices/flashlite.html

In addition to the files listed previously, you may also like to download the sample files provided on this book's web site at www.flashmobileforum.org/samples to follow the examples provided throughout the book.

Now that you know what you need, let's run through the installation process for Flash Lite using the MX 2004 versions of Flash.

Flash MX 2004 Professional

The Flash MX 2004 IDE provides you with everything you need to begin developing Flash content, from design tools to a full-featured code editor. If you have purchased the Flash IDE already, I strongly suggest that you check which version you are running from the Help ➤ About Flash Professional menu option. The minimum required version to author Flash Lite content is 7.0.1, although 7.2 is strongly recommended, as it provides a whole host of improvements to the IDE. If you are running a version of MX 2004 prior to 7.2, you can upgrade to the latest version at

www.macromedia.com/support/flash/downloads.html

At this web site, you can download an updater application for PC or Macintosh that fixes several bugs and problems associated with the previous releases of the IDE, components, and documentation, as well as providing many other noticeable improvements to stability and workflow. This update is free to all users with a valid license and does not alter any projects you have created with a previous version.

The Flash Lite player for the Flash IDE

The Flash Lite player DDL or DMG file provides the Flash IDE with the ability to play back and test Flash Lite 1.1–exported content. It also displays any warnings and error messages associated with Flash Lite development and the many new commands available. To install this file, simply copy FlashLite1_1.dll (or FlashLite1_1 on a Mac) to one of the following hard disk locations:

- **Windows**: C:\Program Files\Macromedia\Flash MX 2004\language\Configuration\players
- **Macintosh**: Macintosh HD::Applications:Macromedia Flash MX 2004:Configuration:players

> *For Windows users,* language *represents your two- or three-letter language code. For example,* en *is used for all English language installations,* es *for Spanish, and so on. For a full listing of language codes, you can refer to the* System.capabilities.language *section in the bundled Flash Help.*

The Flash Lite 1.1 publish profile configuration file

When starting the Flash IDE, the application looks in the aforementioned Players folder for XML-based publish profile configuration files to determine which extra profiles and player versions are available for use when exporting your movies. FlashLite1_1.xml tells the Flash IDE to add a new player version to the export settings screen and contains information on which player file to use to test Flash Lite content, as well as adding extra documentation to the Actions panel to ease development when scripting.

If you open up this file in your favorite general text editor (for example, Notepad2 from www.flos-freeware.ch), you notice that it contains, near the end, information on device capabilities. You can manually alter these values to more accurately emulate your known target device, although this is never as good as actually testing on the device itself. Testing is discussed later in the book; for now, just copy FlashLite1_1.xml into the same folder as the previous player file (FlashLite1_1.dll or FlashLite1_1) and, as before, be careful to enter the correct language code if you are using Windows.

The device's configuration file

DevicesMsg.cfg defines the features that are supported when testing your Flash Lite content in the IDE's Flash Lite player. Again, if you open this file in a text editor, you will notice all of the lines are commented out. Uncommenting these lines enables (or disables depending on the context) features such as support for the four-way navigational pad present on most phones. Most of these options can be switched on by uncommenting a line and setting the variable to on. For example, change the following line:

```
// GetURLOnePerKey=off
```

to this one

```
GetURLOnePerKey=on
```

This setting allows calls to getURL() *only* when called from a keypress event, not a frame or any other scripted event. All of these configuration options and their meanings can be found in the appendixes at the end of this book.

> In Flash 8 Professional, DevicesMsg.cfg *is ignored and is replaced by a series of* XML configuration files for each of the handsets being tested. You can find these files in Flash 8 Professional/<language>/Configuration/Mobile/Devices/.

To complete the installation of the required Flash Lite files for Flash MX 2004, copy DevicesMsg.cfg to one of the following hard disk locations and restart Flash:

- **Windows 2000 or Windows XP**: C:\Documents and Settings*user name*\Local Settings\Application Data\Macromedia\Flash MX 2004*language*\Configuration\

- **Windows 98(SE)**: C:\Windows\Profiles*user name*\Application Data\Macromedia\Flash MX 2004*language*\Configuration\

- **Macintosh**: Macintosh HD::Users:*user name*:Library:Application Support:Macromedia:Flash MX 2004:*language*:Configuration:

> *user name refers to the user for which Macromedia Flash MX 2004 is currently installed. In Windows XP, you can find out the name of the currently logged-in user by pressing Ctrl+Alt+Del and clicking the* Users *tab.*

Device templates

Once you have installed the required Flash Lite authoring files, you may also find it useful to create or download device templates for the devices you wish to develop for. Device templates usually consist of an empty FLA file preset with the Flash Lite 1.1 publish settings, a guide layer containing the device graphic (with a transparent window for the screen), and in certain cases, a guide layer containing device specifications (such as screen size and capabilities). David Mannl, an experienced Flash Lite developer, has created a set of device templates for a wide range of handsets including Nokia, Sony Ericsson, and Siemens. These can be downloaded from the following web site:

www.flash-lite.de/downloads.html

Templates are installed to one of the following locations:

- **Windows**: C:\Program Files\Macromedia\Flash MX 2004*language*\Configuration\ Templates\Mobile Devices
- **Macintosh**: Macintosh HD::Applications:Macromedia Flash MX 2004:Configuration: Templates:Mobile Devices

Placing FLA files in this directory creates new file templates available from the Flash start page or File ➤ New dialog. Figure 3-1 shows the start page with the Mobile Devices category highlighted. You can create template categories of your own by adding subfolders to the Templates folder and placing your FLA files in those folders.

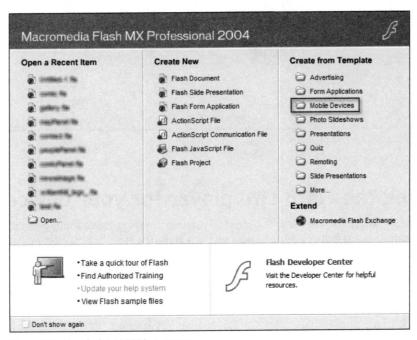

Figure 3-1. The Flash MX 2004 start page

Figure 3-2 shows the Flash IDE just after opening a file created using the Nokia 7610 template. You can see the two guide layers that display the phone graphic and specifications. Testing the movie does not export either of these layers, so it is perfectly safe to keep one or both of these in the FLA throughout production.

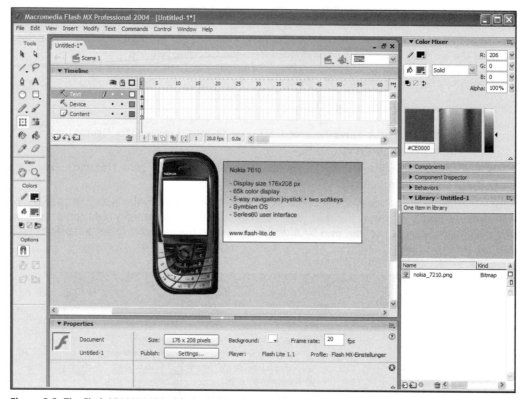

Figure 3-2. The Flash MX 2004 IDE with the Nokia 7610 template

Obtaining the Flash Lite player for your device

Now that your Flash Lite studio setup is complete, you might want to think about getting a Flash Lite player for your handsets and any other devices you may own. The Flash Lite player is available for purchase in the software section of the Adobe Store (www.macromedia.com/store).

The price is nominal (around $8 per device), and you can begin testing on real devices right away. Each Flash Lite player you purchase from the store requires you to send Adobe your device's 15-digit IMEI number. This number uniquely identifies your device and allows the Flash player to be locked for operation on it. On most handsets, you can obtain this number by typing the following into the keypad:

    *#06#

Once the purchase is complete, you receive a Flash Lite player installer file, most likely in the form of a Symbian installer application (a SIS file). Transferring and installing this file depends on the handset or device. Most phones now come with software and cables to transfer and install software from a PC or Mac. Installation can take place over a wide variety of mediums, including Bluetooth, USB/serial cable, infrared, e-mail attachment, and over the air (OTA) via a WAP site link. It is always best to consult your device's manual or manufacturer's web site for specific and full instructions on transferring and installing applications.

As well as purchasing the Flash Lite player for your handsets, I recommend joining the Adobe Mobile Developer Program. Benefits include notifications of events and relevant news, as well as the opportunity to join Flash Lite beta programs, allowing you to obtain the latest Flash Lite player for testing (providing feedback to Adobe is a matter of courtesy, of course). You can join the Mobile Developers Program by e-mailing mobiledeveloper@Adobe.com.

Creating a simple test application

Now, let's test if everything is working as it should. Fire up Flash MX 2004, and choose the Nokia 7610 template discussed previously. With the Text Tool selected, choose a 14-point, blue, sans-serif font such as Arial or Verdana from the Properties panel, or let Flash decide which sans-serif font to use by selecting _sans from the font selection drop-down combo box. Next, simply draw a text field on the stage, and enter the words Hello World. Your screen should now look something like the one in Figure 3-3.

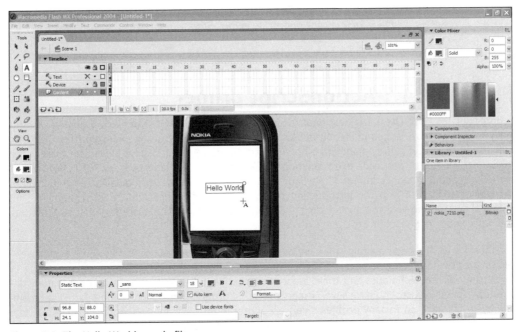

Figure 3-3. The Hello World sample file

You can now test the movie by pressing Ctrl+Enter (or Command+Return on the Mac), or by using the menu system to select Control ➤ Test Movie. You should see the movie displayed in a new window, and the following text should appear in the Output panel:

```
*** Flash Lite Info - FTPS084: Configuration file found.
*** Flash Lite Info - SWFS028: File size: 0.11 kilobytes.
```

The codes FTPS084 and SWF028 represent the various events or errors that can occur when publishing for Flash Lite; a full list of codes and definitions is included in this book's appendixes. If you are having trouble following the previous steps, you can download a premade version of the Hello World file (HelloWorld.fla) from the Chapter 3 samples folder from the book's web site.

> For the remainder of the book, I use the terms "compile" and "test movie" interchangeably to refer to the process of exporting a Flash movie by pressing Ctrl+Enter (or Command+Enter) on the keyboard or using the Control ➤ Test Movie menu option.
>
> Please also make sure that you have selected the correct publish profile to begin with by creating your document from a Flash Lite 1.1–specific template, such as the Nokia 710 template used in the Hello World example, or by manually editing the publish version in the settings interface found in the Properties panel. A common mistake to make at first is to accidentally use the Flash Lite 1.0 profile (which is the default for all included mobile device templates that ship with Flash MX 2004). Using Flash Lite 1.1–specific features when exporting for Flash Lite 1.0 results in the following message appearing in the output window: WARNING: This movie uses features that are not supported in the Flash Lite 1.0 player.

A Flash Lite 1.1 ActionScript primer

ActionScript for Flash Lite 1.1 is best described as Flash 4 ActionScript with Flash 5 objects. All this really means is that it is a combination of Flash 4–style code, such as using on(event) handlers and calls to getProperty(), in conjunction with some of the newer Flash 5 built-in objects such as the Math object, in order to provide extra functionality. When I refer to "later versions" of ActionScript, I am talking about ActionScript for Flash 5 or later, because a lot of the behavior of ActionScript changed after Flash 4 with the introduction of dot syntax and object-oriented programming. This primer is designed to give you a grounding in ActionScript for Flash Lite, from variables to functions, and no previous ActionScript experience is required.

For most of us, it's been a while since we've worked with Flash 4 ActionScript, if we ever have—certainly since before the removal of normal mode from the Actions panel. It's very interesting to revisit some of the techniques and tricks associated with Flash 4–style coding from a completely different perspective. Also, you have several years of Flash 4 programming exploration by the Flash community to fall back on for any problems you encounter. Adobe has made scripting for Flash Lite as easy to use as possible. For example, the compiler allows you to use many of the programming constructs you are already used to, including some dot syntax, and silently converts it to "old school" Flash 4 code behind the scenes. If you have no previous Flash or ActionScript experience, you would benefit from reading *Foundation Flash 8*, mentioned previously, and *Object-Oriented ActionScript for Flash 8* by Peter Elst and Todd Yard (friends of ED, 2006.)

Variables

Variables in Flash Lite behave in exactly the same way as with other Flash player profiles in as far as they allow you to store values to be read and manipulated at runtime. The following types of values can be stored in variables:

- Number
- String
- Boolean: converted to 1 or 0 at runtime
- undefined: cannot be assigned to a variable but is used internally by the player to indicate that a variable has not yet been defined or assigned a value

Unlike in later versions of ActionScript, the use of the keyword var to declare a variable is not supported. You define variables in code simply by assigning them a value. An example of each of the values shown in the previous list can be seen in the following code:

```
age = 50;
apple = "red apple";
isValid = true;
fruit = apple; // stores "red apple";
trace(banana); // outputs: "undefined"
```

The fourth line shows how you can read the value contained in another variable at runtime. The final line shows what happens if you try to read the value of a variable that has not previously been assigned a value. Variable names must contain only alphanumeric characters, underscores (_), and dollar signs ($) and must not begin with a number.

Operators

Flash Lite supports all of the operators found in Flash 4, including eq and gt, but it also supports some of the functionality found in later versions, such as ==. However, rules govern which operators can and should be used with which data types; we discuss these later in this primer. When talking about the variables or values to the left or right of an operator, I use the term **operand**; a set of operands and operators together make up an **expression**.

General operators

In this section, we will look at a couple of general purpose operators that you will be using all the time in your ActionScript coding.

Assignment operator (=) This operator is, perhaps, the simplest to use. The value to the right of this operator is assigned to the variable to the left, for example:

```
lives = 5;
choice = "one";
theirChoice = choice; // theirChoice stores the value "one"
```

The final assignment shows a *variable* to the right of the = operator. When this is the case, the value contained in that variable is assigned to the left-hand side, unless the right-hand variable is a complex object. However, complex objects are not supported in Flash Lite 1.1 ActionScript.

Complex objects can be found in Flash 5 and later, so they are likely to appear in future versions of the Flash Lite player. Complex objects can contain multiple properties, methods, or other objects (known as child objects). An example of a complex object might be a variable named car *that contains properties for* speed *and* bhp. *Access to these properties could be achieved through the use of the dot operator (.), for example,* car.bhp = 297;, *or with the array access operators,* car["bhp"] = 297;. *Arrays and movie clips are also complex objects. In Flash Lite 1.1, we can mimic this behavior using movie clips and the colon (:) operator (discussed later in this chapter). Arrays, however, are not supported.*

The assignment operator can also be used in a compound form alongside arithmetic operators such as +, -, *, /, and % to perform an assignment operation after performing the operation indicated by the first symbol. This makes for easy-to-read, lean code and is often used to increment variables in code loops. An example of this follows:

```
num = 10;
num += 10; // num = num + 10
num /= 5;  // num = num / 5
trace(num); // outputs: 4
```

Ternary operator This operator is a compound form of an if statement when used for conditional assignment (the if statement is discussed further in the section entitled "Control structures"). The following code shows a rational way of acting on a condition:

```
if (vegetarian) {
    pizza = "margerita";
} else {
    pizza = "pepperoni";
}
```

This code can be rewritten using the conditional operator:

```
pizza = (vegetarian) ? "margerita" : "pepperoni";
```

To understand what's going on, take a look at the following psuedo-code:

```
variable = (condition) ? ifTrueVal : ifFalseVal;
```

If condition is true, variable is assigned the value of ifTrueVal; if not, it is assigned the value of ifFalseVal.

Numeric operators

The numeric operators allow you to compare numbers. It is often tempting to use these operators with other primitives such as strings, as you can in later versions of ActionScript. This can lead to unexpected behavior in certain circumstances or a failure to function altogether; the reasons are explained fully for each of the operators that follow.

Numeric equality operator (==) The documentation that comes with the Flash Lite CDK (the *Flash Lite 1.1 Authoring Guidelines*) incorrectly states that the numeric equality operator is a single equals sign (=). If you try to test numeric equality with this operator, you do not get the results you expect. The following code illustrates the problem:

```
a = 10;
trace(a = 12);   // output: 12s
trace(10 = a);   // results in an error being thrown
```

As you can see, the first trace statement simply takes the second operand as the value, as expected with the assignment operator. Instead you need to use the == operator to test whether two numbers are, in fact, equal:

```
b = 20;
trace(b == 10); // outputs: 0 (false)
trace(20 == b); // outputs: 1 (true)
trace("15" == 15); // outputs: 1 (true)
trace("abc" == "abc"); // outputs: 0 (false)
```

Notice that the last two comparisons involve strings. The first shows a string that contains only numerals. When Flash Lite encounters values that do not fit in with the operators being used (in this case a string on one or both sides of a numeric equality operator), it attempts an automatic type conversion and treats the string "15" as the numeric equivalent 15. For more information on this behavior, please refer to the next Focus Point, which discusses automatic type conversion. The second of the string comparisons involves two string literals. Even though the strings are, in fact, the same, the test proves false, because to test alphanumeric strings, you must use one of the string-specific operators, such as eq.

Numeric addition, subtraction, multiplication, and division operators (+, –, *, and /) These operators work as expected in Flash Lite, performing the various arithmetic functions associated with these familiar symbols. The only thing to watch out for is accidentally reverting back to Flash 5–style coding, which you might be used to, and using the + operator with a string. Even though Flash performs automatic type conversion in most cases (discussed later in this chapter), if you attempt to use a string that does not contain only numeric digits, you receive a 1.#QNAN error, as the following example shows:

```
trace("2" + 3);   // outputs: 5
trace("two" + 3);   // outputs: 1.#QNAN
```

Now, of course, you would never intentionally type the second line, but you might accidentally do so when referring to values stored in a variable or values that a user might enter into a text field. The #QNAN message simply indicates that a nonnumeric operand has been used with an arithmetic operator.

Modulo division operator (%) The modulo operator performs a division and returns the remainder of that division:

```
x = 50;
y = 20;
trace(x%y);   // outputs: 10;
```

This operator comes in handy when you want to quickly find out whether a number is even or odd. An example usage of this might be when setting alternating row colors in a table:

```
rows = 10;
for (i=0; i<rows; i++) {
    if (i%2) rowColor = "white";
    else rowColor = "grey";
}
```

In Flash Lite, the modulo operator is expanded as x - int(x/y) * y in the SWF, which is slower and may not be as accurate as with later versions of the player. For those interested in the lower level behavior of the Flash player, you can find out exactly what code your SWF contains after you've exported it using a variety of tools, shown in the section on SWF tools near the end of this chapter.

Increment and decrement operators (++ and --) Adds 1 to or subtracts 1 from the value preceding or following the operator. If the operator appears *after* the variable, the addition or subtraction takes place after the expression has been evaluated, for example:

```
x = 1;
if (x++ == 1) trace("x == 1");   // outputs: x == 1
```

If you place the operator *before* the variable, the increment or decrement takes place before the expression is evaluated:

```
x = 1;
if (++x == 1) trace("x == 1"); // doesn't ouput anything
```

Any strings are treated as a numeric 0 if used with the increment or decrement operator.

Numeric greater than and less than operators (> and <) These operators are used to test whether a value is numerically larger or smaller than the value to the right of the operator. As with the other numeric operators, problems can occur when testing strings:

```
c = 30;
trace(c < 40);  // outputs: 1 (true)
trace(20 > c);  // outputs: 0 (false)
trace("15" > "10");  // outputs: 1 (true, type conversion)
trace("abc" > "abc");'  // outputs: 0 (false, no type conversion)
```

In short, this operator should not be used to test strings. Instead, use gt and lt.

Numeric greater than or equal to and less than or equal to operators (>= and <=) Similar to the > and < operators, these compound operators also evaluate as true in an expression where the values are equal:

```
d = 40;
trace(d <= 40);  // outputs: true
trace(d >= 30);  // outputs: true
trace(d >= 41);  // outputs: false
```

Numeric inequality operator (<>) When used between two values, the expressions evaluates as true, or 1, if the values are not equal, and false, or 0, if they are equal:

```
diceRoll = random(5)+1;
if (diceRoll <> 6) trace("Stay in jail");
```

> *Type conversion differs from Flash 5 or later in Flash Lite. Take, for example, the following code:*
>
> ```
> trace("1"+1);
> ```
>
> *In Flash Lite 1.1 (and Flash 4 for that matter), the* Output *panel traces the number 2. Flash Lite automatically converts the string literal* "1" *to a number, no matter which side of the operator it appears on. In Flash 5 or later, this conversion works the other way around—it traces the string* "11". *This happens because, in Flash Lite, the + operator is used solely for numbers, unlike later versions of ActionScript. In Flash Lite, the* add *keyword is used to concatenate strings.*

String operators

Strings have their own set of operators in Flash Lite; this differs from later versions of the Flash player, but adjusting to the use of these is very straightforward and completely natural once you've used them a few times. Strings are assigned with the assignment operator (=) discussed previously. However, other string operators in Flash Lite and Flash 4 are deprecated in later versions.

String concatenation operator (add) The add operator is used to **concatenate**, or join, strings. Although the *Flash Lite 1.1 Authoring Guidelines* state that the & operator can also be used to concatenate strings, this is not the case and doing so results in an error being thrown. The following code uses the add operator to generate a string containing all of the letters in the alphabet:

```
alphabet = "";
for (i=65; i<91; i++) alphabet = alphabet add chr(i);
trace(alphabet); // outputs: ABCDEFG...XYZ
```

The chr() function is used to return a character string from an ASCII character code.

String equal and not equal operators (eq and ne) The equal operator (eq) tests whether a string is identical to another, and the not equal operator (ne) tests to see if one string is different from another:

```
trace("Apple" eq "Apple");  // outputs: 1 (true)
trace("Apple" ne "Orange");  // outputs: 1 (true)
trace("Apple" eq "apple");  // outputs: 0 (false)
```

A string is case sensitive when used with either of these operators. If you want to test one value against another without worrying about case (for example, a user-input value), you have to write your own lowercase() function. This code can be found in the "Useful functions" section of this chapter.

String greater than and less than operators (gt and lt) Strings can be compared against one another for alphabetical precedence. When comparing strings, the string starting with the numerically higher character code in the Unicode character set is treated as "greater than" the other. For example, "Z" is greater than "N," which, in turn, is greater than "A". If both strings begin with the same character, the next character in the string is considered. In Flash Lite, the string is first converted to lowercase. An example of a string comparison might be as follows:

```
trace("CNN" gt "BBC");
```

While you may not agree with this statement, it does however evaluate as true! For a full listing of the ASCII character set including decimal, octal, and hexadecimal character codes, you can refer to the excellent table at www.asciitable.com.

Boolean operators

Boolean values are treated slightly differently in Flash Lite than in later versions of the player. Flash Lite does not have a runtime or byte code value for true or false like Flash 5 and later versions. In Flash Lite, Booleans are physically converted to their numeric equivalents at compile time. true equates to 1, and false to 0:

```
trace(true); // outputs: 1
trace(false); // outputs: 0

if(1) trace("1 is true"); // outputs: "1 is true"
if(0) trace("0 is false"); // doesn't output at all
```

While you can (and should) use the keywords true and false when writing your code, if you want to use them with arithmetic operators, please bear in mind that you are actually dealing with the numbers 0 and 1, as illustrated by the following example code:

```
playerWins = true;
trace(playerWins > 0);  // outputs: 1 (same as 1>0)
```

Logic operators

Logic operators evaluate expressions against one another. These is useful for combining expressions, allowing you to generate more complex expressions that better model a condition, for example, when one condition is dependent on another.

Logical AND operator (&& and "and") The && or and operators test whether both conditions are true. If so, the entire expression evaluates as true:

```
filledInForm = true;
age = 34;
if (filledInForm && (age>18)) trace("Membership approved!");
```

Notice the extra set of brackets, or, as they are collectively known, the **grouping operator**, used here to separate expressions and improve legibility. Code inside a set of brackets is evaluated before any operators outside of the brackets are taken into consideration.

Logical OR operator (|| and "or") Evaluates as true if either condition is true, for example:

```
theColor = "red";
if (theColor == "red" || theColor == "blue")
    trace("We have the right color for you!");
```

The keyword or can be used, but || is recommended for future compatibility.

Logical NOT operator (! and "not") The logical NOT operator (!) has the effect of inverting the Boolean value of an expression, converting a true into a false, and vice versa:

```
if (!dead) // continue game
else // game over
```

The keyword not can be used in place of the ! operator, but this keyword has been deprecated, like or.

Undefined variables

Although the keyword undefined is not supported for use in the code you write for Flash Lite movies, variables that are not initialized or simply don't exist still take on the value undefined. For proof of this, try out the following sample code:

```
trace(randomNamedVar);  // outputs: "undefined"
```

While it is not possible to test a value to see if it is undefined, it is important to understand the behavior of undefined variables in Flash Lite for debugging purposes. As with Flash 4, undefined variables in Flash Lite take on a value of 0 when used with a numeric operator as shown next:

```
count = count - 10;
trace(count);  // outputs: -10
```

As you can see, even though count was never defined or initialized, the numerical addition assignment operator initializes the variable to 0. This behavior can cause problems in loops, where you may forget to initialize a counter beforehand and fail to see why it fails silently. The same behavior occurs with string operators—the undefined variable takes on the value of an empty string, or "":

```
cra = "BMW";  // mispelt variable "cra"
car = car add " 7 Series";
trace(car);  // outputs: " 7 series";
```

> *Flash Lite 1.1 currently follows Flash 4 behavior where* undefined *is concerned but is likely to change in future revisions. In fact, this behavior changed in Flash 7, where the previous code example outputs* "undefined series 7". *In Flash 7, undefined variables do not take on a default value when used with operators; instead they take on the value* undefined.

Slash notation (targeting movie clips)

The movie clip is a fundamental unit in Flash Lite. Movie clips can contain graphics, animations, sounds, variables, and even child movie clips. We can use them to model parent-child relationships between objects, for example, a car movie clip can contain four wheel movie clips, which, in turn, could each contain a hubcap and five bolt movie clips. When it comes to accessing these movie clips in code, Flash Lite uses a syntax similar to the one used for identifying files and paths on a computer's operating system. Take this Windows file path, for example:

    C:\windows\media\soundfile.wav

It should be fairly easy to see that the path is referring to a file named soundfile.wav stored in a folder named media, which, in turn, is found in another folder named windows, on the C: drive. In Flash Lite, we also use a slash to indicate a difference in the "level" at which a MovieClip can be found, but instead of a backslash (\), we use a forward slash (/).

When the Flash compiler sees a forward slash in code, it examines its context to see whether it needs to be treated as a division operator for arithmetic or a path operator for movie clip access. The first slash indicates the root time line; the root time line is the main time line you see at the top of the screen when creating a new document. Every movie clip you create is a child, grandchild, or great-grandchild of the root time line. Any slashes that follow this root slash indicate a lower level, a child of the movie clip in question. The diagram in Figure 3-4 shows how this relationship works in practice.

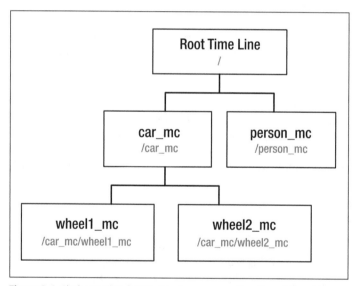

Figure 3-4. Slash notation for movie clips, representing the relationships between parent and child movie clips

The smaller text under each movie clip name shows how that movie clip would be referenced in code. You can see the root time line is always a single /. The movie clip named car_mc has been placed on stage and can be referred to in code as simply /car_mc. Flash also allows us to drop the leading slash in car_mc if we are writing code on the main time line, because Flash allows for relative paths.

Relative paths

A **relative path** is one that does not include a root slash (/). Instead you can refer to a movie clip with a path that is relative to the movie clip you are *currently* working in. I could write the following code on frame 1 of car_mc's time line:

```
xPos = getProperty("/car_mc/wheel1_mc", _x);
trace(xPos);
```

For now, you can just ignore the getProperty() function, which is discussed later. You should notice that we explicitly refer to wheel1_mc with a full, absolute path, and this works as expected. "Wait," I hear you say, "we are already working in car_mc's time line." Because that is true, we can also use a relative path to refer to wheel1_mc—a path indicating where wheel1_mc is *relative* to our current location, inside car_mc:

```
xPos = getProperty("wheel1_mc", _x);
trace(xPos);
```

If we want to refer to bolt_mc, which is inside wheel1_mc, we could simply use the following:

```
boltXPos = getProperty("wheel1_mc/bolt1_mc", _x);
trace(boltXPos);
```

If you would like to take a moment to play around with slash notation, you can find the FLA file for the preceding example (Car.fla) in the Chapter 3 downloads. Figure 3-5 shows how this parent-child relationship might appear on stage.

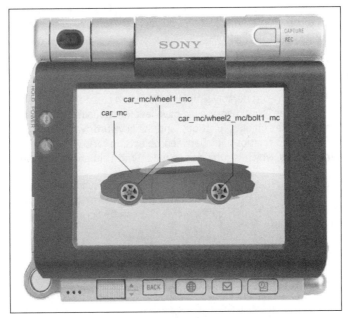

Figure 3-5. The car movie as it might appear on a Sony Clie UX50

What if we want to write code on /car_mc/whee1_mc's time line that referred to a parent movie clip, such as car_mc itself? This is where the dot operator (.) comes in. A double dot (..) allows us to refer to the parent of the current movie clip. Take the following code, for example:

```
trace(getProperty("..", _x));
```

In this case, ".." refers to the parent movie clip wheel1_mc, and as this code appears inside a frame on wheel1_mc's time line, the parent in this case is of course car_mc itself. Now we can find the x position of car_mc from within the wheel clip. Nice. Finding the x position is especially useful if we want to get the properties or variables stored in sibling movie clips:

```
trace(getProperty("../wheel2_mc", _rotation));
```

Here we access the current rotation of the other wheel. We can use this to sync the wheel rotations every frame. You can even build complex paths by using multiple slashes and double dots:

```
trace(getProperty("../wheel2_mc/../wheel1_mc", _x));
```

As you've probably guessed, this is a rather long and useless path that simply refers to the wheel movie clip in which we are actually writing the code in the first place! It could simply be rewritten as follows:

```
trace(getProperty("", _x));
// or
trace(_x);
```

Using a combination of the slash (/) and dot(.) operators, we can access the properties of any other movie clip, which is very powerful indeed. You can even use certain Flash 5 notation such as tellTarget("_root") and getProperty("_level0/car_mc");. Flash Lite is very flexible in this respect and should allow you to develop a coding style you feel comfortable with whether you are coming from a Flash 4 or even a Flash 7 background.

Variable scope

Variable scope in Flash Lite is a considerably simpler affair when compared to the complex scope chain[1] found in later versions of ActionScript, because we have less functionality with which to nest objects, and thus, variables. Without complex objects, functions, and the keywords var and _global, we have very little with which to create nested relationships between objects. In fact, we are limited to nesting objects through the use of movie clips, which is sufficient to model most situations that we encounter.

Access to variables that are defined within another movie clip is achieved with the slash (/), dot (.), and colon (:) operators. The colon operator indicates that the name to follow is not a movie clip but a variable. Variables defined on a time line of a movie clip can be accessed using a combination of the / and : operators, for example:

```
trace(/:$version);
```

---

1. The scope chain is beyond the scope (pun intended) of this chapter, as it generally relates to ActionScript for Flash 5 or later. However, for a full understanding of how Flash uses the scope chain to find variables, please see the excellent article by Timothée Groleau, entitled "Scope Chain and Memory waste in Flash MX," available at http://timotheegroleau.com/Flash/articles/. This article helped me to "crack" Flash, and I would recommend that anyone wanting to understand Flash a little bit more read it several times.

If you try this code, you should see something written to the Output window like "WIN 6,0,99,0" (or "1,0,0,31" in the case of Flash 8's device emulator). $version is a variable that contains the version number for the Flash player being run. If you test $version on a handset running Flash Lite, you see something like "5,2,5,0" (the current version number for the Flash Lite 1.1 player). Going back to our previous car example, you can define a variable in car_mc from the main time line using the following code:

```
/car_mc:speed = 250;
```

Now you can see that we are starting to lay the groundwork for creating one of the games shown later in this book. We can also use this notation to retrieve values for properties like _x (the x position of a movie clip), or _rotation (its rotation, of course):

```
trace(/car_mc:_rotation); // outputs: 0
```

Try adding this code to frame 1 of car.fla's time line, you can even rotate the car symbol using the transform tool and run it again to view the different values for _rotation.

getProperty() and setProperty()

The getProperty() and setProperty() functions allow us to read into and change movie clip properties. MovieClip properties include _x, _y, _rotation, _width, _height and many others. getProperty() takes two parameters. The first parameter is a string containing the path to the target, and the second is the property to obtain, for example:

```
getProperty("smiley_mc", _width);
```

setProperty() takes three parameters. The first two parameters are the same as getProperty()'s: the target path and the property. The last is the new value for the given property.

```
setProperty("smiley_mc", _width, 200);
```

To see these functions in action, open jitterFace.fla from the Chapter 3 samples. In the example, you can see we are using setProperty() to set the smiley's _width and _height properties to a random size every other frame (movies loop back to the first frame unless they find a stop() action); this example illustrates the basics of scripted animation.

set()

set() is the variable equivalent of setProperty(). We can use it to set a variable's contents using the now-familiar slash notation discussed previously. Although it isn't necessary to use set(), as we can simply use the slash and colon notation described earlier, using it allows us to define variables that we do not know the name of until runtime, for example:

```
username = "rleggett";
counter++;
set(username add counter, "loggedIn");
trace(rleggett1);  // outputs: loggedIn
```

This means that we can actually create ranges of variables to mimic Flash 5's arrays. For more on emulating arrays, please see the section entitled "Emulating arrays with eval()."

_target

The _target property can be used to give you an absolute target path for any movie clip. If you type the following code onto any movie clip's time line, you can get trace to output this path, for use elsewhere:

```
trace(_target);
```

As simple as that, we can now trace out the full target path for any movie clip, which is also useful when debugging your applications at runtime.

Control structures

Now that we have a firm grip on manipulating variables and obtaining movie clip properties, you may want to think about acting on these values depending on certain conditions. Flash Lite supports most of the control structures found in the desktop Flash player, including if, if-else, for, for-in, while, and even switch.

if and if . . . else

if and if . . . else are two of the most useful control structures in any programming language. With them, we can evaluate an expression to see whether the outcome is true or false and act on that result. The if statement is formed by following the keyword if with an expression or variable wrapped in parentheses, for example:

```
if (condition) // Do something
```

If the condition evaluates as true, Flash performs the action immediately following the closing parenthesis, for example:

```
if (loggedIn) trace("You are already logged in");
```

We can perform an alternative action if the expression is false using the keyword else:

```
if (age >= 18) trace("You are logged in.");
else trace("Get out of here kid!");
```

You can even have multiple lines of code executed for each of the conditions by using curly brackets:

```
if (loggedIn) {
    trace("Ok you're in");
    gotoAndStop("loggedInFrame");
} else {
    gotoAndStop("loggedOutFrame");
}
```

while and do . . . while

A while loop allows a block of code to iterate while a condition is being met. As soon as the condition evaluates as false, the loop is broken. A simple example of a while loop follows:

```
x = 5;
while (x>0) {
    trace(x);
    x--;
}
```

The previous code would output 5, 4, 3, 2, and 1 in turn. The do . . . while loop, however, allows the condition to be evaluated after the loop iterates, for example:

```
x = 0;
do {
    trace(x);
    x--;
} while (x>0)
```

The output for this code would simply be 0. Notice that even though x is equal to 0 (and therefore does not meet the condition), the code in the loop is still executed once before the condition is evaluated. Although uses for this second type of while loop may not seem obvious right away, a do . . . while loop will prove favorable on many occasions, and remembering the options available is always worthwhile.

switch

The switch statement is great for compacting code and making decisions based on the contents of a single variable. It works alongside the case statement to compare a variable to a number of values (string or number values). First of all, let's look at a typical switch statement as it appears in code:

```
switch (userPrivileges) {
    case "admin": gotoAndPlay("adminLogin");  break;
    case "user" : gotoAndPlay("userLogin");  break;
    case "guest" : gotoAndPlay("guestLogin");
                   userMessage = "Restrictions apply";
                   break;
    default : gotoAndPlay("unrecognizedUser");
}
```

As you can see, the switch statement is followed by an expression (or a single variable), which is evaluated and compared to values that you supply in the various case expressions that follow. These can be strings (as in the previous example), Booleans, or numbers. If a value matches, the code after the colon in the case expression executes until it encounters a break statement. This means that as soon as a value is matched, all of the code for the rest of the case expressions is executed until a break is encountered (it can be easy to forget to add break statements).

In the preceding sample code, the variable userPrivileges might contain the string value "guest". If so, the first two cases ("admin" and "user") are ignored, but the third case matches, causing the gotoAndPlay() and variable assignment for userMessage to execute, stopping when it reaches the break statement.

Finally, the optional default statement can be used to execute code if none of the case expressions match the expression or variable in the switch statement.

Emulating arrays with eval()

Like Flash 4, Flash Lite does not support arrays. This does not mean you cannot use an alternative to arrays in your code, however. When returning data from a server-side source, it is often useful to be able to return a variable number of results. The eval() function allows us to dynamically access the contents of variables that we know the names of. It takes a single parameter—a string indicating the name of the variable to evaluate. An example usage of eval() follows:

```
mammal = "whale";
animal = eval("mammal");
trace(animal);  // outputs: "whale"
```

This is a fair use of eval(), but a better use is to dynamically assign multiple variables with values or read them back. The following code stores n random numbers between 0 and 10 in memory:

```
n = 100;
for (i=0; i<n; i++)
    eval("num" add i) = random(10);
```

We can access these newly created variables in several ways:

```
trace(num0); // outputs: 5 (for example)

// or to list all values
n = 100;
for (i=0; i<n; i++) {
    theNum = eval("num" add i);
    trace(theNum);
}
```

Being able to access the variable in several ways becomes especially useful in loading of external data, where you may want to iterate over several rows of data returned as name-value pairs from a database. Using eval(), you can retrieve an arbitrary number of variables (such as name1, name2 ... nameN) from memory at runtime. This method of data retrieval is examined in depth in Part Two.

Creating custom functions with call()

Flash Lite 1.1 does not support the use of the keyword `function` to define custom functions, but you *can* emulate the use of functions using movie clips, frame labels, and `call()`.

The global `call()` function takes just one parameter, the frame number or frame label for the frame containing your function's ActionScript. You can think of each frame as a function body with the frame label acting as the function's name. Because `call()` does not allow you to target a specific movie clip, it must be used in conjunction with `tellTarget()`, which allows you to send commands to a target clip. This combination directs your target movie clip (containing your functions) to execute the code contained in your specific function. Take the following, for example:

```
tellTarget(functions_mc) {
    call("getHypotenuse");
}
```

This code tells functions_mc to execute the code found on the frame labeled "getHypotenuse". The code on functions_mc's "getHypotenuse" frame consists of just three lines of code:

```
A = 10;
B = 20;
C = Math.sqrt(A*A + B*B);
```

As you have probably guessed, the purpose of this function is to work out the length of the hypotenuse of a triangle based on two known side lengths (A and B) using the Pythagorean theorem. One important thing to note is that `call()` is not the same as `gotoAndStop()`. With `gotoAndStop()`, Flash actually tells the movie clip playhead to move to the desired frame; `call()` simply executes the script attached to that frame. You may also notice that one important thing is missing—parameters. We need the ability to send values for A and B for the function to be useful. We can do this by simply modifying the original code that we wrote to call the function:

```
tellTarget("functions_mc") {
    A = 100;
    B = 200;
    call("getHypotenuse");
}
```

Of course we also have to remove the values for A and B from the function code on the "getHypotenuse" frame; otherwise, we won't be able to set them before calling the function. The code on the "getHypotenuse" frame is now simply

```
C = Math.sqrt(A*A + B*B);
```

That's it; you can now define reusable functions for anything you like. You can view this code in action if you open CustomFunctions.fla from the Chapter 3 downloads. It's also possible to alter the variables or properties of other movie clips from within your functions. This means, for example, you could devise a set of functions that control a spaceship's appearance and position based on its attributes and call that function every frame to update the display, in effect, creating member methods of a spaceship "class." To see this in action, open Spaceship.fla. This file shows you how to monitor a spaceship's health and update the graphics to display damage and a health bar; the screen output for Spaceship.fla is shown in Figure 3-6.

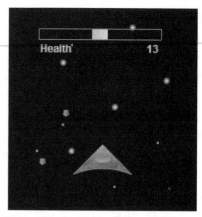

Figure 3-6. Custom functions with call()

There is another way of using the call() function, facilitated by the Flash IDE's intelligent compiler. A sample of this method in action follows:

```
call("MovieClipName:LabelName");
```

As you can see, we eliminate the need for tellTarget() by referencing the label (or function) name using the colon operator within the string. Next, we need to change the way we set the parameters, so the code for the previous Pythagorean example might now be

```
functions_mc.A = 100;
functions_mc.B = 200;
call("functions_mc:getHypotenuse");
```

I think you'll agree this code is much cleaner and easier to read with the colon operator.

Coding conventions

If you are already comfortable scripting with an existing version of ActionScript (AS1, AS2, or AS3), you can pretty much stick with the style you already use; the IDE is intelligent enough to interpret many coding styles. If you are not yet confident in one of these, you may want to follow the coding style in this book. I find it easy to read and consistent with many other programmers' styles, which is a bonus when working in a team or sharing code.

Whitespace and new lines

Making good use of whitespace between variables, expressions, and control statements makes for easy-to-read, easy-to-maintain code. When writing a control statement, I prefer to put a space between the if, else, switch, or while functions and the expression, like so:

```
if (condition) // do this
```

I also prefer to put all curly brackets on their own lines:

```
if (condition)
```

```
{
    // do this
}
```

While the latter isn't the style of code you find in the Adobe documentation, it is very popular, as it makes for easy matching of braces when skimming through code. I use this style of code throughout this book, although I encourage you to use whichever style you find most comfortable. Once you have found a style that matches the way you like to work, you can set the Flash IDE to automatically style the code to match by choosing Auto Format Options from the Actions panel Options menu. Figure 3-7 shows the Actions panel with Auto Format Options circled.

Figure 3-7. The Flash MX 2004 Auto Format Options

Comments

Commenting source code is an invaluable practice. It helps you to understand your code when you come back to it months later and breaks up large chunks of code to summarize the function being performed. Thanks to the MX2004 IDE, Flash Lite supports both the single-line comments indicated with a double slash (//) and the newer, multiline comment styles starting with /* and ending with */:

```
// This is a single line comment
name = "Richard";  // comments can go on the same line

/**
 * Comments can run over multiple lines
 * and even between code...
 */
name = "Michael " add /*surname to follow*/ "Fish";
```

You can over comment, however. If you find you are commenting every line, take a step back, and try to figure out whether the code really does need comments or whether the code explains itself well enough. Take this code snippet for example:

```
// record the users name
username = "jsmith";

// log the user in
loggedIn = true;
```

This is a good example of commenting gone mad. It would have been much better to write a simple, brief multiline comment that summarizes the following few lines, rather than dissect every statement. When in doubt, consider this: Is the comment describing *what* the code does or *why* it does it? The "why" is more important than the "what" in most cases.

Variable naming

Most ActionScript coders favor what is known as **camel case** when naming variables, which is the practice of capitalizing every new word after the first. For example:

```
recordFound = true;
// or
playerMaxLives = 10;
```

It's also important to make sure your variables are descriptive, using verbs rather than nouns to describe what the variable might contain:

```
foundTheRecord = true;  // a little over the top
found = true; // not very descriptive
recordFound = true;  // concise and obvious in function
```

Although variables are not case sensitive in Flash Lite, keeping variable names consistent throughout is considered good practice. Apart from looking more uniform, consistency also prevents variable ambiguity with later versions of Flash Lite (where case does matter, for example, aVar is not the same as avar).

Text field variables

Flash Lite 1.1 does not allow you to name text fields, which means that you cannot refer to a .text property in order to set the text. To get around this, you can give any dynamic or input-type text field (found in the bottom-right corner of the Properties panel) a variable name. Setting this variable to a string or number replaces the text in the text field. When referring to these special text field variables, I like to suffix the variable name with a capital "TF" to distinguish it from regular variables that simply exist on the time line. This practice helps to keep code readable when searching through frames and buttons to see where the someTF variable was first created (the answer being, of course, that it was set in the Properties panel at author time as indicated by the suffix TF). You can also use text field variable names to access the scroll properties of a text field in Flash Lite:

```
trace(textfieldVar.scroll); // outputs a number
```

The number output indicates the current scroll position of the text field, the `.scroll` property can also be set to shift text up or down in a text field. When used in conjunction with the `.maxscroll` property, an efficient scrolling device can be created:

```
scrollOffset = textfieldVar.scroll / textfieldVar.maxscroll;
```

Keywords and reserved words

It is always best to avoid using any keywords and reserved words for your variable names; in fact, I would go as far as to say that it's essential. Take the following line of code for example:

```
color = "blue";
```

At first it may seem perfectly harmless, but if you try to compile this you will receive the following error message:

```
**Warning** Scene=Scene 1, layer=Layer 1, frame=1:Line 1:
Case-insensitive identifier 'color' will obscure built-in object 'Color'.
    color = "blue";
```

Even though Flash Lite 1.1 does not support the Color object (notice the capital "C"), the Flash compiler does not permit you to use the keyword color under any circumstances for variable naming. This also prevents any future keyword conflicts that might arise with later versions of the Flash Lite player. For a full list of keywords in ActionScript, please refer to the ActionScript 2.0 Language Reference, found inside Flash Help.

Statement terminators (semicolons)

Although the Flash compiler assumes that a line break also indicates a statement terminator (a semicolon to you and me), it is good practice to end lines with a semicolon unless the line is part of a control statement such as `if`, `while`, or a curly bracket. All code examples throughout this book follow this practice for consistency.

Dot syntax

Although dot syntax (as used in Flash 5 or later) was not originally available in Flash 4, Flash Lite allows basic use of dot syntax to cut down the amount of code required to access MovieClip properties. Using dot syntax is possible, because the Flash compiler intelligently converts all dot syntax to the Flash 4 equivalent (such as `getProperty()`) at compile time. Dot syntax also helps to maintain more readable code. Take the following code for example:

```
carXPos = getProperty("car_mc", _x);
```

It could be rewritten with dot syntax like so:

```
carXPos = car_mc._x;
```

As you can see, this second line is much easier to read and more logical for those of us who are used to Flash 5 (and later) ActionScript, or AS2. The dot represents the forward slash in a target path string, although you do not need to use a string with dot syntax. You can even use dot syntax to reference child movie clips:

```
boltPosX = car_mc.wheel1_mc.bolt1_mc._x;
```

Throughout this book, I use dot syntax to get and set properties of movie clips and child movie clips, as it produces much shorter code that is also forward compatible with potential advances in the ActionScript of future versions of the Flash Lite player.

FSCommand2 commands

FSCommand was introduced in Flash 3 to provide functionality beyond that offered by the standard Flash player, such as the ability to go full screen, and the ability to execute an external application. It also allows communication with a lower-level application interface, such as C++, Visual Basic, or in our case, the device's own operating system, such as Symbian. FSCommand2 provides an extra set of functions specifically targeted for mobile devices and is only available with Flash Lite. General usage of FSCommand2 is as follows:

```
status = FSCommand2("GetSignalLevel");
```

FSCommand2 returns a status code. A **status code** is a numeric value that usually follows the convention that a value greater than 0 means the command executed successfully, and a value of –1 indicates that the command was not successful or is not supported on the device. (Some functions return 0 for a nonsupported error; please see Appendix C for more information.) There are around 40 FSCommand2 commands for Flash Lite 1.1; a list showing how to use each of them can be found in Appendix C.

> *The difference between* FSCommand *and* FSCommand2 *is that* FSCommand2 *executes immediately, whereas* FSCommand *executes when the end of the frame is reached (and all other code on that frame has been executed).*

Using FSCommand2

You'll probably find that you use some of these functions a lot more than others, so I'm just going over a few of the most useful ones here. First of all, the FullScreen command causes the stand-alone Flash Lite player to maximize to the full dimensions of the screen for a Series 60 mobile device, 176 pixels wide by 208 pixels high. Taking over the entire screen gives you more screen real estate, a crucial commodity when designing for small screens. For the FullScreen command, FSCommand2 takes two parameters: first comes the string "FullScreen", and it's followed by a value indicating whether to switch to full-screen mode (true) or return to windowed mode (false):

```
status = FSCommand2("FullScreen", true);
```

If the call is successful, FSCommand2 immediately returns a value of 0; if the command is unsuccessful, it returns –1. An FSCommand2 command can fail for several reasons: the device may simply not support playing the Flash player full screen, or the Flash Lite movie may be running in a browser window as part of a web page. Some devices do not support the stand-alone player and only offer Flash Lite as part of a web browser plug-in. Although this is true of only a small percentage of handsets, and a decreasing percentage at that, it is important to remember that certain commands can fail at times, and it is better to design around that, if possible, or display a message indicating the compatibility problem.

Another useful command is SetSoftKeys. This FSCommand2 command allows you to remap the soft keys of a mobile phone. The soft keys are usually the two multifunctional keys on the left and right just underneath the screen. SetSoftKeys takes two extra parameters: left and right. These are strings indicating which text to display above the left and right soft keys when the player is running in windowed mode. It is also useful to know that a PageUp keypress event is fired when a user presses the left soft key, and a PageDown keypress event is fired by pressing the right soft key. Let's take a look at how to handle soft key keypresses. The following code is placed on frame 1 of /ch3/FSCommand2.fla:

```
status = FSCommand2("SetSoftKeys", "Next", "Exit");
stop();
```

This code sets up your soft keys, labels them with Next and Exit, respectively, and tells the Flash player to wait at frame 1 for further input. You are now ready to listen for PageUp and PageDown keypress events mapped to your phone's soft keys. To listen for these, you must create a simple button on stage by choosing Insert ➤ New Symbol (or pressing Ctrl+F8) and creating a new button using the dialog box shown in Figure 3-8.

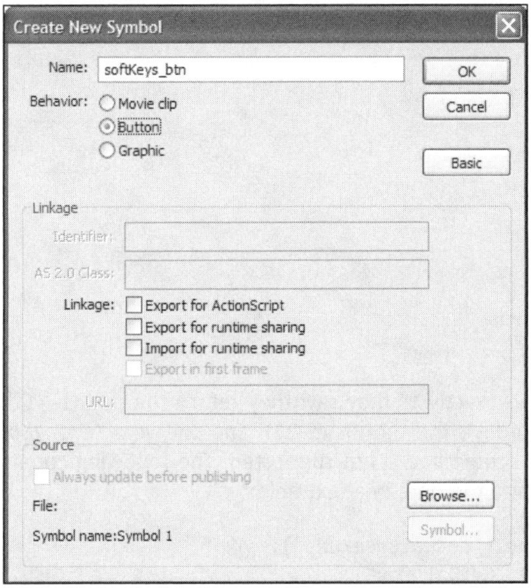

Figure 3-8. Creating a new button

Next, you can click the OK button, come back to the main stage by clicking the Scene 1 button, and drag your newly created (but very empty) button onto the stage anywhere you like. The next step is to add your soft key keypress handler code to this new button. Needing to write keypress handler code on a button may seem strange, but back in the days of Flash 4, this was the only legal way of listening for keypress events. To add the code, you need to click the white dot that represents your new button and type the following into the Actions panel:

```
on (keyPress "<PageUp>")
{
    gotoAndStop(2);
}

on (keyPress "<PageDown>")
{
    FSCommand2("Quit");
}
```

This code tells your Flash player to go to frame 2 should the user press the left soft key (ingeniously labeled Next) and to quit the Flash player if the user presses the right soft key. Please feel free to open /ch3/FSCommand2.fla to see this in action. Remember that commands such as Quit do not work in the Flash IDE, only when tested on a real device.

Getting the date and time

Although the Date object was available in Flash 5, Flash Lite 1.1 does not support the instantiation of objects such as this—you cannot create an instance of Date on which to call methods. To combat this, Adobe exposes several platform date- and time-related functions through FSCommand2.

Date functions

The date functions are as follows:

- GetDateDay
- GetDateWeekday
- GetDateMonth
- GetDateYear
- GetLocaleShortDate
- GetLocaleLongDate

The first four functions do exactly as they say: they return the day (1–31), the weekday (0–6, corresponding to Sunday–Saturday), the month (1–12), and the year (e.g., 2006). All of these functions return a value of –1 if the command is not supported. The following code shows how you might use the date functions to display the date in a text field:

```
wkday = FSCommand2("GetDateWeekday");
day = FSCommand2("GetDateDay");
month = FSCommand2("GetDateMonth");
year = FSCommand2("GetDateYear");

switch(wkday)
{
  case 0: wkday = "Sun"; break;
  case 1: wkday = "Mon"; break;
```

```
        case 2: wkday = "Tue"; break;
        case 3: wkday = "Wed"; break;
        case 4: wkday = "Thur"; break;
        case 5: wkday = "Fri"; break;
        case 6: wkday = "Sat"; break;
    }

    // dateTF is the variable name given for a text field on stage
    dateTF = wkday add " " add day add "-" add month add "-" add year;
```

If you would like to see this in action, you can open /ch3/DisplayDate.fla from the sample files. The final two functions, GetLocaleShortDate and GetLocaleLongDate, behave a little differently. Instead of returning the value, they allow you to set a string variable to the resultant date, for example:

```
    status = FSCommand2("GetLocaleLongDate", "date_str");
    if (status > -1) dateTF = date_str;
    else dateTF = "Unable to read date";
```

You can see in this code that we initialize the variable date_str with the date string returns by the GetLocaleLongDate FSCommand2 command. The date string depends on the device in question, but usual values for GetLocaleLongDate include "October 16, 2004" and "16 October 2004". GetLocaleShortDate returns compound strings such as "10/16/2004" and "16-10-2004". If you need more control over the formatting of these values, it is often better to use the basic date functions to return the component parts of the date, and leave it to your own code to do the formatting.

Time functions

The time functions provide very similar functionality to the date functions. They are

- GetTimeSeconds()
- GetTimeMinutes()
- GetTimeHours()
- GetTimeZoneOffset()
- GetLocaleTime()

The first three functions simply return the value specified: the currently expired seconds (0-59), minutes (0-59), and hours in 24-hour format (0-23). GetTimeZoneOffset provides you with the number of minutes between the UTC (GMT) time and the current local time. It works in much the same way as GetLocaleLongDate, in that it requires that you pass it the name of a string variable:

```
    status = FSCommand2("GetTimeZoneOffset", "offset");
    trace(offset); // outputs 0 for GMT, 540 for Japan standard time
```

The GetLocaleTime function sets a variable to a string that displays the local time in a device-dependent format including hours, minutes, and seconds. Typical formatting might include "6:10:44 PM" and "18:10:44". Its use is similar to the GetTimeZoneOffset function:

```
    status = FSCommand2("GetLocaleTime", "time");
    timeTF = time; // sets the timeTF textfield to 21:39:54
```

For a full list of return values for all of the date and time functions, please refer to Appendix C. You can use your newly acquired time functions to create a miniature Flash Lite project—a digital and analog clock display. Open /ch3/Clock.fla to see the finished item. You can see we have created a code loop between frames 2 and 3. Frame 2 contains the following code:

```
seconds = FSCommand2("GetTimeSeconds");
minutes = FSCommand2("GetTimeMinutes");
hours = FSCommand2("GetTimeHours");

// Update analog output
secondHand_mc._rotation = 360/60 * seconds;
minuteHand_mc._rotation = 360/60 * minutes;
hourHand_mc._rotation = 360/12 * hours;

// Format for digial output
if (length(hours)<2) hours = "0" add hours;
if (length(minutes)<2) minutes = "0" add minutes;
if (length(seconds)<2) seconds = "0" add seconds;
timeTF = hours add ":" add minutes add ":" add seconds;
```

Frame 3 simply contains the following:

```
gotoAndPlay(3);
```

This loop constantly queries the device's time functions and rotates the clock dials depending on the values obtained. For the digital clock display, also make sure the numbers are displayed to two significant figures if, for example, the number of minutes is less than 10—a clock displaying "12:4:55" just doesn't look right! You can do this using the length() function to check the length of the hours, minutes, and seconds when converted to a string and add a leading "0" if it is less than two characters long. The finished clock looks like the one in Figure 3-9 when running in the IDE.

Figure 3-9. The clock application in action

Useful functions

Along with the FSCommand2 commands I've already covered, Flash Lite gives you access to several other built-in functions. Let's go through some of the ones you'll want to use most often.

String functions

While Flash Lite 1.1 does not support the String object (or its built-in string-manipulation methods), it does support several stand-alone functions that can aid you in transforming your strings. Where it is lacking, I try to suggest methods for writing your own string manipulation routines, using some of the methods discussed previously in the section titled "Creating custom functions with call()." You may notice that many of the functions have mb at the beginning. These are multibyte functions and are used where the language you are working with includes multibyte characters in the alphabet (like Arabic).

length() and mblength()

This function simply returns the length of a string:

```
trace(length("twelve")); // outputs: 6
```

If you pass a number to the length() function, it is first converted to its string equivalent.

chr() and mbchr()

chr() and its multibyte equivalent mbchr() return string characters for the numbers you pass to them. It is often useful to have an ASCII table open, or even your computer system's character map application (on Windows, this is accessible from the Start menu, under Accessories ➤ System Tools). The following code displays the entire English alphabet in lowercase:

```
for (i=97; i<123; i++) trace(chr(i));
```

ord() and mbord()

The ord() function can be thought of the opposite of chr(). ord() takes a string character and gives you its ordinal value (its ASCII-code equivalent):

```
trace(ord("f"));   // outputs: 102
trace(ord("fuel")); // outputs: 102
```

If you pass ord() a string that contains more than one character, only the first character is used, as shown in the second line of code here.

substring() and mbsubstring()

The substring() function is used to return a subset of the characters that make up a string. It takes three parameters—the string, the index at which to start counting, and the number of characters to return:

```
str = substring("twenty-six", 8, 3);
trace(str); // outputs: six
```

You can see that the eighth character is actually s, and we're asking substring() to return three characters starting at that point, giving us the returned string six. If you specify that it should return four or more characters (running past the end of the string), only the remaining three characters s, i, and x are returned, with no extra padding characters inserted.

Escape and UnEscape

Strictly speaking these are FSCommand2 commands, but they fit nicely in this section on string manipulation. When sending strings to a server, it is often useful to URL encode, or escape, those strings to preserve spaces and nonalphanumeric ASCII characters, such as the apostrophe (') and ampersand (&), which would otherwise be interpreted in a URL. (These special characters could lead to a malformed URL or, at the very least, corrupt the data being sent.) Flash Lite 1.1 provides us with a function for both escaping and unescaping data. Escaping a string is as simple as replacing these special characters with a hexadecimal escape sequence (e.g., %XX). The following code shows how you would encode a string, ready for sending to a server-side script:

```
sandwich_str = "Ham & cheese; Italian style";
status = FSCommand2("Escape", sandwich_str, "encoded_str");
trace(encoded_str); // outputs: "Ham%20%26%20cheese%3B%20Italian%20style"
```

As you can see, all spaces are replaced with their hexadecimal equivalent %20; the ampersand is replaced with %26, and the semicolon was replaced with %3B. You can visit www.asciitable.com for the full list of hexadecimal codes. Your string is now safe to send to your server-side script for processing or storage in a file or database. Most server-side scripting languages automatically support functions for escaping (and unescaping) strings on the server. In PHP, the functions are simply urlencode() and urldecode(), respectively. If you want to pass long and possibly complicated escaped strings back to your Flash Lite application, you want to unescape those encoded strings using the UnEscape command:

```
sandwich_str = "Ham%20%26%20cheese%3B%20Italian%20style";
status = FSCommand2("UnEscape", sandwich_str, "unEncoded_str");
trace(unEncoded_str); // outputs: "Ham & cheese; Italian style"
```

Now you have the ability to safely pass any string to and from the server, but Escape has other uses. There are several applications that you can use in conjunction with Flash Lite to store data locally on the phone. I cover these applications in depth in Chapter 8, but the Escape function can also be used to encode the string being stored, allowing you to store text files that can contain multiple records. Take the following line for example:

```
no=2&sw1=Ham%20%26%20cheese%3B%20Italian%20style&sw2=Swiss%20Cheese
```

It may not look great for a human to read, but if this text is stored in a text file on a phone, we can use the UnEscape function to read back the two records (sw1 and sw2) using loadVariables(). The loadVariables() function and loading data of this nature are discussed fully in the section on consuming data found in Chapter 5 of this book. Hopefully, the possibilities afforded by escaping and unescaping strings are now becoming clear.

Custom string functions

These functions are not provided as standard, but we can build them using some of the built-in functions described previously. As these are not built in, they run very slowly and should be used rarely or in non–processor-intensive applications. I have supplied the movie clip containing the subroutines for all of the custom string functions in /ch3/StringFunctions.fla.

lowercase()

Using a combination of chr(), ord(), and substring(), we can emulate a string-to-lowercase function by examining every character in a string to determine whether or not the character code indicates a capital letter:

```
input_str = "uSerNAMe";
output_str = "";
len = length(input_str);
```

```
for (i=1; i<len+1; i++)
{
    let = substring(input_str, i, 1);

    if (ord(let)>64 && ord(let)<91)
        let = chr(ord(let)+32);

    output_str = output_str add let;
}

trace(output_str); // outputs: "username"
```

Let's take a look at what's going on. The code in the for loop simply takes one letter at a time from input_str and stores it in the variable let. Once it has the letter, it checks the ASCII value to see if it falls within the range 65–90 (the ASCII codes for A–Z). If this is true, it simply converts let to the character equivalent of that number plus 32 (for a–z). Finally, let is appended to a brand-new string, output_str. Once you put this code in a subroutine inside a movie clip (and execute it with call()), the calling script sets the input_str and retrieves the output_str, as subroutines in Flash Lite cannot accept parameters or return values directly, as discussed previously.

uppercase()

This function is almost identical to lowercase(), except we now check for character codes in the range 97–122 and subtract 32:

```
input_str = "uSerNAMe";
output_str = "";
len = length(input_str);

for (i=1; i<len+1; i++)
{
    let = substring(input_str, i, 1);

    if (ord(let)>96 && ord(let)<123)
        let = chr(ord(let)-32);

    output_str = output_str add let;
}
```

strpos()

Finding a character's position within a string is often useful. One possible use is separating forenames from surnames by locating the space between them. The following code looks for a given character, theChr, and returns the position within a given string, input_str:

```
input_str = "Colin Moock";
theChr = "o";
thePos = -1;
len = length(input_str);
```

```
for (i=1; i<len+1; i++)
{
    let = substring(input_str, i, 1);

    if (let eq theChr)
    {
        thePos = i;
        break;
    }
}
```

In this case, the for loop checks to see if each character matches theChar. If so, it sets thePos to the characters index, i, and exits the for loop with the break statement (ensuring only the first instance of the character is found). If the character is not found in the string, a value -1 is retained for thePos.

strreplace()

This final string function is possibly the most complex. It operates in a similar way to strpos() in that it attempts to find matching characters in the string, but this time, it matches several characters in a row (search_str) and replaces those characters in the output_str with replace_str:

```
input_str = "I enjoy a iced tea or iced coffee";
search_str = "iced";
replace_str = "hot";
output_str = "";

inputLen = length(input_str);
searchLen = length(search_str);

for (i=1; i<inputLen+1; i++)
{
    inputChr = substring(input_str, i, 1);
    searchChr = substring(search_str, 1, 1);

    if(inputChr eq searchChr)
    {
        /**
         * First character matches,
         * attempting to match the rest of search_str
         */
        matchFound = true;
        pos = i;
        k = 1;
        for (j=pos; j<searchLen+pos; j++)
        {
            searchChr = substring(search_str, k++, 1);
            matchChr = substring(input_str, j, 1);
```

```
            if (!(searchChr eq matchChr))
            {
                matchFound = false;
                break;
            }
        }

        if (matchFound)
        {
            // Perform the replace
            i += length(search_str)-1;
            output_str = output_str add replace_str;
        }
        else
        {
            output_str = output_str add inputChr;
        }
    }
    else
    {
        output_str = output_str add inputChr;
    }
}

trace(output_str);  // outputs: I enjoy a hot tea or hot coffee
```

Though rather a lot of code, it does its job well. It even replaces multiple occurrences of a string within a string. If you really want to understand what this code does, the best way is to run your finger through as you manually write down the contents of output_str for each iteration of each for loop. I learned this way back in my first computer science class, and it has served me well when working out simple algorithms such as this. The basic steps follow:

1. Loop through all of the characters of input_str until you find a match for the first character of search_str.

2. If you find a match, loop through the next *n* characters of input_str matching each character of search_str (where *n* is equal to the length of search_str).

3. If no match is found for any of the characters in search_str, go to step 1.

4. If a match *is* found in input_str for *every* character in search_str, go to step 5.

5. Add search_str to the end of output_str, and increment i by the length of replace_str to skip the replaced characters in input_str.

split()

We can emulate the split() function in Flash 4. The split() function typically returns an array of elements based on a delimited string. Take the following Flash 5 code for example:

```
var arr = String("Tom,Joe,Bert").split(",");
```

arr now contains the separate values Tom, Joe, and Bert in a one-dimensional array (minus the commas). We don't have arrays in Flash Lite, as you know, but we can use eval() to give us separate values:

```
input_str = "Tom,Joe,Bert";
delimiter_str = ",";

numItems = 0;
len = length(input_str);
tmp_str = "";

for (i=1; i<len+1; i++)
{
    let = substring(input_str, i, 1);

    if (let eq delimiter_str)
    {
        eval("item" add numItems) = tmp_str;
        tmp_str = "";
        numItems++;
    }
    else
    {
        tmp_str = tmp_str add let;
    }

    // add the last value (if there's no delimiter at the end)
    if (i == len && i ne delimiter_str)
    {
        eval("item" add numItems) = tmp_str;
        tmp_str = "";
        numItems++;
    }
}
for (i=0; i<numItems; i++)
{
    item = eval("item" add i);
    trace(item);
}
```

Using the custom string functions

So far, I have shown these functions as blocks of code, but to make them usable as functions in their own right, they need to be pasted onto the frames of a movie clip and accessed with the call()

function from another block of code. The following code shows how values might be passed to and received from one of these string functions:

```
input = "uSerNAME";

StringFunctions.input_str = input;
call("StringFunctions:lowercase");
output = StringFunctions.output_str;

trace(output); // output: "username"
```

Number functions

Flash Lite allows you to use the Math object and many of its methods. In Flash Lite 1.1, these methods are generally approximated using an expanded form.

int()

The int() function is a stand-alone version of Math.round(). Not only does it round a number to the nearest integer, it also converts any string to numbers:

```
aString = "23.4";
trace(int(aString)); // outputs: 23
```

random()

Before Math.random(), introduced in Flash 5, there was the stand-alone function random(). This function takes one parameter, an integer, and returns an integer number between 0 and one less than the number given as the parameter:

```
trace(random(3)); // outputs 0, 1 or 2
```

In order to generate a number within a certain range, you can use the following code:

```
min = -20;
max = 50;
num = random(max - min + 1) + min;
```

This code assigns any number from –20 (min) up to and including 50 (max) to the variable num.

The Math object

The Math object is fully supported in Flash Lite 1.1, although upon further inspection, its methods are approximated; Flash Lite often uses fixed values for calculations, sometimes producing inaccurate results. Something to be wary of is that many of these approximated methods generate a lot of code when compiled. A single call to Math.cos() is converted into 18 lines of code if the parameter is passed by a variable (if a literal is used, the result of the Math.cos() is hard coded into the SWF file). A good example of this approximation can be seen in the Math.random() function. The following code shows a call to Math.random() function:

```
aNum = Math.random()*10;
```

The code generates a floating-point number between 0 and 10. In Flash Lite 1.1, the preceding code compiles to the following:

```
aNum = (random (2147483647) / 2147483647) * 10;
```

As you can see, the maximum supported integer value (see the "Limitations of ActionScript for Flash Lite" section) is used to generate a floating-point value between 0 and 10.

> Some Math functions require the parameters to be within certain boundaries. One example is Math.acos(), which requires a value between –1 and 1. Any other value results in the following, rather cryptic error message: -1.#IND.

The Number object

Although the Number object's static properties may appear to be supported, the values are, in fact, hard coded into the SWF file as string literals. For example, Number.MAX_VALUE reports an incorrect value of 1.79769313486232e+308, which is far out of reach for the Flash Lite 1.1 player's maximum integer (discussed in the "Limitations of ActionScript for Flash Lite" section of this chapter).

Time line functions

Now let's review the different time line functions available for controlling movement of the playhead.

play() and stop()

These constitute the most basic abilities of the Flash player—the ability to start or stop the playhead that runs along the movie's time line. A movie containing more than one frame automatically starts to play, so having a stop() action on the first frame is often useful:

```
stop();
```

gotoAndStop() and gotoAndPlay()

Similar to the previous two commands, these functions accept one parameter, a number or string indicating the frame number or frame label of the frame to go to before issuing the play() or stop() command, for example:

```
gotoAndStop("pauseFrame");
```

nextFrame() and prevFrame()

These commands simply send the playhead to the next or previous frame, respectively, and are useful for creating simple galleries where pictures are stored across multiple frames. The following button handler code shows how this might be used:

```
on(keyPress "<Right>")
{
    nextFrame();
}
```

nextScene() and prevScene()

These commands are similar to nextFrame() and prevFrame() in that these functions control the movie playhead, except nextScene() and prevScene() move the playhead to the next or previous scene, respectively. To access the scenes contained in a movie, or to add or reorder scenes, press Shift+F2 (or Window ➤ Design Panels ➤ Scenes) to access the Scenes panel.

Movie clip functions

The movie clip functions allow you to access and modify movie clips and their properties. Without these functions, Flash Lite would be limited to performing simple animation rather than having the rich interactivity we currently enjoy.

getProperty() and setProperty()

You can find information on these two essential functions in the "Variable scope" section found in this chapter.

tellTarget()

With tellTarget(), we can instruct a movie clip to perform any number of actions within its own scope. These can be time line actions, actions to set properties or variables, or actions to call frames containing ActionScript with call(), for example:

```
tellTarget("my_mc")
{
    gotoAndStop(5);
    setProperty("", _x, 10);
}
```

This code tells the my_mc movie clip to stop on frame 5 of its time line and move to 10 pixels in on the x axis. The first parameter of setProperty(), when left blank, indicates that you are referring to the current movie clip, like the keyword this in later versions of ActionScript.

duplicateMovieClip()

Creating multiple instances of a movie clip at runtime is often useful, especially when you don't know how many copies are required. Take the following situation as an example: you need to plot a dot on a graph for every record in a result set. There's no way you can know how many dots are required before running the application, but duplicateMovieClip() allows you to create copies of your dot movie clip and place them wherever you require on stage. The following code randomly places 50 instances of dot_mc on stage:

```
for (i=0; i<50; i++)
{
    duplicateMovieClip("dot_mc", "dot" add i add "_mc", i);
    eval("dot" add i add "_mc")._x = random(176);  // eg. dot2_mc._x = 25;
    eval("dot" add i add "_mc")._y = random(208);
}
```

You can look at this code in action by opening /ch3/duplicateMovieClip.fla. You may notice that the original dot_mc is kept off stage. You can use this simple little trick if you don't want the user to see your graphical assets when playing a game. For example, you can store an explosion animation off stage and duplicate it to the correct position when a target gets hit.

removeMovieClip()

This function can only be used to remove movie clips that have been dynamically created using duplicateMovieClip(). Use it as follows:

```
duplicateMovieClip("dot_mc", "anotherDot_mc", 1);
removeMovieClip("anotherDot_mc");
```

loadMovie()

The loadMovie() command allows you to load in external content (in the form of a SWF file) into another movie clip:

```
loadMovie("my_mc", "some.swf");
```

When the call is made, anything previously contained in my_mc is immediately removed. loadMovie() can also accept a third parameter—a string containing the method that loads variables into the external movie clip's time line. This method can either be POST or GET:

```
loadMovie("my_mc", "some.swf", "POST");
```

The variables defined in your base movie's time line are accessible as variables in the some.swf file's time line.

loadMovieNum() and unloadMovieNum()

loadMovieNum() differs from loadMovie() in that, instead of loading a SWF file into a specific movie clip, it loads a SWF file into a separate level. You can think of a **level** as a separate time line that appears in front of the base time line (which resides at level 0). unLoadMovieNum() allows us to remove the movie from a given level. The following code shows how we might load content into level 1:

```
loadMovieNum("some.swf", 1);
```

On a button found on the base (level 0) time line, we might have the following code:

```
on (release)
{
    unloadMovieNum(1);
}
```

This code simply unloads the content we previously loaded using loadMovieNum(). As with loadMovie(), loadMovieNum() also accepts a third parameter indicating the method with which to load variables into the external movie's time line.

ifFrameLoaded()

When loading external movies with loadMovie() or loadMovieNum(), you may want to see just how much of the movie has been loaded before you tell it to start playing or go to a specific frame. ifFrameLoaded() allows you to do this; it can also be used in a frame loop to act as a rudimentary preloader. If you place the following code on frame 2, you can detect when your desired frame (in this case, frame 5) has been fully loaded and then move on to the content:

```
loaded = false;
ifFrameLoaded(5) loaded = true;

if (loaded)
{
    trace("Content loaded");
    gotoAndStop(3);
}
else
{
    gotoAndPlay(1);
}
```

> The simulate download option does not work for Flash Lite 1.1 testing. Instead, you can export for Flash 4 just for testing the preloader code and revert to Flash Lite 1.1 for all other testing.

General functions

Finally, let's look at some miscellaneous functions, which don't really fit into any of the previous sections.

getURL()

getURL() allows for communication with many of the device's built-in communication mechanisms, including web browsing, SMS text messaging, e-mail, and telephone (calling) facilities. Simply prepend your call to getURL() with the communication mechanism you require:

```
getURL("sms:NUMBER?body=Body Text"); // create text message to NUMBER
getURL("http://www.website.com/page.xhtml"); // visit web page in browser
getURL("tel:0123456789"); // call given number
getURL("mailto:email@address.com?subject=Subject&body=Body Here"); // email
```

The telephone (tel:) command accepts international numbers, just leave off the initial 0 and replace it with the country code of your choice, for example, 1 for the United States and 44 for the United Kingdom. Flash Lite applications with a button to "call me now" often have better conversion rates than those with "visit my web site," which requires more effort on the part of the user. In Chapter 5, we'll look at each of the possible uses for getURL() with an example for each.

getTimer()

The getTimer() function returns an integer containing the number of milliseconds (1/1000 of a second) that have elapsed since the SWF file started running. If you continually check this value over several frames and compare it to the previous values, you can work out the time elapsed, and thus the frame rate. For a working example of this, take a look at the FPS speedometer, found in the Flash Lite CDK examples; a brief sample use follows:

```
newTime = getTimer();
timeDiff = ((newTime - oldTime)/1000) add " seconds";
oldTime = newTime;
```

stopAllSounds()

Although you cannot play sounds through code in Flash Lite 1.1, you can still execute sounds by attaching them to keyframes on the time line or by instructing a movie clip to go to and play (gotoAndPlay()) a frame containing a sound effect using tellTarget(). Either way, you may want to stop the sounds that are currently playing; stopAllSounds() does just that, without stopping the movie playhead. However, sounds set to stream continue to play as the playhead moves over the frames containing them.

eval()

eval() allows you to dynamically dereference a variable or movie clip that you know the name of at runtime. For sample uses of eval() in Flash Lite 1.1, please see this chapter's sections entitled "Checking for a movie clip's existence" and "Emulating arrays with eval()."

Limitations of ActionScript for Flash Lite

Now it's time to talk about limitations. For the moment, I don't want to talk about the limitations imposed by working with small, low-powered devices instead of desktops or even the Flash player in general. I'd like to focus on specific limitations that might be overlooked when developing ActionScript for Flash Lite 1.1.

getURL() and loadVariables()

Some handsets support calls to getURL() and loadVariables() on keypress events only (handsets not running the Flash Lite stand-alone player, which are generally Japanese handsets). Most handsets support only one call to getURL() or loadVariables() per frame or per keypress event. This limitation may not be apparent when testing in the Flash IDE; if it's not, you can mimic this behavior by uncommenting one of the lines in each of the two pairs shown in DevicesMsg.cfg:

```
// LoadVarsOnePerKey="model xxxx phones"
// LoadVarsOnePerKeyOrFrame=on

// GetURLOnePerKey=off
// GetURLOnePerKeyOrFrame=on
```

Please note that you cannot set both lines to on in each of the pairs shown, as they are mutually exclusive. If GetURLOnePerKey is on, then GetURLOnePerKeyOrFrame must be off. In Flash 8, the device emulator handles this configuration for you.

GET character limit

When using commands such as loadVariables() and getURL() data can be sent to a server-side script using the GET method for sending variables. However, there is a limitation regarding the length of the URL and thus the amount of data you can send with GET. This limit is usually device dependent. I have successfully sent over 4,000 characters with this method using the Flash Lite 1.1 player on a Nokia Series 60 device, which suggests the limit is imposed by the amount of RAM available to the player (only 750KB is assigned to the player to begin with!). However, when the data exceeds 1,024 bytes (or characters), it is always safer to send the variables using the POST method, which allows for much more data to be sent.

> Remember that you are, quite often, URL encoding your GET variables with FSCommand2 commands (e.g., Escape, varname), which almost always increase the length of the URL string by adding extra characters to escape nonalphanumeric characters.

Local storage

There is no direct method of storing data on the device through ActionScript (such as local system objects, or "Flash Cookies," as they affectionately known). However, there are workarounds, which are explained in detail in Chapter 8. Most of these methods make use of an external and sometimes platform-specific application (the Symbian C++ application or Java socket server) and the loadVariables() command, resulting in asynchronous calls, which require a little bit of work to make them robust enough for deployment—not to mention requiring the use of third-party applications. Using third-party applications for this is usually unfavorable, because these applications introduce extra cost and time into a project.

XML

Flash Lite 1.1 does not have an XML data type, and the limited string manipulation abilities mean that XML is pretty much off the menu. This doesn't mean you can't use XML with Flash Lite though. Later in this book, I will show you how to connect to XML-based web services with a Flash Lite application and a server-side proxy script. This method takes some of the stress off of the Flash Lite application and makes for shorter downloading times (and cheaper data costs for your end users!).

Maximum integer value

There may be situations where you find yourself dealing with rather large (or rather small) numbers. Flash Lite 1.1 imposes a maximum integer value of 2,147,483,647 (and a minimum of −2,147,483,648). Take the following code, for example, which appears in frame 1 of a new movie:

```
max = 2147483640;
```

And on frame 2, you have the following:

```
max++;
gotoAndPlay(2);
```

So now you have a loop that increments max from 2,147,483,640 upward (you also have a text field on stage with a variable property of max, so that you can view the contents of the variable max at runtime). If you would like to try this out, open /ch3/maxNumber.fla in Flash. Testing the movie in the IDE, you can see that max continues to increment well past the maximum integer limit. However, transfer the file to a device, and you can see that as soon as the value exceeds 2,147,483,640, it becomes infinity. This is another thing to watch out for when testing primarily in the Flash IDE.

Version inconsistencies and common pitfalls

Just when you thought you had a firm grasp on ActionScript for Flash Lite 1.1, there are a few more commonly encountered problems associated with working with a Flash 4–based player to deal with. These pitfalls and player inconsistencies are covered in the following sections. Although there may be others, I try to explain those that you are almost certain to encounter and those that are regularly encountered by Flash Lite developers.

Variable initialization and undefined

As you should have noticed by now, we haven't used the keyword var to define any variables. In Flash Lite 1.1, you define new variables by simply initializing them:

```
counter = 0;
trace(++counter); // outputs: 1
```

This code works in all versions of ActionScript, from Flash 4 (and therefore Flash Lite 1.1) to Flash 6. Now, if you take away the line that defines and initializes counter, you can see that it still works; counter is incremented from 0 to 1:

```
trace(++counter); // outputs: 1 (in Flash Lite 1.1 through Flash 6)
```

In Flash 6 or lower, counter is automatically initialized with a value depending on the operation occurring, even though it has not been previously defined. As you are performing a numeric increment, the value assigned to counter will be 0 (for a string operation the value is "", an empty string). This behavior changed in Flash 7, where an undefined variable is *not* initialized with a value; it simply receives the value undefined. If you try to add or increment with an undefined variable, you generate NaN (not a number):

```
trace(++counter); // outputs: NaN (in Flash 7).
```

Although we can assume variables are defined when initialized in Flash Lite 1.1, which means your code works regardless of initializing a variable or not (assuming you are incrementing from a value of 0), it is always better to safeguard against the potential problem in the first place and add in that one extra line.

Checking for a movie clip's existence

Traditionally, if you wanted to test whether ball_mc was on stage, you could write the following code:

```
if (ball_mc) trace("It's here!");
```

This code works fine in Flash 5 or later, but in Flash Lite 1.1 ball_mc returns undefined. What if you want to test whether a dynamically created movie clip exists? You could try the following:

```
i = 1;
if (eval("ball" add i add "_mc")) trace("Ball " add i add " is here!");
```

Again, in Flash 5 or later, this code works, and you get Ball 1 is here! output in theTrace panel. With Flash Lite, however, eval("ball1_mc") returns undefined, even if ball1_mc is clearly on stage, because you cannot directly access a movie clip in code with Flash Lite 1.1. Instead, you must access one of its properties:

```
if (length(ball_mc._target) > 0) trace("Movie clip exists!");
```

The _target property is a good one to use, as every movie clip has a _target string that contains more than zero characters, unless it does not exist. It also leaves the other properties free for you to alter (remembering, of course, that a value of 0 for any property, such as _height, evaluates as false when used as a condition).

> *You may have read "you cannot directly access a movie clip in code with Flash Lite" and thought, "Yes, you can. I can write 'my_mc._x = 50;', and it moves my movie clip on stage." Although it appears that you are accessing my_mc directly and setting one of its properties, the compiler is, in fact, silently converting this code back to the old style setProperty("my_mc", _x, 50);. You can check this using the ActionScript Viewer (ASV), discussed later in this chapter.*

Renaming movie clips

Here's a problem that might leave you stumped for a good half an hour, and it tends to hit when time is running short. For many versions of the Flash player, you are able to assign names to movie clips on stage, so that you may later access or alter their properties in code. You can also change the name of a single movie clip over several keyframes. Say, for example, you have a movie clip named ball_mc on frame 1 (see Figure 3-10).

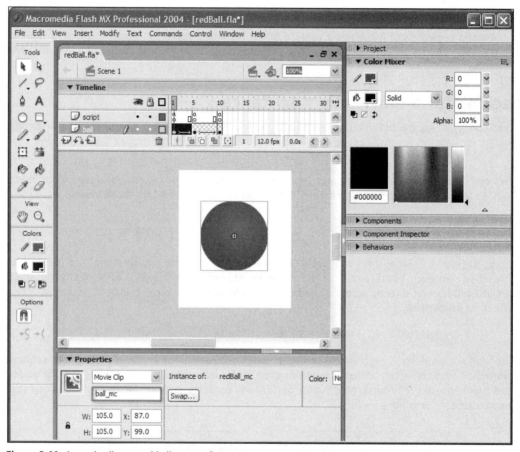

Figure 3-10. A movie clip named ball_mc on frame 1

Next, you decide to animate it over three frames with a motion tween and rename it ballSquished_mc on frame 5 (see Figure 3-11).

Figure 3-11. The same movie clip on frame 5, now named ballSquished_mc

If you need to access ballSquished_mc in code on frame 5, you would normally write

```
trace(ballSquished_mc._x); // works in Flash 6+
```

Regardless of what the movie clip may have been called on frame 1, you might think you can refer to it by its new name on frame 5—wrong! In Flash Lite 1.1, you cannot access the ball movie clip by its new name; it is forever known as ball_mc, its original name. This problem was fixed in Flash 6, so it may have slipped off your radar for the last few years. But Flash Lite 1.1 is based on Flash 4, so this little gem is back! To summarize this conundrum, you cannot name a single movie clip with different names over multiple keyframes and refer to it in code by anything but its initial name. The moral is simply this—make sure a movie clip maintains a consistent name throughout its life span on the time line (and tell animators to be careful when sending you tweaked files!). For an illustrated version of this problem, open /ch3/redBall.fla.

add vs. + (string concatenation)

A common early mistake when writing ActionScript for Flash Lite 1.1 is to use the + operator for string concatenation, as you can in Flash 5 or later. Flash Lite interprets the plus sign (+) as a numeric addition statement, treats your strings as NaN (not a number), and gives the following output:

```
trace("Ford" + " " + "Focus"); // outputs: 1.#QNAN
```

Instead, you need to use the add operator to concatenate strings; it may seem slightly awkward in comparison, but the colored syntax highlighting in the IDE makes it fairly painless to look at.

SWF tools

When dealing with the limited memory and slow processor speeds in many mobile devices, it is often useful to see where any extra CPU cycles are going. Several tools can aid you in this purpose. First and foremost is Burak Kalayci's ActionScript Viewer (ASV), which can be found at www.buraks.com/asv. Version 4.07 or later is capable of decompiling Flash Lite 1.1 SWFs, including the new FSCommand2 commands. Once the code is decompiled, you can see which ActionScript scripts made it to the final SWF. You can test ASV by creating a movie with the following code:

```
x = 50;
y = 20;
trace(x % y);
```

Opening the SWF in ASV, you should see that this code has been converted to the following:

```
trace (x - (int (x / y) * y));
```

This example shows how the modulo operator is, in fact, approximated in Flash Lite 1.1. The Flash MX 2004 IDE allows you to write code in a more modern style than that originally afforded by Flash 4. Take the following code for example:

```
aVar = "someVal";
gotoAndStop (10);
```

By default, ASV decompiles your Flash 4–based SWFs to Flash 5–style code (most likely to the style of code you are using in the IDE). The preceding code is what you might call Flash 5–style. If you press F8, or right-click the code in ASV and choose Force Flash 5 Code, you can view the Flash 4–style of code that we once had to use:

```
Set Variable: "aVar" = "someVal"
Go to and Stop (10)
```

I think you'll agree that the first code snippet is much easier to read! It is a useful feature to be able to see this Flash 4–style code nonetheless. You can also see what the compiler does with this dot syntax written in the Actions panel:

```
xPos = my_mc._x;
```

In ASV Flash 5 mode, you see the following:

```
xPos = getProperty("my_mc", _x);
```

Finally, when you press F8 to view Flash 4–style syntax, you see

```
Set Variable: "xPos" = GetProperty ( "my_mc",_x )
```

Having these three views of the same code really helps you to understand just how the Flash Lite player works and what the IDE does to hide the Flash 4–style implementation from you. If you really want to get fancy, click the byte code button to see the code as a single string of numbers and letters! ASV is an essential tool that provides much more than just a view of the code that makes up a SWF file; it also allows rebuilding an FLA and extracting assets, code, and all manner of information. Figure 3-12 shows ASV in action, displaying a reconstructed time line for a virtual pet game.

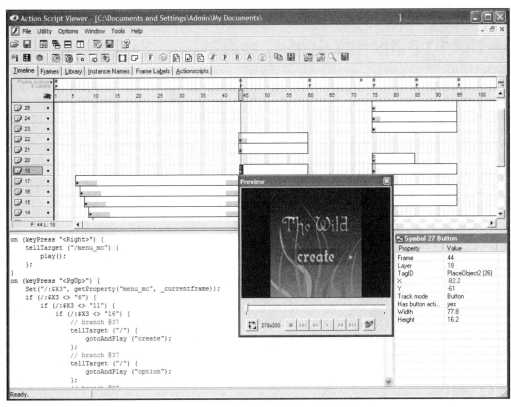

Figure 3-12. ASV and Flash Lite content

Another useful tool is Flasm, available at www.nowrap.de/flasm.html. Flasm disassembles SWFs and allows you to see the contained code. Visit the Flasm web site to see just what you can do with it. Flasm is a little outside the scope of this book, but if you are familiar with assembly language, Flasm allows you to see your individual operations codes that run through the Flash player and optimize them as you see fit to provide the ultimate control over your program flow.

The Adobe Flash Lite 1.1 CDK

The Adobe Flash Lite CDK is a complete collection of materials to get you started in Flash Lite 1.1 development. I discuss the CDK in depth in Chapter 5, but for now, I'd like to give a general overview. The kit can be downloaded in the form of a zip file from the following URL:

> www.macromedia.com/devnet/devices/flashlite.html#cdk

Inside the archive, you find several resources, which include the following:

- **Flash Lite 1.1 Authoring Guidelines**: A PDF file
- **Flash Lite 1.1 authoring updater**: All of the files listed in the "Installation" section of this chapter
- **Example files**: Working, device-ready files for testing
- **Prebuilt Halo interface elements**: Components including buttons, scrollbars, and more

Flash Lite 1.1 Authoring Guidelines

The *Flash Lite 1.1 Authoring Guidelines* contain a wealth of information pertaining to developing content with Flash Lite 1.1 and are a perfect brief introduction to many of the topics covered in this book. At 86 pages, *Authoring Guidelines* is just about short enough to print, but to save some ink and a few trees, I provide versions of its appendixes at the end of this book (including all of the Flash Lite 1.1 error codes and their meanings and all of the FSCommand2 commands). The example files are a great way of learning Flash Lite hands on, in particular capabilities.swf, which allows you to test your chosen device's capabilities (such as connectivity, various FSCommand2 command calls, and platform information).

Interface elements (components)

One of the most useful parts of the CDK is the prebuilt Halo-style component set included. I use the term "component" loosely, as we are really talking about simple movie clips with a consistent visual style and some code that allows them to perform a given function, rather than a real, extendable component framework. Flash 4 ActionScript doesn't really allow us to create a fully reusable component set along the lines of the MX components that come with Flash MX or the version 2 component architecture that comes with Flash MX 2004. There are several reasons for this; for example, we can't assign an on(release) handler (or indeed any other mouse or key event handlers) to movie clip instances, nor can we dynamically set the focus to a specific text field or movie clip. These are essential for creating self-contained, dynamic user-interface elements such as combo boxes.

If you dig into the component FLA files found in <CDK_DIRECTORY>/Components/, you can see that the drop-down list box supplied is actually made up of two separate entities: a button (the clickable bar graphic) and a movie clip (the drop-down options). These entities are not linked in any physical way but rather by a small ActionScript script attached to the button that tells the drop-down movie clip to play its opening or closing animation, thus revealing the drop-down options (which are also buttons). It also uses a time line variable to store the menuOpen state of the drop-down list, which means you have to modify the code to have multiple drop-downs on the same screen. On a positive note, these components are supplied in four different color schemes: Halo green (the default), orange, blue, and silver. These allow you to port desktop applications to the mobile device while maintaining visual cohesion. The Flash Lite CDK interface elements are shown in Figure 3-13.

In Figure 3-13, we have a fairly complete set of Halo-style components that fits in with the existing Halo-themed component set that ships with Flash MX 2004, and these components function perfectly within the boundaries of Flash Lite development. In Part Two of this book, we will look at each of the CDK components in depth, and I will show you how you might use them in real mobile applications.

Summary

This chapter gave you insight into how to get started in Flash Lite development, including how to code with the hybrid Flash 4 ActionScript and Flash 5 objects and some of the common pitfalls in Flash 1.1. In the next chapter, we'll look in detail at Flash Lite 2!

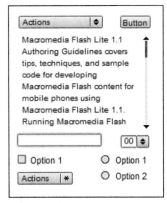

Figure 3-13. The Flash Lite CDK interface elements

Chapter 4

FLASH LITE 2.X

The last chapter included an introduction to Flash Lite in general and offered an in-depth look at the first globally available version of the player, Flash Lite 1.1. This chapter looks into the next major and minor versions of the Flash Lite Player and the myriad changes that have taken place between them and their predecessor. Before you start to think that reading the last chapter might have been a waste of time, *rest assured*, the Flash Lite 2.0 and 2.1 players play back Flash 1.1 movies with 100 percent backward compatibility. Add to that the length of time it took the Flash 1.1 player to go from developer release to being found on a viable number of publicly available handsets, and you can see that you can get very comfortable with Flash Lite 1.1 for the foreseeable future, with all of your accumulated knowledge being directly applicable to Flash Lite 2.X development when you are ready to make the transition.

In this chapter, we look specifically at the following topics:

- The basics of Flash Lite 2.X
- The new objects and constructs available in Flash Lite 2.X, including dynamic movie clips and buttons, mobile shared objects, the System.capabilities object, and the new drawing API
- How best to structure a Flash Lite application
- The classes, methods, and properties not supported in Flash Lite 2
- Improvements over Flash Lite 2.0 available in the Flash Lite 2.1 Player

Flash Lite 2.X ActionScript primer

From here on out, more often than not, I refer to the Flash Lite 2.0 Player, instead of 2.X (which refers to both 2.0 and 2.1), but where you see "2.0," you can be sure that the 2.1 player is also capable of whatever is being described, and I explicitly point out any extra functionality the 2.1 player offers.

Flash Lite 2.0 allows you to write your code using ActionScript 1.0 or 2.0. Each of these languages alone could, and *has*, filled up many books already, so this section gives you a running start into programming, while making sure to highlight any limitations imposed by the Flash Lite 2.0 player. Even though I have stated that you can use either ActionScript 1.0 or 2.0, the real difference between the two is not the core objects, language elements, keywords and constructs but in the physical structure of your code. In fact ActionScript 2.0 code is compiled down to ActionScript 1.0 when you export the SWF file. Last of all, this section does not cover object-oriented programming in ActionScript 1.0 (using the object prototype property), in favor of utilizing ActionScript 2.0, which in my opinion is far easier and designed for that purpose. If you are not already a whiz at AS2, I strongly recommend you also take a look at *Object-Oriented ActionScript for Flash 8* (Elst, Peter and Todd Yard. Berkeley: friends of ED, 2006), which goes far and above what I cover here with regard to programming in AS2 and how to best architect your applications and classes. If you are an AS2 veteran, please feel free to skip right through this primer and on to the "Structuring a Flash Lite 2.0 application" section.

Variables and strict data typing

As with Flash Lite 1.1, you can utilize variables to store and manipulate values in your application. Flash Lite 2.0 uses the following types of variables:

- `String`
- `Number`
- `Boolean`
- `Array`
- `MovieClip`
- `Object`
- `Function`

You can see immediately that, in addition to those found in Flash Lite 1.1, we also have the `Array`, `MovieClip`, and `Object` types. These are what we like to call **composite data types** (the others are **primitive**). Composite data types can contain not just a single value but multiple values and, indeed, can contain other complex objects forming a parent-child hierarchy. The `Function` class is a new addition to AS2 and is used for variables that point to function definitions. The following example uses some of these new variable types in a Flash Lite 2 application:

```
var myName:String = "Jim";
var myFavNo:Number = 7;
myName = "Actually it's Richard"; // accessing a previously declared variable
```

Notice the use of the keyword var to create a local variable in a Flash Lite 2.0 application. It creates a variable in a given scope (we talk more about scope later on). However, var is a very useful construct that we simply don't have in Flash Lite 1.1, and one we will use throughout this book. You may also notice the variable's type is given after a colon when it is declared. This is known as **data typing**, and we will go into that in depth shortly.

Along with the previously listed types, you can also assign any variable one of the following special values:

- null
- undefined

These values are used to indicate a lack of value. undefined is the value returned when you attempt to access a variable or an object that does not exist (such as a movie clip that has been removed) or a variable that has been deleted using the delete statement. You can also use undefined or null to remove references to functions that you no longer wish to run, as in the following commonly used example:

```
my_mc.onEnterFrame = undefined;
```

This statement removes the reference to my_mc's onEnterFrame function, which may have been defined elsewhere, thus stopping it from executing every frame. In general, it is considered good practice to assign null rather than undefined to variables, such as those you wish to declare without yet knowing which value they need to have assigned. Or you can use the delete statement to remove references and allow the Flash Player to perform some cleanup operations, so the player can run a little bit better.

> What's a reference? A **reference** is the term given when a variable points to a location (think "container") in the computer's memory that stores a value, such as "hello world". When we assign simple values, such as numbers and strings, to a variable, what actually happens is that the content of the memory location the variable points to is modified. When a variable references another variable (for example, var a = b;) or a complex object (for example, a movie clip), that variable's memory location actually stores the address of another memory location where the object is found. This allows for the dynamic and flexible nature of the Flash player.

ActionScript 2.0 allows **strictly typed** variables, which means that you are able to let the compiler know what *type* of data variables should hold *ahead of time*. This allows it to run a quick check to see if you are attempting to assign a string to a number variable, for example, and enables you to catch a variety of errors as soon as you compile. As you can probably guess, this very useful feature can end up saving you a lot of headaches, especially when applications contain dozens (sometimes hundreds!) of classes, and you don't want to have to spend hours tracking down one line of code that is causing the application to fail silently. You can instruct the compiler of a variable's data type by using the colon symbol followed by the desired data type. The following snippet of code shows how this might work in practice:

```
var myLV:LoadVars = null;
myLV = new LoadVars(); // OK
myLV = 123;  // Error: "Line 3: Type Mismatch -
                  // Found Number where LoadVars expected"
```

In this example, we have created a new variable named myLV and instructed the compiler to assume only a value that is a LoadVars object. When, on line 3, we assign it a number, an error appears in the Output panel when we test the movie. In ActionScript, all classes extend the base class Object; with strict data typing, we are permitted to also assign values that are of superclasses to a variable, so in this case, we could assign myLV an Object and get no error.

> *Please note that, in order to take advantage of strict typing, your code must reside in external ActionScript classes.*

Operators

The previous chapter covered a range of simple operators ActionScript allows for manipulating variables, so if you aren't already up to speed on how you can manipulate variables in ActionScript, that chapter might be worth reviewing quickly. One thing that differs in ActionScript for Flash Lite 2.0 is the lack of a distinction between operators for strings and operators for numbers. In Flash Lite 2.0, we no longer use add, eq, gt, lt, and ne. Instead, we use the standard operators, which are also used for numeric comparison: +, ==, >, <, and !=. The player knows how to make the distinction between a number and a string and performs the correct operation at runtime. Take the following expressions for example:

```
var a = "john";
var b = 150;
trace(a == "joe"); // false
trace(b < 200);    // true
trace(5 == "5");   // true
```

It's worth noting that, in the last trace(), automatic type conversion occurred causing the expression to evaluate as true. Automatic type conversion happens between simple data types like strings and numbers, and while it can be a blessing, it can also be something to watch out for. My advice here is to trace well, and trace often!

Classes

Perhaps one of the biggest paradigm shifts from Flash Lite 1.X (or, indeed, ActionScript 1.0) is the introduction of classes in ActionScript 2.0. While it was possible to emulate classes in ActionScript 1 utilizing the prototype and constructor properties of an object, classes are now laid out in the language itself, which makes for easy object-oriented programming.

If you are unfamiliar with the term, a **class** can be thought of as a "type of" something. For example, a member of the Aircraft class might be a plane, a blimp, or a hot air balloon. They all share some things in common, like the ability to rise, fall, and eventually land or crash back down to Earth. A more abstract class is the Object class, the class that all other classes are derived from.

A simple ActionScript 2.0 class follows for your viewing pleasure:

```
class CandyBar
{
    public function melt() : Void
    {
        // I'm melting!
    }
}
```

Inheritance

I mentioned previously that all classes are derived from the base class Object. This leads us nicely to the subject of **inheritance**. You can think of the Object class as the granddaddy of all others, having its own children and grandchildren. A sample object relationship could be Object ➤ Aircraft ➤ Blimp.

Here we have a three-tier relationship that might continue to include more-specialized types of Blimp and so on. This relationship forms the basis of inheritance; the Blimp includes all of the functionality of an Aircraft, which includes all of the functionality of an Object. In code, this relationship might be modeled as follows:

```
class Aircraft
{
    function fly() : Void
    {
        this._y -= 100;
    }
}

class Blimp extends Aircraft
{
    function inflate() : Void
    {
        this._xscale = this._yscale = 200;
        fly();
    }
}
```

You might notice the keyword extends. This simply lets Flash know that, for the class Blimp, we want to take everything from Aircraft and add to it everything defined in Blimp.as, which includes any overridden functionality that we might decide needs rewriting for a more-specific purpose. For example, we may redefine the fly() method. You can always refer to methods of a superclass using the keyword super.

Casting

Taking this idea one step further, the process of **casting** involves telling the compiler that an object should be treated as a different type. This may be useful when we have, say, a base class Animal and two subclasses, Amphibian and Mammal. We may have a rather simple method that just accepts as a parameter a reference to an Animal, so we can use this function for multiple objects where the user might actually dictate which value is going to be passed in. We can then use casting to treat the object as a particular subclass, which might include more-specific functionality, thus avoiding compiler-type checking errors. We cast an object by wrapping the desired object in brackets preceded by the name of the class to which we wish to cast it:

```
function displayAnimal(animal:Animal) : Void
{
    if(animal instanceof Mammal)
    {
        // casting to Mammal
        displayMammal( Mammal(animal) );
    }
}

displayMammal(mammal:Mammal) : Void
{
  // ah, a lovely Mammal
}
```

This example shows *down-casting*—we are taking an object of a particular superclass and instructing the compiler to treat it as a more-specific subclass. *Up-casting*, the more-common reverse of this, involves taking an instance of a subclass and treating it as a member of its base class, for example:

```
function displayMammal(mammal:Mammal)
{
    convertAnyObjectToXML( Object(mammal) );
}

function convertAnyObjectToXML(obj:Object) { … }
```

Trust me when I say that you need to use both types of casting frequently in a well-written game or application. Even if doing so doesn't seem very obvious right now, the reasons for casting just click into place when you find a need for it, so there's no need to spend the rest of today dreaming them up.

> *When you attempt to cast to certain core data types* (Array, Number, *and* String), *a conversion takes place instead. For example,* Number("123") *physically converts the string* "123" *to the numeric value* 123.

Visibility (access control modifiers)

I like to explain visibility with an analogy: I have a set-top box for my TV, and that box knows all about what channels are receivable, the frequencies they are broadcast in, the current date and time, the TV listings for the next week, and a whole range of miniscule details that are required to turn a boring digital signal into a viewing pleasure. What it allows me to see, however, is just enough to be able to usefully interact with it. Things like the current time and the current channel number are *publicly* viewable to anyone in the room just by looking at the box, but things like the frequency that a channel is being broadcast in are *private* to the box; after all, only the box really needs to know that in order to do its job.

If we boil down the function of something, we can work out which properties and methods that it has at its disposal should be public or private. But why is this useful and what does it have to do with Flash? Well, by marking things as "private," we are limiting what the external world of the object is being exposed to, thus simplifying the operation of the object in question. In programming, this is often called **defining the interface** or **API**.

In ActionScript 2.0, we define classes by listing methods (functions) and properties, we add the public and private keywords (known as **access control modifiers**) before them to set their visibility, and we have a very limited range of visibilities at our disposal:

- public
- private
- Not specified (public)

The following code snippet shows a simple class with several visibilities defined:

```
class Animal
{
    public var isBreathing:Boolean = false;

    function giveLife() : Void
    {
        startBreathing();
    }

    private function startBreathing () : Void
    {
        isBreathing = true;
    }
}
```

This example might be a little abstract, but it does illustrate a few things. In our Animal class, we have a Boolean property, isBreathing. I've defined this property as public. This means that any classes creating instances of Animal can get and set the value of isBreathing to true or false. Next, I've defined a method, giveLife, but I haven't specified whether it is public or private, so it will take on the default value of public, meaning that any classes creating instances of Animal can call this method. If you try to call someAnimal.startBreathing() directly from another block of code outside of this class you will get the following error:

```
The member is private and cannot be accessed.
```

However, a class that subclasses another is automatically able to access all privately and publicly defined attributes of its parent class; for example, a Cow class that extends Animal could call startBreathing() in its own methods. It is also able to redefine the visibility of all attributes to make them public if they were previously private or vice versa. Table 4-1 shows how the different visibilities affect the behavior of your classes.

Table 4-1. Visibilities and their behaviors

Modifier/Visibility	Behavior
public	No restrictions between classes or subclasses
private	Only the class itself and subclasses can access these
Not specified	Acts the same as public

Variable scope

If you followed the last section easily enough, this one will seem fairly familiar. Again, let's start with an analogy. If a subject is out of the *scope* of this book, it means that I am not able to include it. In programming, when a *variable* is **out of scope**, it isn't visible to a certain block of code. Variables are scoped to a particular block of code when they are declared. You can create blocks of code by using braces ({ and }). The following piece of code declares a variable in a function block that shows just how this works in practice:

```
function helloWorld()
{
    var a = 5;
    trace(a); // 5
}

function helloAgain()
{
    trace(a); // undefined
}
```

In the preceding code, the variable a is scoped to the function helloWorld() and the subsequent function helloAgain() is unable to see or use it. In ActionScript 2.0, variables that are defined as properties of a class, otherwise known as **member variables**, are accessible to all of the functions defined in that class, for example:

```
class TestClass
{
    var a:Number = 5;

    function helloWorld() : Void
    {
        var a:Number = 10;
        trace(a); // 10
        delete a;
        trace(a); // 5
    }
}
```

This code shows two things. The first is that the functions (or methods) within the class can access the member variable a. And second, we can also declare variables within a function using var, even if those variables have the same name as previously defined member variables. These **local** variables take precedence over the member variables within the scope of that particular block until you delete them or leave the block, in which case the member variable is again what the function sees when you write a. This behavior takes place in what we call the **scope chain**.

Programming constructs new to Flash Lite 2.0

This section examines programming constructs that are not found in Flash Lite 1.0 programming. These new constructs provide us with more power to quickly develop games and applications using less time and while writing less code.

typeof and instanceof

These operators can be used to determine the class of an object. When placed before an object or variable, typeof evaluates to a string indicating its type, for example:

```
var myNum:Number = 12;
trace( typeof myNum ); // "number"
```

All of the values typeof evaluates to are listed in the Flash Help system and include string, object, movieclip, function, and Boolean. One thing to watch out for, however, is that an Array evaluates as object when using typeof. On the other hand, instanceof returns true or false when used between two objects in an expression. It returns true if the first object is of the same class, or a subclass, as the second. Given that Dog extends Animal, the following is true:

```
trace( myDog instanceof Dog ); // true
trace( myDog instanceof Animal ); // true
trace( myDog instanceof Number ); // false
trace( myDog instanceof Object ); // true
```

The last line shows that all classes automatically extend Object and, therefore, are all instances of the Object superclass.

When teamed up with a switch() or if . . . else statement, these operators can be great in determining the type of value being presented to a function and then acting on that determination. One particular scenario might include a screen full of items, each of a different class, including an umbrella, a ball, and a frog, that the user might click. Now, you might want to do something different depending on which object the user clicks, but you don't want to have to write lots of separate functions to handle each object specifically. It would be a lot better to just listen for all of these clicks in one function, so you can write this single function and determine the type of object the user clicked. Take this typical click handler, for example:

```
function onClickItem( event:Object )
{
    var item:Object = event.target;

    if( item instanceof Umbrella ) item.open();
    else if( item instanceof Frog ) item.croak();
    else if( item instanceof Ball ) item.bounce();
}
```

undefined and null

In Flash Lite 1.1, you can see traces of undefined in the Output panel, but in reality, that player simply doesn't know what undefined or null really is. In Flash Lite 2.0, we can use these values at runtime. For more information on what these values mean please refer to the "Variables and strict data typing" section in this chapter.

One thing I would like to point out is that, when defining properties in a class, those properties take on a value of null unless they are **initialized** (set for the first time). So you can always check this.someProp == null, if you are not sure if it has been set yet.

for . . . in

We have a new type of for loop to play with in 2.0—the for . . . in loop. This loop deals with objects by iterating through all properties and methods in an object. Here's how to use it:

```
var obj:Object = new Object();
obj.abc = 123;
obj.someFunc = function() { }
for( var i:String in obj ) trace( obj + " - " + obj[i] );
```

The preceding code first traces out abc = 123 and then someFunc = [Function function]. You can use for . . . in to iterate through arrays, to examine the contents of object for debugging (as with this example), and to do a whole variety of other things. One thing to note is that certain properties and methods have been intentionally hidden from the for . . . in loop, and you can undo this with the ASSetPropFlags function. This function is undocumented officially, but Guy Watson, also known as "FlashGuru," put up an excellent summary some time ago, and you can view this at www.flashguru.co.uk/assetpropflags.

The article is over four years old (and must have cost a good amount of bandwidth), but the information it contains is as fresh as ever!

New objects in Flash Lite 2.0

I'd like to examine some of the new objects available to you in Flash Lite 2.0. I will discuss some of these objects in detail in other chapters, so when this is the case, I'll point it out. In particular, the new classes that are also common data types, like Array, have already been covered in this chapter. This section is by no means a definitive reference. The Flash Lite 2.X documentation in the Flash 8 IDE contains all of the required information to use these classes, but I'm going to point out the ones you can use now and, where relevant, give some typical use cases.

Date

The Date object takes over for some of the FSCommand2 commands in Flash Lite 1.1. Not only that, it provides a whole lot more information about the current date and time and universal date and time. Best of all, it's a data type that you can use for performing operations such as getting the difference between two dates to check for time elapsed or, as in the following example, checking whether someone's date of birth makes them old enough to visit my site on vodka:

```
function isOlderThan (theDate:Date, age:Number):Boolean
{
    var isOlderThan:Boolean = false;
    var today:Date = new Date();

    if (today.getFullYear() - theDate.getFullYear() > age)
    {
        isOlderThan = true;
    }
    else if (today.getFullYear() - theDate.getFullYear() == age)
    {
        // Year just about ok, check month
        if (today.getMonth() > theDate.getMonth())
        {
            isOlderThan = true;
        }
        else if (today.getMonth() == theDate.getMonth())
        {
            // Month just about ok, check day
            if (today.getDate() > theDate.getDate())
            {
                isOlderThan = true;
            }
            else if (today.getDate() == theDate.getDate())
            {
                // Happy birthday
                isOlderThan = true;
            }
        }
    }

    return isOlderThan;
}

var dob:Date = new Date(1984, 2, 6);
trace( isOlderThan( dob, 18 ) ); // true
```

Color

How bland the world would be without color. In Flash Lite 2, we can use the Color object to dynamically adjust the color and alpha (opacity) of movie clips to perform a variety of cool effects like tints, photographic negatives, and whiteouts. You can fire up ColorExamples.fla to follow along, but all you really need here is a movie clip on stage named my_mc. Let's take a simple, complete color change example first of all:

```
var c:Color = new Color( my_mc );
c.setRGB( 0x00FF00 );
```

The effect is that a solid color replaces your object following its original outline. That's useful in, say, a coloring book where you have chopped up your images into individual movie clips, but a more subtle tint might be preferred in other situations. To apply a tint, or indeed any sort of color transformations, you need to employ a **transform** object. The next example inverts every color in the original movie clip:

```
var c:Color = new Color( my_mc );
var t:Object = { ra: -100, rb: 255, ga: -100, gb: 255,
                         ba: -100, bb: 255, aa: 100, ab: 100};
c.setTransform(t);
```

t is our transform object, and we are setting lots of properties on it. If this is confusing right now, don't worry. It confuses everyone, but the Help is very thorough. The gist is that each color has an a value and a b value, so we get ra, ga, ba and aa (red, green, blue, and alpha values for a). These a values represent the color percentage and range between –100 and 100, so in our example, setting these values to –100 for red, green, and blue causes a complete inversion. The b values, rb, gb, bb, and ab, are the color offsets and range between –255 and 255. If you think of all colors as residing on a long rainbow strip, you can see how the color offset value comes into play by shifting the rainbow horizontally. The confusion tends to come about with just how the offsets affect the percentages, but check out the following Focus Point for a helping hand.

> If the color and color offset values still confuse you, select a movie clip on stage, and fire up the Advanced Color panel from the Color drop-down box in the Properties panel. You can play around with the values visually and write them down to apply them in your code.

Key and ExtendKey

We cover these objects and how to use them in detail in Chapter 5. For now, know that Flash Lite 1.1 key catchers are a thing of the past (thank goodness)! Feel free to skip ahead momentarily if you'd like to see just how Key and ExtendKey make your life easier.

TextField and TextFormat

Text fields in Flash Lite 1.1 are extremely limited. In fact, they are so limited they really impact what is possible with the player, and the biggest drawbacks are that you can't have them automatically resize to fit the text, and you can't measure the text metrics to lay out your content dynamically.

With the TextField class, we are able to check a variety of properties and methods such as textHeight, which returns the number of vertical pixels the text within the TextField actually uses. With this information, you could, for example, shift down an article in a news reader application to make sure the previous article appears without overlap or a gap.

Stage

The Stage object is your way of tapping into the user's screen. You can use it to find out how tall and wide the Flash player currently is, align your content on the screen, and listen for when the Flash player is resized (perhaps when changing from standard to full-screen mode) in order to lay out your application to suit the new size. Note that I've found that Stage.width and Stage.height do not report the true values in cases where the content is being automatically scaled to fill the screen (although this shouldn't affect your application, because your sizing is also automatically relative to the given width and height). One other thing to note is that you must set Stage.scaleMode to "noScale" in order to listen for stage resize events.

MovieClipLoader

Well, now that we have a MovieClip class that represents our on-screen elements, we find ourselves looking for a convenient way of dealing with loading other SWFs into container movie clips. Traditionally, we would have set up a frame loop to monitor the loading progress through MovieClip.getBytesLoaded() and MovieClip.getBytesTotal(), but with MovieClipLoader, we can save on the mess and just listen for when the SWF has loaded:

```
createEmptyMovieClip( "holder_mc", 1 );

var listener:Object = new Object();
listener.onLoadComplete = function( mc:MovieClip )
{
    trace( "MovieClip " + mc " loaded");
}

var mcl:MovieClipLoader = new MovieClipLoader();
mcl.addListener( listener );
mcl.loadClip( "my.swf", holder_mc );
```

> While onLoadComplete *might be the event you'd think to be most useful,* onLoadInit *is the one broadcast afterward, when the SWF has fully loaded and rendered the first frame. This is the event you should tie into if you need to do things like call methods or access objects that are defined in the SWF being loaded.* onLoadProgress *is also broadcast as the SWF streams in and is good for displaying a progress update.*

LoadVars

No doubt a lot of people reading this book have used Flash before and have had to load in data from the Net. Those who have probably used LoadVars instead of the older (Flash Lite 1.1) loadVariables() command, because LoadVars wraps up the whole process of specifying the data, sending and receiving data, and notifying you of when it is received into a single object. If you'd like to understand how to use LoadVars, you can skip ahead to Chapter 5, where we look at this object in detail.

XML and XMLNode

This is another object that I cover in Chapter 5, so for now, I'll just say that it is similar to LoadVars but aimed more specifically at sending and receiving the most prolific data-exchange format on the Net, XML. XMLNode can be used to build up an XML document in RAM through a DOM-like interface and can be treated as an XML object for the most part, as they share a lot of the same properties and methods. In fact, XML extends XMLNode.

Video

We've had video in Flash Lite for some time, but now you can dynamically attach video objects to the screen and control them with code. This means you can move them, resize them, and control the playback directly from your code. The most important thing to realize with video in Flash Lite is that, unlike with the desktop player, the video is not rendered by the Flash Player but by the underlying hardware. This means that you cannot do things like layer movie clips on top of video; video always appears above everything else, but you *can* have elements frame it.

Structuring a Flash Lite 2.0 application

I'm sure by now you've had enough dry theory and want to get going. Before we start, though, Flash Lite 2.0 gives us two main ways of building applications. We have the time-line–based approach we are used to in Flash Lite 1.1, but now, we also have the ability to write all program logic in code, attaching items directly from the library when required and keeping the FLA's time line completely empty. They both have their uses, so I explain both methods in this section.

The time-line–based method

I'm going to keep this section fairly brief, as we are going to cover using the time line to build applications in depth in Chapter 5. To summarize, this option involves using labeled keyframes to define states that the application can exist in, such as main menu, in-game, and high score table. You then write code directly in frames on the time line that can control the playhead, moving between these states and controlling variables, objects, and movie clips that exist within them to react to user input or employ game logic. I recommend this method to people who are new to AS2 and aren't used to defining their entire applications in code alone. I also recommend this method to people who have limited timeframes or small-scale applications, or to people who need to rapidly prototype content. Nothing beats this method for speed, as you can literally get your application roughed out in a matter of hours and just build in functionality as you go. This method is not good for people working on more-complicated applications, people working in teams (perhaps even just a designer and a coder), and those working on projects where the code needs to be maintained over an extended period of time or to utilize reusable modules in several applications.

The pure code method

Well, if you already know AS2 and skipped the last few sections, this method is probably for you. This is my method of choice. In the last few years, I've received FLAs full of assets, sometimes code, animations and so on, but the first thing I do is start fresh with a new blank file. I've wasted enough time digging through spaghetti code, and I'm sure you have too—the only way to combat this is the pure code approach. By this, I mean utilizing AS2 classes to structure the application's logic, flow, and entry point, more often than not with only a single line of code in the FLA and nothing on the stage. This enables you to very clearly finger trace your way through an application. You can work out where *that* gets attached, why *that* runs and so on, because you have a clearly defined entry point, which is something you can lose when working on the time line. With Flash Lite 1.1, we had nothing but the FLA to work with for all of our assets and our code. With Flash Lite 2.0, we can finally re-enter the wonderful world of classes!

Let's start off by creating a new FLA file and choosing a mobile template from the New File dialog. When the stage appears, notice that, in the Properties panel, we have a new button, Device Settings, as seen in Figure 4-1.

Figure 4-1. Extra options become enabled in the Properties panel.

Before we look into that, the first job is to click Publish Settings, which is just below Device Settings, and choose Flash Lite 2.0 from the available profiles, if it isn't already selected. Next, choose ActionScript 2.0 from the ActionScript version drop-down. Now, back to the Device Settings button—click this button to bring up the device selection screen, as seen in Figure 4-2.

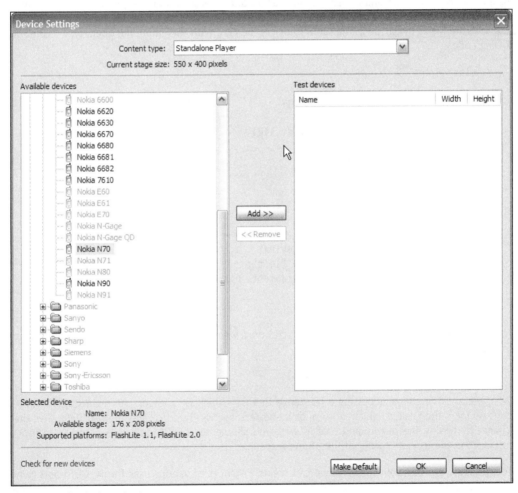

Figure 4-2. The device selection screen

111

We can use this screen to let Flash know which devices we'd like to test the content on, from European Nokias to Japanese Samsungs, and which mode, from Stand-alone mode to Wallpaper mode. Although it is likely that your content will work on most devices and in most of the available modes, it is useful to pick a few types that you know you need to support, so that you can test accurately how it might look and function when used in the real world.

For this first application, we'll select the Standalone content type from the content type drop-down and add the Nokia 6680 to the list of test devices. This is the mode that the developer edition of the Flash Lite Player runs in by default, and it gives us the option to go to full-screen mode at any point. You can see that the Device Settings dialog only allows you to add phones that support the type of content you are testing, but you can switch the content type or phone at any point without changing the rest of your file. Finally, save the FLA, and give it a test run by pressing Ctrl+Enter.

So now we have a rather uninteresting blank canvas that runs on a phone—great. It's time for some ActionScript! Create a new ActionScript file by choosing File ➤ New ➤ General Tab ➤ ActionScript File, and save the file as MyApp.as in the same folder as the FLA. With the empty file open, type in the following code:

```
class MyApp
{
    private var canvas:MovieClip;

    public function MyApp(mc:MovieClip)
    {
        this.canvas = mc;
        showWelcomeMsg();
    }

    private function showWelcomeMsg() : Void
    {
        canvas.createTextField("myText", 1, 0, 0, 0, 0);
        canvas.myText.autoSize = "left";
        canvas.myText.text = "Welcome to Flash Lite 2.0";
    }
}
```

That class isn't linked to anything in our FLA right now; we need to create a new MyApp in the FLA. On the first frame, type the following code:

```
var app:MyApp = new MyApp( this );
```

What we are doing here is passing a reference to this (which is _root on the main stage). MyApp's constructor is then called, which, in turn, calls showWelcomeMsg() and creates the text field. Give that a whirl by testing the movie, and if all is well, you should see the string Welcome to Flash Lite 2.0 displayed in the top-left corner of the phone's screen.

Technically, from this point onward, we can create instances of various user forms, GUIs, and game screens by attaching movie clips to the canvas. The aim is to break down classes, so that they do only a specific job; in this case, our application could attach an instance of a GameScreen movie clip, which could then contain further logic to handle keyboard input, or attach instances of Enemy movie clips within itself, using an Array to keep track of them.

There's nothing to stop you from just using MyApp to extend MovieClip in the class definition; that way, you can simply drop an instance of MyApp from the library onto your stage. The constructor then runs automatically, allowing you to attach things directly to this in the class, instead of having a third-party canvas element.

Let me take that idea and show you how you might start to structure a basic application in this way (the files for this are in the MyLoginApp folder). A listing of MyLoginApp.as follows:

```
import LoginScreen;
import mx.utils.Delegate;

class MyLoginApp extends MovieClip
{
    private var myText:TextField;
    private var loginScreen:LoginScreen; // symbol in library

    public function MyLoginApp()
    {
        showWelcomeMsg();
    }

    private function showWelcomeMsg() : Void
    {
        createTextField("myText", 1, 0, 0, 0, 0);
        myText.autoSize = "left";
        myText.text = "Showing Login Screen";

            var mc:MovieClip = attachMovie("LoginScreen", "loginScreen",➥
                getNextHighestDepth());
        loginScreen = LoginScreen( mc );
        loginScreen.addEventListener( "onLogin", Delegate.create(this, onLogin)➥
);
    }

    private function onLogin(evt:Object) : Void
    {
        myText.text = "Thanks for logging in!";
    }
}
```

To go with that, we have a new class, LoginScreen.as:

```
import mx.events.EventDispatcher;
import mx.utils.Delegate;

class LoginScreen extends MovieClip
{
  private var login_btn:Button;
  private var username_txt:TextField;
  private var password_txt:TextField;
```

```
        public function LoginScreen()
        {
            EventDispatcher.initialize(this);

            login_btn.onRelease = Delegate.create(this, onClickLogin);
        }

        private function onClickLogin()
        {
            dispatchEvent( {type:"onLogin", target:this} );
        }

        public function addEventListener(type:String, obj:Object) {}
        public function removeEventListener(type:String, obj:Object) {}
        private function dispatchEvent(event:Object) {}
    }
```

There's quite a bit to take in here, but nothing that hasn't been covered. I am pointing things out here, and you can flip back to find more information earlier in this chapter. If we look at the MyLoginApp class first, you can see we are using inheritance by saying the MyLoginApp class *extends* MovieClip, which allows us to create a movie clip symbol for it in the library. If you look in the FLA, we have linked the movie clip symbol to the MyLoginApp class in the Symbol Properties screen, thus giving our MyLoginApp class all of the abilities of the MovieClip class but allowing us to add extra functionality within the class file. We've done the same for our LoginScreen movie clip, because that's also a visual class, unlike a UserDetails or Temperature class might be.

The visual nature of the class brings about our first issue. When we use attachMovie() with the LoginScreen clip, the compiler is expecting an instance of LoginScreen, not MovieClip, because we've typed our loginScreen property as LoginScreen in the class definition. However, attachMovie() normally returns MovieClip, so here we use LoginScreen(. . .) around the MovieClip object returned by attachMovie() to perform a *casting*. We know that LoginScreen *is* still a MovieClip, but a somewhat more-specialized one; in this case, it contains a button and a couple of text inputs. You could just wrap attachMovie() directly in the cast, but I have broken it down into steps for illustrative purposes.

Let's jump now to the LoginScreen.as file. In this file, we don't have much code. We are defining a few properties—login_btn, username_txt, and password_txt—all of which are on stage in the symbol library. We also set an onRelease handler for the login_btn in the constructor, so we can respond to the user clicking it. For the moment, ignore Delegate.create(); I'll explain exactly what this does later, in the section entitled "MovieClip buttons and the Delegate class." For now, it suffices to say that it allows us to respond to the button click within our LoginScreen class.

Now we have two classes, with an instance of one (LoginScreen) attached inside the other (MyLoginApp). Next, I cover the way that we provide communication between the LoginScreen and its parent MyLoginApp, so that we get some user interaction going on.

The EventDispatcher class

Among the principles of good object-oriented design are encapsulation and the ability to modularize your code, so that it is portable and not a spaghetti junction. One way to encapsulate code is to dispatch events, so that only classes that want to register for those events actually receive them. We do this by using the EventDispatcher model, which is a popular way of communicating between movie clips and classes in AS2. Essentially, you endow a movie clip or any class with extra EventDispatcher methods, giving it the ability to tell anything wanting to listen to it that an event has occurred. In this case, we are "dispatching" an event from the LoginScreen as soon as the user clicks the Login button.

Looking at the code in LoginScreen, you can see that we prepare the class for having these EventDispatcher methods by defining three empty methods: addEventListener, removeEventListener and dispatchEvent (which is private, because it is only used from within the class). With these defined, we use EventDispatcher.initialize() in the constructor to mix in those methods, so that they are not empty at runtime. I'm not a big fan of mixing in methods at runtime, but without being able to build those methods into the MovieClip class ourselves, one way to inject code into other classes is to use mix-ins. Using mix-ins also means we can give EventDispatching powers to any class we like, regardless of what class it inherits.

> *A lot of people prefer to write event dispatching methods in a special subclass of* MovieClip, *for example,* EventDispatcherMC, *and extend that class each time rather than use the mix-in approach. I don't take the mix-in approach myself, but it is not as popular as using* EventDispatcher.initialize(), *so for the purpose of this book, I'll stick to the most widespread implementation.*

Now that our LoginScreen class has the ability to add listeners and inform them of events, you can see in the onClickLogin method that we construct what is known as an **event object**, in this case a generic object with two properties, type and target: {type:"onLogin", target:this}. The type property is used to allow other objects to register for this particular event. The target is always specified, so that when an object listening for a particular type of event receives one, it can determine precisely where it came from. We then dispatch that event using our mixed-in EventDispatcher method, so that anything listening for it can receive it:

```
dispatchEvent( {type:"onLogin", target:this} );
```

Now let's look at the MyLoginApp class to see how we go about listening for and reacting to an event:

```
loginScreen.addEventListener( "onLogin", Delegate.create(this, onLogin) );
```

You can see that we use that same string, "onLogin", to link the event listener (myLoginApp) to the event dispatcher (loginScreen). Again we use Delegate.create() to pass in a function that we'd like to run when we get that event. This function is as follows:

```
private function onLogin(evt:Object) : Void
{
    myText.text = "Thanks for logging in!";
}
```

Whenever we want AS2 to listen for an event, we write an event handler. The event handler always takes the event object that is being thrown as the parameter. If you were to trace out evt.target, you would get _level0.loginScreen. You can use this target object to call methods or retrieve public properties of objects once they have dispatched an event. Alternatively, you can add extra properties to the event object that might contain data associated with the event.

> When you get accustomed to how event dispatching works, you'll want to make things a little more strict by defining actual classes for the event objects we are, at the moment, creating on the fly. This allows you to use static "constants" for the event types, so that you don't lose hours of time, because you accidentally tried to listen out for an onLogn event instead of onLogin.

If you'd like another example of structuring an application or game with AS2, jump ahead to the games chapter (Chapter 6) and take a look at the blackjack game.

Dynamic MovieClips and buttons

The MovieClip class is a core type in the Flash Lite 2.0 player and one that has many uses. You already know from Flash Lite 1.X that you can put movie clips on stage, give them instance names, nest them, and create graphics and animation within them.

In Flash Lite 1.1, you can only create duplicates of an existing movie clip that is already placed on stage using the duplicateMovieClip() function. This is your only way to dynamically create a variable amount of content on screen in response to loaded data or user input. With Flash Lite 2.0, you have two other functions that allow you to achieve variable content.

createEmptyMovieClip()

The first, and perhaps simplest means of incorporating dynamic content is createEmptyMovieClip(). This method simply creates a movie clip on stage with a given name at a given depth. Take the following code placed on frame 1 of a new FLA for example:

```
var my_mc = createEmptyMovieClip("my_mc", 1);
```

Notice that createEmptyMovieClip() takes two parameters: the first being the name to give the movie clip instance and the second the depth at which to display it. The higher the depth number, the sooner it displays. createEmptyMovieClip() also returns a reference to the movie clip you are creating. In this example, I'm simply assigning that to a variable with the same name as the movie clip, which is overkill, of course, as createEmptyMovieClip() was already going to create a variable with that name when it created the empty clip. But I consider it good practice to always make my intent as clear as possible, and it is often easier to grab a reference to your new movie clip, so you can modify it a little without worrying about its real instance name, especially when you are creating movie clips in a loop with names that are not known until runtime (such as mc1 through mc23).

Well, that single line isn't very exciting, so let's use some drawing API to put something in our movie! I explain the drawing API in depth later in this chapter, so for now, let's just modify our code as follows:

```
var my_mc = createEmptyMovieClip("my_mc", 1);
my_mc.lineStyle(1, 0x000000, 100);
```

```
for(var i=0; i<=176; i++)
{
    my_mc.lineTo(i, Math.random()*50+75);
}
```

What we have now should look something like the sound wave of a cymbal crashing. You can find this example as DynamicMovieClips.fla in the Chapter 4 downloads.

attachMovie()

This function is much more exciting (you heard it here first). It allows you to attach any movie clip symbol from your Library panel on stage at runtime. You could create a library of game characters, sprites, for example, and attach them as and when needed. It works much in the same way as createEmptyMovieClip() with one extra parameter at the start:

```
var myBall_mc = attachMovie("StrangeBall", "myBall_mc", 1);
```

The extra parameter, in this case "StrangeBall", is what is known as the **linkage ID** for the clip in the library. You can assign a linkage ID to any movie clip in your FLA's library by right-clicking it and choosing linkage. Figure 4-3 shows myBall_mc in the emulator.

You may also notice an option on this screen for linking an AS2 class to the movie clip, but we'll discuss that in good time.

One optional parameter that attachMovie() takes is an object containing properties to assign to the newly created movie clip when it is instantiated, which can include the usual _x, _y, _xscale, and so on:

```
var initObj = {_x:50, _y:30}
```

If you are unfamiliar with the use of { and } to define an object, this notation is just ActionScript shorthand for the following code:

```
var initObj = new Object();
initObj._x = 50;
initObj._y = 30;
```

Figure 4-3. You should see something like this in the emulator.

You can then pass that in to your attachMovie():

```
var myBall_mc = attachMovie("StrangeBall", "myBall_mc", 1, initObj);
```

Bingo! You can see that as soon as the ball appears on stage, it is at the correct position horizontally and vertically. Personally, I prefer to not use init objects in favor of explicitly setting those properties after it has been attached, so that others can follow the code a bit more easily, but there may be cases where it is beneficial. The decision is completely up to you and depends on your style.

getNextHighestDepth()

As Flash Lite 2.0 is based on the Flash 7 player, we can make use of some extra niceties that come with it. getNextHighestDepth() is a MovieClip method that keeps track of the highest depth at which you have attached anything and always returns a number greater. In the previous createEmptyMovieClip() and attachMovie() calls, I simply pass in a value of 1 for the depth. One thing to note is that if I attach another movie clip at depth 1, the first disappears. To combat this, we used to have to increment a (sometimes global) numeric variable each time we attached something, just to make sure we got no overlaps. That extra bit of effort, which is prone to error, has been superseded by getNextHighestDepth(). This method is available for any movie clip that you might want to attach something inside, and it works out this depth value for you—with the added benefit of the number it returns being one more than the highest previously given as a movie clip's depth. It thus avoids any possible overlaps (which result in the existing movie clip at that depth being destroyed). A quick example follows:

```
attachMovie("StrangeBall", "myBall", getNetHighestDepth());
```

There are times, however, when you want to control at which depths movie clips are being created or attached. This is fine; use getNextHighestDepth() in combination with swapDepths() (which does what it says—it swaps the depth of a movie clip with another depth or movie clip), and utilize your own depth counter. One scenario in which you might want control is when you randomly attach movie clips. You know there will never be more than 1,000, and you want to attach labels above each piece for all of those. With this in mind, you can allocate depths 1 to 1000 for those movie clips, and depths 1001 to 2000 for the labels.

> If you are designing for the Sony PSP, bear in mind it only has Flash 6, so getNextHighestDepth() is not supported. I find that most content I make in Flash Lite 2.0 plays back fine (features permitting), but this little function can be the cause of some headaches, so beware.

onEnterFrame()

Now that we can attach movie clips all over the place, we can move on to doing something with them. One thing I like to do with movie clips is animate them over several frames. You can do that on the time line, but with dynamic applications like games, you need to modify their positions and sizes in code.

Open OnEnterFrame.fla to follow along. All we have in this file is a movie clip in the library, which has been given a linkage ID (so we can attach it at runtime) and some code on frame 1:

```
var myBall_mc = attachMovie("StrangeBall", "myBall_mc", 1);

myBall_mc.onEnterFrame = function()
{
    this._x++;
    this._y++;
    this._rotation++;
}
```

Here we have an instance of StrangeBall being attached on stage and given the name myBall_mc. We then give it a function to run as its onEnterFrame loop, which runs at the frames-per-second (FPS) rate the Flash movie has been set to, in this case, 12 times a second. 12 FPS is a good speed to stick to in mobile applications at the moment, as you don't usually get any more than 12 frames even when you choose 20 or 30 because of the limited CPU power. Within the loop, we alter the x and y positions and the rotation, so when we test this movie, we can see a slow rotation (from 0 degrees to 180 degrees to −180 degrees and around again) along with a translation diagonally across the screen.

We could have created a class for the ball symbol and overridden the onEnterFrame method in the class to provide this animation, but it's often more efficient to animate movie clips from within the onEnterFrame loop of their parent. Doing this enables you to animate as many clips as you like in just one onEnterFrame loop, saving some processing power. Typically the onEnterFrame loop makes up your continuing game loop in most Flash-based action games.

MovieClip buttons and the Delegate class

One new thing in Flash Lite 2.0 is the ability to use movie clips as buttons. This may sound like a strange thing to do at first, but trust me; once you've started doing this, you'll soon see it makes things much more controllable. For example, you can't dynamically create buttons, only movie clips, so with this in mind, let's take a look at how you might attach a movie clip on screen and use it as a button.

The first job is to create a new movie clip in the library. Next, create three keyframes on the time line, and label them up, over, and down in the Properties panel. With that done, put a stop() action on the first frame, and fill each frame with graphics that represent your three states. For example, you might have a solid blue rectangle on the first frame, with a light blue one on the second for when the user hovers over it, and a dark blue one on the third for when the user's mouse button is down. You may even have some text on a new layer that spans all three frames.

Now, in the library, give the new movie clip symbol the linkage ID TestButton. Go back to your main (empty) time line in scene 1, and on the first frame, enter the following code:

```
var btn:MovieClip = attachMovie( "TestButton", "btn", 1 );

btn.onRelease = function() {
   this.gotoAndStop( 1 );
   trace( "clicked!" );
}

btn.onRollOver = function() {
  this.gotoAndStop( 2 );
}

btn.onPress = function() {
   this.gotoAndStop( 3 );
}
```

What you've done here is attach a movie clip on stage and define three different mouse handlers for it. The second you define a mouse handler for a movie clip, the clip becomes a button and gains the hand cursor when a user rolls over it (or in the case of Flash Lite, the user can tab to it with the arrow keys). The handlers deal with telling the button to go to the correct frame to give the visual effect of being a button. One thing to note here is that this refers to the movie clip in question within the handlers, so be aware that you might need to use this._parent to call methods on the button's parent movie clip or use mx.utils.Delegate to handle the button in the scope of the parent clip:

```
import mx.utils.Delegate;

var btn:MovieClip = attachMovie( "TestButton", "btn", 1 );
btn.onRelease = Delegate.create( this, onClickButton );

function onClickButton() {
    btn.gotoAndStop( 1 );
    trace( this ); // _level0
}
```

The Delegate.create() method takes an object and a function. It returns that same function but scoped to the object you pass it. That's the quick definition, but it's easier to explain with an example:

```
var btn:MovieClip = attachMovie( "TestButton", "btn", 1 );
btn.onRelease = onClickButton;

function onClickButton() {
    trace( this ); // _level0.btn
}
```

Notice in this example that we do not use Delegate. We get the onClickButton run in the scope of the btn instance, which actually refers to btn instead of _level0, where the onClickButton function is actually written. This way of reference can limit what other objects or instances are visible inside your handler function, and it can sometimes be misleading to the uninitiated. Imagine, for example, you need to disable btn2, btn3, and btn4 when you click btn. Without running the onRelease handler in the scope of the parent object (in this case, _level0, where these hypothetical buttons exist), those child buttons might not be *visible* to that handler. In Chapter 3, I mentioned an article written by Timothée Groleau on the scope chain, and the scope chain can probably help give you a better understanding on why we need Delegate (if you haven't already taken a peek at that article, this would be a perfect time).

> Delegate.create() *modifies the scope of the function by using the built-in* Function.apply() *method of the ActionScript language, which has been there since AS1. For future reference, AS3 automatically delegates functions, so* Delegate.create() *is required in this particular situation.*

Unsupported code

With Flash Lite 2, we now have so many of the classes and functions that are available in Flash 7 that we sometimes forget about those that didn't make it to the mobile player. This section lists the classes, methods, and properties not available in Flash Lite 2. Some classes and methods not shown here are only partially supported; here I list only those that are not supported at all.

Classes

The following classes are either not suitable for Flash Lite or simply didn't make it into Flash Lite 2.0; where possible, I have tried to list alternatives:

- Accessibility: This class includes features for users with disabilities and is not very practical on handsets.

- Camera: For now, Flash Lite cannot access a device's camera directly.

- ContextMenu and ContextMenuItem: With no mouse for a right-click, there's no need for a context menu!

- CustomActions: CustomActions contains methods pertaining to SWF files running inside the Flash IDE, which are not required in the Flash Lite player.

- LocalConnection: LocalConnection is used to communicate between two Flash movies embedded in a single page or running simultaneously on a computer, but the use cases for such a thing on a mobile device are very few.

- Microphone: As with the camera, the current Flash Lite player isn't able to tap into the device's microphone.

- NetConnection and NetStream: Used in Flash's AMF, remoting, and streaming video functionality, these protocols are not supported in Flash Lite. Instead, you can use LoadVars, XML, loadVariables(), or loadVariablesNum() to get data in and out of your applications and games.

- PrintJob: Even though some phones are able to send documents to printers using IR or Bluetooth, it has yet to catch on, so it isn't supported in the current Flash Lite player.

- TextField.StyleSheet: TextField in Flash Lite 2.0 supports only a subset of the desktop's available HTML, and style sheets didn't make it. An important thing to note is that you can only embed one.

- TextSnapshot: The TextSnapShot class is used to retrieve text stored in static text fields within a movie clip. There is no Flash Lite alternative.

- XMLSocket: Sockets are not supported in Flash Lite 1.1 or 2.0, instead you must either poll using one of the other data retrieval classes or methods, or poll a local socket server written in C++ or Java (as shown later in this book). However, XMLSocket is supported by Flash Lite 2.1.

- Selection: The most useful methods of this object (addListener, removeListener, setFocus, and getFocus) are available. The remaining methods, which are used much less frequently (such as getCaretIndex()), are not available. However, Selection is supported by Flash Lite 2.1.

Methods

The following methods cannot be used in your Flash Lite 2.0 code:

- Mouse.hide and Mouse.show: The Mouse class is supported for devices with stylus or touch screen input. However, you cannot hide or show the cursor (as the cursor never displays anyway!).

- MovieClip.attachAudio: You cannot attach audio in this way, but you can make use of the Sound object in Flash Lite 2.0.

- MovieClip.getTextSnapshot: This method returns all of the static text in a given movie clip and is not supported by Flash Lite.

- System.setClipboard: Most devices don't support the clipboard metaphor; therefore, the Flash Lite player does not allow you to set it.

- System.showSettings: The Settings panel allows users to enable or disable access to devices like webcams, which is why this panel isn't required in the mobile player.

- TextField.getFontList: Usually devices have a limited number of installed fonts, around four on current Series 60 devices. However, you cannot retrieve a listing of these; instead, use _sans, _serif, and _typewriter where applicable.

- TextField.replaceSel: As Selection.setSelection() is not supported, this function has no context in which to operate.

Mobile shared objects

One thing you can't do with Flash Lite 1.1 is store any data locally without some heavyweight Java or Symbian application running in the background. With Flash Lite 2.0, you can now make use of **mobile shared objects** (MSOs), which are known as **local shared objects** in the desktop Flash player. With MSOs, you can store text, numbers, and even complex objects, like record sets or high-score tables, in a file on the phone itself, ready to be loaded in the next time the game or application is launched.

MSO example

If you'd like to follow along with the example, open MSO.fla from the Chapter 4 downloads. MSOs differ from local shared objects found in the desktop player, because they cannot be accessed synchronously. Instead, you must add listeners when you wish to retrieve information. The general theory of MSOs is as follows:

- Add a listener to the SharedObject class.
- Get a handle to a local shared object.
- Inform the user that the shared object has loaded via the listener.
- The user can read, write, or clear the shared object's data object.

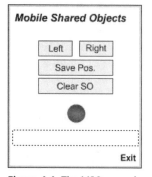

Figure 4-4. The MSO example

One important thing to note here is that, when dealing with shared objects in Flash Lite, you are accessing them asynchronously—they take a split second to load before you can use them. Let's look at the example; it looks like the screen shown in Figure 4-4.

Let's go through the code that appears on frame 1 a few lines at a time:

```
// Setup movie
fscommand2("fullscreen", true);
save_btn.enabled = false;
clear_btn.enabled = false;
```

```
// Load in MSO
SharedObject.addListener("ballSO", this, "onMSO");
var so:SharedObject = SharedObject.getLocal("ballSO");
```

The first thing we do here is set up the movie by going to full-screen mode and disabling a couple of buttons that we don't want the user to access until the shared object is ready for use. Next, we add an event listener to the SharedObject class, so that we can find out when our object has loaded. Then, we load in the shared object. SharedObject.getLocal("ballSO") asks the Flash Lite player to give us the SharedObject in the file system that has been named "ballSO", which allows us to request the same shared object each time we run the application.

```
// Called when MSO loads
function onMSO(so:SharedObject)
{
    // If this is not the first time
    if ( 0 != so.getSize() )
    {
        ball_mc._x = so.data.ballX;
    }

    output_txt.text = "Ball x: " + ball_mc._x;

    // Enable buttons
    save_btn.enabled = true;
    clear_btn.enabled = true;

    SharedObject.removeListener("ballSO");
}
```

The function onMSO is called when the shared object has loaded; its arguments include a reference to the shared object that we have asked the system to load. The first thing this function does is check whether the size of the shared object is 0. If it is 0, we know that it doesn't yet exist (therefore, it is automatically created). It also means that this is the first time we have run the application. If it isn't 0, we know we have already run the application and saved some data, so we can load in the value ballX that we have stored in the shared object's data object. That value is then used to position our ball movie clip ball_mc.

```
save_btn.onRelease = function()
{
    so.data.ballX = ball_mc._x;
    so.flush();
    output_txt.text = "Ball position saved.";
}

clear_btn.onRelease = function()
{
    so.clear();
    output_txt.text = "Ball position cleared.";
}

left_btn.onRelease = function()
{
    ball_mc._x -= 5;
    output_txt.text = "Ball x: " + ball_mc._x;
}
```

```
right_btn.onRelease = function()
{
    ball_mc._x += 5;
    output_txt.text = "Ball x: " + ball_mc._x;
}
```

The final few functions are simply button handlers that run when you click the various buttons. The first contains the onRelease handler for the Save button. It sets a property on the shared object's data object, in this case ballX—the x position of ball_mc. We call SharedObject.flush() to write the data to file. In the handler for the Clear SO button, we call SharedObject.clear() to remove all properties from the shared object and set its size back to 0 by deleting it from disk. Finally, the last two functions simply update the x position of ball_mc and update the on-screen text field.

There we have it—simple! You can use shared objects to keep track of anything from high scores to game progress or login details, for example:

```
var highScores = {weyert:1000, scott:1250, rich:1337};
my_so.data.date = new Date().toString();
my_so.data.highScores = highScores;
```

More on mobile shared objects

Not all devices support MSOs. You can test for this with System.capabilities.hasSharedObjects; more on the System.capabilities object follows in the next section.

Even if the device has the capability to store and retrieve shared objects, it might be out of allocated space. You can check to see if there is enough space as follows:

```
var maxSize = SharedObject.getMaxSize()
```

This returns the maximum amount of space you can use across multiple shared objects, in kilobytes. If you need to check how much space your SharedObject is currently using, you can do so as follows:

```
var size = SharedObject.getSize()
```

You can call this method on any SharedObject to find out its exact size, in kilobytes, so that you can warn the user that their file is oversized if need be.

The System.capabilities object

The System.capabilities object exposes a lot of the hardware's abilities to your applications at run-time. These include which types of video, images, and sounds the device can render and play back, as well as other technical capabilities including MMS and e-mail. The System.capabilities object also replaces a lot of the capabilities variables used in Flash Lite 1.1 development. For example, you would now use the Boolean variable System.capabilities.hasEmail in place of the global variable _capEmail to check whether the device supports e-mail.

There are far too many properties on the System.capabilities object to list here, but you can find a full list in the documentation that comes with the Flash IDE, the Flash Lite CDK, or on the Adobe LiveDocs. For now, let's go over a simple case, in which we are testing to see whether the device is capable of playing 3GP video files.

Device functionality

As with Flash Lite 1.1, we can tap into some of the device's native abilities, such as playing video or sound. Using the System.capabilities object discussed previously, we are able to see just what capabilities a device has. Now I'd like to take you through displaying a video after checking whether the video type you are trying to play is supported.

If you'd like to follow along with this one, open 3GPTest.fla (this video of a jet car was taken at the Santa Pod Raceway about a year ago with a Nokia 7610, which doesn't have a particularly sharp camera).

The file contains code on two frames. The first contains

```
FSCommand2("FullScreen", true);
```

We put this line on its own frame, because the Flash Lite 2 player has issues when switching between normal and full-screen modes at the same time as starting to play a video.

On frame 2, we have the following, beautifully simple video code:

```
stop();

if (System.capabilities.videoMIMETypes["video/3gpp"])
{
    vid.play("vid.3gp");
}
else
{
    output_txt.text = "3GP un-supported";
}
```

There's really nothing to it. First we check whether the phone has 3GP support, and if so, we tell our video object (which we created in the library and placed on stage) to play the given 3GP video file. That file can be online, and you can use the rtsp:// protocol to stream video from a RealServer if you have one, or you can simply point to an http:// address if you want your end user to download the video instead of embedding it. You may like to take a moment to flip through the frames in the FLA to see what we have on stage. Essentially, you can skin this example and use it as a demonstration show reel for your company.

Drawing API

The ability to dynamically create content with the drawing API tends to excite people about Flash Lite 2. If you are old enough to remember LOGO (the little on-screen turtle that you could tell to move forward 20, turn right 45, and move forward another 20), you'll grasp the concept of what the drawing API offers, but it also offers a lot more. Without further ado, fire up the Flash IDE, jump into a new Flash Lite 2.0 project, and type the following code into the ActionScript editor for the first frame:

```
var my_mc = createEmptyMovieClip("my_mc", 1);
my_mc.moveTo( 80, 50 );
my_mc.beginFill(0x00FF00, 100);
my_mc.lineStyle(1, 0x000000, 100);
my_mc.lineTo(10, 20);
my_mc.lineTo(80, 80);
my_mc.lineTo(10, 50);
my_mc.endFill();
```

You can also find this in the file DrawingAPI.fla in the Chapter 4 downloads. When you run this code, you should see a green kite shape with a black outline. I specifically want to show a shape whose outline actually crosses over itself, so you can see that Flash deals with fills, but this could just as easily be a simple convex shape like a triangle, square, or hexagon.

Try it out; it works well. You might want to try other things, such as drawing dashed lines, complex shapes and so, and we will look at these in a second. For now, you can understand the drawing API a little better by reading Ric Ewing's informative article "Advanced Drawing Methods in Macromedia Flash MX" at Macromedia DevNet:

www.macromedia.com/devnet/flash/articles/adv_draw_methods.html

Extending the drawing API

The drawing API might appear limited at first. For example, there is no built-in single-pixel plotting. Never fear, you can easily plot a single dot of any size from 1 pixel in diameter to a large circle with a very simple lineStyle() followed by lineTo():

```
moveTo(10, 10);
lineStyle(1, 0x000000, 100);
lineTo(11, 11);
```

If you'd like to reuse this code throughout a project, it is often useful to wrap it up inside a function. That's fine, but odds are you'd like to be in a position to access that function everywhere in your code. The possible solutions are to add this function to a utility class, so that you can call a static method and pass to it the movie clip to draw onto; adjust the the x position, the y position, and the point size; or to add it to the MovieClip class directly:

```
MovieClip.prototype.plotPoint = function(x, y, size, color)
{
    moveTo(x, y);
    lineStyle(size, color, 100);
    lineTo(x+1, y+1);
}
```

```
createEmptyMovieClip("my_mc", 1);
my_mc.plotPoint(10, 10, 1, 0x000000);
```

Now, anywhere in your code, you can call the plotPoint() method on any MovieClip. One problem here is that when you are developing games and applications that use AS2 code in class files, you need to make sure to run this code at the beginning, when the application initializes, so that it actually does something when you call it. MovieClip is a dynamic class and is prone to silent failures when you try to call methods that don't exist, so watch out.

With a few lines, you can now plot dots and circles, but why stop there? You can easily add code to plot a variety of shapes including stars, gears, polygons, and more. The following web page is dedicated to draw methods:

http://formequalsfunction.com/downloads/drawmethods.html

This page contains all of the code required to do just about any kind of drawing operation you need.

Improvements and changes in Flash Lite 2.1

The Flash Lite 2.1 player builds upon the 2.0 player in several ways. This section explains the major additions that have been included in this release but not the minor bug fixes between the versions.

XMLSocket

Perhaps *the* most eagerly anticipated feature, in my eyes anyway, is XMLSocket. One of my biggest gripes with Flash Lite is that you can't really make any robust multiuser applications while maintaining efficient data transfer. In Flash Lite 1.1, you have to continually poll a server every time you receive a response to keep the connection open; whenever it slips, the user receives a modal dialog box asking the user if he or she wishes to connect to the GPRS or 3G connection. In 2.0, things improve slightly. This message only appears the very first time the user tries to access the Internet, so it's less infuriating, as you can poll only when it's required. In 2.1, we get the icing on the cake—XMLSocket.

An XMLSocket object opens and gives you access to a socket connection between the client and server that doesn't die when you send a request and receive a response; it remains open until you are finished with it. This persistent connection between client and server provides a robust pipe down which you can both send and receive data. More importantly, the server can push data to the client whenever it wishes—this goes against the previous methodology of continually polling (and pulling data from) the server. The server is able to retain a pool of information on all of its connected clients and maybe perform logic between requests, giving the impression of a set of rules that make the world that binds the clients. Then the server can send out data to synchronize its clients and inform them of virtual or real events that may occur as and when they happen. Think multiplayer games here. To add to this, XMLSocket in Flash Lite 2.1 is compatible with the myriad of free and commercial XML socket servers designed for use with Flash that are already out there, including the following ones:

- **Oregano**: This Java-based, completely free, extendable, open source, multiuser server is available at www.oregano-server.org.
- **SUSHI**: This Java-based, commercial, extendable, Flash Lite SDK–compatible socket server is free for up 30 users and is available at www.rawfish-software.com/index.php.

- **Unity**: This Java-based, commercial, extendable socket server is available at www. moock.org/unity.

- **ElectroServer**: This Java-based, commercial, extendable socket server is available at www. electrotank.com.

There are others, but I've included the most-popular and widely used ones. The servers I list here are not only easy to set up, run, and use (on Windows, Mac, or Linux), they are all outstanding in terms of the documentation and the feature sets they include. SUSHI also includes HTTP tunneling, so that it is compatible with Flash Lite 1.1 through the use of loadVariables() and polling. One other server that deserves a mention, although it doesn't fit exactly in the same category as the previous ones (as it is aimed at providing custom, large-scale solutions and, at present, is not available off-the-shelf) is one that I have used with Flash Lite 1.1—Monterosa's enMasse. enMasse is a very fast, C++-based server that can handle many thousands of clients; you can find out more about it at www.monterosa.co.uk.

If you'd like to take some time to download any of these servers, they all come with sample Flash files that are Flash 6 or 7 compatible. Publish these as Flash Lite 2.1, and you are ready to get exploring! If you'd like to see how to use this new class with Flash Lite specifically, take a look at the blackjack game at the end of Chapter 6.

In-line text fields

Another issue I have with the Flash Lite 1.X and 2.0 players is how they deal with text fields. Users of phones aren't really used to having to tab to a text field *and* press Enter to begin inputting text; like with a text message, they expect to tab to it and begin writing. Adobe addressed this in Flash Lite 2.1; now you can enter text into text fields simply by tabbing to them (using the arrow keys), and you can begin typing, press the usual keys to switch between input modes (numeric, alphabetical, capitals, and so on), and tab away when finished. Visually, this process may differ between phones; for example, on a Nokia Series 60, users can see a little input-mode icon appearing over text fields when they are able to enter text into them. It's important to note that you do not have to change your existing movies, as this new behavior is a bonus and does not break existing functionality.

Beware that when a user starts a text-input session, your movie's animations and scripts pause until the user finishes. There are other options when it comes to in-line text input, such as a software-only solution. I have written one that you are free to use that's available at

```
http://richardleggett.co.uk/blog/index.php/2006/02/21/flash_lite_
2_0_inline_textfield
```

One other thing to be aware of is that this in-line text input does not currently support right-to-left languages. However, you can adapt the preceding software solution to cater to those languages.

TextField variables

With Flash Lite 1.1, you may be accustomed to using variable names for text fields to set, read, and scroll them, for example:

```
myTFVar = "Some text" add newline add "Another Line";
myTFVar.scroll = 2;
```

With Flash Lite 2.0, the recommended practice is to give TextFields an instance name in the Properties panel and access the text and scroll properties as follows:

```
myTextField.text = "Some text" + newline + "Another Line";
myTextField.scroll = 2;
```

You can, of course, also use special escape characters like \n and \r to insert new lines and carriage returns into text.

Escape/Unescape changes

In Flash Lite 1.1, you are also required to use special FSCommand2 commands to perform some operations that are not found traditionally in Flash 4 ActionScript, such as when **escaping** (URL-encoding) text to send to a server. This would be written as follows:

```
FSCommand2("Escape", myText, "myNewText");
```

As Flash Lite 2.0 supports the use of ActionScript 1.0 and 2.0, you can make use of new global functions that replace these workarounds. The previous example can now be written as follows:

```
myNewText = escape(myText);
```

In addition to escaping text, you also have unescape() to do just the opposite.

File locations

The locations in which the Flash Player looks for files have changed for Series 60 phones in later models (including the Nokia N and E series phones). The new locations follow:

```
c:\nokia\others
e:\others
```

This change tends to affect only developers. That's because, when you are deploying a real application with installer and menu icons, it is almost always better to install the SWF file to a known location that isn't in the usual Flash Player–accessible file path and use the operating system's built-in file-type association to launch the Flash Player (via a small Symbian application for example.) This way users can't accidentally delete your file without going through the proper uninstall process.

Summary

In this chapter, we've gone on a whirlwind tour of AS2, and seen how to build a basic Flash Lite 2 file, some common pitfalls, and the differences you'll find with Flash Lite 2. Hopefully, now you feel a lot more confident as we go into the details of how to create applications and games. If you feel you need a quick refresher, you might skim through this chapter a couple of times just to set the basics right in your mind before carrying on. Otherwise, turn the page, and let's look at some mobile application development techniques!

Part Two

LET'S GET DEVELOPING!

Chapter 5

APPLICATION DEVELOPMENT

Until now, we have discussed both applications and games rather generally. This chapter will focus squarely on applications for mobile devices, from tax calculators to e-mail clients—all of these things are possible with Flash and Flash Lite. Although the majority of applications are created for business users (for productivity, travel, and finance), many areas have yet to be explored. This chapter will give you a better understanding of how to go about creating applications, from the design of the UI to loading the data, so you can use this information to put new ideas into action. Although I cover both Flash Lite 1.1 and 2.X in this chapter, I tend to focus a little more on Flash 1.1, because that version will be the prominent one to develop for to maintain the largest viewership across the board for at least a year to come.

In this chapter, I cover the following topics:

- UI design
- The Flash Lite 1.1 and 2.X CDKs
- Consuming data
- Integrating with the phone
- An example application for a stock quote client

User interface design

When it comes to interacting with your application the UI is probably going to play *the* biggest role in how usable it is. Although we have several limitations imposed when designing for mobile devices, such as the smaller screen real estate and out-of-the-norm input devices mentioned in Chapter 2, we can, thankfully, shift these limitations from something that can get in the way to something that can give us a clear set of rules to abide by.

Navigation and interaction

Knowing the user is something that we developers often find difficult. We see the applications that we create not only from a tech-savvy perspective but also from the creator's perspective. This creates two distinct problems. The first problem is that we might make assumptions; we might know that, in order to type text into an input text field in a Flash Lite application, we have to use the arrow keys to first highlight the text field and then press Enter or the select key to begin entering the text. A nontechnical person might spend a few seconds grappling with the buttons, perhaps moving the keyboard focus around with the arrow keys and hitting all of the letters with no sign of the text field responding, before coming to the conclusion that the application must be broken. The second problem is that, although we know precisely what our application does, someone new to it may not have this insight. For this reason, we need to make the application's UI function extremely blatant; large buttons that are clearly labeled, a clear order of operations (discussed later in the section titled "Prioritization"), adhering to common device UI guidelines, and adding fail-safe mechanisms throughout the application provide ways of achieving this clarity without sacrificing too much of the visual appeal.

When reading through the rest of this section on UI design, keep a few key questions in mind:

- What are the users' goals?
- What environment are they operating in? What is the application's context?
- What are their previous experience and skill levels?

Aesthetics vs. functionality

Striking a balance between making your application look good and having it run well is one of the hardest aspects of mobile development. The small screens do not permit us the same level of flexibility when it comes to customization or artistic flair as desktop application designers have. More often than not, we have to keep things extremely basic just to keep the application usable and the text legible. Minimalism is a trump card in mobile development—not only does it provide a clearer UI, it also means that in general the UI enables the application to run a lot better on the device's frequently underpowered processor. Many of the Flash Lite applications you create will run a phone's battery down in no time at all if left unchecked. As an added bonus, a minimalist design might also mean less work when it comes to the design and layout!

For an example of effective design for the small screen, let's look at the screenshots of Paul Wilson's Traffic Lite application, shown in Figure 5-1.

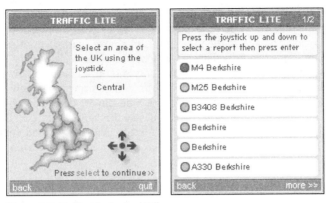

Figure 5-1. Traffic Lite by Paul Wilson

Traffic Lite is a Flash Lite client for obtaining United Kingdom road travel news on the go. You can select from various parts of the country and choose from a list of roads to read about delays and traffic congestion, all supplied via data from the BBC's Backstage service at http://backstage.bbc.co.uk. As you can see, no part of the screen is wasted, and every screen contains instructions on how to navigate the UI. When it comes to mobile development, the UI is very much content driven. Space is precious, so avoid fancy borders and flashy touches unless they are essential to branding. Also, always attempt to provide some visual indicator of what the user needs to do to navigate the UI, such as a visual representation of the arrow keys. This need for the UI elements to be as compact and obvious in function as possible is something the experience design team at Adobe took very seriously when designing the Flash Lite 1.1 CDK components, as we will discuss later in the chapter.

Text and fonts

Flash affords us two main types of fonts: TrueType and pixel fonts. Both are accessible from the fonts listing in the Properties panel, and both are embedded in the exported SWF file. Flash Lite also enables us to specify one other type of font—device fonts. Let's go over each of these font types to see their merits and drawbacks.

TrueType TrueType fonts were created to fill the need of accurately representing a printed font for on-screen viewing. Storing just the font outline, the computer displaying the text creates a screen version of the outline, and in the case of Flash, this text is be **antialiased** (smoothed) by default to improve the appearance and readability. As of Flash MX 2004, this antialiasing can be switched on or off in the Properties panel, which can be great when you are working with small font sizes where the antialiasing causes the text to appear blurred. Prior to 2004, the only ways around using antialiasing were to switch the player quality down to low or to use one of the other font types described in this section. On the upside, TrueType fonts give you scalable text that can include entirely custom styles and characters. On the downside, these font outlines need to be embedded into the SWF, and in the case of dynamic text fields, entire character ranges need to be included in the export, increasing the file size. Some examples of popular TrueType fonts include Arial, Helvetica, Times New Roman, and Courier.

Pixel fonts This type of font is essentially a TrueType font, but it is designed for use at a specific point size by constructing the font from a series of squares on whole pixel coordinates, and it has a **rasterized** (nonsmoothed) look. The aim of the pixel font is to enable sharp fonts at small sizes (10 points or less). The downside of pixel fonts is that they cannot usually be scaled to any other size, and they suffer from the same problems as regular TrueType fonts in terms of file size. However, these fonts are perfect for both Flash Lite and Flash for Pocket PC, where maximizing the screen usage is paramount. Some freely available and commercial pixel fonts are available for download on the Web; the most well-known outlets are www.meantangerine.com and www.fontsforflash.com. To keep pixel fonts appearing crisp and sharp, make sure the text field is left-aligned and situated on whole pixels (alternatively, check the Antialias check box in MX 2004, or select Bitmap Text from the Font Rendering Method drop-down in Flash 8).

Device fonts The final type of font in our typographic arsenal is the device font. In the IDE, this option can be checked on or off in the Properties panel when editing a text field. If you wish to use a device font, select _sans, _serif, or _typewriter from the font list, and check the Device Font check box (Flash 8 has no check box, although you can specify Use Device Fonts in the font rendering method drop-down if you enter the name of a custom font). A device font uses the font rendering built into the device to display crisp fonts at small sizes and incurs no additional file size for font outlines. This type of font is perfect for large areas of text that might need scrolling, but you do need to test on the actual device to see just how it really appears.

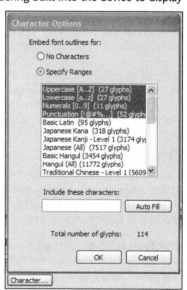

Extended characters When you need to include extended Latin characters, such as "é", or even Cyrillic characters, such as "Ж", you need to consider embedding those particular font outlines in your movie when using dynamic text fields. You can do this with the Character button in the Properties panel (Embed in Flash 8), which opens the Character Options panel shown in Figure 5-2.

With this panel, you can embed certain ranges of characters from various character sets by holding down the Ctrl key and clicking the various list options to highlight them. When creating content for i-mode, it is important to note that i-mode–enabled phones support a few extra characters (known as **emoji**) that you might want to take advantage of. These characters are normally little emoticon-type graphics, such as fast food or smiley faces. For more information, you can check out the *Flash Lite Authoring Guidelines for the i-mode Service* at

Figure 5-2. The Character (Embed) Options panel

```
http://download.macromedia.com/pub/documentation/en/flash/mx2004/
fl_docomo_author_guidelines.pdf
```

> *Flash Lite 1.1 accepts text encoded in ANSI or UTF8 format. UTF16 is not currently supported; this includes both Little Endian (LE) and Big Endian (BE) byte-order marks. For character sets that include double character codes, the device's system code page is used. Japanese, for example, uses Shift+JIS; other languages use their multibyte character set (MBCS) equivalents.*

Keyboard focus

Focus is the term given when a particular visual component, be it a button, a text field, or a movie clip, has the attention of the keyboard or keypad. When a component has focus, it receives events from the keyboard, such as a press event when the user presses the Enter key. The usual method for changing the keyboard focus in a Flash application is by pressing the Tab key. However, in Flash Lite, focus is changed by using the arrow keys only, because of the obvious lack of a tab key on the handset! Flash displays a visual indicator of focus in the form of the focus rectangle, a yellow rectangle that surrounds the given component. In the case of buttons, the button also displays its over state, which is useful when you have multiple components on stage, and you would like the user to be able to select between them. Figure 5-3 shows three buttons arranged vertically in a quiz application. In this example, the middle button, labeled Rambutan, has the current keyboard focus.

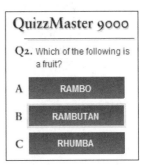

Figure 5-3. QuizzMaster 9000

Although it doesn't do anything other than illustrate the yellow focus rectangle, you can download this example (ButtonFocus.fla) as part of the Chapter 5 downloads. When testing this file in the Flash Lite emulator for Flash MX 2004, be sure to disable keyboard shortcuts from the Control menu. Disabling the keyboard shortcuts allows you to navigate your movie's UI with the Tab and arrow keys and prevents the movie playhead from moving when you press the Enter key. If you are using Flash 8 Professional or later, this is already done for you with the introduction of the new Flash Lite emulator (the Tab key is not required for changing focus under any circumstances).

The yellow focus rectangle is actually an optional feature and, as such, it can be switched off. The following code disables it:

```
_focusrect = false;
```

Setting it back to true, of course, re-enables the rectangle. If you have a screen full of buttons, as shown in Figure 5-3, disabling the focus rectangle can benefit the visual appeal of your application, and the buttons still show their over state to indicate which has focus. The problem comes when you have text fields on the same screen as buttons. A text field does not show that it has focus without the focus rectangle being enabled in a Flash Lite application (however, the desktop and MX 2004 IDE players display a blinking cursor inside the text field). In these cases, the focus rectangle is a must. You can always enable or disable it for specific screens or components by placing the previous code in relevant frames.

In Flash Lite, the tab (focus) order for buttons and text fields is defined by the following equation:

```
index = cx + cy * 6
```

where cx and cy represent the center of the button's hit area. Of course, the higher the value of index, the lower down the tab order the component goes. The coefficient of cy (6) means that vertical positioning takes priority over horizontal positioning when it comes to ordering the components, so components that are below others on stage are further down the tab order, and more key presses are required to reach them.

> *In Flash MX 2004, you first have to disable keyboard shortcuts* (Control ➤ Disable Keyboard Shortcuts) *to use the arrow keys to navigate the UI. In cases where you also have a text field on stage, Shift+Tab cycles backward in the tab order, and Tab on its own cycles forward.*

While this works well and feels fairly intuitive when navigating the UI, the arrow keys also give us the added control of being able to skip through columns of components with the left and right keys. Additionally, some handsets support what is known as **wraparound navigation**, where repeatedly pressing the down key, for example, returns the focus to the first component after leaving the last (this feature is not currently supported in Series 60 handsets). You can enable this behavior when testing in Flash MX 2004 by uncommenting and changing the value of the following line in `<Flash MX 2004>/<Language Code>/First Run/DevicesMsg.cfg` to on (further configuration of this file is covered later in this book):

```
// Navi4WayWrapAround=off
```

Flash 8, on the other hand, automatically has the correct settings, depending on which handset is being tested. Sometimes however, this built-in tab control doesn't suit our needs. At these times, we can create our own custom tab order. Creating a custom tab order is covered later in this chapter and makes use of intercepting key events from the user.

Key events and key catcher buttons

Although phones don't have as many keys as a standard PC keyboard, their keys are even more important because of the lack of a mouse for an alternative user input device. This section covers how to listen for user input from the keyboard or keypad and how that differs between versions of Flash Lite.

Key catchers (Flash Lite 1.X)

In Flash Lite 1.1, the only way you can register keyboard input is by listening for key press events on buttons. This may seem a strange concept for those of you coming from a Flash 5 or greater background, but there are ways to keep things nice and orderly.

Let's now create a document that displays which key is being pressed in the output panel. Open Flash, and create a new document from the mobile templates described in Chapter 3. Create a rectangle on stage with the rectangle tool, and with the newly created shape selected, choose Modify ➤ Convert to Symbol (F8), and select Button from the list of options. There's no need to edit the button's up, over, or hit states; we aren't going to use this button in the conventional sense. Your screen should now look something like the one shown in Figure 5-4.

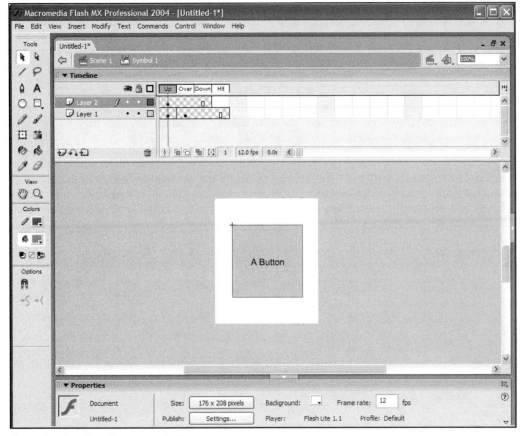

Figure 5-4. Creating a key catcher button

Return to the main time line (either by double-clicking the button's surrounding area or clicking the button labeled Scene 1 just above the time line), select our new button by clicking it, and open the Actions panel with Window ➤ Development Panels ➤ Actions (F9). Next, enter the following code:

```
on(keyPress "<Left>")
{
    trace("left");
}

on(keyPress "4")
{
    trace("4");
}
```

Now, if you test the movie (by pressing Ctrl/Command+Enter), you can begin pressing the left arrow and number 4 keys to see some output being generated in the Output panel. Although writing the code to catch key presses for each individual key is time consuming, there aren't many keys on a phone to worry about; in fact, most of the time the only keys being used are the arrow keys, the soft keys, and Select/Enter.

> *If you are developing content for i-mode services, you are unable to use the left and right keys for navigation, as these are reserved for forward and back behavior in the built-in browser.*

While this button works well, you may not want to have a big ugly button occupying the middle of your application just to allow for keyboard input, so it's often better to place your key catcher buttons offstage, and perhaps represent them with just some text, like KeyCatcher, instead of the rectangle graphic, as shown in Figure 5-5.

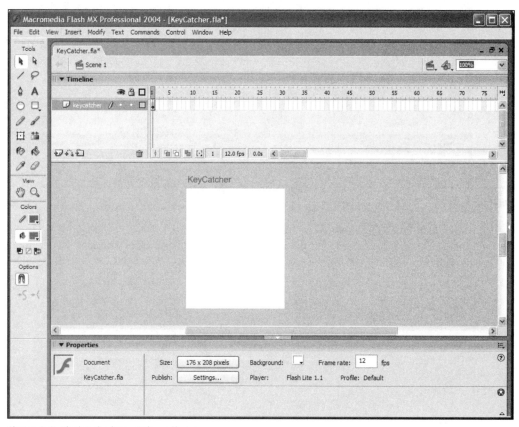

Figure 5-5. Placing the key catcher off stage

The text field in the key catcher has been set to use the _sans font; as discussed earlier, selecting _sans automatically uses one of the device fonts installed on the handset or PDA and, therefore, does not incur any additional file size for the font. In addition to detecting the left and number 4 keys, we can also detect soft key input. The soft keys are usually placed directly beneath the screen, to the left and right sides of the phone. Their purpose is usually dynamic in nature; the phone's OS and the applications that run on it change the labels that appear above the soft keys and their functions. We can do the same in Flash Lite using the FSCommand2 command SetSoftKeys. The following code, when placed on frame 1, changes the labels shown above our soft keys from the standard Flash Lite labels Options and Back to Apple and Orange:

```
status = fscommand2("SetSoftKeys", "Apple", "Orange");
```

With this change applied, we can now listen for soft key presses by adding the following code to our key catcher button:

```
on(keyPress "<PageUp>")
{
    trace("Apple!");
}

on(keyPress "<PageDown>")
{
    trace("Orange! Exiting app...");
    fscommand2("Quit");
}
```

You might notice that for the right soft key, not only do we display Orange! in the output panel, we also exit the application with the FSCommand2 command Quit. Otherwise, if this file was tested on a handset, there would be no way of exiting the application through normal means, as the Flash Player's option for exiting the file has been overwritten. This file can be found in the Chapter 5 downloads as KeyCatcher.fla.

> *Here's a tip for terminating your applications when you are testing on a device and you find you have not given the user a way of exiting, because you have overridden the functionality of the soft keys: press and hold the Symbian/Menu key to bring up a list of the currently running applications (similar to Alt+Tab on Windows), and press the C key to terminate the currently selected application.*

The Key object (Flash Lite 2)

In Flash Lite 2, you are able to listen for keyboard events (press, release) by creating a listener for the global Key object, for example:

```
var listener = new Object();
listener.onKeyDown = function()
{
    trace("a key was pressed");
}
Key.addListener(listener);
```

What we have here is a plain-vanilla object being created—listener. To that we add an onKeyDown function; the name of this function is important, so be sure to type it carefully. We can then use the Key object to add our listener object as a listener for all Key events. With that done, our onKeyDown function is called whenever the user presses a key and before he or she releases it (see onKeyUp in the Flash documentation for more information on responding to key-up events).

Now that we have a way of responding to keyboard input, we can check to see which key is pressed by using two callback functions invoked by the Key object, onKeyDown and onKeyUp:

```
var listener = new Object();
listener.onKeyDown = function()
{
    trace(Key.getAscii());
    trace(Key.getCode());
}
Key.addListener(listener);
```

Key.getAscii() returns the ASCII value of the last key pressed, so if the user pressed the number 1 key on the keypad, Key.getAscii() returns the string "1". Alternatively, you can use the Key.getCode() method to return the key code for the last key pressed; this is useful for comparing the key value against built-in constants defined in the Key object, for example:

```
if(Key.getCode() == Key.ENTER) trace("user pressed select");
```

Other useful values include Key.LEFT for the left-directional key, and many others defined in the Key object that are instantly accessible by typing Key. in the Flash IDE. You can find an example of this code in action in KeyObject.fla.

ExtendedKey (Flash Lite 2)

If you have skipped the section titled "Key Catchers (Flash Lite 1.X)," I'd advise you to read the part near the end that discusses the function of soft keys on phones. With that in mind, just how do we listen for soft keys in Flash Lite 2? We can't use Key.PGUP, and there is no Key.LEFTSOFTKEY constant. Instead, we have been provided a brand-new global object—ExtendedKey. ExtendedKey provides a whole range of extra keys, including the standard left and right soft keys.

These key constants are intuitively named: ExtendedKey.SOFT1 is the left soft key, and ExtendedKey.SOFT2 is the right. Here's some sample code for handling soft key events in Flash Lite 2:

```
var listener = new Object();
listener.onKeyDown = function()
{
    var code = Key.getCode()
    if (code == ExtendedKey.SOFT1)
    {
        // left soft key pressed
    }
    else if (code == ExtendedKey.SOFT2 )
    {
```

```
        // right soft key pressed
    }
}
Key.addListener( listener );
```

However, ExtendedKey doesn't just contain two constants; it contains constants for twelve soft keys, from SOFT1 through SOFT12, enough to support future devices, or devices that are not phones but media players, which would have several keys unique to that particular device.

Custom tab order

Previously, I mentioned the need to facilitate a custom tab order for buttons in some applications, where the default tab order calculated by Flash Lite may not be desirable. Another reason for doing this is so that, in both Flash Lite 1.X, we can automatically select a menu option or button when the user enters a screen. Without a custom tab handler, the user would have to navigate to a button using the arrow keys before selecting anything.

Now that we can listen for keyboard events, we can act on those key presses to provide our custom tab order. In this example, we are creating an application with four vertically arranged buttons. These buttons will be labeled one through four but not in that order. In Figure 5-6, you can see a screenshot of our application running.

Figure 5-6. A custom tab order application in Flash Lite

As you can see, the twist here is that the button order is mixed up. Although it is ultimately unrealistic to want to achieve this exact situation, there may be times when you want to control the tab order yourself, for example, when using dynamically duplicated buttons (only movie clips can be duplicated), or buttons that need to contain dynamic text (as you cannot name regular buttons to set the text on any text fields they contain). It is important to note that none of the buttons in this example are real buttons; they are, in fact, movie clips set up to mimic buttons by having several frames, one for each of the button states. One more thing to note is that these movie clips are named btn1 through btn4 in the Properties panel. You can also see our now-familiar Key Catcher just above the main movie. Now let's go through the code involved in creating this example. If you open CustomFocus.fla from the Chapter 5 downloads, you can see exactly where the code lies. For those happy just reading for now, the following code is found on frame 1 of the root time line:

```
_focusrect = false;

order = "1324";
currentFocus = 1;
totalButtons = 4;

tellTarget("btn" add substring(order, currentFocus,1)) { gotoAndStop(2);  }
```

The first line tells Flash to disable the focus rectangle, so we can rely solely on our button's over state (frame 2 of our movie clip). Lines 2 to 5 simply set up some variables on _root that we use in our button catcher code, but note that currentFocus does not refer to the actual button number (that is, 1 is not necessarily referring to btn1). Instead, it refers to the index of the button within our button order. Notice that the order is defined as a series of numbers with no delimiter between. This was done for two reasons: we don't want to complicate things by having to employ our custom split function (created in Chapter 3) to deal with chopping out the commas or whatever we use to delimit the numbers, and we are not likely to be able to fit more than 10 buttons (0–9) on stage at any one time. The final line tells our currently selected button (indicated by whichever number is at position currentFocus in the order) to go to frame 2 and show its over state.

The code attached to that button catcher follows:

```
on(keyPress "<Up>")
{
    if (--currentFocus == 0) currentFocus = totalButtons;

    for (i=1; i<totalButtons+1; i++)
    {
        tellTarget("btn" add i) { gotoAndStop(1); }
    }
    tellTarget("btn" add currentFocus) { gotoAndStop(2); }
}

on(keyPress "<Down>")
{
    if (++currentFocus > totalButtons) currentFocus = 1;

    for (i=1; i<totalButtons+1; i++)
    {
        tellTarget("btn" add i) { gotoAndStop(1); }
    }
    tellTarget("btn" add currentFocus) { gotoAndStop(2); }
}

on(keyPress "<Enter>")
{
    output = "Button " add currentFocus;
}
```

If we take each of the on(*event*) handlers in turn, the first, on(keyPress "<Up>"), listens for the use of the up key:

```
    if (--currentFocus == 0) currentFocus = totalButtons;
```

This line does two things. First of all, --currentFocus deducts 1 from currentFocus via the prefix decrement operator, regardless of anything else that may occur. For example, if the current focus was 1 (as it is when we first run the application), currentFocus is now set to 0, and the second part of the expression is evaluated. The second thing it does is reset the currentFocus to the total number of buttons (totalButtons) should our currentFocus equal 0 (which does not exist as a button), thus selecting the last button in the tab order and giving us our wraparound navigation. The following block of code deals with the visual appearance of the buttons:

```
for (i=1; i<totalButtons+1; i++)
{
    tellTarget("btn" add i) { gotoAndStop(1); }
}
tellTarget("btn" add substring(order, currentFocus,1)) { gotoAndStop(2); }
```

First of all, it cycles through all buttons on stage and sets them all to the regular up state (frame 1). The last line tells the button at index, currentFocus, to go to its over state (frame 2), completing the effect. The on(keyPress <"Down">) handler does exactly the same thing, except the first line wraps the navigation the other way, setting currentFocus to 1 should it exceed totalButtons. The final block of code, on(keyPress "<Enter>"), simply displays the currently selected button name upon pressing the Select (or Enter) key on the keyboard. This is a very handy method to have at hand (and one that I use in almost all of my Flash Lite applications), as it allows you much more control over how your menu systems and navigation works.

> Remember that, in Flash Lite 2.X, we can make use of Selection.setFocus() to automatically give a button focus.

Prioritization is a concept that can be applied to any facet of human-computer interaction (HCI). It's used when designing any kind of interface through which a user gives commands *to* or receive feed-back *from* a mechanical or computerized device, from the electrical thermostat control in your home to a full-blown web site. Before we take a look at just how to use prioritization in our applications, let's give it some context by explaining another key idea to emerge in the world of HCI—Fitts's Law. Published in 1954 by Paul Fitts, Fitts's Law is a principle used to predict the time required to move from a starting position to a target area, for example, on a computer desktop. In fact, Fitts's law was used in 1978 by Card, English, and Burr to work out which computer input device was most effective; of course, the mouse came out on top, proven by its unrivaled popularity nearly 30 years later. You may have instantly realized the implications for our mobile UI; no matter how small the distances involved, we can use this principle to aid in our design phase and create a better, more effective UI.

Factors that affect the time taken by a user to perform an activity include the distance moved and the size of the target area. For mobile content, this relates to the distance the eye has to move, the num-ber of key presses required to reach the target (when tabbing), and the amount of scrolling required. With this in mind, we can formulate a more specific list of factors that might contribute to the time it takes a user to perform an action:

- Distance and frequency of eye movement
- Number of button clicks and key presses required
- Amount of scrolling required
- Size of the target area
- Absolute position of the target on the screen
- Position of target relative to other screen elements (visual grouping)
- Familiarity of UI
- Accessibility of target (for example, via shortcut keys)

145

To expand on some of these points, the distance and frequency of eye movement is linked with the position of the target, in terms of its absolute position and about the way components are grouped visually. As a general rule, it's good to try to organize the components, so that the eye follows the program flow and order of operations, while also trying to group them by function. The number of key presses required to reach the target can be minimized through the use of the final point on the list, shortcut, or accessor keys. With Flash Lite, we can utilize the phone's soft keys to accomplish this through the FSCommand2 command SetSoftKeys explained previously in this chapter. We can also utilize the infrequently used * and # keys to the same effect and provide quick access to operations such as zooming. After all, this is a phone; people are used to everything working without delay. Accessor keys allow power users to become very proficient at using your application just as they are when text messaging with predictive text.

Prioritization gives us a way of applying these factors directly to our interfaces. We simply assign a priority to each of the UI elements in terms of how important it is to the user. For example, the Exit button almost certainly has a higher priority than an About button, because users should not be forced to search for a way of exiting your application; they may not have meant to start it in the first place.

Context also plays a very important role in how an interface is used and which of the listed factors affects a component's priority. Take, for example, a route-finder application. This is likely to be used when driving, so one-handed operation is key. Also, the user might be in direct sunlight, in which case the most important buttons need to be large, clearly labeled, and readable at a glance. When considering these external factors, our priority listing may change; nevertheless, it is always useful to evaluate first attempts at a UI to see if it could be organized better, and this means testing on the device itself as often as possible.

Let's take another example of a mobile application—the fictitious e-mail client application pictured in Figure 5-7.

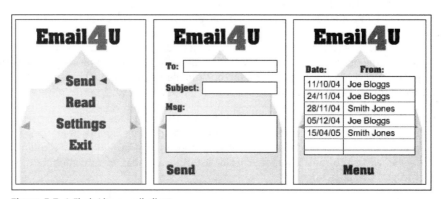

Figure 5-7. A Flash Lite e-mail client

If we list the visual elements for the menu screen in order of priority, we might end up with a list that looks something like this: Read, Send, Exit, and Settings, with Read being the most commonly used. When we apply our knowledge of priority based on context and a little common sense, we can start to swap around the positioning of our buttons and components, eventually deciding on the final design shown in Figure 5-8.

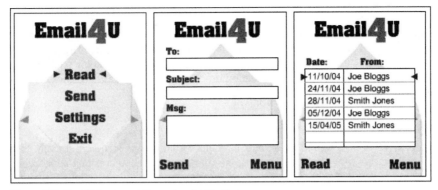

Figure 5-8. The UI, improved through prioritization

Notice that although Exit appeared higher in the list of priorities than Settings, we have placed it at the end of the menu listing on screen. This is because when a list of components is arranged vertically or horizontally on screen, components in the middle are more obscured by their surrounding complexity. Placing the Exit button on the outer edge increases its visibility—not to mention the fact that the last item on a menu is usually the first place people look for a way of exiting the application. We can also employ our wraparound navigation trick to make Exit even more accessible. On the second screen, we have attempted to reduce the amount the eye needs to move to follow the program flow when entering values into to:, subject:, and msg: by aligning all of the input boxes and giving them fixed widths. The final screen shows an improvement to the inbox, with a visual indicator of which e-mail is selected (shown as two dark arrows on either side of the message), as opposed to a slight highlight that might not even be visible in sunny conditions. The last change is to respect the common UI guidelines by including the most important two commands as soft key options (the bottom-left and bottom-right options).

Common UI guidelines and feedback

With the graphical flexibility offered by the Flash Player, it's easy to create interfaces that are extremely difficult to use. This section aims to outline some of the key UI best practices that should ensure easy operation of your applications. To aid developers in creating applications for the Series 60 platform, Nokia released the "Nokia Series 60 UI Style Guide" white paper[1] detailing some common guidelines to follow. Although many of these do not apply to Flash Lite at present, we try to include those that are relevant in the following sections outlining UI elements.

Fonts

When using text, be sure to keep the size at 10 point or larger to maintain readability. When a lot of text needs to be shown at once, introduce scrolling text fields or pages, and make use of the device or bitmap fonts described previously for extra clarity.

---

1. This white paper can be found at http://ncsp.forum.nokia.com/download/?asset_id=10131.

Color

Some people say that sticking to the web-safe 216-color palette is a good idea. While this isn't a bad idea at all, most (if not all) handsets that are currently shipped with the Flash Lite player include full-color screens (at least 4,096 colors, usually 256,000), and with PDAs, full-color screens are standard. Still, keeping the contrast to a maximum is a good practice; gray text on a white background is hard to read in any condition, and red on yellow is designer suicide.

Soft keys

Soft keys are there to be assigned important functions within an application. Generally speaking, the right soft key is reserved for "negative" actions, including going back and exiting applications. The left soft key is used to confirm dialogs, make selections, and any other "positive" actions. It is also frequently used to bring up a menu (such as the CDK's Action menu component). As a note to developers wishing to quickly port their applications from Flash Lite to Pocket PC or desktop, having a button underneath soft key labels allows you to use the stylus or mouse to perform that soft key action (as long as you duplicate the code assigned to that soft key in the button's on(press) event). This way you can also embed Flash Lite applications in regular web pages, and users can try out your applications using the mouse (instead of having to explain about the page up and page down keyboard shortcuts), as shown at http://richardleggett.co.uk/downloads/flashlite/mxna/MXNALite.html.

Full screen

Most of the applications I create utilize the FSCommand2 command FullScreen. While it is nice to be able to take over the entire screen, if your application *can* run in the limited space afforded by the Flash Player when running out of full-screen mode, it is a good idea to go with that option. Running in standard mode allows you to use the actual soft key labels created by the phone and doesn't encroach as much on the user (just as web sites that pop up and take over the full screen can be annoying). Games, on the other hand, are widely accepted as needing to take over the entire screen, because with limited screen real estate, this is sometimes unavoidable.

Soft notifications

Many interruptions might occur when someone is using your application, so if it is a game, users might expect a Pause button. But in an application where this is not usually needed because of an event-driven nature, we need to have things like bubble notifications (little speech bubbles that tell the user an event has occurred during absence, such as E-mail received) that remain on screen until the user physically dismisses them.

Navigation

Navigation on a phone occurs in three main forms: tabs (along the top of the screen), lists (as in our Email4U menu), and grids (as seen in the Main menu of Series 60 phones). Flash Lite allows for easy reproduction of all of these mechanisms, and it is a good idea to follow on from the phone's UI in this respect to increase familiarity, which, in turn, decreases the time it takes someone to learn how to use your application.

Help

For a full-featured application, a Help screen should always be accessible either from a menu option, or better yet, from a shortcut key throughout the application (that is, context-sensitive help). This could be as simple as a Help movie clip that is hidden at runtime with visibility that is toggled on and off by pressing the * key. This way you can simply lay Help over the UI.

Visual feedback

When an operation is going to take more than about two seconds, such as retrieving information from a server, be sure to show some sort of loading message, preferably animated. This stops the user from thinking the application has crashed and is proven to mentally reduce perceived the amount of time an operation takes from the user's perspective. The most important feedback is perhaps when an operation has failed; silent failure frustrates many Flash programmers, so we shouldn't really inflict this on our users.

Feedback can also be used to draw attention to an object, for example, a slight, pulsating glow draws the eye, which is great when we want to user to press a confirmation button before continuing. With mobile applications, we can use Flash to create modal dialog boxes. The example in Figure 5-9 asks the user to acknowledge a prompt before being allowed to continue.

Figure 5-9. A modal dialog prompt

You can download this file, named `ModalDialog.fla`, as part of the Chapter 5 downloads. A **modal dialog** (window) is one which prevents all other interaction from occurring without first acknowledging it. This is hard to pull off in Flash Lite, because most of our keyboard interaction is dealt with using key catchers on the time line, which we cannot easily disable, unlike a Flash 6 (or later) key listener. To achieve this in Flash Lite, we must physically move the playhead to a frame that does not contain our key catcher—in fact, it contains a key catcher with completely different code—and then move the user to the relevant frame depending on the input.

Audio feedback

In a similar vein to visual feedback, an audible beep can be a good way of letting the user know an event has occurred or a button has been clicked. Although I wouldn't recommend having a beep for each key press, important buttons would do well to give some sort of extra feedback. Whenever sounds are used in a game or application, an option to disable the sounds is usually a good idea. In Flash, we can make use of MP3s to include a variety of sounds in very small file sizes; for Flash Lite, we can also take advantage of device sounds, as outlined in Chapter 8.

Fail safes

Fail safes are mechanisms put into place to deal with uncommon occurrences that can affect the running of your application. The following list includes a few things that might affect the successful execution of an application:

- Battery dying or phone being dropped
- Connection not available or signal lost
- Finger slipping and pressing the wrong key
- Incoming phone call
- Memory limit being reached

All of these factors have the potential to occur whenever your application is run. To combat the negative effects of these, you can build in a few fail safes to prevent a negative impact should the event occur. When it comes to the battery dying, prevention of data loss is the only thing we can do. With a lack of local file storage to serialize and store some of the data in the application's memory, we must turn to either regularly uploading the data to a server or saving to local file storage (see Chapter 10).

When it comes to connectivity, two main sets of issues arise. The first is that the user might not have a data connection at all, it might not be set up properly, or the device may be limited in that respect. This is why it is good to have prompts, such as the one illustrated in previous section on visual feedback, to give users the opportunity to back out of an operation before they go ahead with it. Second, if the user goes ahead with it and the connection fails or hangs because of a server issue, we can offer the option to abort the attempt (a simple soft key function with Abort above it suffices for cell phones, as does a similar button for Pocket PC applications). This button simply goes back to a previous frame and gives control back to the user. In certain cases, the Flash Player gives an error; for Flash Lite, this is Unable to load data, which is thrown when a connection cannot be established for various reasons. When this occurs, the user is prompted to either abort the application or continue. At that point, your own fail safe button can be used to restore order and give the user another chance to repeat the attempt if the lack of connectivity that caused the problem is only temporary.

This same prompting mechanism can be used to prevent finger slippage and is useful for buttons that perform irreversible changes such as deleting a record. For most applications, however, where external data is not changed, this sort of fail safe isn't really needed.

When an incoming phone call is received, the stand-alone Flash Lite Player is hidden, and the user is returned to the phone's main UI until the call is complete, at which point the Flash movie regains focus (full-screen or otherwise). There is currently no way of detecting an incoming phone call from within Flash, but the application *is* paused (frame loops do not take place), until either the call is complete or the caller hangs up.

The final point on that list is "memory limit being reached." Most often, this is caused by bitmap data being too large for the Flash Lite player to cope with, which is not usually fatal (the bitmap is simply replaced with a red rectangle). However, when it *is* fatal (such as the memory stack limit being reached), the only thing we can do is create the application in a manner that's as stateless as possible.

The Flash Lite 1.1 CDK

The Flash Lite 1.1 CDK has been covered briefly in Chapter 3, but I'd now like to go through just what this kit contains and how it can help you in creating your mobile applications.

The example files

If you open the Flash Lite 1.1 CDK zip file and extract the contents to a folder, you find a subfolder inside named Examples. In this folder, you can find several FLA source files that contain a variety of goodies for getting you started, including an application that displays a device's capabilities (found in <CDK Folder>/Examples/Device Capabilities/capabilities.fla). This application tests out the various FSCommand2 commands discussed in Chapter 3, as well as other device-specific capabilities, such as MMS and e-mail functionality, and can help you to better gauge just what a device can offer before you start. I have adapted this file to automatically send this data to a server, where a publicly available database listing shows the various device capabilities of other handsets and devices that people have run the modified file on. You can find the adapted version of this file and view the device capabilities database at http://flashlite.richardleggett.co.uk/capabilities/. The listing of example files includes the following:

- **Device capabilities**: This example illustrates listing device-specific capabilities using FSCommand2 and other system calls.

- **Connection detection**: This example shows how you go about loading variables from a text file stored on a remote server.

- **CPU detection**: Using a timer and a frame loop to detect CPU lag, this example detects which type of device is running the application, from a mobile phone to PDA or desktop.

- **FPS speedometer**: This example displays the number of frames rendering every second (we will learn how to adapt and use this file to measure the performance of our games in the next chapter).

- **Landscape orientation**: This example shows how to display content for landscape viewing by dynamically rotating a movie clip on stage.

- **Font examples**: These illustrate examples of various freely available bitmap fonts and the use of TrueType and system fonts in an application (discussed later in this chapter).

- **Import files**: This example shows the dynamic loading of a SWF animation from a remote server.

- **Vibrate**: This example is sample use of the vibrate command (not supported on all devices, including Series 60 handsets).

Have a good look through these examples, and don't worry if there are any code listings or concepts in them that don't make sense. By the end of this book, these examples will be child's play.

The components

The Experience Design Team at Adobe did a great job of porting their famous Halo component design to the mobile platform. Keeping these components faithful to their desktop counterparts allows us to benefit from a prebuilt component set, and the instantly recognizable style allows users accustomed to Flash RIAs to know exactly what each component does at a glance (aiding UI familiarity, as discussed earlier). Moreover, the team has also created all of the components in the four Halo colors: blue, green, orange, and silver. Figure 5-10 shows a listing of the Flash Lite 1.1 CDK components.

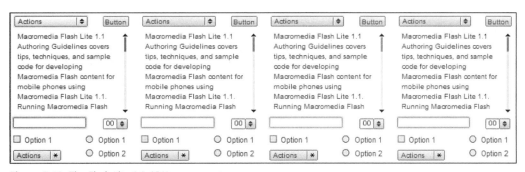

Figure 5-10. The Flash Lite 1.1 CDK components

> *To retain the visual sharpness shown in the screenshots, you must place all of these components on an exact pixel location. Therefore, the x or y coordinate cannot be 8.9; instead, choose 9. This keeps the lines and the text as sharp as possible.*

One of the main use cases for Flash Lite is for the rapid prototyping of mobile applications. With the CDK components, we can make this happen in even less time. Now, let's go through each of the components in turn, considering some information on how it works and where it is best used.

Button

The button component shown in Figure 5-11 is the most commonly used of all the components. It is actually an instance of a Flash button (as opposed to movie clip like the some of the other components). One thing that lets the button down is customizability, but this is discussed in the next section. Usage is as simple as dropping the button on stage and opening the Actions panel to enter your own custom actions in the prewritten on(press) handler.

Figure 5-11. The button component

Text field

The text field component (see Figure 5-12) is simply a movie clip containing a text field and background graphic to represent the text field state: up, over, or disabled. However, there is no way of detecting when a text field gets focus in Flash Lite, and for this reason, this component is somewhat weak (you can't switch the visual state to display or hide the Halo glow when the component gains or loses focus). Usage is as simple as copying the text field component to the stage and accessing the contents of the text field with myTFComponent_mc.myInput.

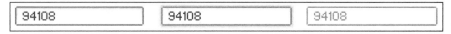

Figure 5-12. The text field component

Radio button

The radio button, shown in Figure 5-13, is a little more complex and contains some custom code of its own to allow it to interact with other instances of radio buttons in order for selections to be mutually exclusive.

Figure 5-13. The radio button component

The radio button is actually a two-frame movie clip, with each frame containing a simple button (one showing the check box checked, the other showing it unchecked); each button also has some code attached. The code on the unchecked button in the radio button example (<CDK>/Interface Elements/Radio Button/) reads as follows:

```
on (release) {
    _level0.selectedRB = _name;
    if (_level0.selectedRB eq "myRB_01") {
        gotoAndStop(2);
        trace("selected radio button is option 1");
        trace(_name);
        tellTarget ("_level0/myRB_02") {
            gotoAndStop(1);
        }
    } else if (_level0.selectedRB eq "myRB_02") {
        gotoAndStop(2);
        trace("selected radio button is option 2");
        trace(_name);
        tellTarget ("_level0/myRB_01") {
            gotoAndStop(1);
        }
    }
}
```

As you can see, the action of making the radio buttons mutually exclusive is hard-coded onto each radio button. When you click one radio button, the if() statement sets itself as the selected component and manually tells the others to display their regular (nonselected) states. This could be improved to make it a lot more flexible and reusable, and we will look at that in the section titled "Improving the radio button" later in this chapter.

Numeric stepper

The numeric stepper, shown in Figure 5-14, is designed to be used with the up and down arrow keys, so with this component on stage, it is important that you do not have a need for these keys until the user presses Enter on the numeric value selected.

Figure 5-14. The numeric stepper component

The stepper is a simple movie clip containing a text field and button; the button contains the following code:

```
on (keyPress "<Up>") {
    stepValue++;
}

on (keyPress "<Down>") {
    stepValue--;
}
```

stepValue is the name of the dynamic text field contained in the numeric stepper movie clip. With this in mind, you can see that the operation of the stepper is fairly simple, and we can introduce limits into the previous code should we need to. One other piece of code we should add follows:

```
on (keyPress "<Enter>") {
    _root.theValue = stepValue;
    tellTarget("/") gotoAndStop("someFrame");
}
```

This way we can detect when the user is done with the stepper and move on to another frame to do something else. This doesn't give much flexibility; a new instance of the numeric stepper is needed for each action with this method, but with Flash Lite, it is very hard to make a component flexible unless it is very simple.

Check box

The check box, shown in Figure 5-15, works in much the same way as the radio button in that it is a movie clip containing two frames—one with a checked button and one with an unchecked button.

Figure 5-15. The check box component

The checked button contains the following code:

```
on (release) {
    _level0.selectedCB = _name;
    trace("selected checkbox is " add _name);
    gotoAndStop(2);
}
```

As you can see, the code simply sets a variable on _root (_level0 to be precise), to the name of the currently selected check box. In the section titled "Improving the radio button" later in this chapter, you will see that, using the same method of adapting the code, you can make this component a lot more flexible, allowing for multiple selected check boxes on stage. However, with this method, we can act on the action of checking a check box (and perhaps display some extra components), simply by adding extra code in the previously shown on(release) handler.

Drop-down (pop-up) menu

The drop-down menu (see Figure 5-16) is used it to display a list of values from which you can make a selection. It is also good for pop-up navigation (perhaps accessible from a soft key).

Figure 5-16. The drop-down menu component

The menu itself is made up of two component parts: a simple button that controls the opening and closing of the menu and the menu itself, a movie clip containing a given number of buttons (the default is three) with opening and closing animation. Clicking the Menu button executes the following code:

```
on (press) {
    if (menuOpen eq false) {
        tellTarget ("_level0/dropDown") {
            play();
        }
        menuOpen = true
    } else {
        tellTarget ("_level0/dropDown") {
            gotoAndPlay(6);
        }
        menuOpen = false
    }
}
```

When the previous code is run, the menu movie clip (dropDown) plays and display the new buttons, which can now be tabbed to using the arrow keys. When the buttons are clicked, the following code closes the menu again:

```
on (press) {
    _level0:menuOpen = false
    tellTarget ("_level0/dropDown") {
        gotoAndPlay(6);
    }
}
```

Now is probably good time to spend a few minutes playing around with this component to get a feel for how it works. Remember that you have to duplicate the component in the library for each instance you want on stage. The sample file in the CDK also contains some code for the menu item buttons' on(press) event to show just how this component might be used to load in content, depending on which item is selected. To convert the drop-down menu to a pop-up menu, simply move the menu buttons upward in the menu tween and republish.

Actions menu

The Actions menu, shown in Figure 5-17, is very similar to the drop-down menu, except that it is designed to pop upwards, and it is invoked with the * key (on(press) is replaced with on(keyPress "*") in the button code). Other than that, it is essentially the same component. As the name suggests, the intended use is to perform actions such as loading in data, moving the playhead to a different frame, or opening a URL, video, or sound with the phone's built-in mechanism.

Figure 5-17. The Actions menu component

Scrollbar

The scrollbar (see Figure 5-18) is not so much a component in its own right as a script that you place on a button (a key catcher button, to give it a name), along with a movie clip containing the scrollbar's visual components.

Figure 5-18. The scrollbar component

The script you place on the time line follows:

```
on (keyPress "<Up>") {
    tellTarget("text_mc") {
        text.scroll--;
    }
    if (scrollBar_mc.thumb_mc._y > "6"){
        scrollBar_mc.thumb_mc._y=scrollBar_mc.thumb_mc._y-6;
    }
}

on (keyPress "<Down>") {
    tellTarget("text_mc") {
        text.scroll++;
    }
    if (scrollBar_mc.thumb_mc._y <= "81") {
        scrollBar_mc.thumb_mc._y=scrollBar_mc.thumb_mc._y+6;
    }
}
```

This code moves the thumb graphic (thumb_mc) inside the scrollbar component (scrollBar_mc) in order to reflect the scroll in the text field. There's no trickery going on here; it does exactly as it says on the box—the thumb moves six pixels down every time you press the down key until it reaches 81 pixels, and performs a similar reverse operation for the up key. This isn't very flexible, as you can imagine. The text field isn't linked with the behavior of the scrollbar in any way. In the following section, we build on the scrollbar to tie the text field and the scrollbar together.

Improving the CDK components

While the components in the CDK are great for most uses, their operation lacks a certain amount of flexibility because of a lot of hard-coded values that don't really tie the components together in an elegant manner. For this reason, we've decided to create custom versions of some of the components to address some usage issues.

Using the Push Button more effectively

While the Halo button is great in some situations, it is very limiting in that the width is fixed, and in order to have buttons with different labels, you have to duplicate the button clip in the library. To fix the latter, we can remove the label layer from the button component and place labels not inside the button itself but directly above the buttons on stage. This saves on file size, as only one instance of the button is in the library, and you can still assign custom button actions to each instance you place on stage.

When it comes to altering the width of the button, the current implementation of the Halo style doesn't allow us to change the width of the button very easily. The only way to get around this is to duplicate the button in the library and duplicate all of the symbols that are used in making up the central portion of the button, the section that we want to stretch. To save us some time later on, double-click the Push Button symbol in the library to edit it, and for each of the three frames in the time line, select the contents of the frame on stage and press Ctrl+B (or select Modify ➤ Break Apart). Doing this removes the need for the following movie clips in the library: Push Button–Down, Push Button–Up, and Push Button–Over. These can now be deleted from the library altogether. The next logical step is to duplicate the button symbol in the library, perhaps giving it the name Wide Push Button. Your new library should look something like the one shown in Figure 5-19.

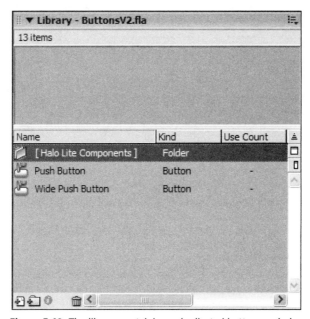

Figure 5-19. The library containing a duplicated button symbol

The next step is to edit our new Wide Push Button by double-clicking it in the library. We then need to spend some time stretching and shifting the middle and right portion, respectively, for each of the button states. The screenshot in Figure 5-20 illustrates the process.

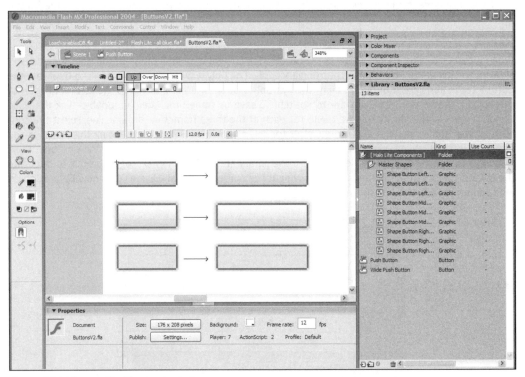

Figure 5-20. The modified button symbols

To see this yourself, open ButtonV2.fla, which includes an example of each of the methods described in this section.

Improving the radio button

This section takes you through the process of turning the CDK radio button into a reusable component by abandoning some of the code and making it easier to use in the long run. It may be beneficial to go back and read the section on the CDK's radio button one more time, so that it is fresh in your mind. You should note that, in order to complete this improvement, no changes need to be made to the library, and no movie clips or buttons need to be duplicated. At this point, opening RadioButtonV2.fla from the Chapter 5 downloads might be the easiest way to follow the process more closely, and opening the CDK in another window just for comparison might be helpful.

With RadioButtonV2.fla open, the first thing to note is the names of the radio button movie clips on stage. The first two, labeled red and blue, are named colorsRG_1 and colorsRG_2 respectively. The part before the underscore (_) represents the group name for the radio button group. The number after the underscore uniquely identifies the radio button in that group. With this in mind, double-click the first radio button component on stage, so that we can edit the code attached to the buttons contained within. Your screen should now look something like the one shown in Figure 5-21.

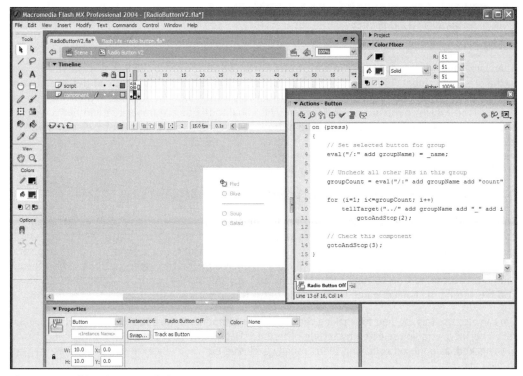

Figure 5-21. Editing the CDK radio button

As you can see, we now have three frames on the time line, as opposed to the two in the CDK version. If we look at the code on frame 1, we can see why:

```
groupName = substring(_name, 0, length(_name)-2);
eval("/:" add groupName add "count") += 1;
```

The first line simply works out the name for the radio button group that the component belongs to, so if we have named the radio button colorsRG_1, we know that this is the first radio button in the group named colorsRG. This group name is stored as a variable in each radio button movie clip for use later on. The second line increments a counter on _root; this counter will be named colorsRGcount for the colorsRG radio group. This way you can drop as many as nine radio buttons per group on stage, and the count will be updated automatically.

Now select the radio button on frame 2. This is the deselected radio button state. If you open the Actions panel, you should see the changes we have made:

```
on (press) {
    groupCount = eval("/:" add groupName add "count");

    for (i=1; i<=groupCount; i++)
        tellTarget("../" add groupName add "_" add i)
            gotoAndStop(2);
```

```
eval("/:" add groupName) = substring(_name, length(_name), 2);
gotoAndStop(3);
}
```

There are quite a few lines of code in here, so let's break them down into the three blocks you can see in the previous snippet. The first line in the on(press) event obtains a local copy of the groupCount, the number of radio buttons in the particular group. This is used in the next block as the condition for the for loop, which counts from 1 to N, where N is equal to the total number of radio buttons in the group. The tellTarget() then tells *all* radio buttons in that group to display their deselected states by going to frame 2.

The final two lines of code set the currently selected radio button:

```
eval("/:" add groupName) = substring(_name, length(_name), 2);
```

This line sets a variable on _root to the unique index of the current radio button; for example, colorsRG_2 sets _root.colorsRG to 2. This way we can always check _root.colorsRG to see which radio button has been checked and act upon it. That's it, RadioButtonv2 is complete, and I hope you find it as useful as I do. The sample file includes two groups of two radio buttons, but with this method, you can add up to nine radio buttons and any number of groups. All you need to worry about is setting the correct name for the radio buttons, and you're ready to go.

We can also use this method for making the check box component more flexible by allowing for multiple check boxes being selected by setting different variables on _root to identify which check boxes are checked, as opposed to having them visually exclusive but mutually exclusive in code as they are in the CDK.

Improving the scrollbar

The scrollbar in the CDK components discussed previously is a little too hard-coded for my liking, and it doesn't take into account how much text is in the text field. Imagine the text was loaded in from some external source; we need a way of determining the scroll position based on how much the text field has had to scroll. The following code is a replacement for the code attached to the key catcher button in the scrollbar sample; to view this code in action, open ScrollbarV2.fla from the chapter for downloads:

```
on (keyPress "<Up>") {
    theText.scroll--;
    scrollAmt = (theText.scroll-1)/theText.maxscroll;
    scrollHeight = sb_mc.track_mc._height - sb_mc.thumb_mc._height;
    sb_mc.thumb_mc._y = int(scrollHeight*scrollAmt);
}

on (keyPress "<Down>") {
    theText.scroll++;
    scrollAmt = (theText.scroll-1)/theText.maxscroll;
    scrollHeight = sb_mc.track_mc._height - sb_mc.thumb_mc._height;
    sb_mc.thumb_mc._y = int(scrollHeight *scrollAmt);
}
```

One other thing I have changed is the name of the text field variable; it is now theText, and I've removed it from its movie clip container and placed it directly on the main stage. I've also renamed the scrollbar sb_mc for the purpose of fitting the code into this book without the line wrapping. In the preceding code, you can see that we determine a value for scrollAmt (this is the ratio between the maximum scroll amount for the text field and the current scroll amount). We can then multiply that by the scroll track height minus the height of the thumb graphic to get a position for the scroll thumb. The new code now allows you to change the height of the scroll track and the amount of text entered into the text field without changing a single line.

Creating a data grid

One component that is missing from the CDK is the data grid. Of course, you won't want to use a data grid in a mobile application on as many occasions as you would a button. Nevertheless, building this component can help you to better understand how to go about coding for Flash Lite, and you can use it wherever you want to display tabular data in your applications.

The data grid component we are going to build is simple—nine text fields, each with a variable name incorporating a letter and a number. Text fields in the first column have a variable beginning with an "A", in column two with a "B", and so on. The rows are then labeled with a number, so column 1, row 1 would be cell A1. When we select all of these text fields and convert them to a movie clip, we have our data grid. To use the data grid, simply assign values to those variable names, as shown in the following code:

```
myGrid.A1 = 1;
myGrid.A2 = 2;
myGrid.A3 = 3;

for (i=1; i<=3; i++)
{
    eval("myGrid:B" add i) = random(100);
    eval("myGrid:C" add i) = eval("myGrid:A" add i)*eval("myGrid:B" add i);
}
```

The first three lines are straight variable assigns. However, the for loop has been set up to add in dynamically generated random numbers for the fields in row B. We then use those values by multiplying them by the values in column A, and we get a total column. You could, of course, use this grid with data loaded in on the fly, and you can create as many rows and columns as you can fit in your application. The source file for this component is available in the Chapter 5 downloads under DataGrid.fla.

The Flash Lite 2.0 CDK

As with the Flash Lite 1.1 CDK, the Flash Lite 2.0 CDK contains a wide variety of documents and samples aimed at getting you off to a running start in Flash Lite development. Unlike the 1.1 CDK, the concentration in this release is on documentation, with no new Flash Lite 2–specific components this time around.

The documents

The Flash Lite 2.0 CDK has a wealth of documentation. These documents come in the form of several PDF files, including the following ones:

- **The CDK "read me" file**: Outlines the contents of the CDK ZIP package.

- **"Introduction to Flash Lite 2.X ActionScript"**: This file includes fairly in-depth information on the Flash Lite 2 classes with a focus on what classes and methods are not supported in Flash Lite 2.

- **"Flash Lite 2.X ActionScript Language Reference"**: This file pretty much replicates what you get in the documentation that comes with the Flash IDE—in-depth information on each class and function available to Flash Lite 2. It's a good reference, although, at 780 pages in length, it's probably too many pages to print.

- **"Developing Flash Lite 2.X Applications"**: Some practical examples of solving Flash Lite 2 problems are included in this file, many of which are covered in this book, but it is a valuable reference to have also.

- **"Getting Started with Flash Lite 2.X"**: This file includes a sample Hello World application. If you've found this book a little too fast-paced up until now, perhaps try reading through this PDF and coming back to this book to try out some of the more difficult examples.

The example files

The 2.0 CDK comes with several examples to sink your teeth into. This time there is also a PDF explaining each. For your convenience, the examples are listed here:

- **Custom input text focus manager**: Not happy with the default yellow focus rectangles in Flash Lite? This gives you more options.

- **SoftKey**: This example provides some very useful keys. I often try to avoid these keys if at all possible, because some implementations of the Flash Lite player don't have access to them. But if you know your target audience uses Nokia, for example, go ahead!

- **Simple button menu**: This very basic example shows how to use buttons in Flash Lite.

- **Text field**: This example demonstrates how to read in and manipulate text entered by a user. Remember that in Flash Lite 2.1, we have new and improved in-line text input to boot.

- **Two- and four-way navigation**: These examples show how different types of phones support varied navigation styles—one gives a full, four-directional input, the other just up and down.

- **Shared object**: With this example, you can make use of the phone's memory card or internal memory to store your applications state for later use.

- **Media playback**: You can find out how to load audio, images, and video into a Flash Lite movie in this example.

- **Dynamic menu**: It's often the case that you don't know how many menu items you need to display, for example, with data loaded from the Internet. This example shows how to dynamically generate a menu system.

These examples are possibly more advanced than those found in the Flash Lite 1.1 CDK. But not to worry, most of this information is covered in this chapter, and any that isn't you can find in the next chapter on game development.

The tutorial

The tutorial included with the Flash Lite 2.0 CDK comes in the form of a nice, complete sample application for a fictional restaurant. The sample file shows you how to make use of the time line for structuring an application (discussed in Chapter 4), using the soft keys for user input and external video. The tutorial file nicely rounds off another excellent CDK from the creators of Flash Lite, and we encourage you to download the files and experiment with them at the same time as reading this book. The more tactile experience you have with Flash Lite, the more the content of this chapter will make sense.

Consuming data

Having your application running on a mobile device is one thing, but the real use comes from the ability to send and load data to and from external sources. This turns a rather static application into something dynamic, something that can change depending on what information the user inputs. After all, we are talking about connected devices for the most part; these devices were designed to aid in communication, be it voice or data. As well as the ability to send and load data from a remote location, Flash also gives us the ability to load in data from local storage somewhere on the device's built-in memory or on an expandable storage device, such as a memory card. A good use for this might be to load in text depending on the language selected by the user; an example of this is presented later on.

loadVariables() (Flash Lite 1.0+)

Flash movies have been able to load in data from external files for several versions now, since the introduction of the `loadVariables()` command in Flash 4. These files are plain text, although they do not need to have a .txt extension; you could use .dat, for example, to better hide how your application works. There are two forms of the `loadVariables()` command, and both are available for Flash Lite 1.0 and later versions: loadVariables(*url, target, method*) and loadVariablesNum(*url, level, method*).

loadVariables(url, target, method)

This form of the `loadVariables()` command takes three parameters, all of which are text strings. The first is the URL, the location, of the file containing the data (for example, file:///c:/ folder/file.txt). This can be the location of a text file in local storage, remote storage (via HTTP), or even a server-side script that dynamically generates the data output (for example, http://server.com/getDetails.php?id=21). The file must contain the data in URL encoded format, for example:

    myVariable=someValue

Multiple variables can be strung together with the use of the ampersand symbol (&) in the following manner:

    date=10/10/2005&name=Joe&highscore=300

When including text in the data, the text should also be URL-encoded to prevent characters like the ampersand from prematurely terminating a string:

```
myString=Dolce%20%26%20Gabanna    // Would read: Dolce & Gabanna
```

You can use Flash to generate this encoded text using the FSCommand2 Escape command in Flash Lite, or the escape(); function in Flash 5 (or higher) or any other language that supports URL encoding strings (almost all server-side languages do).

The second parameter is the target movie clip into which the variables defined in the text file are to be created, written in slash notation relative to whichever movie clip you are calling the function from. Remembering that the _root time line is also a movie clip, some possible values for this parameter are: "/" (_root), "" (_root again via use of empty speech marks), "/my_mc", or just "my_mc" to indicate a child movie clip relative to the calling context. In fact, that last example of loading the variables into a child movie clip can be very useful for keeping your data in one place; you could use a movie clip to represent a record set, for example, and just read out the values for my_mc.val1 ... valN as required (an example of this is given later in the section titled "Interaction with a database").

The final parameter is optional; it indicates which method to use when sending variables *from* Flash (GET or POST), as one other thing the loadVariables() function does is send all variables stored in the current movie clip to the given URL. This can be useful if you are using loadVariables() with a server side script that dynamically generates the response based on some variables supplied in the GET scope. However, you can always append these to the URL string itself (for example, http://example.com/script.php?id=200) and cut out the need for any other variables being sent (data costs for mobiles are sky high!). Variables sent by specifying GET as the final parameter are automatically URL encoded. If you omit the final parameter altogether, no variables are sent other than those explicitly referenced in the URL string.

To view this function in action, let's open LoadVariables.fla from the Chapter 5 downloads. You can see that we have a dynamic text field on stage, with the variable name myVar assigned to it in the Properties panel, and in frame 1, we have the following code:

```
loadVariables("dummyData.txt", "");
```

I've left out the optional third parameter; we don't want to send any variables, and the text file probably wouldn't know what to do with them if we did! Testing the movie should display Lorem ipsum dolor sit amet, consectetur adipisicing elit. in our solitary text field.

loadVariablesNum(url, level, method)

This function is perhaps a little more simple than the previous one. The first and last parameters are identical to the previous function, but the second is a number that indicates which level to load the variables into. While it may, at first, seem that this function isn't quite as useful as the previous one, it can be very useful when you have SWFs loaded into various levels (beginning at level 0 for your stub movie), and you wish to target a specific level to inject variables into. Sample usage includes the following:

```
loadVariablesNum("myTextFile.dat", 0);
```

LoadVars (Flash Lite 2.X)

The LoadVars object provides us with a nicely wrapped-up way of both passing data to and requesting data from a server-side script. With LoadVars, we create an instance of the LoadVars class, instruct it to request a data source, be it a text file or script, and automatically convert the name/value pairs it returns into a usable plain object. Take the following code for example:

```
var lv = new LoadVars();
lv.bookId = 123;
lv.onLoad = function(success:Boolean)
{
    if(success) trace(this.bookTitle);
}
lv.sendAndLoad("http://localhost/getBookWithId.php", lv, "POST");
```

Now there's a lot going on here, so if you are already familiar with the LoadVars object, feel free to go on as it works in Flash Lite 2, exactly as it does in the desktop Flash player. If not, I'll go through the process in detail here.

In the first line, we simply create an instance of the LoadVars object and call it lv. With that done, we assign it a dynamic property, bookId, and give it the very original value of 123. This is used to send a value to the server, so that it might examine this value and query a database. The next step is to create an onLoad handler that executes when our LoadVars instance receives data back from the server. This is a simple function; in the preceding code, we have created an anonymous function, but you could just as easily write a function elsewhere (perhaps another method in an AS2 class), and simply assign a reference to it or use Delegate.create() to proxy the call and modify the scope. The function accepts one parameter, success, which is set automatically by the Flash player when onLoad is invoked. If it is true, we are able to trace any variables returned by the script as properties of our LoadVars instance. If it is false, we know that the sendAndLoad operation has failed, and we can take action as necessary.

In reality, the script might return a string such as "bookTitle=Gattica&bookPrice=12". The LoadVars object takes those name/value pairs and adds them as properties to whichever object you set as the target for the sendAndLoad operation. sendAndLoad is one of three methods LoadVars has that allows for client-server communication. sendAndLoad not only receives data from the script but sends any properties of the LoadVars object as parameters to the script in question. The first parameter sendAndLoad accepts is a URL containing the location of the data source. Next, it takes a reference to an object to inject the results into; to keep the sample short we're using the very same LoadVars object, lv, but this could be any plain old object. Last, it requires you to tell it which method to use to send any variables in: GET or POST. In this case, we specify POST. We won't get into HTTP communication in detail or into the benefits of using either; it suffices to say that your server-side script may require prior knowledge of which method you are using (PHP utilizes the $_GET and $_POST arrays to receive the values for example). The other two methods LoadVars uses to communicate with the server include send(), which simply sends data and cares nothing about the return value, and load(), which does the opposite and simply loads in data from a data source.

> *If you have a text file containing name/value pairs,* LoadVars *has a lesser-known method that can help you out.* LoadVars.decode() *accepts a string containing name/value pairs and automatically adds each variable as a property to the* LoadVars *object being used, ready for access in the usual manner, for example:*
>
> ```
> var lv = new LoadVars();
> lv.decode("result=5&name=jimmy");
> trace(lv.name); // jimmy
> ```

XML (Flash Lite 2.X)

When it comes to actually sending and loading data, you can think of the XML object in a similar way to the LoadVars object. The differences are that when the data returns it must be as a well-formed XML document and that you access the results slightly differently.

One area where you might want to use XML over LoadVars is when consuming a web service or an RSS feed. Take the following code for example, which traces the titles of the latest Adobe News Aggregator collected posts:

```
var xml:XML = new XML();
xml.ignoreWhite = true;
xml.onLoad = function( success )
{
  var nodes:Array = this.firstChild.childNodes;

  for( var i in nodes )
  {
    if( nodes[i].nodeName == "item" )
      trace( nodes[i].firstChild.firstChild );
  }
}

xml.load( "http://weblogs.macromedia.com/mxna/xml/➥
        rss.cfm  _?query=byMostRecent&languages=1" );
```

That might look a little cryptic, but what we are doing in the first two lines is creating and setting up a new XML object. In the third line, we define a handler for when the data is returned, and in the final line, we make the request for the data, in this case from a ColdFusion page by passing it a few parameters. At this point, I strongly suggest visiting the following link to get a feel for what the XML should look like:

http://weblogs.macromedia.com/mxna/xml/rss.cfm?query=byMostRecent&languages=1

Inside the onLoad handler function, we are using some very basic constructs to first retrieve a list of child nodes that are within the outermost tag in our returned XML. We then loop through those until we find nodes with the name item. If you look at the XML, you can see that these contain the individual news items in the listing. When we do find a match, we trace the child node of the child node, in other words, the text within the *title* node.

In the early days of Flash, people used to work with XML this way a lot, but it's not very robust. The second someone makes a change to the XML format on the server, the whole thing breaks. After a short time, we began to write functions that loop through the XML Document Object Model (DOM) systematically, utilizing firstChild, the childNodes array, and the attributes property to accurately parse XML even if the format changes a little. This method is probably the most widely used, and in certain cases, I still use it, but like most coders I know, I also utilize some functions that convert XML into an ActionScript object with properties that match the names of the XML nodes in a hierarchical structure (you can find code to do this at one of the original Flash resource sites, http://proto.layer51.com). But a still better option, for the most part, is to use a set of classes designed for data retrieval from XML and the query language we use with it, known as XPath.

XPath is a language used to create rules that can select single or multiple nodes and attributes from some XML with just a single string. Some sample XML data follows:

```
<data>
  <item name="one" relevance="100" />
  <item name="two" relevance="42" />
  <item name="three" relevance="1" />
</data>
```

Here's an example of an XPath that selects *all* nodes with the node name item:

```
//item
```

It's simple—the double slash tells us that it is going to select all items regardless of their positions. You can use a single slash at the start to target nodes with an absolute location, for example:

```
/data/item
```

Now, with the XPath classes from Adobe (search the Web for mx.xpath.XPathAPI) or using our recommended XFactor Studio (www.xfactorstudio.com), we can use the XPath.selectNodes() method to select nodes from XML objects and attributes:

```
import com.xfactorstudio.xml.xpath.XPath;
//  my_xml is defined previously
var nodes:Array = XPath.selectNodes( my_xml, "//item" );
```

Now nodes contain an array of XMLNodes matching the criteria—magic! Let's say that you'd like to just get a single item node with a name attribute of one—no problem:

```
var node:XMLNode = XPath.selectNodes( my_xml, "//item[@name='one']" )[0];
```

You can get more and more complex with XPath. XFactor Studio's implementation, for example, allows you to use functions in XPath to build in simple conditions like contains() to see whether a node name or attribute name/value contains certain words. For a great tutorial on XPath, you can visit the following URL:

```
www.w3schools.com/xpath/default.asp
```

It may look pretty magical, but those XPath paths can get almost as complex as regular expressions, and that can mean a significant Flash performance hit. As with most aspects of computing, we have a power-to-weight struggle going on. XPath provides a lot of power and produces much less code than other available solutions in most cases; thus it is more maintainable, but this is at the cost of processing power. The XML is interrogated each time you wish to retrieve data, and with a big XML file, this just isn't a practical option. Alternatively, converting the XML to an ActionScript object when it is loaded means taking a big CPU hit for a short period, but then lookups are lightning fast thereafter. In summary, I recommend using XPath for most situations where the XML is less than about 50KB and looking to the alternative methods if you think the application is going to be sluggish.

Interaction with server-side scripts

Using the `loadVariables()` command, we can bring in data from a remote location on the Internet just as easily as bringing in data from a text file. The only thing we need change is the URL, and, if we are sending any parameters, we *can* specify the third parameter, the method with which to send variables (GET or POST). However, it can be a lot more efficient to specify the parameters in the URL if you are sending the variables via GET, for example:

```
baseUrl = "http://richardleggett.co.uk/script.php?";
url = baseUrl add "myParam=" add someValue;
loadVariables(url, "");
```

Using GET gives us the added benefit of being able to switch the URL from a local server to a live server in one place. By specifying the baseUrl on frame 1 of our application, we can refer to it throughout and only need change in once, perhaps by commenting out or uncommenting a line of code depending on whether we are testing locally or not.

A lot of people, when first trying this, get confused about what *form* their server-side script needs to output the data in and how they go about using that form. We discussed the correct forms when talking about text files: name/value pairs with no spaces, and URL encoded strings. The following list gives options for generating this sort of output in various server-side languages:

- **PHP:** `echo()`, `print()`
- **ColdFusion:** `<output />`, `WriteOutput()`
- **JSP (servlets):** `<%= value />`, `out.print()` (or a variation thereof)
- **ASP:** `Response.Write()`
- **C#:** `Console.WriteLine()`

An important thing to note when using these output mechanisms is that you should not need to specify any special page headers such as mime types; this output should be in plain text format, not UTF16 for Flash Lite.

Interaction with a database

Earlier in this chapter, I mentioned using a movie clip to represent a record set. This little trick can be expanded to provide what we might call a **data access object** (DAO) in the object-oriented world of AS2. The idea behind the DAO is this: not only does our movie clip store the returned data from the server, it also contains frames that represent the methods we can call to obtain this data.

For now, let's consider a fictitious movie database that can be represented by Table 5-1.

Table 5-1. A movie database

ID	Title	Rating
1	*Jaws*	PG
2	*Speed*	R
3	*Fight Club*	R
4	*Vanilla Sky*	R
5	*Tron*	PG

When returning data for use in Flash Lite 1.1, we cannot use for(var i in obj) to check for return values in a LoadVars object, nor can we use XML. Instead, we must return all data in a URL-formatted string, using the emulated arrays described in Chapter 3 to separate the results to use them. For this reason, the return string from the script needs to include three things:

- The number of records returned
- Values for each record (title, certification)
- A terminator variable

The first item is fairly obvious; we use this to let Flash know how many records are to be found in our emulated arrays (0 would indicate no records are being returned). The second is a listing of the actual values, one for each record, and the last lets us check to see if we have received all of the data. Using the information from Table 5-1, we can write a sample return string:

```
rows=2&t1=Jaws&t2=Vanilla%20Sky&c1=PG&c2=R&end=1
```

Breaking this down, we can see that rows is set to 2, indicating that we should find variables for two records to follow. The variables t1 and t2 are shorthand for title1 and title2; reducing the number of characters returned saves on data costs and speeds up transmission. Notice that the titles are URL encoded, with the space in Vanilla Sky being converted to %20 on the server side. c1 and c2 refer, of course, to the certifications for the given films, and finally, end=1 signifies that the data transfer is complete. This return string would most likely be dynamically generated based on some form of SQL query taking place on the server. We might even send some variables to the script for it to use to generate a response. For example, the script might return *N* random films, where *N* is equal to the number stored in a GET variable named no that we pass to it.

With this in mind, we can create our Flash Lite application to retrieve and display the results. For the purpose of this sample, we are simply loading dummy data from a text file that represents a typical return string to save on creating and populating a real database on your machine. But for all intents and purposes, the Flash side of things does not change; the only thing that would need changing for a live application is the URL, for example:

```
numRecords = 2;
end=0;
loadVariables("http://server.com/getRandomMovies.cfm?no=" add numRecords, "");
```

169

If you open LoadVariablesDB.fla from the Chapter 5 downloads, you should find the finished application to follow along with. Figure 5-22 shows a screenshot of our application when first opened.

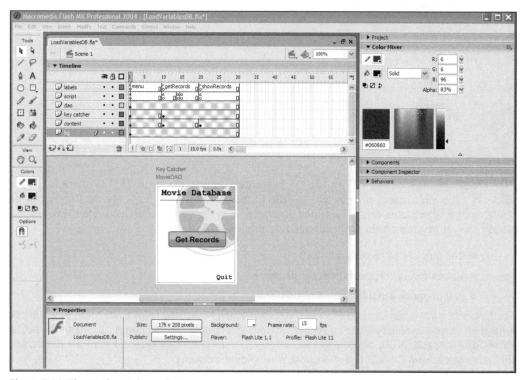

Figure 5-22. The Movie Database client

We have three key states indicated by the frame labels. First up is the menu, which contains the following code on the time line in frame 1:

```
fscommand2("SetSoftKeys", "", "Exit");
stop();
```

All we do here is set up the movie and pause at the menu, waiting for the user to click the button that has the following ActionScript attached:

```
on(press)
{
    gotoAndPlay("getRecords");
}
```

When the user clicks the button, and the playhead reaches the frame labeled getRecords, we enter the second state of our application, in which our DAO is called to retrieve the details from the script (or text file in this case). This is achieved with the following code on frame 10 of the time line:

```
call("MovieDAO:getRecords");
```

This code is a shortcut for telling our MovieDAO movie clip to execute the ActionScript contained on *its* frame also labeled getRecords. The alternative is to use tellTarget() followed by call(). The following code is contained on that frame:

```
rows = 0;
end = 0;
loadVariables("movieData.txt", "");
```

This code resets (or initializes) two of the variables we are looking to be returned by the script: rows and end. With these reset, we call for the data to be loaded. At this point, we replace the previous text file name with the URL for our script followed by any additional GET variables, possibly read from a text field on stage.

If we return now to the main time line, you can see that once this code has been called, we enter a two-frame loop between frames 14 and 15, in which we constantly check to see if MovieDAO.end has been set to 1, indicating that the data has been fully loaded. If everything goes OK, the script detects the change to end and moves onto the third and final state, marked by the frame label showRecords. As a side note, if the call to the script *does* fail and no error has occurred, we have implemented a fail safe in the Back soft key button that allows the user to return to the menu and try again. If it is successful, however, we want to be able to display the results. The results are displayed by the final piece of code, found on frame 20:

```
for (i=1; i<=MovieDAO.rows; i++)
{
    if (i!=1) duplicateMovieClip("movie1", "movie" add i, i);
    eval("movie" add i)._y = i*movie1._height;
    eval("movie" add i).title = eval("MovieDAO:t" add i);
    eval("movie" add i).certificate = eval("MovieDAO:c" add i);
}
```

All we are doing here is using a for loop to go from 1 to the figure stored in rows and duplicating the movie clip named movie1 for each record after the first. Next, we set the text fields contained within these duplicated movie clips to the values now stored in our emulated arrays in MovieDAO. The end result is a clean way of separating the data from the presentation; we use our MovieDAO movie clip as an object that not only retrieves the data but also stores it for later usage.

For a more-advanced version of this concept, please take a look at my MXNALite application, which makes use of Macromedia's live MXNA Flash services and is found in the Chapter 5 downloads. This example uses several of the concepts in this chapter, including wraparound navigation, key catchers, custom tab order, and record sets that can be displayed in pages through a DAO.

Integrating with the phone

Several functions are accessible through getURL() and FSCommand2 that enable us to tap into some of the phone's native functionality, including e-mail and battery-level indicators. With these functions, you can add extra value to your Flash applications and integrate them more seamlessly with the phone itself.

getURL()

getURL() is a command that instructs a Flash movie's container application to pass arguments to the OS to deal with. You can mimic this behavior on your computer by opening up a web browser and entering the following into the address bar: mailto:contact@richardleggett.co.uk. Next, press Enter to open your default mail client (Outlook, Thunderbird, or otherwise) with a blank e-mail addressed to the given e-mail address. We can use the mailto: protocol in our getURL() too, along with several other protocols explained in the following sections.

mailto:

An example is mailto:email@address.com. This command opens the phone's e-mail composition application (if it has one) with a blank e-mail. Optional parameters can be included to fill in certain fields of the e-mail, for example, mailto:email@address.com?subject=Subject&body=Body%20Text, which fills in both the subject and body fields with the text given in the name/value pairs.

http:

An example of this command is http://www.google.com. It simply opens up the device's built-in web browser, which is usually XHTML (or cHTML) compliant. The MXNALite RSS Aggregator application discussed in Chapter 6 makes use of this command to visit blog posts listed in the feed.

sms: and mms:

These commands perform similar operations, this time opening the SMS or MMS editor. sms:07967111000 is an example. Again, we can supply optional parameters such as sms:000000?body=Visit%20my%20site to fill in the message body, perhaps with the URL to our application download. This command is great for spreading the application through the phone itself.

tel:

This command, for example, tel:012345678, simply dials the number following the command. It may be useful not only to have your contact details in your application but also to provide a direct link to call your office!

Other resources

You can also use getURL() to launch files with their associated programs, for example:

```
getURL("file:///e:\\muvee\\muvee003.3gp");
```

This command attempts to play the 3GP video file at that location in the phone's movie player, such as the Real Player. This is sometimes a safer option than launching a video or audio file with an application that you know resides in a certain location, for example on the Symbian OS. Applications tend to move between different versions of the same mobile OS, and this way you are not reliant on a particular mobile OS.

FSCommand2

FSCommand2 exposes several native functions and some of the information pertaining to its current status. These range from URL encoding strings to getting the current date and time. There are more than 40 FSCommand2 commands; these are all covered in detail in this book's appendixes, and in Chapter 3, we went through the date and time functions in detail. However, let's go over a couple of functions that we can use to make our applications blend in a little better with the phone's normal operation.

SetInputTextType

This FSCommand2 command allows us to specify which type of text input to allow for our text fields by taking advantage of the phone's built-in input mechanism. These types include Numeric (numbers only); Alpha (letters only); Alphanumeric; Latin (includes punctuation); Non-Latin (for example, kanji), which allows for extended characters; and NoRestriction, which has no limitations. The following example sets the input to Numeric only:

```
fscommand2("SetInputTextType", "Numeric");
```

We might use this for a screen where we are asking the user to enter their ZIP code. Alternatively, we can change the input text mode upon pressing the up or down keys to allow different input modes for different text fields on the same screen. If you attempt to set the input to Latin or Non-Latin and that mode is not supported, NoRestriction is used instead.

GetBatteryLevel

It's sometimes nice to include a battery level indicator at the top of your application, so that the user won't get unexpected low-battery messages, especially because Flash Lite applications drain the battery at a much quicker rate than leaving the phone in standby mode. A sample use follows:

```
level = fscommand2("GetBatteryLevel");
max = fscommand2("GetMaxBatteryLevel");
percent = level/max*100;
```

GetSignalLevel

In much the same way, we can also display a symbol to show the current signal strength, letting the user know why he or she may not be able to connect to the Internet through your application. When using these functions, it's easiest to create a movie clip that contains, say, five frames (one for each bar of signal) and use the resulting signal strength to tell that movie clip to stop on a particular frame, for example:

```
strength = fscommand2("GetSignalLevel");
max = fscommand2("GetMaxSignalLevel");
frame = Math.ceil(strength/max*5);
tellTarget("signal_mc") gotoAndStop(frame);
```

If we run this example in a simple frame loop, we get a constantly updated value displayed on the screen. When using these FSCommand2 commands, be sure to check for fail values (for example, –1 is returned if GetSignalLevel isn't supported), and show an alternative instead, perhaps a question mark overlaying the symbol.

Example application: Stock quote client

To illustrate some of the ideas covered in this chapter, let's go through the process of developing a simple application that makes use of data stored on a server (in the form of a web service). This application needs to run on both mobile phone (Flash Lite 1.1) and Pocket PC (Flash Player 6).

The application itself is a front end for retrieving 20-minute–delayed stock quotes from the web service at XMethods.net (the description can be found at http://services.xmethods.net/soap/urn:xmethods-delayed-quotes.wsdl). We are going to include a number of predefined stock symbols displayed as buttons on the UI to save typing, but any symbol on the NASDAQ index can be entered and the resulting value fetched from the web service. Before we go through the client side of things, we need to create a server-side script to act as a proxy for consuming the web service.

The server side

Flash Lite 1.1 does not support the direct consumption of web services over SOAP or otherwise, so we need our script to make the request and return the result in a Flash Lite–friendly format. Let's go through several examples to show just how simple consuming web services can be. All of these scripts accept one URL/GET parameter and one symbol, and return the result in the following format:

```
result=00.0
```

PHP

The PHP example requires only one extra file, nusoap.php , available from http://sourceforge.net/projects/nusoap/. With this in the same folder as our script, we can use it as follows:

```php
<?php
    // Include the nusoap library
    include("nusoap.php");

    // Get symbol name to check
    $params = array("symbol" => $_GET["symbol"]);
    $sc = new soapclient("http://services.xmethods.net/soap/ _
            urn:xmethods-delayed-quotes.wsdl", true);
    $result = $sc->call("getQuote", $params);

    // Return result to Flash
    echo("result=" . $result);
?>
```

NuSOAP is dealing with the complicated formation and parsing the SOAP envelopes sent to and received from the server; all we need do is read out the result and echo it back to Flash!

ColdFusion

This sample really does show how ColdFusion excels at making the programmers' lives easier. Using the CFINVOKE tag, we can directly access the result from the web service described by the given WSDL file:

```
<cfinvoke
    webservice = "http://services.xmethods.net/soap/urn:xmethods-delayed-quotes.wsdl"
```

```
    method = "getQuote"
    symbol = "#URL.symbol#"
    returnVariable = "val">
<cfoutput>result=#val#</cfoutput>
```

Java Servlet

Java on the Web is renowned for having a steeper learning curve than the two languages previously mentioned, but there are libraries out there to make our lives easier. This example makes use of the Apache project's AXIS library for creating and consuming SOAP-based web services. Full instructions on how to download and install AXIS are included in the "read me" file that comes with the downloads for this particular example:

```java
import java.io.*;
import javax.servlet.*;
import javax.servlet.http.*;

import org.apache.axis.client.Call;
import org.apache.axis.client.Service;
import javax.xml.namespace.QName;

public class StockQuoteServlet extends HttpServlet
{
    public void doGet(HttpServletRequest req, HttpServletResponse res)
        throws ServletException, IOException
    {

        res.setContentType("text/html");
        PrintWriter out = res.getWriter();

        try
        {
            String symbol = req.getParameter("symbol");
            String endpoint = "http://services.xmethods.net/soap/ _
                urn:xmethods-delayed-quotes";

            Service service = new Service();
            Call call = (Call) service.createCall();

            call.setTargetEndpointAddress(new java.net.URL(endpoint));
            call.setOperationName(new QName("getQuote"));

            Float ret = (Float) call.invoke(new Object[] { symbol });
            out.println("result=" + ret);
        }
        catch (Exception e)
        {
            System.err.println(e.toString());
        }
    }
}
```

175

It is a lot more complicated than the previous examples, but for those used to working with servlets, this code should all be second nature, with the only new bit being the instantiation of an instance of the Service and Call classes.

With our server side in place, we can now use these scripts to proxy our calls to the web service. Let's move on and start creating our Flash clients.

Stock quote client for Flash Lite

Our Flash Lite client makes use of several of the concepts discussed in this chapter and should be thought of as an easy first step into Flash Lite application development. When you're ready, open StockQuoteLite.fla from the Chapter 5 downloads and test the movie. You should see the image shown in Figure 5-23 on stage.

Here we have a very simple UI, entirely laid out on stage (there are no dynamically duplicated elements in this example). If you would like to spend a minute playing with the application and getting a feel for what it does, please do. You can navigate the predefined symbols with the arrow keys and press Enter to change the symbol written in the input text field, or you can change it manually with the keyboard, entering any other stock symbols you might know. Click the Get Quote button to retrieve a value for the quote for display in the text field on the right.

Figure 5-23. StockQuote Lite

Setting up the movie

The first step in creating a Flash Lite application is always to create a new blank document using one of the mobile device templates. In my case, I usually go for the Nokia 7610 and delete the two guide layers that are created, giving me a blank canvas to work on. With the new document ready, the best way to understand how to set up this movie is to take a look at the time line of the finished file and scrub through it, viewing the various screens that occur throughout the lifespan of the application. On the time line, you should see that there are three states in this application, indicated by the labels on the top-most layer. The home frame contains the main UI; this is where almost all user interaction takes place. The getQuote frame is where we call our server-side script to retrieve the values. Finally, the pollForQuote state is a simple frame loop, similar to the loop used previously in the section titled "Interaction with a database" that checked for the return value from the script. After creating these application states as labels in your new file, the time line should look just like the one shown in Figure 5-24.

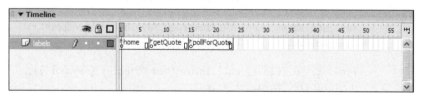

Figure 5-24. StockQuote Lite time line

Now that we have something solid to work with, we can start creating the other layers that contain the buttons, key catcher, and ActionScript. These layers, from the top, should be named script, keycatcher, please wait, ui, and gfx.

Creating the UI

With our stage ready, we can now begin adding the graphics to the gfx layer. This contains a few border graphics and the logo. To save time, you can simply copy these elements from the finished file, or if you wish, you can create your own to give the application a new style. Next, copy the buttons and text fields onto the ui layer, or re-create them from scratch using the techniques described earlier in this chapter. This includes adding in the buttons for the predefined stock symbols (and the text labels that go on top), the input text field for the symbol name, and the text field for the result and the buttons that go below. Note the variable names given to the text fields—we have set the variable name of the results text field to result, as shown in Figure 5-25. This allows us to set the text in the text field as soon as the variable result is returned from the script.

Figure 5-25. The text Properties panel

Accordingly, we also need to set the symbol text field to have the variable name symbol. The final stage of creating the UI is to add in our key catcher button somewhere off stage, as shown in Figure 5-23.

For the getQuote state on frame 7, we need to add some loading text on the please wait layer. I've also added in a semitransparent white rectangle just behind the loading text to obscure the rest of the UI until the loading is complete. The loading text and the rectangle need to go on a new key frame on frame 7, as shown in Figure 5-26.

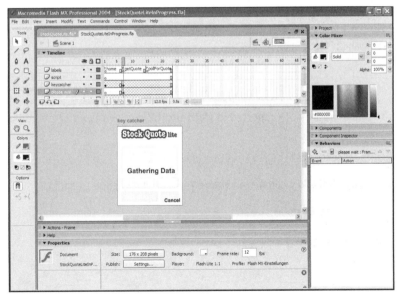

Figure 5-26. The loading screen

As the soft key actions need to change when the data is loading, we also need to create another key frame at frame 7 for the keycatcher layer. This allows the user to go back to the menu should the call to the server-side script fail. At this point, we can also add a text field containing the word Back to the keycatcher layer, just above the right soft key, to let the user know that this is an option. Remember that, at the moment, we have no ActionScript anywhere. That comes next.

Adding the code

Before we add the code to the time line, let's first deal with all of the button and soft key actions. Select the first button in the predefined stock symbols area. You might want to move the button labels to another layer, so that you can hide them to make selecting the small buttons a little bit easier. With the Actions panel open and the first button labeled MACR selected, enter the following ActionScript:

```
on(press)
{
    symbol = "MACR";
}
```

As simple as that, we can change the text in the symbol text field to any other value. You'll need to repeat this for each of the other buttons, changing the symbol text to the relevant symbol. Again, feel free to save some time by copying the buttons from the completed file. The other button code that needs adding is for the key catcher buttons on frames 1 and 7. For the button on frame 1, we need to attach the following code:

```
on(keyPress "<PageUp>")
{
    gotoAndPlay("getQuote");
}

on(keyPress "<PageDown>")
{
    fscommand2("Quit");
}
```

This code allows us to exit the application with the right soft key and provides a shortcut to the Get Quote button with the left one. Unfortunately, you cannot actually execute the buttons' onPress events, because functions are not supported in Flash Lite 1.1, but you *can* run the same code, which in this case is just a single line:

```
gotoAndPlay("getQuote");
```

For the other instance of the key catcher on frame 7, we have less code to add:

```
on(keyPress "<PageDown>")
{
    gotoAndStop("home");
}
```

This code is our fail safe for allowing the user to return to the home screen should the phone not receive a return value from the script or throw a connection error. You could test the movie at this point and see how the application responds to user input, but with no more to be done to the UI, we can now concentrate solely on the script layer and get this thing working.

Select the first key frame on the script layer, and open the Actions panel by entering the following ActionScript:

```
baseURL = "http://localhost/flashMobile/stockQuote/php/getQuote.php";
fscommand2("SetSoftKeys", "Get Quote", "Quit");
stop();
```

You can see that we are using the baseURL variable described previously to point to the actual location of the script. Here you can specify the location for the script of your choice, perhaps one of the examples (PHP, ColdFusion, or Java) given previously. Next, we set the soft key labels, enabling the key catcher Page Up and Page Down events to register, and pause on this frame awaiting user input.

In frame 7, the first frame in our getQuote state, we add the following script on a new key frame:

```
fscommand2("SetSoftKeys", "", "Cancel");

result = "";
url = baseUrl add "?symbol=" add symbol;
loadVariables(url, "");
```

The first line simply sets the soft key labels to the appropriate values to match our key catcher code. But the next three lines actually perform the server request. First, we reset the value of result, so we can detect the new return value and append the variable symbol to the end of the script, so the application is ready for our call to loadVariables(). With that done, there is only one more script to write—the two-frame loop between frames 15 and 16 that makes up our pollForQuote state. Frame 15 contains the following code on the script layer:

```
if (result ne "")
{
    if (result eq "-1") result = "ERR";
    gotoAndStop("home");
}
```

And frame 16's code follows:

```
gotoAndPlay("pollForQuote");
```

Taking the code on frame 16 first, we simply loop back to frame 15, where we look for the value of result to equal something other than the empty string ("") we set it to. If it remains an empty string, the script continues to frame 16 and loops back. If the value has changed, we check whether our script has generated a result of –1, indicating the symbol did not exist on NASDAQ (this is defined in the web service definition). If a –1 is found, we set the result to the error string ERR to let the user know a problem has occurred, and return to the home screen to display the result. If everything went OK, the result on the home screen displays both the symbol and associated stock value.

At this point, it might be good to adapt the example to include some extra functionality found earlier in this chapter. Some things to try might include the following:

- Showing the current time for the quote
- Displaying a list of previous values in a ticker-type listing
- Limiting user input to Alpha only

StockQuote Lite for Flash Lite 2

If you're thinking, "Great, I have to make a whole other version for Flash Lite 2," then stop. Flash Lite 1.1 applications run without problems on a device with Flash Lite 2. I want to include this example, as you may not be interested in developing for Flash Lite 1.1 and may prefer to concentrate only on Flash Lite 2 development, in particular, for handsets likely to come with Flash Lite 2 from 2007 onward. You can find the files for this example in the Chapter 5 downloads, StockQuoteLite2.fla.

The Flash Lite 2 version probably looks very different at first glance. When it comes down to it, I've barely touched the UI, but now everything is on just one frame, with all code on frame 1:

```
import mx.utils.Delegate;

// Uncomment the relevant URL and be sure to check the path for your machine
var baseURL = "http://localhost/flashMobile/stockQuote/php/getQuote.php";
//var baseURL = "http://localhost/flashMobile/stockQuote/cf/getQuote.cfm";
//var baseURL = "http://localhost/flashMobile/servlet/StockQuoteServlet";

// This time we use LoadVars over loadVariables()
// and Delegate the onLoad handler to _root's scope
var lv:LoadVars = new LoadVars();
lv.onLoad = Delegate.create( this, onQuoteReceived );

// Hide the loading animation and set the softkeys
gatheringData_mc._visible = false;
FSCommand2("SetSoftKeys", "Get Quote", "Quit");

stop();

// Define a button handler for the get quote btn
getQuote_btn.onRelease = Delegate.create( this, getQuote );

// Retrieve a quote and show the loading anim
function getQuote() {
    gatheringData_mc._visible = true;
    lv.load( baseURL + "?symbol=" + symbol_txt.text );
}

// Check the result and display it
function onQuoteReceived( success ) {
    gatheringData_mc._visible = false;
```

```
        if(success) {
            if (lv.result == -1) result_txt.text = "ERR";
            else result_txt.text = lv.result;
        } else {
            result_txt.text = "ERR";
        }

        gotoAndStop("home");
    }
```

As you can see, I've made use of the Delegate class to change the scope functions run in. I think it makes for cleaner code, but if you are unsure of how this works, take a look at the section on the Delegate class in Chapter 4.

Adapting StockQuote Lite for Flash for Pocket PC

Most of the discussion so far has been about developing for Flash Lite. You should note, however, that content developed for Flash Lite also works on a PDA, such as a Pocket PC, which uses the Flash 6 or Flash 7 Player (depending on which device you own). You may need to redesign the interface to suit the larger screen and perform a few minor tweaks, but the code doesn't need to change for the most part (with the exception of some Flash Lite–only commands such as FSCommand2, which are ignored at worst). This is facilitated by the backward compatibility of the Flash Player (with Flash Lite 1.1 being based on the Flash 4 format), and the Flash Player's ability to display as much of a SWF as it understands (and leave out the rest). Indeed, you can still visit sites containing Flash 1.0 content and play that content back without any issues at all.

To help with this process, I have also included a version of the StockQuote application for Pocket PC (see Figure 5-27) in the Chapter 5 downloads under StockQuotePocketPC.fla.

Some key points to take into account when converting applications for use on Pocket PC include the following:

Figure 5-27. StockQuote for Pocket PC

- Use a Pocket PC device template (screen size differs).
- Replace soft key functionality with buttons.
- Make sure everything is accessible through the stylus and on-screen keyboard.
- Take advantage of ActionScript 1 or 2 to create shorter, cleaner code.

I'd like to point out one thing: in order to make this version different from the Flash Lite 2 version (and it could have been almost identical), I've utilized a style that bridges the gap between the time-line–heavy Flash Lite 1.1 style and the completely code-driven Flash Lite 2 version. Hopefully, this Pocket PC version allows you to make the shift a little more gently.

Summary

In this chapter, we discussed a lot of techniques, tips, and best practices for dealing with many aspects of mobile application development. In the next chapter, we will look at creating games for mobile devices. We will explore which work best, how to optimize graphics and logic, and some step-by-step sample games, including blackjack.

Chapter 6

MOBILE GAMING

Mobile gaming is *big*. Every year, the Game Developers' Conference (GDC) in San Francisco (www.gdconf.com) brings together something in the region of 10,000 developers for a week-long event. In 2005, the GDC opened itself to the mobile gaming arena with GDC Mobile (www.gdconf.com/conference/gdcmobile.htm), an event geared specifically for mobile game developers to teach, to learn, and to discuss the future of the industry. Shortly after that, big players such as Electronic Arts started to look into taking a piece of this pie; EA began developing games for mobile devices and created a mobile division, EA Mobile. By this time, THQ and Midway were already sporting a pair of veteran wings with an acclaimed mobile gaming history, which gives a very good indication that mobile gaming was, and still is, a seriously viable and profitable industry. With all eyes firmly fixed on this sector, the time for early adopters to cash in may have passed, but the demand for games on devices is bigger than ever and continues to rise.

This chapter includes the following topics:

- An introduction to the mobile game scene
- Platforms and game genres
- Moving game elements with code
- The physics of motion
- Player input
- Collision detection and reactions
- Efficient math
- Game assets (including graphics, sound, and video)
- Saving and loading high scores
- Sample games

Introduction to the mobile game scene

Let's begin with no illusions. We are not going to port Quake III to Flash for mobile devices any time soon, but we *can* make an endless variety of engaging, educational, exciting, and profitable games that make use of limited resources and can compete well with titles written in any other mobile technology, including Java and even native system code. There are several reasons for this, so I'll expand a little on just how this is possible in the current and future market by first taking a little look back at the evolution of games over the last ten years.

About the summer of 1995, when Sony's PlayStation was released, all of a sudden every game being released seemed to make use of 3-D graphics. Previously, some pseudo-3-D and some basic 3-D were used with isometric games, such as Nintendo's Super FX chip for its Super Nintendo Entertainment System (SNES), and some very clever ray-casting engines, such as the one found in Doom. But such raw power had never been used to push hundreds and thousands of dynamically lit, texture-mapped polygons around the screen at over 60 FPS; it was a defining moment for the game industry. With that said, even when it seemed suicidal to release a game that wasn't 3-D in case the public rejected it as old school, 2-D games, such as Team 17's Worms series, never stopped being released. Their popularity continued, and some of the best games today are highly original and absolutely two-dimensional. You may be asking yourself, "Where is this going?" Well, when you consider what is possible with Flash and Flash Lite, you need not worry about pure graphical prowess. Your games can be just as popular as those incorporating the latest and greatest graphics; it all depends on the game play and execution.

Tetris is one game that has stood the test of time; it has suffered very little from the countless technological advances since its conception some 18 years ago and is considered by many as the "ultimate" game, ported to every known system, including the mobile phone. When a version of Tetris was released for digital TV services in the United Kingdom, it received one million plays, each costing £0.25 ($0.44), in the first week alone. A digital set-top box is a limited device, in much the same way a mobile phone is: the processor is slow, the keypad (remote) is awkward, and it is considered a semi-connected device in that it has to dial up via a phone line to make payments. Nevertheless, these 2-D, often very simple games are obviously generating a steady revenue stream for television service operators, and the same mentality can be applied to mobile devices.

Platforms

With our boosted confidence in Flash for mobile gaming, we might want to spend some time scoping out the competition. I'm talking about competition not just in terms of which technology you should use to make your games (I covered that briefly in Chapter 2) but also which devices people will choose to play their games as they move around. The ever-increasing power of phones and PDAs opens up other competition in the mobile gaming space, namely handheld consoles.

There are several types of devices a consumer might choose to play games on. Some options available are PDAs, phones, and handheld consoles such as Nintendo's GameBoy series and Sony's PSP. PDAs offer the option of developing with Java or native operating-system code using C++ (or even C# or VB.NET for the .NET Framework on Pocket PC), as well as with Flash.

PDAs and phones

With PDA and mobile phone platforms, J2ME and native applications generally make up the majority of what is found at present, because until now, these were the only options. Also, J2ME, for one, made it at least somewhat practical to develop for more than one device without a large game studio's budget. Native applications, however, provide the raw power required for these devices to compete with some handheld consoles in terms of graphical complexity. Unfortunately, these devices are still not great for games, as the controls tend to limit the games' ability to make the experience enjoyable for the user. This is improving, however, and one device (indeed, now a series of devices) is aimed specifically at tackling this issue—the N-Gage, later evolving into the N-Series.

N-Gage and N-Series gaming phones

Although some great examples of 3-D games are written in Java, native code is where the speed of newer handsets really shines. With specific math coprocessors boosting performance through the roof, the N-Gage is an example of such a device. Early console games can literally be tweaked to run on a handset with virtually no performance hit. In fact, I've seen Doom 2 run on a mobile device a lot faster than I remember it running on my Pentium PC. But this is where the cookie crumbles, as the technical requirements become higher and higher, fragmentation between device manufacturers increases. With the case of hardware-accelerated gaming, games will experience even more compatibility issues between handsets than you see on the considerably more open architecture of the PC, where you still have constant releases of patches to allow games to work with the wide array of graphics cards now available.

Handheld consoles

The term **handheld console** refers specifically to devices whose primary function is to play games. They may also provide functionality such as movie and MP3 playback and Internet browsing, but fundamentally their form factor is to accommodate game play. At present, the two main leaders in this field are Nintendo's ever-successful GameBoy series and Sony's PSP.

One thing these devices do very well is communicate with their parent systems, such as the PlayStation and Wii; what I am talking about here is *convergence*. Convergence is something that Flash is very good at providing. One thing I like to do with my PSP is control my XBox Media Center playback utilizing a simple Flash movie that is run in the PSP's web browser. As long as the two devices are on my home wireless network, Flash can be used to good effect in these sorts of situations. The PSP homebrew scene has taken to Flash on the PSP surprisingly well, porting a lot of good web games to build up a nice catalog of free games. I say "surprisingly well," because most of the guys producing games had to be hardcore C++ coders to make most of the homebrewed games, so perhaps Flash is helping to let more people get their own stuff out there.

This ease of development is really where Flash shines. We can dramatically increase the return on investment (ROI) because of the significantly reduced development time and human resources involved in creating content. There are absolutely thousands of great Flash games on the Web. If you pick the cream of the crop, port those to PSP (sometimes, porting is not even required), and make these accessible through a web portal page, you'd already have a healthy back catalog for people to enjoy with minimal effort. With WiFi proliferating around cafés, airports, and public transportation, you're never far from being able to enjoy these.

If you already use Flash as a web designer, perhaps one of the most pleasing aspects of choosing Flash over any other technology for creating mobile applications is that you get instant satisfaction for your effort, because you don't have to trawl through reams of documentation and SDKs that are entirely platform dependent or learn a great deal of new things—you can apply what you already know.

Game genres

Before we look into which sorts of games work and which simply do not, it might be useful to break down just how people use games on their mobile devices. We can break these people into two reasonably distinct camps: hardcore gamers and casual gamers. With mobile devices, the casual gamers make up the vast majority of the total gamers. This might show a lack of truly great games; more likely, it shows that people turn to their handsets for a quick distraction and little more. On the bus, on the train, or when waiting for somebody, the first thing a person with a little time and no friends to chat to will do quite often is take a phone out and begin tapping away; it's almost some sort of reflex action. Next time you are on public transportation, look at individuals getting on and sitting down to see just how many reach for their phones to avoid conversation with strangers!

Both hardcore and casual gamers play games that fall into several main genres, though. I'd like to list some typical game genres for your consideration:

- **Action**: These are difficult to pull off because of player speed, but this limitation will improve over time. Example: Space shooters.
- **Role-Playing Games (RPG)**: RPG games are great overall; plus, you have the option to make use of MSOs in Flash Lite 2 to save progress. Example: Final Fantasy.
- **Sports**: We aren't talking 3-D soccer, but strategy and management simulations can do well (especially when used with up-to-date, accurate data feeds). Example: Football Manager.
- **Strategy and Logic**: These games work well; minor variations in strategy games can add value for players without costing too much extra development time. Example: Minesweeper.
- **Skill**: Skill games can work well; we will look at an example of this later in the chapter. Example: Tower of Pisa.

- **Multiplayer**: Multiplayer games offer a potential sweet spot yet to be proven in the mainstream, but phones are, of course, social devices. Example: Mad Bomber.
- **2-D Racers**: These are on par with action games speed-wise. They're technically possible, but limited controls can make these problematic. Example: Micro Machines.
- **Card and Board Games**: These games are great for longevity, and distractions don't affect game play much. They're not so good to just quickly pick up and play. Example: Monopoly.
- **First-Person Shooter (FPS)**: Creating these games in Flash Lite is almost impossible, although it has been done with limited success (the results come closer to Wolfenstein in terms of 2-D billboard sprites than true FPS games). Example: Quake.

Regardless of the game type you choose, the key is to find the balance between making the game play as engaging as possible and bludgeoning the CPU to death with a million operations per second. The Flash Player deals with poor CPU treatment by either throwing an error and quitting, or more commonly, running at a fraction of the desired FPS rate and resulting in a less-than-desirable experience.

Code samples

As with previous chapters, this chapter covers both Flash Lite 1.1 and 2.0 ActionScript, on a per-case basis. The aim is to make you comfortable with whichever format you may find in examples, articles, and tutorials online. By now, you should be finding it easier to distinguish between the two, and it is always good practice to be able to, with minimal effort, convert between them where required.

Making things move

"Making things move" is not just the name of an outstanding book on this very subject—of course, I'm referring to *Foundation ActionScript Animation: Making Things Move* by Keith Peters (Berkeley: friends of ED, 2005). I'd like to now briefly look at how you can listen for user input to move a single object or several objects at the same time on screen, and I'd like to look into how this continuous movement might be achieved for the one-button game concept described later in the section entitled "Player input."

Moving an item directly

Let's try placing a movie clip on stage and moving it every frame; that's 12 times a second at the default 12FPS setting. Fire up Flash, start a new Flash Lite 2 stand-alone mode project, and create yourself a movie clip; it contain absolutely anything you desire, including our faithful old red ball. Now, place that on stage, and name it my_mc in the Properties panel. To get this moving, you can take one of the two approaches that I'll describe in this section. First of all, let's look at assigning a function to the movie clip's onEnterFrame loop on frame 1 of the main timeline:

```
my_mc.onEnterFrame = function()
{
    this._x += 1;
}
```

Quite simply, this function moves our movie clip 1 pixel to the right every 1/12 of a second. The preceding code is known as an **anonymous** function; we are assigning something a function that has no name. Alternatively, we could have written

```
my_mc.onEnterFrame = moveMe;

function moveMe()
{
    this._x += 1;
}
```

The important thing to note here is that, just like with the anonymous function, when the function moveMe() runs, it runs in the *scope* of my_mc; so the keyword this refers to my_mc itself, and not _root, which is where we are actually declaring the function. We could have ten movie clips on stage, all with their onEnterFrame assigned to moveMe(). They would all move independently, as this would refer to each one separately as they each run the moveMe() function. The better alternative is to have another object governing the motion of my_mc (indeed, all of our ten movie clips), so we can have one loop function that can control the position of lots of clips at once without those clips necessarily all moving at the exact same speed.

Moving several items at once

Let's take our movie clip, and give it a linkage ID in the library (e.g., "ball") so that we can use attachMovie() to dynamically add some to the stage:

```
var ball1 = attachMovie( "ball", "ball1", 1 );
var ball2 = attachMovie( "ball", "ball2", 2 );
onEnterFrame = function()
{
    ball1._x += 1;
    ball2._y += 1;
}
```

Here we have our two ball instances moving independently, controlled by just a single onEnterFrame. In this case, it belongs to the main timeline, _root, which is useful for several reasons. Not only could we compare positions of the ball instances to each other in this one loop (for example, in collision detection between them), but if we had 100 balls, bullets, or sprites of any kind, giving each one its own onEnterFrame would seriously bog down the CPU. Having one onEnterFrame to govern them all is a more efficient way of tackling animation and can make for easier-to-follow code.

Moving items around a point

Now you can animate objects moving in two directions, you can expand your capabilities a little. Let's think about some situations we might need to model in a game. Take orbiting, for example, where one or more objects orbit another. An example of this might be a shield made up of several sprites that rotate around the player's ship. If you'd like to follow along with this example in Flash, open RotateAroundAPoint.fla. You should find the following code on frame 1:

```
    var orbitPos = 0;

    onEnterFrame = animate;
    function animate()
    {
        var xPos = Math.sin( orbitPos * Math.PI/180 ) * 50;
        var yPos = Math.cos( orbitPos * Math.PI/180 ) * 50;

        planet_mc._x = xPos + star_mc._x;
        planet_mc._y = yPos + star_mc._y;

        orbitPos += 2;
        if( orbitPos > 359 ) orbitPos = 0;
    }
```

We have another familiar onEnterFrame loop here. This could also be written this.onEnterFrame = animate;, but I chose to leave out the explicit scoping of the variables and function in question to give you a feeling for how Flash figures it out by following some standard rules. This time, the aim is to orbit planet_mc around star_mc. The first thing to do is define a variable to store the current orbit position, orbitPos; this is how far around the star the planet has orbited, ranging from 0 to 359 degrees. At the end of the loop, you will notice that we are incrementing this value by 2 each frame, until it reaches anything over 359 degrees, at which point, the orbit resets, as the planet must have come full circle!

Our next step in the loop is to work out the next x position and y position of our planet. We do this by multiplying the distance away from the planet, a whole 50 pixels(!) by the sine or cosine of the orbit angle in radians for x and y, respectively. The multiplication by Math.PI/180 just converts degrees to radians, which the sine and cosine functions expect.

The second block of code in the onEnterFrame function applies these values to the _x and _y properties of the planet, also adding the _x and _y of the star, so that we are, indeed, rotating around that and not just the point (0, 0) at the top-left corner of the screen.

The physics of motion

Now that you can move things around at a constant speed, you might want to branch out a bit and look at how things move in the real world. In reality, it's almost impossible for something to remain still (on microscopic and quantum levels, nothing is ever *completely* still). But we can assume that, for our purpose, every object has a certain velocity ranging between negative infinity and positive infinity, including zero. Notice that I use the term velocity instead of speed, because a *velocity* can be negative as well as positive, for example, when reversing a car instead of driving forward.

Velocity, direction, and momentum

With velocity, we can also take into account in which direction an object is traveling. For example, I might have a pedometer that tells me I'm running at 12mph down a windy road. At the same time, it might be said that, because I'm running toward the northeast, overall I'm actually traveling at, say, 7mph in a northerly direction and 10mph in an easterly direction. I'm still going 12mph toward the northeast, but we can break it down into these individual directions also. In a 2-D game, we might represent this break-down with an objects x velocity (from left to right) and y velocity (from top to bottom). Breaking down what we know as a single value for velocity into individual velocities in certain directions is also known as breaking it down into its **components**.

> In math, when we take a velocity and a direction, what we get is usually called a **vector**. A vector can be thought of as a line that has both magnitude (e.g., length or speed) and direction (e.g., an angle). We can use some simple math to do things like add up 100 vectors that represent the speed and direction of 100 particles within a sphere to get the overall speed and direction for that sphere in its entirety.

Let's take a look at how we might apply velocity to a movie clip in Flash Lite 2. You can follow along with this one using Velocity.fla. First of all, create a movie clip on stage, and give it the instance name my_mc. Next comes the code for frame 1 of the root timeline:

```
my_mc.xVel = 3;
my_mc.yVel = 0;
my_mc.onEnterFrame = animate;
function animate()
{
    this.xVel -= 0.11;
    this.yVel += 0.1;

    this._x += this.xVel;
    this._y += this.yVel;
}
```

> Flash Lite 1.1 developers take note! This Flash Lite 2 code requires minimal mod-ification to work in Flash Lite 1.1. Instead of writing the onEnterFrame function as it appears in the preceding code snippet, simply create a two-frame loop inside the my_mc symbol and place the code within one of those frames instead of in the previously-defined function. This is covered in Chapter 3, so feel free to jump back if you need a refresher on creating code loops in Flash Lite 1.1.

OK, so that example is fairly boring. We can see the ball curving back on itself as we alter its velocity in the x and y directions and apply those values to each frame. You can think of -= 0.11 and += 0.1 as applying acceleration (or deceleration) to the object's velocity. Now, you can start to think about how you can control not only the direction something is traveling in but also how fast it is accelerat-ing in that direction. We'll look at a real-world use for this with the jumping sheep example a little later on. For now, I'd like to look at one more useful way of animating objects with code.

Creating an ease out tween

One of the most common ways of animating a movie clip from one position to the other is with the ease out tween. This is available from the motion tween options in the Properties panel when animating on the time line, but here, we are going to see how it is done with code. You might recognize an ease out without knowing its name; it's characterised by a rapid initial speed that slows to a full stop upon reaching the target. Modifying the previous code, we get the following ease out code:

```
endX = 100;
endY = 100;
my_mc.onEnterFrame = function()
{
    this._x = this._x + (endX-this._x)/10;
    this._y = this._y + (endY-this._y)/10;
}
```

You may notice I haven't used the var keyword to declare my variables. You can and should use this for Flash Lite 2, as it clearly defines in which scope a variable is being created. For the purpose of this example, I'm leaving it off just to show you that you can still write code in a Flash Lite 1.1 style with only minor differences. Going through the code, you can see we have set up a couple of variables to determine the target x and y positions for our movie clip to reach. Inside the onEnterFrame loop, we simply move toward that target by following a simple equation:

```
New X Position = Current X Position + ➡
                    ((Target X Position - Current X Position) / Divisor)
```

If you break down the equation, you can see that our new x position is the sum of the current x position plus the difference between the target x and the current x position, divided by a value I've called Divisor. By taking the target x position and subtracting the current x position, you get the distance you need to move the object. That distance starts off great, and as the object gets closer, diminishes in size. Divisor is there to stop you from reaching the target position all at once. The larger the value, the slower the target position is reached; a lower value, thus, increases the speed. The magic happens as the distance to the target reduces. We are still using the same divisor, but it is operating on increasingly smaller values, leaving the object less distance to travel each time, until the value eventually gets near enough to 0. This slows the object as it reaches the target. We can apply exactly the same equation to the y position and, thus, have the ability to ease out to any location we like.

Player input

A lot of the stuff covered in this chapter is purely code based, things that you can just leave running to show various game-related concepts. But it's good to remember that in games all of these things are directly related to some sort of user input. This section will look at taking that user input and doing something with it. I've mentioned before that the keys on most mobile devices aren't the best for gaming; they're usually small and fiddly. Let's now talk about some ways to make sure this isn't too much of an issue.

One-button games

That may sound like a crazy claim to make, but it is possible to make games that have just a single button for all user input. In fact, you can find a whole lot of these designed by the game gurus over at globz.com. With only one button for input, you have to rely on one thing to make the game interesting—*time*. Effectively, this sort of game relies on something automatic occurring as time passes, and the user presses a button to interact at given points. Take, for example, a base jumper jumping out of a building. As she falls, the user sees windows rushing past and has to choose when to open the parachute; the further the jumper drops, the more points the user gets, but if she drops too far, she'll crash into the ground and have a really bad day. It's true the user might also need another button to access the menu or quit the game, but what we have here is just one example of how you can use time to make up for the poor buttons available on phones, which make it difficult to perform rapid button presses in games.

This same concept is good for another Flash Lite limitation—the inability to detect a keyUp event. Normally, we'd listen for the keyDown, start moving a character, for example, and stop moving her on the keyUp (alternatively, we could use Key.isDown() to check whether a key is still being depressed). Without being able to listen for a keyUp or check Key.isDown(), we have no way of knowing when to stop the character, so any movement must, instead, be done by individual increments every time you press the key. This makes for jerky and delayed movement. If the character can be allowed to constantly move (perhaps using an onEnterFrame loop), we can listen for keyDown events to change the direction of that motion. This constant movement brings the feeling of accurate control over an on-screen element.

Using input with motion in a jump example

It's time to apply some of what you've learned. In this example, we are going to take a simple side-on hero character, something like Mario from the Nintendo game series, but in this case, we will use a sheep to avoid any nasty copyright issues. We are going to get him running and jumping with key presses, and we are going to take the constant movement approach, so when you release the key he will keep running unless you change direction, jump, or hit a wall.

To follow along please open jump.fla from the Chapter 6 examples. The screen for jump.fla is shown in Figure 6-1.

There's not a lot going on here. We have some dummy background graphics, and our hero movie clip containing a sheep, named hero_mc. All of our code is on one frame as usual, to make it easier to explain. With practice, you will find that you prefer to separate code into separate files where possible, using some of the techniques described in Chapter 4. For now, let's concentrate on the raw code. There's quite a bit this time, so I'm going to go through it in segments, from top to bottom. The first segment follows:

Figure 6-1. The jumping sheep example

```
var direction = "";
var gravity = 0.8;
var yspeed = 0;
var floorHeight = hero_mc._y;
hero_mc.gotoAndStop(1);
```

You should be fairly familiar with the process of setting up the scene at the start. We create a couple of variables, the first being the initial direction of the hero (which we initialize as a blank string, as the user has yet to press a directional key). The next two variables are part of our jump code, and we will look at those later. Next, we measure the vertical position of the hero character, so we know where the floor is (assuming the hero is on the floor when the game starts, based on where we position him on stage). Finally, we tell hero_mc to go to frame 1 and stop using gotoAndStop(). This prevents the walking animation from occurring while the character is not moving at the start. If you drill down into the hero_mc movie clip, you can see a simple time line with just enough frames to give the impression of walking animation when played back, so this gotoAndStop() action prevents this loop from playing through at the start. Next, we have the key listener code on frame 1:

```
// Create listener object
var keyListener = {};

// Add listener object to the Key object's listeners array
Key.addListener( keyListener );

// Define the onKeyDown event called when a user presses a key
keyListener.onKeyDown = function()
{
        // Check which key they pressed
        if( Key.getCode() == Key.RIGHT )
        {
            direction = "right";
            hero_mc.gotoAndPlay("walk");
        }
        else if( Key.getCode() == Key.LEFT )
        {
            direction = "left";
            hero_mc.gotoAndPlay("walk");
        }
        else if( Key.getCode() == Key.UP )
        {
            if( hero_mc._y >= floorHeight ) jumpPressed = true;
        }
}
```

The usual practice is to create a simple object to listen for any keypresses (in this case, called keyListener). Then, add it as a listener to the Key object itself. This means that whenever the user presses a key, a function named onKeyDown will be executed on any listening objects, so we must define onKeyDown in order to intercept these keypresses. Within this function, we make use of the if statement to check the key code for whichever key was pressed, for example, Key.RIGHT or Key.LEFT.

Let's take each block of this triple if statement in turn. The first checks to see if the user pressed the right button. If so, we simply set the direction to "right", and start the walk animation contained within hero_mc. You may wonder what could possibly change just by setting this direction variable to a string—all will be revealed in the game loop, which we will come to shortly. If the user did not press right, we check the same for Key.LEFT and, accordingly, set the direction to "left". If neither of these keys were pressed, we check whether the up key, Key.UP, was pressed, and quite simply, we set another variable jumpPressed to true, but only if hero_mc is not above the value stored for the ground level, floorHeight. Now, let's move on to the penultimate piece of the puzzle, the game loop:

```
onEnterFrame = function()
{
    if( direction == "right" )
    {
        if( hero_mc._x+hero_mc._width/2 < Stage.width )
            hero_mc._x += 2;
        else
            hero_mc.gotoAndStop(1);

            hero_mc._xscale = 100;
    }
    else if( direction == "left" )
    {
        if( hero_mc._x-hero_mc._width/2 > 0 )
            hero_mc._x -= 2;
        else
            hero_mc.gotoAndStop(1);

        hero_mc._xscale = -100;
    }

    if( jumpPressed )
    {
        yspeed = -8;
        hero_mc.onEnterFrame = jump;
        jumpPressed = false;
    }
}
```

The first part of this onEnterFrame (game) loop takes into account that variable we set when the user presses left or right, direction. If the direction is "right", the game loop does two things. The first is to check whether our hero is hitting the right-hand side of the screen with if(hero_mc._x+hero_mc._width/2 < Stage.width). This evaluates to true if the center point of our hero graphic is at or past the right-hand edge of the screen. If not then, the _x position is incremented by 2 pixels. Also, the _xscale is set to positive 100; this may already be the case, but essentially, this just makes our hero face to the right. If we find that the hero is past the edge of the right of the screen (even by just half a pixel), the running animation stops and his _x position is not incremented. The next part of the code just repeats this for the "left" direction, but instead decrements _x and sets _xscale to -100, flipping the character.

Now, let's look at the jump code. If we find that the jumpPressed variable is set to true (meaning the user has pressed Key.UP), we set our yspeed variable to -8; initially, this was 0. We will use yspeed to actually move our hero along his path up and back down to earth just by changing this value. Next, we are setting hero_mc's onEnterFrame function to point to another function, named jump. Finally, we revert jumpPressed to false, so that this code doesn't execute again until the user presses the jump key another time.

OK, we are almost there, but we have one last bit to examine. In the game loop, you will remember we set our hero_mc's onEnterFrame to a function called jump. This is the last piece of code we need to get the jumping in there:

```
function jump()
{
        yspeed += gravity;
        this._y += yspeed;

        if( this._y >= floorHeight )
        {
            yspeed = 0;
            this._y = floorHeight;
            delete this.onEnterFrame;
        }
}
```

If you look back, you can see that we set yspeed to -8 when the user pressed the up key. Now, we are going to make use of that variable, adding to it our arbitrary value for the effect of gravity, which we set to be 0.8 at the start. This will bring yspeed up from its initial -8, closer to 0 and beyond, each time this loop runs through. Now you will see why we did this. In the next line, we increment this._y by yspeed. It's important to note that, because we set the jump function to the onEnterFrame of hero_mc, this will refer to hero_mc itself. So the first time this is code run, hero_mc._y will have added to it -8 plus 0.8; in other words, we're raising the character vertically by 7.2 pixels. That will make our character jump, and when yspeed eventually becomes positive, fall back down to earth. But there's nothing in there yet to stop him from passing right through the floor.

The final bit of code here does just that. We check to see if this._y is greater than or equal to floorHeight. Remember, in Flash, _y increases toward the bottom of the screen. If this._y is greater, we know we overshot the floor or at least met it, so we can stop the movement by resetting yspeed, positioning hero_mc exactly at floor level and deleting the onEnterFrame to prevent the jump loop from continuing to execute until next time. Phew, such a simple example takes quite some explanation, but hopefully running through it a few times yourself should help it sink in nicely.

We also touched on our next topic briefly here, when we prevented our sheepy hero from passing the walls of the screen; the next topic is collision detection.

Collision detection

Collision detection plays a vital role in many types of games—not just action games, in which we want to see if maybe a bullet has hit a target, but also in platform games, in which we want to see if our character is standing on a surface or jumping in the air, and in many more situations where we have multiple objects on screen at any time. The subject of collision detection has been covered in many books, but with the added limitations of Flash 4 ActionScript with Flash Lite 1.1, we need to take another look at just how this can be achieved. There are many types of collision detection to fit the various situations you might encounter when making a game. In this section, I try to cover some of the main methods that best suit mobile gaming where processing speed is limited, this includes several options for detecting collisions between objects using both Flash's built-in mechanism and math alone.

MovieClip.hitTest() (Flash Lite 2.0+)

If you are looking to develop for Flash Lite 2, you can take advantage of the very useful MovieClip.hitTest() function introduced in Flash 5. The following code shows this function being used to detect whether two movie clips are overlapping, or as we refer to it in games, colliding. Should mc2 overlap mc1, bang! will be displayed in the output window:

```
if (mc1.hitTest(mc2)) trace ("bang!");
```

For a moment imagine that mc1 was a player, and mc2 was, maybe, some hot coals. We might have this code running every other frame in a frame loop, and if the condition evaluates as true, we could deduct some health from a player's health gauge, for example. hitTest() will, by default, check if the objects' bounding boxes are overlapping. The bounding box is an imaginary rectangle that is just large enough to encompass the entirety of the graphics contained in a movie clip. The problem with this is that a circular or irregularly shaped movie clip might register a collision with another even if the visible shape itself isn't touching, because their rectangular bounding boxes *are* still overlapping, as shown in Figure 6-2.

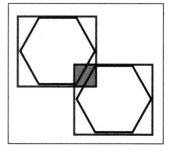

Figure 6-2. Overlapping bounding boxes around hexagons

The solution is to use the second form of the hitTest() function, which allows us to set a shape flag, telling Flash to examine the actual outline shape of the movie clip when testing for a collision. The only drawback here is that with our new accuracy, we must test the shape collision against a single point as opposed to two separate objects, or the Flash Player would probably crash because of all of the necessary calculations involved in detecting every possible point of contact along the two outlines. This form of hitTest() is illustrated in Figure 6-3.

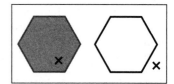

Figure 6-3. Two hexagons showing point-based hit tests

The hexagon on the left in Figure 6-3 shows that the hit test is true, because the point is inside its shape boundary, unlike the one on the right. The code to detect whether our point is anywhere inside the shape follows:

```
if( shape_mc.hitTest( point.x, point.y, true ) )
    trace("point x,y is within shape");
```

This is great for detecting whether a crosshair is over an irregularly shaped target, for example. Check out the Shape Burst sample from the Chapter 5 downloads to see this in action (ShapeBurst.fla). The game (shown in Figure 6-4) isn't much fun, as there is no way to win, but it *does* illustrate how to perform hitTest() checks on a regular basis within a game.

With Flash Lite 1.1, we do not have the luxury of the hitTest() function. This is a drawback, but not a fatal one, when it comes to collision detection in games, as we are about to find out.

The registration point

Flash uses something called a **registration point**, an invisible point indicated by the crosshair you see on stage when editing a movie clip or button symbol, for its _x and _y properties at run-time. It's important to always check the position of the registration point, because it may throw some of the calculations off in the remaining parts of this section. Unless otherwise stated, I will be positioning the registration point of a movie clip directly at its center, or as close as possible for irregularly shaped objects. Once graphics have been converted to symbols, it isn't possible to move a registration point; instead, you move the content around the point until it sits in the right place. Say, for example, you needed to move a registration point to the tip of a missile graphic, so that when performing a hitTest() check on a player against a point, that point is at the very front of the missile and will be the first thing to hit the player. To do this, you'd have to edit the missile clip by double-clicking it in the library and moving the shapes or bitmaps that make up the missile to make sure the tip resides precisely on the registration point, as shown in Figure 6-5.

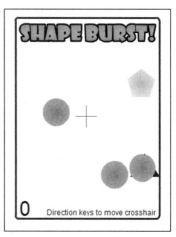

Figure 6-4. The Shape Burst example

Figure 6-5. Missile showing the position of the registration point (at the top, in the center)

Bounding box collisions (Flash Lite 1.1)

Without hitTest() to rely on in Flash Lite 1.1, we have to manually check the boundaries of a movie clip to perform collision detection. The properties we need are _x, _y, _width, and _height. With these four properties, we can calculate a bounding rectangle like so:

```
mcTop = mc._y - mc._height/2;
mcBottom = mc._y + mc._height/2;
mcLeft = mc._x - mc._width/2;
mcRight = mc._x + mc._width/2;
```

Those four variables mark the boundaries that can then be compared with another object's to see if there is any overlap. Let's rename our movie clip from mc to mc1, and imagine we have another movie clip named mc2 on screen that can be moved around with the arrow keys. Our movie might look like the one in Figure 6-6.

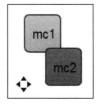

Figure 6-6. Bounding box example

199

> *Flash's coordinate system starts from the top-left corner of the screen and the y axis increments as you move down the screen. Therefore, a movie clip with _y property of 50 will appear vertically below a movie clip with _y equal to 10. The x axis, on the other hand, starts at the left and increments to the right as with many other coordinate systems.*

We can go about testing for an overlap by running code that examines these two movie clips' boundaries every frame, with the simple two-frame loop mechanism that we used previously. Here is how it is done in Flash Lite 1.1:

```
isColliding = false;

mc1Top = mc1._y - mc1._height/2;
mc1Bottom = mc1._y + mc1._height/2;
mc1Left = mc1._x - mc1._width/2;
mc1Right = mc1._x + mc1._width/2;

mc2Top = mc2._y - mc2._height/2;
mc2Bottom = mc2._y + mc2._height/2;
mc2Left = mc2._x - mc2._width/2;
mc2Right = mc2._x + mc2._width/2;

topOverlap = (mc2Bottom >= mc1Top && mc1Bottom >= mc2Bottom);
bottomOverlap = (mc2Top <= mc1Bottom && mc1Top <= mc2Top);
leftOverlap = (mc2Left <= mc1Left && mc2Right >= mc1Left);
rightOverlap = (mc2Left <= mc1Right && mc1Left <= mc2Left);

if (rightOverlap && bottomOverlap || rightOverlap && topOverlap _
      || leftOverlap && bottomOverlap || leftOverlap && topOverlap)
    isColliding = true;

if (isColliding) tellTarget("mc1") gotoAndStop(2);
else tellTarget("mc1") gotoAndStop(1);
```

That's quite a bit of code just to get a simple bounding-box collision test going, but the odds are you will only be checking one particular object against a few others, in which case you can put this code in a simple for loop and make use of the eval() command (or use the array access operators in Flash Lite 2) to check the movie clip's boundaries against the other movie clips. To view this code in action, open BoundingBox.fla from the Chapter 6 downloads. If you are using ActionScript 1 or 2 in Flash Lite 2, you can simplify things a lot with the hitTest() command mentioned previously. Still, there is an easier way to get basic collision detection into your games, and the next example we are going to look at is perfect for just that.

Circle-to-circle(s) collisions (Flash Lite 1.1+)

One of the quickest and cleanest methods for collision detection in games is to use bounding circles to test for an overlap. A circle is often a good shape to fit the outline of a variety of objects, from balls, to helicopters, and the math involved is actually a lot simpler than when dealing with rectangles!

In Figure 6-7, you can see a pool table with a few balls left to sink.

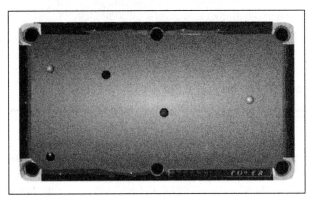

Figure 6-7. A pool table for the circle-to-circle collusion example

If we imagine that the ball on the far right (let's call it ball1) is traveling towards the ball directly in the center (say, ball3), we can work out the distance between them with the following equation:

$$c = \sqrt{a^2 + b^2}$$

Many of you will instantly recognize this as the Pythagorean theorem, which is used to work out the length of the hypotenuse, *c*, of a right-angled triangle with side lengths *a* and *b*. While our triangle isn't visible in the game, it is still there in the math. Side lengths *a* and *b* are nothing more than the vertical and horizontal distances between our two objects, and *c* is the distance between them. We can apply Pythagoras's theorem in ActionScript by working out the vertical and horizontal, and slotting those figures into the previous formula as follows:

```
vertDist = Math.abs(ball1._x - ball2._x);
horizDist = Math.abs(ball1._y - ball2._y);
totalDist = Math.sqrt(horizDist*horizDist + vertDist*vertDist);
```

There you have it—the distance between the centers of ball1 and ball3 are slotted into the equation in the third line, giving us the total distance between the balls. Now, to work out if these balls are colliding, we just need to see if they are closer than the sum of their radii (the radius stretches from the center of the ball, to any point along the bounding circle):

```
radius = ball1._width/2; // assume the same for ball2
if (totalDist <= radius*2) trace("balls are colliding");
```

The balls in the previous example fit with the idea of having a bounding circle that matches exactly the outline of the shape that we are performing the collision test on. But we can also use circles to detect collisions between objects with more-complex shapes, such as vehicles. An example can be found in JetFighter.fla (see Figure 6-8).

Figure 6-8 shows the unlikely situation of a jet fighter and a helicopter that are about to collide head on. You might notice that the jet fighter has not one but two circles over it. By using several bounding circles, we can perform more-accurate collision detection with minimal cost to the execution speed of our game, when compared with more-detailed techniques, such as detecting collisions on a per-pixel basis. Using multiple circles allows for more-realistic collisions as the player weaves in and out of enemy fire and ships, minimizing the occurrence of some very frustrating collisions that tend to happen in the unused white space around graphics that also lie within the circular or rectangular boundaries.

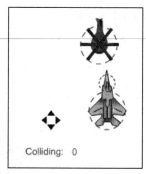

Figure 6-8. A jet plane and a helicopter about to collide

The dotted circles in the illustration are actually child movie clips of the vehicle clips, so everything stays together when moving the vehicles around the screen. The helicopter movie clip is named heli, and its bounding circle is named circ, whereas the jet fighter is named, unsurprisingly, jet, with bounding circles circ1 and circ2. What we need to do is check the bounding circle of the helicopter against each of the circles that surround the jet to see if we have any overlaps. We can do this with a simple for loop:

```
isColliding = false;

// loop through 2 circles
for (i=1; i<=2; i++)
{
    heliRad = heli.circ._width/2;
    jetRad = eval("jet/circ" add i)._width/2;

    heliX = heli.circ._x + heli._x;
    heliY = heli.circ._y + heli._y;

    jetX = eval("jet/circ" add i)._x + jet._x;
    jetY = eval("jet/circ" add i)._y + jet._y;

    horizDist = Math.abs(heliX - jetX);
    vertDist = Math.abs(heliY - jetY);
    totalDist = Math.sqrt(horizDist*horizDist + vertDist*vertDist);

    if (totalDist <= heliRad+jetRad) isColliding = true;
}
```

There are more lines of code there than are strictly necessary, because I've expanded certain things like the calculation of heliRad, which I could have used without creating an extra variable by placing the code for the helicopter radius directly in the final if statement. But I wanted to lay it out like this to make sure it was as easy to follow as possible. The other thing to note is that this isn't the most efficient code, as everything is evaluated several times inside the for loop. For example, I could have assigned a value to heliRad outside of the for loop, as it will never change, whereas jetRad *will* change, depending on which circle, circ1 or circ2, you are looking at. I've put together a little sample that you can run to see just how this works in JetFighter.fla in the Chapter 6 downloads.

> *As a side note, you can also use circle-to-point collisions. You can easily substitute one of the circles for a point, if you want to see whether any object that's actual size is unimportant—something like a projectile, crosshair, or particle—is inside a circle. To do this, simply check whether the total distance is less than or equal to the radius of the one circle that concerns us, the target, for example,* if (totalDist <= jetRad) trace("Hit by bullet").

If you are using Flash Lite 2, you might be more familiar with the use of the array access operators in place of the eval() function. You might also be aware that we don't need the physical two-frame loop; instead we can use a simple onEnterFrame function loop:

```
this.onEnterFrame = function()
{
    var isColliding = false;

    // loop through 2 circles
    for ( var i=1; i<=2; i++)
    {
        var heliRad = heli.circ._width/2;
        var jetRad = jet["circ"+i]._width/2;

        var heliX = heli.circ._x + heli._x;
        var heliY = heli.circ._y + heli._y;

        var jetX = jet["circ"+i]._x + jet._x;
        var jetY = jet["circ"+i]._y + jet._y;

        var horizDist = Math.abs(heliX - jetX);
        var vertDist = Math.abs(heliY - jetY);
        var totalDist = Math.sqrt(horizDist*horizDist + ➥
                                  vertDist*vertDist);

        if (totalDist <= heliRad+jetRad) isColliding = true;
    }
}
```

As you can see, there's not much of a difference between the code here, and the code listed previously, but hopefully, this side-by-side comparison shows that using dot syntax in Flash Lite 1.1 can produce quite similar code to the more-modern ActionScript 1 and 2. This is particularly true when the code is written in the IDE where you can get away with not specifying var to declare variables (although it is recommended to avoid confusion about where the variable is declared!). This would not have been possible back when Flash 4 was out; the IDE improvements since then make it feasible.

Line-to-circle collisions (Flash Lite 1.1+)

Think back to our pool table example; we don't just have collisions occurring between the balls (circle-to-circle collisions). We also have collisions between the balls and the cushions (line-to-circle collisions) that we need to perform some collision checking on, so that the balls don't simply float off the edge of the table. If you have some game programming experience already, you will know that this isn't so tricky; we just see if a ball reaches a certain _x or _y position and bounce it back in the opposite direction by switching it's vertical and/or horizontal velocity. So to make it a little more difficult for ourselves, let us imagine a situation where the lines *aren't* perpendicular or creating a perfect box. Instead, let's have our lines at various angles, such as those found on a miniature golf course (see Figure 6-9).

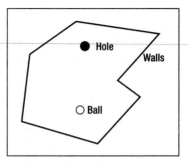

Figure 6-9. A hole for an imaginary miniature golf course

We can't just check whether the _x or _y position has reached a certain value now. We need to come up with another way to see if the ball is touching (or passing through) a point on the line—we need to employ a little trigonometry to solve this one.

Get your graph paper ready

Take a look at Figure 6-10, which shows a simple line drawn on a graph.

In addition to drawing the line alongside a pair of axes, we can define it with the following equation:

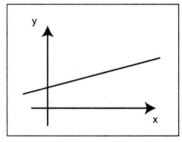

Figure 6-10. A simple line on a graph

$$y = mx + b$$

Now, you may remember plotting lines on graph paper at school, or for those lucky enough, entering an equation into your calculator to have it magically drawn for you. Either way, recall that this general equation allows us to describe any straight line that we might want to represent. The *x* and *y* variables are fairly self-explanatory: *y* represents the given vertical position of a point along the line, depending on the values to the right of the equals sign, and *x* relates to the horizontal position depending on *y*. The *m* represents the **gradient** of the line; the gradient is simply the slope of the line. You can get a value for that by first imagining that along our line we have a right-angled triangle, as shown in the triangles in Figure 6-11.

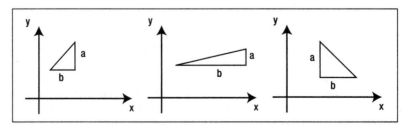

Figure 6-11. Three triangles plotted on graphs

To get the slope, or gradient, we just divide the height of the triangle by the width (*a* over *b*). Our triangle is of an arbitrary size, because technically speaking, our line is infinitely long, so we have to pick just a portion of the line to measure. The line in the far-right image actually has a negative gradient, because it is sloping downward. You can test this by dividing, say, -1 (the triangle's height) by 4 (the triangle's width) to get -0.25.

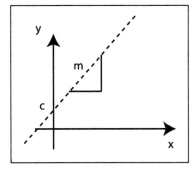

The final part of the equation is *c*, the intercept along the y axis. That may sound complicated, but it simply refers to the point at which the line passes through the y axis. Therefore, a value of 0 for *c*, would mean the line passes through the origin. Figure 6-12 ties together all of these ideas.

Figure 6-12. Triangle showing gradient (*m*) and intercept (*c*)

With that piece of rather dry theory out of the way, it's time to see how we can use this to actually detect a collision in our games.

Line intersection

This section relates to detecting whether a circle is touching a line—well, that's only half the story. In reality, we need to think of the circle as traveling along *another* line, a line that will, at some point, pass through the line that is our wall or obstacle, that is, if we extend the two infinitely. This second line is the circle's **path**. It's not guaranteed that the path our circle is traveling along *will* intersect the other line, however, as the lines might run directly parallel to each other. But for the moment, let's work on the premise that the lines are *not* parallel, and at some point along these infinite lines, they will cross and form an intersection point (see Figure 6-13).

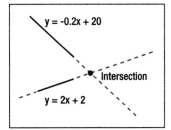

Figure 6-13. Lines intersecting at a point

> For those wishing to dig into trigonometry a little more, just as you can find out whether two lines are parallel by seeing if their gradients are equal, you can also find out if they are perpendicular by multiplying the gradients together. If the result is -1, your lines are at right angles to each other!

The intersection is the key, at this single point the x and y values in both line equations will be the same. This is the point we need to find. In Figure 6-13, I have labeled both lines with their corresponding equations:

```
y = -0.2x + 20  (for the wall)
y = 2x + 2      (for the circle's path)
```

If we go back to our general equation, we can think of these lines as follows:

```
y = m1*x + c1   (for the wall)
y = m2*x + c2   (for the circle's path)
```

Now that we have some pure algebra to play with, all we have to do is rearrange these equations to give us a value for *x*:

```
x = (c2-c1) / (m1-m2)
```

So, for our lines in Figure 6-13, this would be

```
x = (2-20) / (2+0.2)
```

which gives us x = -8.19 (approximately). Plugging the value for *x* back into either one of our original line equations we get the following:

```
y = -14.37 (approximately)
```

I've rounded these numbers to save ink, but nevertheless, we now know that our two lines cross at the point with the coordinates (-8.19, -14.37). With that in mind, now we only need to figure out if our circle is closer to that point than the length of its radius, just as we did when dealing with our circle collisions earlier on. As a result, this code may look a little familiar:

```
xDist = circleX - x;
yDist = circleY - y;
totalDist = Math.sqrt(xDist*xDist + yDist*yDist);
isColliding = (totalDist <= circleRadius); // true or false
```

If isColliding is true, we know that our circle's perimeter is breaching the line we are detecting against, so you can act on that in a suitable manner; for example, bounce the circle off the line as if it were a ball on a wall. We will look at doing just that shortly.

The line equations

There's one thing missing from our method; just how do we obtain these line equations in the first place? Not just guesswork or a protractor and ruler combination, that's for sure. Let's backtrack for a second, and look at how we can work out line equations. At this point, you might find it helpful to open LineCircle.fla from the Chapter 6 downloads (see Figure 6-14).

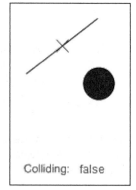

For the moment, let's not concern ourselves with the line equation for the path that the circle moves along. Instead, let's look at our wall's line; this solitary line is nothing more than a black stroke within a movie clip. What is important, however, is the location of this line in relation to the movie clip's registration point. Double-click the line_mc symbol *in the library* to open it for editing. The left-hand point of the line is exactly on top of the registration point, and the line extends 100 pixels to the right. This positioning gives us something concrete to work with in the next stage of the process, working out the equation.

Figure 6-14. The LineCircle collision test example

Go to the main stage, and you can see I've rotated the line movie clip counterclockwise; to be precise, its _rotation property now reads around -37.24786377 at runtime (you can check this in the Transform palette, available by pressing Ctrl+T or Cmd+T). Armed with the knowledge that Flash uses values ranging from -180 to 180 for a movie clip's _rotation property, we can use this very angle to work out the gradient of the line; the code is very simple:

```
lineRot = line_mc._rotation * Math.PI/180;
line_x1 = line_mc._x;
line_y1 = line_mc._y;
line_x2 = lineLen * Math.cos(lineRot) + line_x1;
line_y2 = lineLen * Math.sin(lineRot) + line_y1;
line_m = (line_y2-line_y1)/(line_x2-line_x1);
```

Where lineRot is the rotation of the line in *radians*, line_x1 and line_y1 mark the registration point in the line (the start of the line); line_x2 and line_y2 mark the end point of the line; and line_m is the gradient that we get as a result. Again, we need to convert the degrees into radians, because they are much more natural for trigonometric functions, and therefore, radians are what Math.cos() and Math.sin() expect!

Now we have the target line's equation, but our work isn't quite finished. If you think back to the start of this section, I said you can define a straight line by the equation $y = mx + c$. We have *m*, but we need *c*, the y axis intercept. To get *c*, we need only the following equation:

```
line_c = line_y1 - line_m*line_x1;
```

That's it! We take the line's gradient multiplied by the starting x coordinate and subtract that from the starting y coordinate. I don't blame you if you are thinking, "Great. We have a bunch of numbers." But it will all make sense soon. Next, we need to follow the same process for the circle itself:

```
circRot = Math.atan2(yVel, xVel);

circ_x1 = circle_mc._x;
circ_y1 = circle_mc._y;
circ_x2 = circRad * Math.cos(circRot) + circ_x1;
circ_y2 = circRad * Math.sin(circRot) + circ_y1;

circ_m = (circ_y2-circ_y1)/(circ_x2-circ_x1);
circ_c = circ_y2 - circ_m*circ_x2;
```

The only difference here is that, in the first line, we use Math.atan2(). Because we don't have a line as such, we need to derive our imaginary line/path from the movement of the circle, in this case its x and y velocities. Math.atan2() will take our two figures, the values for y and x, and it will give us the angle the circle is headed!

> Remember, if `line_m`, the line's gradient, is equal to `circ_m`, the circle's path-line gradient, you know the lines are parallel and will never cross, so beware—put a check in to make sure you don't continue with the detection if these lines are parallel.

Putting it all together

We now have the figures required to build the line equations for the wall and the path the circle is traveling along. Let's plug those values into our line intersection algorithm and see what we get:

```
intersectX = (circ_c-line_c)/(line_m-circ_m);
intersectY = line_m*intersectX + line_c;
xDist = Math.abs(circ_x1 - intersectX);
yDist = Math.abs(circ_y1 - intersectY);
totalDist = Math.sqrt(xDist*xDist + yDist*yDist);
```

Well, there we have it, a value for intersectX, intersectY, and for good measure, the total distance between the center of the circle and the point on the line where that intersection occurs (totalDistance). To clearly mark that point, I'm moving a crosshair to the intercept position in the example with the following code:

```
intercept_mc._x = intersectX;
intercept_mc._y = intersectY;
```

This gives us a visual representation on the point that we've worked out for the circle to cross the wall line. The final step is to check whether the point at which the circle is supposed to collide with the line is actually on the line. Remember that we extended the line infinitely in the math, so we need to rein that back in to see whether the intersection point is along the stretch that is displayed on the screen:

```
if (   (intersectX >= line_x1 && intersectX <= line_x2)
    && (intersectY <= line_y1 && intersectY >= line_y2)

    || (intersectX >= line_x1 && intersectX <= line_x2)
    && (intersectY >= line_y1 && intersectY <= line_y2)

    || (intersectX <= line_x1 && intersectX >= line_x2)
    && (intersectY <= line_y1 && intersectY >= line_y2)

    || (intersectX <= line_x1 && intersectX >= line_x2)
    && (intersectY >= line_y1 && intersectY <= line_y2)  )
{
    // Now for the old circle radius distance test
    isColliding = (totalDist<=circRad);
}
```

I think you'll agree that is a pretty verbose `if` statement in Flash Lite 1.1 syntax, but it works and runs fairly quickly.

Collision reactions

So far, all of the talk regarding collisions has been about the detection. This is great if your objects are programmed to vaporize or explode on contact, but you might want to model other reactions, such as an object bouncing off of a surface or the collisions several objects affecting each others' directions and velocities. One statement you may remember from school is

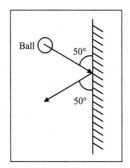

Figure 6-15. Ball hitting a wall and rebounding

```
Angle of Incidence = Angle of Reflection
```

Figure 6-15 illustrates this with a ball bouncing against a wall.

Of course, this doesn't take into account gravity or other forces, but another example might be a pool ball on a pool table hitting the cushion and rebounding. The thing to note is that the reaction is equal and opposite. When we don't take into account things like friction, what we have is an elastic collision.

Elastic collisions are collisions where no momentum is lost. As you can imagine, this means we have less to compute in the game, making it a little easier on the processor. If we wanted to model the real world more accurately we would have to make all collisions inelastic, energy is always lost in a collision between objects of size;[1] the lost energy is converted to another form such as heat or light. But in the interests of fun, we are not going to concern ourselves with such details.

The final part of our line-to-circle collision detection example actually shows a little more code—the code that makes the circle (or ball) bounce off the line (or wall). Here is that code:

```
if (isColliding)
{
    // grab the angle for the line's tangent/gradient
    alpha = Math.atan(line_m);

    // apply velocities to gradient/tangent line
    yVel2 = yVel * Math.cos(alpha) - xVel * Math.sin(alpha);
    xVel2 = xVel * Math.cos(alpha) + yVel * Math.sin(alpha);

    yVel2 = -yVel2; // flip vel along ball path

    // re-apply velocities to original trajectory/path line
    xVel = xVel2 * Math.cos(alpha) - yVel2 * Math.sin(alpha);
    yVel = yVel2 * Math.cos(alpha) + xVel2 * Math.sin(alpha);
}
```

---

1. By "collisions of size," I mean the macroscopic collisions we are modeling in our games between cars, missiles, billiard balls, and such. We aren't concerned with the strange goings-on that can occur at the microscopic level.

Thankfully, there's not too much here. Essentially, what we are doing is what the diagram at the start of this section showed—making the ball bounce *back* at the opposite angle at which it struck while keeping its momentum. The first line of code here gets an angle, alpha. alpha is the angle of the line's gradient (or tangent, with it being a straight line and not a curve). We get this using Math.atan(); the result is in radians.

We next create a couple of temporary x and y velocities, xVel2 and yVel2. These are made by plugging the angle alpha into two sets of equations. The first multiplies the existing velocity by the cosine of the angle, subtracting the same value by the sine of alpha. The second performs a similar operation, but it *adds* the sine instead. If this doesn't make sense, do not worry; I had to go back to my geometry books before I remembered why we do this. Simply put, this works out the velocity of the ball in relation to the line, you might say it was "mapping" the x and y velocity onto the equation of the wall line.

The next line flips the y velocity, yVel2. We do this so that the ball actually bounces off of the wall and doesn't just pass through it! This bit technically does the real work we set out to do. The final couple of lines take our new x and y velocities and map them back onto the original path line, so that we can apply our new xVel and yVel to the ball to see the reaction take place, and voilà, a collision reaction.

If you would like to sap some of the momentum out of the ball when it hits the wall, just multiply xVel and yVel by a number less than 1, like 0.5. On top of that, you might be applying a friction value to these two figures every frame that naturally reduces the velocity, like we had with gravity in the jumping sheep example when dealing with the jump velocity.

Why so slow?

If you've taken a moment to test the previous sample on your device, you will notice that it runs at a leisurely pace. The phone's CPU is just not up to the challenge yet. In the next section, we will make a little headway with optimizations, but I have included the previous examples regardless of speed, because there is no doubt at all about the increasing speed of handsets. Personal tests have shown that the speed of Flash Lite–capable phones has doubled in the last six months, so this code will be useful in the long run when processor speed is less of an issue. This applies even more so for PDA devices, which are already fast enough to run the previous example and already support Flash Lite 2. Detecting collisions against just one or two lines as opposed to five (for example, in something like Pong) is another example of where this is still useful without hampering performance. One thing using only two lines doesn't solve, however, is the need to figure out all of the properties of these lines at runtime, so that we can plug those values into the equations.

One immediate solution is to realize that the lines are never moving, so we can simply hard code the values for their rotation, their length, and any other information we might need. In fact, we can perform what is known as precalculation, and I'd like to cover that in the next section.

Efficient math

We've already looked at a few things that you can do with code to speed up the performance of your applications. One example is to use circle-to-circle collision detection between a player and another sprite or two vehicles. This is far more efficient than using the line math or even bounding-box collision approach, which technically could be more accurate. Another technique we can use that used to be the norm back in the Flash 4 days is something called precalculation.

Precalculation

Precalculation is the process of working out, ahead of time, all the possible values an expression can generate. To put it another way, if we want to convert an angle in degrees to radians, using pi/180, to the angle in radians, we could also generate an array of 360 values one time only before we begin running our game or application. This means less accuracy, of course; with 360 values we have only enough for one per degree, so any values in between would need to be rounded up or down to a whole degree. However, precalculating gives us an *accurate enough* set of numbers to use without needing to perform the multiplication perhaps several times every second. This works in any case where a simple array lookup (using the array access operators or eval()) is faster than evaluating an expression. Let's run through this example first in Flash Lite 2 code:

```
var radians = [];
for( var i=0; i<360; i++ )
    radians[i] = i*Math.PI/180;
```

Later on, we might use this like so:

```
var valueInRadians = radians[ int(degreeValue) ];
```

This is not a great example of using precalculation to good effect, because the equation we are calculating a table for is very simple. But in our circle-to-line collision example, we can make good use of pregenerating values for later use.

If you remember our circle to line collision example was pretty slow going. So let's take a look at WallsCircleOptimized.fla, where I've gone through and performed a bit of optimization. The first thing you might notice is the hard coding of a couple of values:

```
lineLen = 100;
circRad = circle_mc._width/2;
d2r = Math.PI/180;
```

By hard coding these values, we reduce the number of instructions the Flash Player needs to execute in the loop. Things like Math.PI/180 are never going to change, so make use of this wherever possible.

Next, we precalculate some information about the lines:

```
for (i=1;i<=5;i++)
{
    lineRot = eval("r_" add i) ➥
            = eval("line" add i add "_mc")._rotation * d2r;

    line_x1 = eval("x1_" add i) ➥
            = eval("line" add i add "_mc")._x;

    line_y1 = eval("y1_" add i) ➥
            = eval("line" add i add "_mc")._y;

    line_x2 = eval("x2_" add i) ➥
            = lineLen * Math.cos(lineRot) + line_x1;

    line_y2 = eval("y2_" add i) ➥
            = lineLen * Math.sin(lineRot) + line_y1;
```

```
line_m = eval("m_" add i) ↦
         = (line_y2-line_y1)/(line_x2-line_x1);

line_c = eval("c_" add i) ↦
         = line_y1 - line_m*line_x1;
}
```

This might look a little convoluted, but it is essentially fairly simple. What we have here is a loop that runs through each of our five lines, using the eval() statement to create short variable names like r_1, r_2 and so on and assigning values like the rotation of each of the lines. Next, we assign that rotation value to another local variable for use later in the loop. What we end up with is perhaps 35 new variables (40 if you include the local ones) that can be accessed in our collision detection, without having to constantly recalculate all of these rotations, gradients, and so on, which are fixed and never change in this particular case. This has a dramatic impact on how fast the code executes. The balance really is to keep it readable without sacrificing too much speed. Test the sample on a phone to see the difference; it runs at approximately twice the speed!

Profiling

On the desktop, I find it useful to use what is known as a **profiler** to check how long my programs are spending in the various functions that comprise them. A profiler can be started and stopped wherever required and lists the number of milliseconds each function takes. A very simple example of this follows:

```
startTime = getTimer();
// profiled code here
for( var i=0; i<1000; i++ ) { trace(i); }
// profiled code ends
trace(getTimer() - startTime);
```

What we have here is the number of milliseconds our simple for loop took to execute. An alternative is to use ASProf by David Chang, which is written for ActionScript 1.0 but also works for ActionScript 2.0 in Flash Lite. You can download ASProf as an extension for Flash from www.nochump.com/asprof.

To use ASProf, you simply include the ASProf ActionScript include file, which is automatically transferred to the correct place, when you install the extension and specify which classes or methods you wish to profile. This works for ActionScript 1 prototypes or ActionScript 2 classes:

```
#include "ASProf.as"

import com.test.MyClass;

ASProf.profileObject("com.test.MyClass.prototype");

ASProf.begin("a test");
tester = new MyClass();
tester.test();
tester.test2();
ASProf.end();

trace( ASProf.getFlatGraph() );
```

In this example, we're creating a new instance of the `MyClass` class and setting the profiler to examine its prototype. For those of you who have never known the delights of working with the `prototype` object, this is how classes in ActionScript 1 and (behind the scenes) in ActionScript 2, are actually achieved. Telling ASProf to profile the `prototype` of a class means that it will examine all functions you call on it. Alternatively, you can just specify one method and examine that. You can run this example yourself from the `Profiling.fla` FLA in the Profiling folder of the Chapter 6 downloads. The `test()` and `test2()` methods don't do much, but when you call `ASProf.getFlatGraph()`, you get a nice table showing the exact number of seconds spent in each function. You can also tell that `test2()` is taking 98 percent of the total time. It is pretty obvious why when you look at the actual functions (`test2()` has a for loop that goes around 99,999 times!); nevertheless, in the wild, this is a great way to find bottlenecks and optimize code.

Using short variable names

This tip is going to sound a little bit strange, but the age-old practice of short variable names really does have a noticeable impact on code that is run in Flash Lite, and you even save a bit on file size. We use this exact technique in the previous example of the optimized wall (circle-to-line) collision test. I know it can be a lot of effort, but if you are using external ActionScript files and a good editor like Eclipse with the ActionScript Development Tool (ASDT), which is available for free at www.osflash.org/asdt or FDT, which is available commercially at http://fdt.powerflasher.com/flashsite/flash.htm, you can quite easily find and replace multiple files to take out a lot of the effort. This technique is best used in small blocks of code that you have determined are processor hogs by profiling, rather by than applying this across your whole application.

Game assets

Assets are any bitmap images, sounds, videos, or vector graphics used in your games. If you were a J2ME developer, you'd probably be using mainly small bitmap images, with the occasional sound to build your games. Thankfully with Flash, we also get the option to quickly build scalable graphics using the tools available in the IDE. These sorts of graphics are best when kept simple; a lot of vector lines can really slow down your game (think back to our circle-to-line collision vector math earlier in this chapter). In this section, we will look at the various types of assets you can use in your games and how you can go about optimizing them.

Vector graphics

This is what made Flash famous at the start. Vector graphics are most commonly created in the Flash IDE or another program like Adobe Illustrator. All lines and fills used to make up an image are described mathematically behind the scenes; we just manipulate them using tools like the pen and fill bucket. This method of defining graphics means that they can scale to any size without losing clarity. They can give you better-looking graphics at virtually any resolution, and you can rotate these graphics without the bitmap pixilation and zigzags associated with rotated bitmaps—not to mention that the file size can be kept down, but this is something of a balance. When you use vectors, the odds are that you are not creating very detailed images, which means the file size will be less than the bitmap equivalent. But with smaller images and images that contain many vectors, sometimes vector drawings will result in larger files than their bitmap equivalents.

I work with designers on a daily basis, and there's a distinct difference between how most designers think about Flash when compared with coders. Many designers, for very good reasons, only care about the end result and how it looks. But it is our responsibility as developers to make sure we are making best use of the tools available. This means splitting up parts of a graphic into symbols (like movie clips), so that you can reuse or animate those symbols without having to create new graphics.

A real example of this is shown by the two files ArmAnim.fla and ArmAnimOptimized.fla. The first file shows an animation of an arm bending, done simply by drawing each position of the arm as it moves. That's quite a classic approach, but the file size is a whopping 3KB just for that one tiny piece of animation. Imagine an entire game's animation! The second file shows what would happen if we split the arm into three separate graphic symbols (see Figure 6-16). Not only is it quicker to make the animation, but the file is one-third of the size. We could also reuse these parts without adding much to the file size at all!

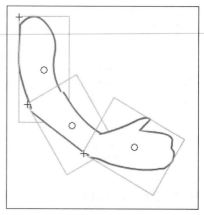

Figure 6-16. The arm animation broken up into graphic symbols

When it comes to optimizing our vectors, we can use one of two tools that Flash offers. The first is the smooth tool. Just select some vector graphics in the IDE, and press the S-shaped button with an arrow on it that appears at the bottom of the Tools palette to perform a simple smooth operation. Alternatively, press the button showing an angled line, which is to the right of the button you used to smooth, to do the opposite. Both operations usually result in fewer lines in your vector graphics, and thus, better-optimized graphics. Taking this one step further, you can also access the second tool available to us, the optimize operation, available from the Modify ➤ Shape ➤ Optimize menu shortcut. This actually sets about reducing the number of curves and lines used to make up your vector graphics. Take a moment to play around with the settings; you can adjust the slider to perform varying levels of simplification to your graphics until you are happy with the final result.

> *Another tip for avoiding sluggish animation is to stay clear of the _alpha property. Using _alpha is a sure-fire way to slow things down, especially when the graphics are complex. If at all possible, it is recommended that you alter the colors in your graphics to match your background instead of altering their opacity to allow the background to show through.*

Bitmap graphics

Bitmap graphics can be imported into Flash in a couple of ways. You can use the File ➤ Import menu item, and selecting your bitmap file, such as a PNG, BMP, or JPG. Or you can simply copy and paste the data from the clipboard in, say, Photoshop. I recommend the first way, so that you can make use of the update command. The update command is available by right-clicking any bitmap asset in the library and choosing update. This will automatically reimport a bitmap file if you have edited the file on the hard disk and automatically update any other library symbols that may use it.

With bitmaps, the rule is to keep them as small as you can. We already have a smaller screen, which helps, but keeping the sheer amount of bitmap data to a minimum is a good way to avoid memory hogging. Remember that in order to display even a 1KB JPG, the Flash Player must completely decompress the data into red, green, and blue (RGB) pixels at runtime, so the actual amount of RAM used is something like this:

```
RAM used in bytes = width * height * 3
```

One thing we can do to optimize bitmaps is to split them up into tiles. This means we can reuse individual tiles, or sprites, in various places. But it also means that with larger bitmaps, we don't necessarily have to have all of it decompressed in memory at once.

I've included a file to show this. Open pano.fla from the Panorama folder. You can see that I've split up the wide image into four parts. Without splitting the image, it actually uses too much RAM for my Nokia to cope with. Splitting up the image allows the effect to be achieved, because we are only ever showing two of the bitmaps at once. One final tip that deserves mention is that it helps to import your graphics at the size you wish to use them instead of scaling them down. It's an extra step but well worth it ultimately.

Sounds and music

There are two main types of sound you can use in Flash Lite, device sounds (such as MIDI or MFi) and standard sounds (such as MP3). The major distinction to make here is that with Flash Lite 1.1, we must embed the sounds in the SWF. With Flash Lite 2.X, we can use the Sound object to dynamically load sounds from the phone or over HTTP.

Device sounds are formats that are native to a device like MIDI or MFi. These are not supported in the desktop player, but we can use them on a mobile device if it already supports them, as most do now for things like ring tones. As with video (see the example in the following section), you should check the System.capabilities object to see which types of device sound are supported. In Flash Lite, we must use proxy sounds to represent our device sounds. **Proxy sounds** are regular Flash audio files (like MP3 or WAV) that you include in your library as usual. When you right-click these and choose Properties, you will notice a few more options when publishing for Flash Lite, as shown in Figure 6-17.

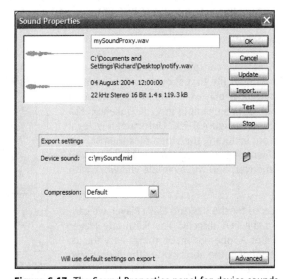

Figure 6-17. The Sound Properties panel for device sounds

The options in this panel let you link your MP3 or WAV file to a device sound, so that when the SWF is actually built, your native sound gets replaced with the device sound (usually meaning it has a smaller file size), and when it's played in the emulator or on the handset, you hear the right thing!

Standard Flash sounds, as I mentioned, are usually MP3 or WAV files. In the library, you can access the Properties dialog for these to choose the actual compression used when compiling your SWF, for example, ADPCM or RAW. These sorts of sounds are played back in a similar fashion to the way they are played back on the desktop player, usually by placing them on keyframes. We can also load them at runtime using the Sound object in Flash Lite 2, in particular, using the Sound.load() function, which can be used to load a sound from a given location, and Sound.start(), which can play the loaded sound. The Flash documentation includes a help book on Flash Lite 2, which goes into details on using the Sound object. But you can also use them in the regular keyframe fashion by selecting any keyframe on the time line, and in the Properties panel, choosing an option from the Sound drop-down menu, as shown in Figure 6-18.

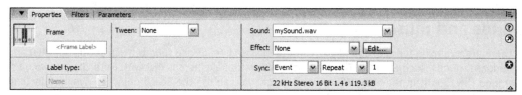

Figure 6-18. The Sound options drop-down menu

The Sound drop-down menu also gives you options to repeat the sound, for example, with a background loop. My biggest tip regarding sounds in games is that you give the user an option to turn them off. Perhaps make use of an MSO (described in the next section) to save that particular preference.

Video

There are three main ways to play video files on a mobile phone using Flash Lite. The first is really a hack—you can simply fill a time line with a series of PNGs or JPGs and play back that animation as normal. This method is required for Flash Lite 1.1, but it is not very efficient and results in some large files, so if possible, it is to be avoided.

In terms of actual video files, we can play video using 3GP and MP4 files. I've included a sample file that shows a video jukebox application capable of playing a playlist of video files included with the SWF. You can look at this example in VideoJukeBox.fla in the Chapter 6 downloads (see Figure 6-19). Unfortunately, legal restrictions prevent me from including the video files themselves, but you can replace the filenames with any 3GP or MP4 files you can download freely on the Net, and the example will work with those too.

Unlike with SWF files prepared for the desktop Flash Player, we cannot embed Flash video in the FLA directly. The Flash Lite Player cannot render FLV video. But Adobe has made things easy for us. Just create a blank video symbol in the library using the drop-down menu at the top-right corner of the Library panel, drop it onto the

Figure 6-19. The minitoobr video jukebox application

stage, give it a name (myVideoInstance), and then simply use myVideoInstance.play(filename) to actually begin rendering the video to screen. It's much easier than messing with NetConnection and NetStream, as we have to with desktop Flash!

In terms of size and compression ratios, I'd recommend keeping video to a standard known as Quarter Common Intermediate Format (QCIF), which is 176×144 pixels. There is a smaller standard size of Sub QCIF (128×96 pixels) that you should try if you would like to support older handsets, but with the standard QCIF, you can pretty much guarantee problem-free rendering on modern handsets. There are many tools that can compress files for you. One is the Nokia Multimedia Converter, downloadable from http://forum.nokia.com. Other tools include FFmpeg (http://sourceforge.net/projects/ffmpeg), which is a free and open source video conversion tool.

Saving and loading high scores

We can make use of MSOs to load and save data from the phone's memory. I think the best way to show the use of MSOs is with an example. This example will demonstrate adding a new high score, saving all the high scores, and loading them back in when the application restarts.

On stage, we need four things: a large dynamic text field named output_txt, and three simple buttons named add_btn, save_btn, and clear_btn. These can look however you wish, or you could just open Highscores.fla from the downloads and dig right in. Now for some code, let's begin on frame 1 as usual:

```
// Set up movie
fscommand2("fullscreen", true);
var scores:Array = new Array();
```

There's not too much to take in so far; the only thing of interest here is that we create a new Array to store our high scores in. Next, we have the code required to set up our MSO and load it:

```
// Load in MSO
SharedObject.addListener("scoresSO", this, "onLoadMSO");
var so:SharedObject = SharedObject.getLocal("scoresSO");

// Called when MSO loads
function onLoadMSO(so:SharedObject)
{
    output_txt.text = "Scores loaded:\n";

    // If this is not the first time
        if ( 0 != so.getSize() )
    {
        scores = so.data.scores;
        displayScores();
    }

    SharedObject.removeListener("scoresSO");
}
```

The first line adds a listener to the SharedObject class. This is different from the desktop version, because shared objects are not instantly accessible in Flash Lite. We also define the scope and the function name to call when the scoresSO shared object is loaded. The next line begins loading the shared object with a call to SharedObject.getLocal(). Finally, the function onLoadMSO is called when our MSO is available; inside this function, we check the size of the SharedObject being loaded. If it is 0, we know it is the first time around, so we do not interrogate its .data property for our high scores array. However, if it is larger than 0 bytes, we know to grab a copy of the so.data.scores array and call the displayScores() function to loop through it and output the values to our text field. The final line in this function just removes the listener from the scoresSO shared object. This is not really needed, but it is always good practice to clean up after yourself when you know you won't be loading it again in the application's lifetime. This applies to any time where you find yourself adding event listeners to objects.

Next, we have our button-click handlers, starting with add_btn:

```
add_btn.onRelease = function()
{
    scores.push( {name:"name"+random(9),
                        score:random(999)} );

    displayScores();
}
```

Having already created a blank scores array (or loaded one in from an MSO), we simply append to it a new random name and score wrapped up in an anonymous simple object with .name and .score properties, respectively, and call displayScores() just so that the user knows what we added.

Next, we add the functionality for save_btn:

```
save_btn.onRelease = function()
{
    so.data.scores = scores;
    so.flush();
    output_txt.text = "Please close and restart app.";
}
```

The Save button's job is to assign our (possibly) modified scores array to the .data property of our MSO and then call SharedObject.flush(), which writes the data to the phone. Giving the user feedback on the next line is always good practice.

Now, let's look at clear_btn:

```
clear_btn.onRelease = function()
{
    so.clear();
    output_txt.text = "Scores cleared.";
}
```

I put this button in just to show that you can always call SharedObject.clear() to delete a SharedObject from the phone's memory. Finally, we have the displayScores() function we called a few times previously:

```
function displayScores()
{
    output_txt.text = "";

    for( var i=0; i<scores.length; i++ )
    {
        output_txt.text += scores[i].name;
        output_txt.text += "\t\t";
        output_txt.text += scores[i].score;
        output_txt.text += "\n";
    }
}
```

In this function, we simply loop through the scores array and append the name and score values to our output text field. Note the use of "\t" and "\n" to insert tab stops and new lines, respectively.

That's all there is to it. The ability to save a Flash native Array without having to parse it or convert it to a string and save it on the server is a massive bonus to Flash Lite development. Remember that you can add almost anything to the .data object of the SharedObject class, including maybe the total playing time in minutes or the number of times the player has opened the game!

Sample games

We've had a few small examples along the way in this chapter, but I thought it would be a good idea to include some complete examples of games for you to dissect and adapt at your leisure. Hopefully, you can spot all of the techniques introduced in this chapter in these games. Feel free to customize them or introduce new elements as you wish. I'd recommend reading through this chapter again once you've had a chance to look at these games, just to help build a good solid foundation to work from.

Mad Bomber (Flash Lite 1.1)

Mad Bomber is a version of a classic arcade game called Kaboom!, originally made for the Atari 2600. Not only is this game addictive but it's easy to make. The concept is simple: a deranged maniac is dropping bombs from the top of a wall. You, the hero, must stop the bombs from reaching the ground by catching them in your bucket of water, of course.

You can find Mad Bomber (as well as all of the other games) in the Chapter 6 downloads. The controls to this game are very straightforward—just a left and right arrow system and simple menu buttons for further interaction (see Figure 6-20). This should remind you of some of the key catcher code from previous chapters.

Figure 6-20. Mad Bomber

Snake (Flash Lite 2.0)

The second game for your perusal is based on the famous game that came with the earlier Nokia mobile phones, Snake (originally called Nibbles!). Snake, shown in Figure 6-21, leverages the Flash Lite 2 pure-code approach described in Chapter 3. The use of ActionScript 2.0 makes it very easy to develop and reuse this code for other games. You can find the source in the ch6/Snake folder. Each of the class files is fully commented.

The game consists of the following four classes:

- SnakeGame: Controls the game
- SnakeWorld: Draws the world of the game
- Snake: Draws the snake on the screen
- FoodPiece: Draws food pieces on the screen

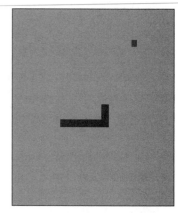

Figure 6-21. Snake

Let's take a brief look at the classes; you may wish to have them open in Flash while reading this, so that it is easier to follow along.

SnakeGame

The SnakeGame class is the daddy, responsible for controlling the interaction in the game. It keeps track of the score and overall state of play, and it creates an instance of the SnakeWorld class. The communication between the SnakeGame and SnakeWorld classes is handled via events using the EventDispatcher model.

SnakeWorld

The SnakeWorld class is a visual class used to draw all the graphics of the game, such as the background, the food pieces, and the snake itself. The SnakeWorld class also receives events from the Snake instance that it creates, in order to know when the snake eats a food piece, but also when it hits the sides of the screen; or, of course, itself. The SnakeWorld class also tells the Snake instance to update its physical position every frame.

Snake

The Snake class is the most important class of the game, perhaps. It includes most of the logic found in the game, for sure. Its main job is to draw the snake graphics, though, and make them move. When the Snake class gets created, the head of the Snake is added to an array of items that need to be drawn on the stage. The items in this array make up the segments in the snake. Each time the snake has to update itself, the following steps are executed:

1. The positions of the segments of the snake get shifted forward.
2. The position of the snake head is updated based on the current direction.
3. The snake is checked to see if it has collided with the sides of the screen.
4. The snake is checked to see if it has collided with a food piece, itself, or its tail.

The snake moves by looping through its segments' array, shifting each part of the body into the position of the next, right up to the head before finally moving the head to a brand new location, depending on which direction it is heading in. If any of the collisions in step 3 or step 4 occur, an event will be dispatched to give a signal to SnakeWorld that something has happened. If the snake eats or collides with a food piece, a FoodPiece event will be dispatched; each time this event gets caught by the SnakeWorld class, a new FoodPiece will be drawn on the screen.

FoodPiece

The FoodPiece class is a simple class attached to a MovieClip symbol. It is used only to draw the food graphic on stage, using the attachMovie() function and the linkage ID specified by the LINKAGE variable in the class. Using something like a LINKAGE static string for each class linked to a library symbol is good practice, because it allows for automatic checking of the first parameter when using attachMovie() (meaning if you mistyped SomeClass.LINKAGE, you get a compile error, whereas if you mistype a plain linkage ID string, you merely don't get anything on stage).

BlackJack (Flash Lite 2.1)

The BlackJack example, shown in Figure 6-22, is perhaps the most complicated example in this chapter. It makes use of the Flash Lite 2.1 XMLSocket connection to connect to a Java server that could be running online anywhere. The Java server acts as the dealer in a game of blackjack. This example is a very simple form of the game, but you could use this to develop a very polished version complete with nice graphics for the cards (instead of just numeric values) as well as animations for going bust or winning.

The game works by establishing a connection with the server using XMLSocket. Then, messages are sent as XML objects. The server reads these as plain text, but it could just as easily parse these into, say, a Java XML class, so that it can read the individual nodes. In our case, the XML messages are simple enough for us not to need this, but it is always there just in case. The server then responds with more XML messages (constructed and sent as strings), which the

Figure 6-22. BlackJack

Flash client can parse and react to. There's not too much code on the client; you can find it all in two frames on the main time line.

To start up the Java server make sure you have a Java Development Kit (JDK) installed; you can get the latest, JDK 5, at http://java.sun.com/javase/downloads/index.jsp.

I recommend the version with the NetBeans IDE, if you don't have an editor already, unless you prefer to use an IDE like Eclipse to edit your Java code, as I do. Either way, you can use the source provided without any other tools. First, you need to add the JDK bin folder to your systems PATH or Environment variables, so that you can run java.exe (the Java virtual machine) and javac.exe (the Java compiler) from any command-line window and any folder. If you don't know how to do this, please search online for "setting path in Windows", or "setting environment variables Mac", depending on which system you use, for several useful articles on the subject. You can test whether the JDK is all set up by opening a command prompt, navigating to the folder containing the sample .java files included, and typing

```
java -version
```

If you see something like java version 1.5.0, you know you are on track. With that done, you need to compile the .java files into Java byte code (.class) files, so that we can run them in the Java virtual machine. To do this, type the following:

```
javac BlackJackServer.java
```

I've also included a batch file to run this for you (compile_server.bat). This file generates the class files, ready to run. To run them, type the following:

```
java BlackJackServer
```

You should see BlackJackServer running on port: 2048. Alternatively, I've included another batch file to do this for you. You can terminate the server at any time using Ctrl+C or closing the Command window. You are now ready to compile and run the FLA! Be sure to check out the Command window; it will show the messages coming through.

Summary

In this chapter, we have explored a whole range of game-related topics. There is enough in the subject of Flash game programming alone to fill several large books, so hopefully, this chapter gives you a good foundation to get started making some games for yourself, having covered getting your game assets together, optimizing coding, building in logic and physics, and more.

In the next chapter, we will look at mobile content such as screensavers and wallpapers, another area where Flash Lite can be used.

Chapter 7

FLASH LITE MOBILE ENTERTAINMENT BASICS

In Chapter 6, we covered Flash Lite as it pertains to mobile gaming. This is one of the fastest growing and most popular areas for Flash Mobile content today; it's second only to mobile entertainment, the subject of this chapter. Here, we'll explore what Flash Lite has to offer this rapidly growing industry. In particular, I'll cover some Flash Lite content types, including wallpaper and screen savers. Later in this chapter, we'll actually design and develop some examples for each these content types using Flash Lite 1.1.

Yes, this chapter requires some Flash Lite 1.1 ActionScript knowledge, which, by now, you should be comfortable with. However, those that require a bit of a refresher in Flash 4 syntax will be happy to know that I have included a short review of Flash Lite 1.1 ActionScript as part of this chapter. It covers the basic syntax you need to know to complete the walkthrough exercises included in this chapter.

In the unlikely event that you have skipped ahead to this chapter and have with no prior Flash Lite 1.1 experience, I do encourage you to visit the previous chapters of this book on Flash Lite programming, especially the one focused on designing and developing Flash Mobile applications (Chapter 5). After reading that, you can tackle the upcoming Flash Lite 1.1 wallpaper and screen saver exercises in this chapter without a hitch.

Before we start jumping into content types, such as wallpaper and screen savers, I'd first like to discuss the history of Flash Lite as it pertains to mobile entertainment. This will give you a better idea of how Flash Lite has evolved over the past few years and where it might be headed in regards to this particular industry.

Evolution of Flash Lite

Flash Lite was commercially introduced in the Japanese market in 2003 as part of the NTT DoCoMo i-mode rollout. I'll cover i-mode in greater detail in Chapter 11. For now, you can think of i-mode as a wireless Internet service for mobile users with portable devices, such as cell phones.

In 2003, Flash Lite 1.0 was put into place, so that operators who offer i-mode service could provide content such as animations, simple applications, and, to some degree, very basic games to i-mode users. It met with a lot of success. Over the next year, Flash Lite continued to steadily evolve with i-mode as it grew in both size and popularity. As the i-mode infrastructure continued to mature, so did the need for more sophisticated content distributed through this service.

In 2004, Flash Lite 1.1 was introduced with a more-elaborate feature set and Application Programming Interface (API). More complex applications, games, and other content were then possible. A critical transformation was under way. Content utilizing Flash Lite 1.1 was evolving from merely animations to much more interactive and robust content, such as fully featured applications and more compelling games.

As Flash Lite evolved, new content types also became available and continued to expand outside of the realm of browser-based and stand alone–based Flash Lite content. These content types included such things as wallpaper, screen savers, and animated ring tones (referred to as "Chaku Flash") to name just a few! All of this has had quite an impact on the mobile entertainment industry in the Asian-Pacific region. Flash Lite was proving to be a success for mobile multimedia content.

At about this time, Flash Lite 1.1 also started to proliferate. It was becoming a global phenomenon, rather than occupying the exclusive niche market it once had in the Asian-Pacific region. Macromedia (now Adobe) began touting Flash Lite to the masses, including other mobile operators, carriers, and device manufacturers all over the world. Many Flash developers and other mobile professionals, such as yourself, began using Flash Lite to create applications, games, and other innovative content.

The introduction of Flash Lite 1.1 in 2004 was followed by Flash Lite 2 in 2006. Flash Lite 2 offers more common ground between desktop and mobile device development. Since this newest player is roughly based on the Flash 7 Player specifications, it supports most of ActionScript 2. Therefore, it has been much better received by hardcore developers who wish to transition to mobile device development from desktop Flash. You, yourself, may be such an individual. The Flash Lite development community is finally starting to leverage Flash Lite 2 in all sorts of new and exciting ways.

Potential impact of Flash Lite 2

Because of the fact that Flash Lite 2 content types, such as screen savers and wallpaper, have not penetrated the market on a global scale, I will not discuss them in any length here. However, I fully expect Flash Lite 2 to play an important role in the next generation of multimedia content types delivered on mobile devices.

As evidence of this, Verizon Wireless (in the United States) has announced plans to offer Flash Lite–based screen savers to its subscriber base through the BREW implementation of Flash Lite 2. With the adopters of Flash Lite 2 and support from carriers such as Verizon Wireless, this really opens the door to new and quite exciting content possibilities!

I have high hopes that innovative Flash Lite 2 content types will emerge as more device manufacturers and carriers choose to license this latest version of Flash Lite. Eventually, there will be a switch to Flash Lite 2—it's just a question of when! Until that time, content types based on Flash Lite 1.1 will be continue to be created, utilized, and distributed.

In fact, Flash Lite 1.1 multimedia content, such as wallpaper and screen savers, remains one of the most lucrative businesses in the Flash Lite ecosystem for certain areas of the world. The Asian-Pacific region (particularly Japan) is the most notable example of this. We hope that this successful trend in Flash Lite 1.1 multimedia content types started in the Asian-Pacific region will have a greater global impact in the near future with Flash Lite 2.

Market trends in mobile entertainment

Before we jump into the technical aspects of Flash Lite and mobile entertainment, it is important to look at some of the trends today. I will try not to bore you with too many statistics or fancy graphics. They'd be outdated by the time you read this anyway. Rather, I will briefly talk about various regions and how each culture relates to the mobile entertainment industry. I'll also talk about how Flash Lite is starting to play a part in all of these cultural trends. I'll present some compelling examples of how Flash is helping define the trends within the mobile cultures in the following three geographic areas:

- Asian-Pacific region (APAC)
- North American region
- European region

Other areas are sure to have their own particular mobile trends. However, for the purposes of our discussion, I'll be concentrating on only these three specific areas.

Asian-Pacific region

Mobile technology is a huge business in Japan. It is interesting to note that many more Japanese people have phones than personal computers these days. They use handsets and portable devices for everything from retrieving information online, to playing games, to paying for items in stores. For these users, handsets are much more than voice-capable devices—they are data-delivery devices as well as access points to online services. They are very much a part of their lifestyle and culture. With the proliferation of services such as i-mode, Flash Lite has taken the lead in delivering new and exciting rich user experiences to mobile users in this region.

As we discussed previously, starting in 2003, Flash Lite 1.0 was preinstalled on i-mode–enabled handsets. Flash Lite has come along way since then. It has become a standard for next generation interactive content such as animations, games, and other entertainment-based applications, such as wallpaper and screen savers. I'll cover some of these in the upcoming section on Flash Lite media content types.

As i-mode has evolved, so have the services. i-mode subscribers are demanding more personalized, engaging, and interactive content. Today, Flash Lite is able to deliver on all of this very successfully.

Flash Lite content consisting of animated ring tones (Chaku Flash), screen savers, standby screens, as well as casual games has since become a significant portion of the mobile economy in Japan. It is rare that a handset does not provide some sort of entertainment value. Flash Cast is another great Flash Lite success in the APAC region; we'll talk more about this Flash Lite mobile content distribution service in Chapter 11.

Flash Lite has had a major impact on mobile entertainment and, for all intents and purposes, continues to do so in this region. Japan is the epicenter for much of the Flash Lite entertainment-based content out there to date.

North American region

The United States in particular is is just beginning to see the impacts of Flash on mobile devices. This is primarily because of technical reasons, such as the lack of adoption for Flash Lite, but also cultural differences. In Japan, it seems that everyone has a handset, but not necessarily a computer. The reverse is true in the United States. However, more-sophisticated mobile handsets are becoming more commonplace. The device capabilities and services are becoming more advanced as the mobile technology improves and people become more mobile savvy.

Today, the United States is experiencing significant growth in the areas of mobile entertainment in regards to streaming TV services and music. It is interesting to note that the United States, which is an entertainment Mecca of the world (just think of Hollywood movies!), has lagged in this area for far too long, but it is quickly catching up.

Mobile providers and, more recently, Mobile Virtual Network Operators (MVNOs) are scrambling to figure out how to best deliver multimedia such as music, video, and games to their mobile customers. Although phones are the most popular consumer items, for most entertainment purposes, Americans are more likely to buy a mobile consumer electronic device, such an MP3 player. This may even include the IRiver u10, IRiver clix, IRiver e10, viliv p1, or a portable gaming device, such as a Sony PlayStation Portable (PSP), to some degree. Of course, these coincidentally all run Flash! They fit into the unique category of portable consumer electronic entertainment devices. A great number of these are Portable Media Players (PMPs). However, this is changing as phones start to incorporate more and more entertainment-based features (video and music, for example).

The United States is quickly gathering steam as it starts to establish a Flash Mobile ecosystem. It is only a matter of time before mobile entertainment becomes more commonplace in the United States. The newly formed relationship between Adobe and Verizon Wireless to distribute Flash Lite content is evidence of this. Further proof of this is that Verizon is shipping a device that utilizes a Flash Lite user interface. I fully expect Flash Lite to be a success for Verizon Wireless, as one of the first companies to offer Flash Lite content such as games, applications, wallpaper, and screen savers.

European region

The European market very closely resembles the United States market in terms of mobile entertainment. From mobile games and video to ring tones, wallpaper, and text-messaging marketing campaigns, the mobile entertainment industry seems to be growing in popularity among the heavily populated regions of Europe, most notably including the United Kingdom, Italy, and France. In these regions a large majority of ring tones and wallpaper are specifically designed and created for publicity events such as movie premieres and marketing campaigns. In this regard, marketing is a significant part of the mobile content economy when it comes to these content types.

It is clear that this region is just starting to see the impact of the mobile entertainment industry. The possibility for Flash Mobile to play a part in all of this is very promising.

What are the global trends?

From my perspective, Flash Lite has clearly been extremely successful in several key areas. In regards to mobile entertainment, I believe that the majority of popular Flash mobile content revolves around animations, user interfaces, games, ring tones, wallpaper, and screen savers. We need to briefly discuss some of the various content types that are available within Flash Lite. As you will soon see, there quite a few of them!

Flash Lite content types

Flash Lite can export several content types. You can think of a content type as simply a specialized version of a published SWF file. Depending on the region you are in, a few examples of popular content types for Flash Lite 1.1 might be Stand-alone Player, Browser, Wallpaper, Screen Saver, or Sub-LCD. However, this depends highly on the devices available to you and their respective Flash Lite capabilities. Not all Flash Lite devices support all content types; they typically offer only a unique subset.

Up until this point, you have been working with one exclusive content type, the stand-alone player. Flash Lite stand-alone content always runs in a modal state. What does this mean? It means that the Flash Lite content is launched in its own window or **shell**. For the most part, the content acts as an independent application from the rest of the device. This is not always the case, however. Some content types run more like embedded applications. They integrate with the actual device user interface or communicate with the operating system on a low level. Wallpaper is an excellent example of this. It runs inline as a background for devices that support it. With other specific content types, there is even a greater level of intercommunication between Flash Lite and the device. Typically this is accomplished through what's referred to as a Man-Machine Interface (MMI). Chaku Flash (an animated ring tone) is one such example of this found on a few devices in Japan. However, for the purposes of this chapter, I will not cover such region-specific content types, as they are device dependent.

In Flash Lite, there are numerous content types. Figure 7-1 shows the current Flash Lite 1.1 content types available on various handsets dispersed throughout the world. A majority of these content types are focused on entertainment—the topic for this chapter. The content types available depend on a device's set of capabilities. Unfortunately, for this reason, we will not be able to discuss every single Flash Lite content type in this one chapter. Covering each and every content type available would require an entire book!

Instead, the walkthroughs that I have provided you in this chapter can be universally applied. I'll stick with two popular content types: wallpaper and screen savers. No matter where you are, a screen saver is still very much a screen saver, and wallpaper is very much wallpaper. Besides some minor implementation details, these types are generic enough for us to cover in this chapter.

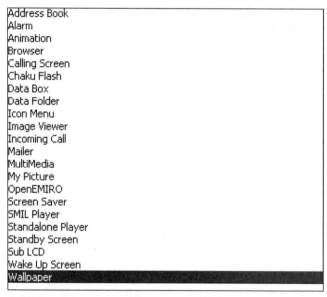

Figure 7-1. Flash Lite 1.1 content types available in Flash Professional 8

What content types are available?

As of this writing, Flash Lite–enabled content types such as wallpaper and screen savers have made their way into the US, European, and other markets apart from Japan. However, for the most part, the APAC region still dominates when it comes to this particular type of mobile entertainment content.

Table 1-1 lists all the current content types for Flash Lite as they are found in Flash Professional 8. Note that a lot of the content types are specific to DoCoMo, KDDI, and Vodafone KK, which are all major operators in Japan. Many of these types only work on i-mode–capable devices. Again, in this chapter, we will concentrate on more globally accessible content types, such as wallpaper and screen savers, because many of the other content types, such as Chaku Flash, are too region- and device-specific to cover with complete depth and accuracy here.

Flash Lite 1.1 content types

Again, Table 1-1 lists the currently available content types within the Flash Professional 8 authoring tool.

Table 1-1. Flash Lite 1.1 content type capabilities (subject to change over time)

Content Type	Description	Availability
Address Book	Uses Flash Lite to let users associate a SWF file with an entry in their device's address book application.	DoCoMo and Vodafone KK (Japan only)
Alarm	Uses Flash Lite to let the user select a SWF file to play for the device's alarm.	KDDI and Vodafone KK (Japan only)
Browser	Uses Flash Lite to render Flash content embedded in mobile web pages and viewed in the device's web browser.	Global (when operator and/or target devices support it)
Calling History	Uses Flash Lite to display an image or animation associated with each entry in the user's address book, along with the name and phone number.	KDDI (Casio phones in Japan only)
Calling Screen	Uses Flash Lite to display an animation when the user receives or makes a call.	DoCoMo and KDDI (Japan only)
Chaku Flash	Uses Flash Lite to let the user select a SWF file to play as the ring tone for incoming calls.	KDDI (Japan only)
Data Box	Uses Flash Lite to render Flash content in the device's data box application, which lets the user manage and preview multimedia files on the device.	DoCoMo, KDDI, and Vodafone KK (Japan only)
Data Folder	Uses Flash Lite to render Flash content in the device's data folder application, which lets the user manage and preview multimedia files on the device.	KDDI (Japan only)

continued

Table 1-1. Continued

Content Type	Description	Availability
Icon Menu	Uses Flash Lite to let the user select custom icon menus for the device's launcher application (used by the UILauncher content type).	KDDI (Casio phones in Japan only)
Image Viewer	Uses the image viewer application that lets the user manage and preview multimedia files on the device, including SWF files.	DoCoMo (Japan only)
Incoming Call	Uses Flash Lite to display an animation when the user receives a call.	DoCoMo, KDDI, and Vodafone KK (Japan only)
Mailer	Uses Flash Lite to display an animation when the user sends or receives an e-mail message.	Vodafone KK (Japan only)
Multimedia	Uses Flash Lite to preview SWF files (as well as other multimedia formats).	KDDI (Japan only)
My Picture	Uses the My Picture application that lets the user manage and preview SWF files, as well as other image formats, on the device.	DoCoMo (Japan only)
OPEN EMIRO	Displays Flash Lite content when the device is returning from standby mode. This is similar to the wake-up screen content type on other devices.	KDDI (Casio devices only)
Screen Saver	Uses Flash Lite to display the device's screen saver.	Global (when target devices support it)
SMIL Player	Uses Flash Lite to preview SWF files (as well as other multimedia formats).	KDDI (Japan only)
Stand-alone Player	Makes Flash Lite available as a stand-alone application, so the user can start and view arbitrary SWF files that reside on the device or that the user receives in the messaging inbox.	Global (where target devices support it); available for select Symbian Series 40, 60, and UIQ devices

Content Type	Description	Availability
Standby Screen	Uses Flash Lite to display the device's Standby Screen (or wallpaper screen).	Global (when target devices support it)
Sub-LCD	Uses Flash Lite to display content on the external or secondary screen available on some flip phones.	Global (when target devices support it)
UILauncher	Uses Flash Lite for the device's application launcher and to display the device's launcher application (i.e., the application that lets the user start other applications).	N/A (device specific)
Wake Screen	Uses Flash Lite to display an animation as the phone is starting.	DoCoMo (Japan only)
Wallpaper	Displays Flash content in the background of a device's user interface menu.	Global (when target devices support it)

As Flash Lite continues to evolve so shall this list. You should also be conscious that devices that support these specific content types are also subject to change. Available content types may vary from device model to device model. This is an excellent reason why you should be vigilant about keeping your Flash authoring environment updated. The way to do this is to periodically check out the latest mobile device profile updates available from Adobe at the following web site: www.adobe.com/products/flash/download/device_profiles.

These mobile device profile updates will help keep you better in sync with the various content types and their support on Flash Lite devices. These updates are provided in MXP (Macromedia Extension format) files. They allow you to update your mobile device profiles both quickly and easily.

i-mode–specific content types

Because of the broad nature of this book's audience, I have kept the examples thus far very Westernized for. However, it should be noted that many of the other Flash Lite content types available are specific to i-mode and hence only accessible to the Eastern hemisphere (Japan!). Depending on the operator (e.g., KDDI, NTT DoCoMo), some rules apply to development of other entertainment-based content types for i-mode. Restrictions and limitations may also apply for Flash Lite. For instance, some Flash Lite ActionScript may be limited in functionality or disabled entirely. In some cases, there may be new functionality that extends outside of the Flash Lite 1.1 specification.

If you are developing for this particular area of content, I suggest you reference the official i-mode CDKs provided by Adobe. These give you the exact specifications you need when developing under the i-mode platform. Where does one acquire these? Download the latest CDKs and documentation from the following location: www.adobe.com/devnet/devices/development_kits.html.

233

You need to download the KDDI or NTT DoCoMo Flash Lite CDKs if you are working on content within the APAC region. In this chapter, I will not go into specific details, as we are considering Flash Lite content types available in a global landscape.

Flash Lite 1.1 content types vs. Flash Lite 2 content types

Thus far we've talked about Flash Lite 1.1 content types, so you may be wondering, "What about Flash Lite 2?" Good question. All the content types we have discussed have been for Flash Lite 1.1–enabled devices. Flash Lite 2, at the time of this writing, has not had a sufficient penetration rate in the mobile world as a preinstalled player, so almost all types are Flash Lite 1.1 based. For the most part, this includes wallpaper and screen savers.

As I mentioned previously, however, this is quickly changing. With the recent Verizon Wireless announcement and the rollout of Flash Lite for BREW on the horizon, there will soon be support for Flash Lite 2 screen savers on BREW-enabled handsets. This United States–based carrier may be the first to offer this Flash Lite content to the market place.

It may only a matter of time before we start seeing other new and exciting types of content based on the capabilities of the Flash Lite 2 player. However, all of the Flash Lite 1.1 content we will discuss in the sections to follow should (for the most part) work as expected in Flash Lite 2 player. Much of what we discuss from here on out should, for all intents and purposes, be compatible with future versions of the Flash Lite player.

Flash Lite 1.1 ActionScript review

Before we dive into some of the examples contained in this chapter, I just want to quickly recap some of the Flash 4 ActionScript you may encounter in the following sections. Since Flash Lite 1.1 is based on a Flash 4/Flash 5 hybrid player, it's important to recall some important commands and syntax that were covered in previous chapters of this book.

However, there is no need to panic. You need to recall only a bit of ActionScript from the previous chapters to be able to complete the upcoming wallpaper and screen saver, including knowing and understanding the following four basic Flash Lite 1.1 statements and operators:

- add
- random()
- setProperty()
- tellTarget()

add

The add operator provides string concatenation in the Flash Lite 1.1 examples that follow shortly. Prior to Flash Lite 2 and ActionScript 2 (with the + operator being able to automatically cast to different data types), add was the only command used to combine two or more strings together. The + operator is reserved for number values in Flash Lite 1.1 ActionScript. You should use add to concatenate strings in Flash Lite 1.1, as seen in the following example:

```
s = "a" add "b" add "c"; //-- this will set the variable s to "abc"
```

random()

The random() function returns a positive integer 0 to the parameter specified, minus a value of one. So random(10) really returns 0 through 9, and not 1 to 10, or 0 to 10, as you might think. Thus random(10) + 1 returns the values 1 to 10. Keep in mind that, with Flash Lite 1.1, random() is not the same as the ActionScript 2–based Math.random() function that returns a number 0 to 1. Let's quickly look at the usage of this statement:

```
//-- picks a number 0 to 45 and then adds 5 to that number
totaltwinklestars = random( 46 ) + 5;
```

setProperty()

setProperty() is a custom function that allows properties of objects to be set in Flash Lite 1.1 content. Values such as _alpha, _y, _x, and _rotation can be set using this function. For example, setProperty("moon_mc", _x, 20) would set the x coordinate position of the moon_mc movie clip on a stage to the value of 20. You can think of this as a longhand way of using ActionScript 1–type (Flash 5 and greater) dot syntax to set values (i.e., _parent.moon_mc._x). An example follows:

```
//-- sets the moon's x coordinate to 10
setProperty( "moon_mc", _x, 10 );
```

Note, however, that in certain instances in Flash Lite 1.1, it is permissible to use dot syntax to refer to variables. For the purposes of this chapter, we'll stick with using setProperty(), as it keeps our minds focused on Flash Lite 4 syntax, which is required for our upcoming Flash Lite 1.1 content.

tellTarget()

tellTarget() is perhaps the most frequently used statement in Flash Lite 1.1 ActionScript. It has already been used quite a bit in previous chapters. However, it is good to review it again here. tellTarget() acts as a way to designate an object, such as a movie clip, within Flash Lite content to receive variables and other commands. Therefore, tellTarget("moon_mc") { i++ } actually increments the value of a variable called i within a movie clip named moon_mc. Again, dot syntax support is limited in Flash Lite 1.1 content, so we must resort to using the tellTarget() command.

It's important to remember that the parameter fed into tellTarget() has to be a string value and not an instance value. This is quite different than one would expect with ActionScript 2, where an instance name is used. tellTarget() does not take in an instance name but rather a string. This is an important tip.

As you can see, telling targets is equivalent to using dot syntax in newer versions of ActionScript. We'll use it in some of our examples later on in this chapter. The following example combines all of the ActionScript you have seen thus far. This targets a specific movie clip on the screen and adjusts its x and y coordinates with random values. It also sets the alpha value of the target movie clip to a random number.

```
tellTarget( "s" add i add "_mc" ) {
  setProperty( eval( "s" add i add "_mc" ), _x, random( 220 ) );
  setProperty( eval( "s" add i add "_mc" ), _y, 0 - random( 100 ) );
  setProperty( eval( "s" add i add "_mc" ), _alpha, 50 + random( 50 ) );
}
```

235

All of the commands I have mentioned are nearly deprecated in implementations of ActionScript outside of Flash Lite. However, within Flash Lite 1.1 content, they are used quite a bit. Flash Lite 1.1 content is still prevalent in the marketplace, so these commands are good to know and use when they are called for.

After reviewing this section, if you're still having trouble with Flash Lite 1.1 ActionScript syntax, I recommend revisiting Chapter 5, which covers a lot of the syntax for Flash Lite 1.1 ActionScript. It can sometimes be easy to forget or confuse the ActionScript syntax you are working with in Flash Lite. This is especially true when switching back and forth between Flash Lite 1.1 and Flash Lite 2 development. For this reason, I've made the Flash Lite 1.1 examples in this chapter as straightforward as possible.

Now that we've reviewed some of the Flash Lite 1.1 ActionScript you will encounter, it's time to move on to your very first Flash Lite 1.1 content type: Flash Lite wallpaper. First, we need to consider a target device to deploy our content on.

Choosing your target device

Up to this point, you have only read about Flash Lite wallpaper. You are probably itching to get some content under way. Perhaps one of the easiest things to create in Flash Lite is animated wallpaper. Later, we'll also tackle how to create a screen saver from start to finish.

Where should you begin? Well, first of all, you're going to need to select a Flash Lite 1.1–enabled device that supports these content types. Several factors, including your geographic location, device capabilities, and network operator all play a factor in whether you can actually deploy these content types on a physical device. This does not stop you from practicing the creation and testing process, however. After all, there's always the Flash mobile emulator if you can't find a device that supports wallpaper or screen savers. Working within the Flash authoring tool will work for the most part.

You'll need to perform a little bit of research to figure out what target device makes the most sense. The best way is to search the Web for device documentation or browse through the latest device templates available in the Flash emulator. This information is also available online through Adobe at www.adobe.com/mobile/supported_devices/handsets.html.

Consulting other online device documentation is also recommended, as devices sometimes appear more quickly than this page is updated. If you don't have access to a device that supports wallpaper, remember that you have your trusty Flash mobile emulator. With it, you can make believe, so to speak, by choosing from the available device templates and working with the stand-alone content type.

I am choosing a Sony Ericsson Flash Lite 1.1–enabled device to facilitate the design, development, and testing of our Flash Lite wallpaper and screen saver content. I will be using the Sony Ericsson k608i shown in Figure 7-2. At the time of this writing, this device supports browser, stand-alone, wallpaper, and screen saver modes.

Figure 7-2. The Sony Ericsson k608i

Sony Ericsson phones are available in the US and European markets and have Flash Lite 1.1 prein-stalled. Some of these support the content types we need. If you have access to these, you should be in good shape. However, be aware that Nokia is also shipping phones that are Flash Lite 1.1 enabled. Some of these also support screen saver and wallpaper modes natively, including some of the Nokia Series 40 third edition handsets that are on the market. Check out www.adobe.com/devnet/devices/nokia.html for more information on these devices. For those in the Asian-Pacific region, wallpaper and screen saver mode should not be a problem. Again, the content types available vary from device to device and region to region.

Also, an important fact you should be aware of is that service capabilities can and do sometimes change. For example, by the time you are reading this chapter, new devices may be available and old devices may have become obsolete. All devices have an expected shelf life before they are discontin-ued or replaced with newer models. It is imperative to check around and see what's available if you are serious about deploying and testing your content on an actual device. If you are completely satis-fied with using the Flash mobile emulator, then there is no reason to purchase a device for the con-tent we will create in this chapter.

Developing Flash Lite wallpaper

The first wallpaper we are creating is a dynamically generated star background, shown in Figure 7-3. I'll cover the steps needed to replicate this wallpaper. After you complete it, you'll have a chance to use your own creative flare to add some sim-ple animation to it. But let's start at the beginning.

As a general rule, it is a good idea to keep the wallpaper and screen saver content that you create as simple as possible. As we have discussed throughout this book, performance and memory are important to pay attention to when developing for the Flash Lite. This is also true for wallpaper and screen savers, as they are not always stand-alone applications. Always think about CPU, memory, and screen size when developing Flash Lite content, whether it's Flash Lite 1.1 or even Flash Lite 2. This is incredibly important, even for the simple con-tent I cover here. With that said, let's create our very first wallpaper—a static-based wallpaper.

Figure 7-3. The star field wallpaper

Star field static wallpaper

The actual implementation of wallpaper varies from device to device. Therefore, planning is a crucial step in designing and developing your wallpaper content. You need to think about things like screen size, frames per second, and device capabilities.

You also need to find out if your target device supports Flash Lite wallpaper at all. As I have stressed previously, not all devices support this specific content type. Other criteria to consider include the fol-lowing: What is the screen size? What is an acceptable setting for frames per second? How might the wallpaper background interfere with the user interface on the phone? These are just some of the important considerations to take into account when planning and developing your wallpaper content.

What about our target device? As I said earlier, the target device we will be using is a Sony Ericsson k608i. It's a Flash Lite 1.1–enabled handset with both screen saver and wallpaper modes. The default size for this device is 176×220 pixels, and the Flash Lite Player for this device typically runs under 12 FPS, depending on the content. For this reason, I will keep the examples in this chapter straightforward and not overly complex.

The general steps to creating Flash Lite–based wallpaper do not significantly change from device to device. So, if you're inclined to get a better model that is available on the market, you'll most likely want to check out Adobe's supported devices that I mentioned previously. At the time of this writing, a few of the Sony Ericsson models are capable of Flash Lite 1.1–enabled browser, wallpaper, and screen saver modes. It is always a good idea to verify this information by checking your target device's documentation.

Setting up the environment

Now that we have all the planning complete, we begin by opening the Flash Professional 8 authoring tool. Since we are using the Sony Ericsson, you'll want to select the Global Phones option from the Create from Template pane as shown in Figure 7-4.

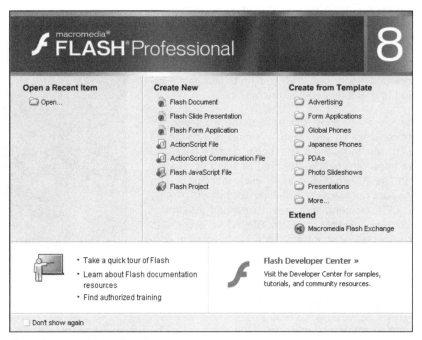

Figure 7-4. Create From Template pane

If you are looking to create Japanese-targeted content, you select Japanese Phones, as shown in Figure 7-5. In our case, we deploying content destined for the US and European markets, so we won't be dealing with Japanese phones at all. We'll be using the Global Phones template, since we are developing for the Sony Ericsson k608i phone. Even though it might seem tempting, do not use the Japanese Flash Lite 1.1 wallpaper profile unless you plan to deploy your content for those specific target devices.

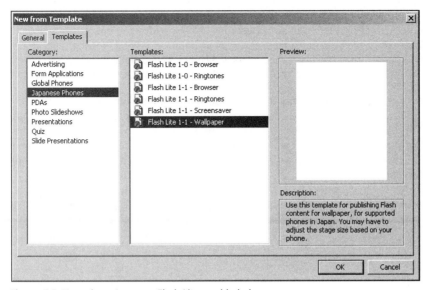

Figure 7-5. Targeting a Japanese Flash Lite–enabled phone

Our next step is to target the Flash Lite 1.1 Symbian Series 60 template. Remember, the wallpaper content we want to re-create is Flash Lite 1.1, since Flash Lite 2 wallpaper is not an option at this time. Again, we want to avoid using the Japanese Flash Lite 1.1 content type, since it's specifically designed for a completely different target device.

At the New from Template dialog, you'll want to select Flash Lite 1-1 - Symbian Series 60, as shown in Figure 7-6.

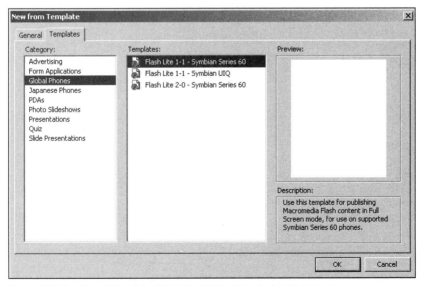

Figure 7-6. New from Template (Flash Lite 1.1 Symbian Series 60 device)

You also want to select the content type you are targeting here. If you click Stage and select the Device Settings button from the Properties panel, you are able to switch the content type from Standalone Player to Wallpaper. Select the k608i from the Sony Ericsson category under the Manufacturers folder, and add it to your list of available device profiles. Also, make it a default device, since we'll be working with it from here on out. To do this, simply click the Make Default button shown in Figure 7-7.

In our case, we are creating wallpaper, so choose that from the drop-down menu. For the Sony Ericsson k608i, Wallpaper should be a selectable from the available content types list, as shown in Figure 7-7. If it isn't, try the Standby Screen selection from the list of available content types. If your target device does not support wallpaper or the standby screen mode (i.e., if they are grayed out and inaccessible), just stick to using the Standalone or Browser content type to follow along with the examples to follow.

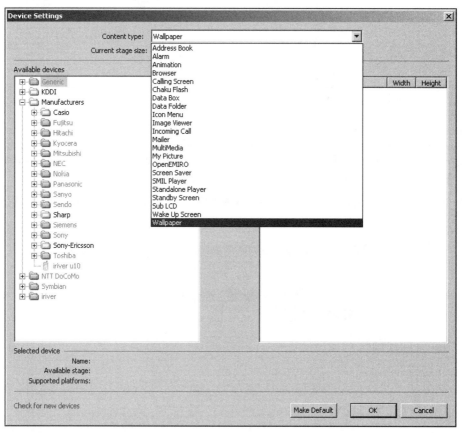

Figure 7-7. Choose Wallpaper mode from the Content type list.

As mentioned previously, it is usually a good idea to check for the latest mobile templates from Adobe in case changes have been made to existing mobile template profiles or new devices have been added. The process is simple. Click the Check for new devices link on the device profile page (as shown in Figure 7-8).

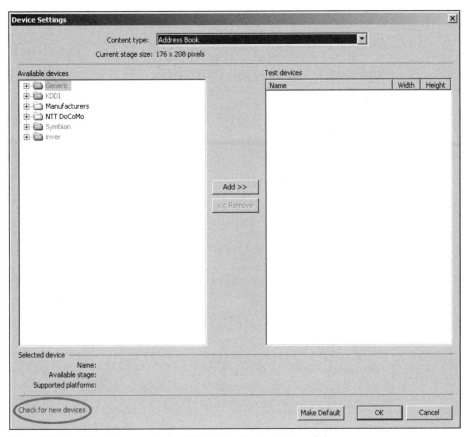

Figure 7-8. The "Check for new devices" link in the Device Settings dialog

This opens a URL and brings you to a web page where you can select and download mobile device templates that have been released and/or recently updated. It's critical that you use new templates as they arrive; otherwise, what you see in the emulator may differ dramatically from what occurs on the actual device itself.

Downloading and installing these mobile device files is a snap and only requires running the MXP file via the Macromedia Extension Manager application. Figure 7-9 shows the Device Profile Updates page maintained by Adobe, where these downloads are posted. Now that you have a Flash Lite template and profile configured and ready to go, it's finally time to start building the wallpaper.

Figure 7-9. The device profile updates page.

Creating your wallpaper

The steps to complete our very first wallpaper are very straightforward indeed. The wallpaper is a randomly generated star field background. This is simple example will get you started quickly building your own wallpaper. The final star field is pictured in Figure 7-10. As you can see in Figure 7-11, the time line for this particular example is going to be very minimal to begin with, consisting of only a few layers and some ActionScript. Yes, the background is generated by code. We could use a static image for the background, but I chose to make the stars a bit more dynamic in their configuration. We can get this effect by using a bit of ActionScript.

Figure 7-10. Our star field wallpaper on the Sony Ericsson k608i

Let's get started developing. It's time to make the first adjustment for the wallpaper. You need to change the default document frames per second. You can find this setting by choosing Modify ➤ Documents or accessing the Properties panel on the main stage. Your background for this example is going to be a dynamically generated movie clip. However, there will be little animation to begin with. You can set the frames-per-second rate to 1 FPS, as seen in Figure 7-12. Later, when you create animated wallpaper, you'll tweak the frame rate to attain the best playback performance with animation you add.

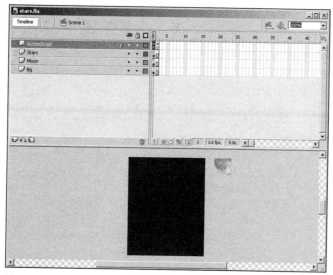

Figure 7-11. The time line and stage of the star field we will walk through in this example

Next, you'll want to change the default background to a solid color. Let's just choose black; the hexadecimal color (hex color) is 0x000000. You can choose whatever color you'd like as long as it doesn't interfere with the color of the stars generated later. I chose black, because it will give a nice contrast when used as wallpaper on the target device. Also make sure that the dimensions are set to the proper dimensions of your target device. In our case, the width is 176 pixels and the height is 220 pixels. Please refer to Figure 7-12 for the final document settings.

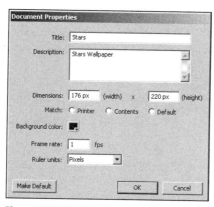

Figure 7-12. The Document Properties dialog

Next, you should also create a layer on the main stage called Bg that has a black, box-shaped vector that occupies all of the background. Make the size of the black shape 176×220 pixels, the dimensions of the target device (your dimensions may vary). For this layer, you can really add any content you'd like, for example, a space station or any other asset you might find. It's a good habit to always have a solid background as its own separate layer, in case you want to change or add content later. Having multiple layers is always a good organization tip for any Flash development.

Now that we have our device profile all set up and the appropriate document properties are in place, it's time to get down to business and start coding. As we mentioned previously, we are going to use code to build our wallpaper. We could use a vector or graphic image, but as you'll see shortly, using a code-driven approach to generating our wallpaper allows us to have a random background every time it is run.

We are creating a star field, so the first thing we need to do is create a star movie clip. This is very easy. Simply press Ctrl+F8 (Windows) or Option+F8 (Macintosh) or select Insert ➤ New Symbol to create a new movie clip. Give it an instance name of star_mc, as depicted in Figure 7-13. Fill in the rest of the properties as shown in Figure 7-13, and click the OK button.

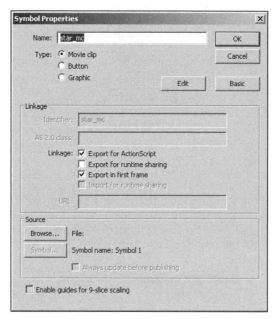

Figure 7-13. Create a star movie clip.

Now that you have your star movie clip, you need to actually create a star and assign it a name. This can be anything you want (within reason). For our purposes, we're just going to use the drawing pen tool to create a single point or dot colored white (the hexadecimal color is 0xffffff, by the way) on the first layer of the star_mc movie clip.

Why use such a simple dot? Adding more detail here wouldn't add much more to the overall effect we are trying to achieve. Besides, too much going on in the wallpaper might interfere with the overall user experience of the phone. When dealing with Flash Lite wallpaper and other such embedded content types, keep (simultaneous) animations to a minimum, and be considerate of what is going outside of the wallpaper, such as the interaction between the user and the device interface.

Think about this: You might imagine a scenario where a menu is convoluted by annoying background graphics, noncontrasting color schemes, and other nasty design problems. It's important to keep the main focus on the user's actions, not the background! It should be subtle, and it should not be too obtrusive. Our star field wallpaper fits these criteria. It's simple, but it helps you get acquainted with wallpaper construction. Don't worry—we're going to spruce up the stars in a bit. After we finish creating the static wallpaper, we'll add some really straightforward code to periodically adjust the brightness of a few of the stars. This will add a bit of realism to them; it will be a kind of twinkle effect. This will be a very simple behavior for our wallpaper that will not detract too much from the user's experience. We'll also add a bit of animation. But, first let's get back to creating our star.

With your star_mc now in your Flash library, you need to actually move one instance of it to your stage. Drag and drop the star_mc from the library to the stage. Give it an instance name of star_mc. You need one instance on the stage to be able to duplicate the movie clip. Remember in Flash Lite 1.1, there are no createEmptyMovieClip or attachMovie statements as there are in Flash Lite 2. We need to utilize the duplicateMovieClip command to make copies of the star. This will eventually be our star field.

Next, you should place the star_mc off the main stage area, as we will be using this single static instance of the star to duplicate other stars dynamically. You may also want to cut and paste your star in a new Layer called stars to help consolidate where everything is kept. Time line management is completely up to your own style and preferences. However, I highly recommend staying away from having everything within one layer for the sake of running into asset placement issues later on. Separate your assets on their own layers.

Adding the code

Great! Now that we have our single star instance just off of the stage, we get to the actual coding part. On frame 1, we want to first set the content to full-screen mode. This content is a background, so we want the whole screen to be occupied. Thus, we need our very first piece of code to set the Flash Lite content to full-screen mode. The device might do this automatically; however, it is not a problem to leave it in as precaution, in case someone decides to run this exercise as a stand-alone application:

```
//-- this ActionScript sets your content to be full screen
fscommand2( "FullScreen", true );
```

We now want to create a second frame on the time line. It will contain our duplication code. Why are we using two frames? We just want to wait a frame until we start populating the stars on the stage. This is a minor detail, and if you want, you could keep everything on frame 1. I just like the effect of having a blank screen before the stars are drawn.

How many stars do we want to be populated? It depends on the effect you are going after. Also, you don't want to stress out the Flash Lite player by having a lengthy processor-intensive loop. Having thousands of movie clips taking up precious memory or CPU cycles is generally a bad idea (even if they are, in fact, duplicated). Instead, we set the total stars to the conservative number of 100, which gives a nice overall effect for our first wallpaper and works well with our device dimensions.

Add the following to frame 2:

```
totalstars = 100; //-- total # of stars to output on screen
```

On frame 2, we also want to add the code that generates the stars randomly on the stage. Create a simple for loop to generate the total numbers of stars:

```
for ( i = 0; i < totalstars; i++ ) {
  //-- duplicate the star clip on the stage!
  duplicateMovieClip( "star_mc", "s" add i add "_mc", i );

  //-- now assign the star clips to a random x,y position and
  //-- also give the star a "distance" effect
  setProperty( "s" add i add "_mc", _x, random( 176 ) );
  setProperty( "s" add i add "_mc", _y, random( 220 ) );
  setProperty( "s" add i add "_mc", _alpha, random( 100 ) );
}
```

As you can see, we are currently duplicating the stars on the screen at random x and y coordinates. We are also setting the random alpha values, or the equivalent of star brightness, for each individual star movie clip. This gives each star an overall perceived distance when the wallpaper is run.

Next, we move on to deal with our moon graphic. Since the moon is not already in the library or stage, we need to first import the graphic. To import the graphic, simply choose File ➤ Import ➤ Import to Stage, and select the moon.gif graphic found in the assets folder located within the WallPaper folder. Once on the stage, cut and paste it onto a new layer called moon that you create on the main time line. Then convert it to a movie clip by selecting it, and using Modify ➤ Convert to Symbol. Assign it an instance name of moon_mc in the properties dialog. Also assign the instance name of the moon movie clip on the stage by selecting it and entering the instance name into the movie clip Properties window. Again, call it moon_mc. Select Window ➤ Properties if that panel is not already open. It's crucial to make sure the moon on the stage has an instance name, since we'll need to refer to this movie clip shortly. We will be duplicating the movie clip and will require an instance to target this clip on the stage.

Next, we need to move it into its final position. Why not just position it where it needs to be from the beginning? Well, remember we are duplicating stars on the screen, so if we position the moon at the outset, the stars could potentially populate directly over the moon. We want to avoid that. To do so, we want to add the moon movie clip to the stage by dynamically duplicating the moon offscreen and placing it above all the stars on the stage at a higher depth. We do this simply by adding the following ActionScript code:

```
//-- add the moon
duplicateMovieClip( "moon_mc", "m_mc", totalstars+100 );
setProperty( "m_mc", _x, 137 );
setProperty( "m_mc", _y, 0 );
```

The duplicated moon will be positioned in the upper right-hand corner, above all the possible stars populated on the screen. Note that the depth of the moon is assigned to a value greater than the last star that is populated on the screen. This is what we wanted to achieve. The moon appears in front of the stars—excellent. Let's continue.

The last step in coding is to insert a stop( ) action on the main time line. If we didn't add this, the wallpaper would continually loop back to frame 1, and everything would start all over again after a few seconds have elapsed. If you leave out the stop( ) command, you'll notice that the stars get randomly generated over a period of time. Quite a different effect than the static wallpaper we were going after! This might just be a little too annoying for our tastes. It may distract the user from the interface of the device, but it might work with a few tweaks (expanding the time line to increase the delay between updates and adding some alpha fades). It really all depends on your preference. We will add the stop( ) action for convenience and overall effect:

```
stop(); //-- remove this and you'll get a different effect
```

The final code follows; you'll want to test to make sure that all of the ActionScript is in place and that there are no syntax errors. To do this, simply press Ctrl+T (Windows) or Option+T (Macintosh) from within the ActionScript panel. This will run a syntax check (you can also use the check mark icon at the top of the ActionScript panel window). Your final ActionScript code should be as follows:

```
totalstars = 100; //-- total # of stars to output on screen

for ( i = 0; i < totalstars; i++ ) {
    //-- duplicate the star clip on the stage!
    duplicateMovieClip( "star_mc", "s" add i add "_mc", i );

    //-- now assign the star clips to a random x,y position and
    //-- also give the star a "distance" effect
    setProperty( "s" add i add "_mc", _x, random( 176 ) );
    setProperty( "s" add i add "_mc", _y, random( 220 ) );
    setProperty( "s" add i add "_mc", _alpha, random( 100 ) );
}

//-- add the moon
duplicateMovieClip( "moon_mc", "m_mc", totalstars+100 );
setProperty( "m_mc", _x, 137 );
setProperty( "m_mc", _y, 0 );

stop(); //-- remove this and you'll get a different effect
```

The final output is going to look something like Figure 7-14.

If you had any trouble with the example, you can always open \WallPapers\stars_final.fla for the final source file for Chapter 7. This is the final star wallpaper for our example here. That's it! You should be ready to test it now.

Testing and deploying your first wallpaper

Congratulations! You have completed your first wallpaper. It's now ready to be tested. Test within the emulator to see how it looks before pushing it to the real target device and setting it as the wallpaper of choice (see Figure 7-15).

Figure 7-14. The final star wallpaper

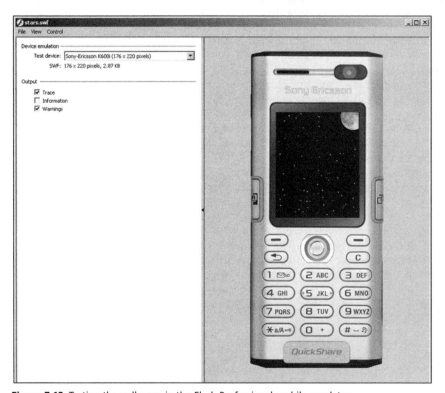

Figure 7-15. Testing the wallpaper in the Flash Professional mobile emulator

Once you are ready to deploy, it's just a matter of transferring to your phone and setting your wallpaper to the star.swf wallpaper. For the k608i, Flash Lite screen savers and wallpaper can be activated by going through a few easy steps. First, access the main Menu of the device, and select the File Manager icon. Next, select the Pictures entry. Any Flash Lite 1.1 SWF files found under the Pictures folder on the device can be used as either screen savers or wallpaper by selecting the More button and using the Set As option. This prompts you to select between the two different content modes. Once applied, the wallpaper should take effect immediately. No reboot of the device is required here. If you are using another device and not the k608i, the process of setting content types is going to be different on your device. However, typically this is a feature found under the themes portion or your target device. Your configuration may vary, so you'll need to consult your target device documentation.

Once you've figured out how to set your star content as the wallpaper, I think you'll agree that creating simple wallpaper is both quick and easy with Flash Lite. Although I agree that this specific example is trivial in nature, I didn't want to overcomplicate things for your first Flash Lite 1.1 wallpaper experience. I wanted to keep it short and sweet. You also have to think about the overall user experience impact the wallpaper will have. Will it add or detract from the everyday usage of the device? Considering that our target device was a Sony Ericsson k608i (a low-FPS Flash Lite player), I decided to keep things at a minimum. Of course, from here, you may have many ideas for what to do this Flash Lite wallpaper. Animate an alien, or show the phases of the moon. These are all things I leave to you to do as exercises. Use your imagination to experiment and have a bit of fun!

Does nothing come to mind? Browse the WallPaper folder, and open the stars_withalien.fla file if you don't have any ideas off the top of your head. Contained within the new source file are a randomly moving alien as well as a twinkle effect for the stars. To achieve the moving alien, I added a tween to move the alien back and forth. I also added a bit of ActionScript to adjust the y position of alien, so it appears to move up and down the screen. If you look on the first frame of the alienmove_mc clip, you'll notice the following code to randomly position it on the ActionScript layer:

```
_y = 60 + random( 160 );
```

I've also added code to frame 2 in the main time line to dynamically add the alien from an existing alien movie clip off of the stage. I do this so it appears above all the other assets on the screen when duplicated. I target frame 2 in that movie clip to start it moving after it has been dynamically added to the background of stars:

```
duplicateMovieClip( "alienmove_mc", "a_mc", totalstars + totaltwinklestars + 200 );
tellTarget( "a_mc" ) {
 gotoAndPlay( 2 );
}
```

In addition, to get the twinkling star effect, I added code to populate a few stars on the screen at random positions:

```
//-- total # of stars to twinkle
totaltwinklestars = random( 46 ) + 5;

//-- populate the stars to twinkle
for ( j = totalstars + 1; j <= totalstars + totaltwinklestars; j++ ) {
  //-- duplicate the star clip on the stage!
  duplicateMovieClip( "twinklestar_mc", "t" add j add "_mc", j );

  setProperty( "t" add j add "_mc", _x, random( 176 ) );
      setProperty( "t" add j add "_mc", _y, random( 220 ) );
}
```

Notice, in the Flash library, that I've created a new movie clip called twinklestar_mc used specifically for this purpose. If you open the twinklestar_mc movie clip and look at the time line, you'll notice we have a fairly lengthy period of time where nothing happens, and then the star's brightness is brought up and down. This gives the appearance of the star twinkling. To make it even more convincing, I added some code to make each twinkle occur at a random times. If you look at frame 1, you'll notice the ActionScript to take care of this:

```
gotoAndPlay( random( _totalframes ) + 1 );
```

The preceding code is used to jump to a random frame on the time line, so that not all the stars are twinkling at the exact same time. Such a simple piece of code can add a lot to the overall effect.

Now that you've seen how you can create a simple wallpaper, let's now take a look at our next wallpaper. This time, instead of creating static wallpaper and converting it to an animated piece, we'll be animating it right off the bat.

As I said before, a significant portion of mobile entertainment content today is made up of simple content types like animated wallpaper. Our next content example continues to show you how fun, easy, and quick it is to generate this sort of content with Flash Lite.

Animated snowfall wallpaper

After the previous example, you should now feel comfortable with creating basic Flash Lite wallpaper. In our next example, we are going to generate another dynamic Flash Lite wallpaper—the snowfall pictured in Figure 7-16.

You should all ready be familiar with environment setup process that we covered in the previous wallpaper sample in the "Setting up the environment" section. Once your Flash environment setup is complete, it's time to get down to business with your second wallpaper.

Figure 7-16. Animated snowfall wallpaper

250

Much like our previous wallpaper, we'll be duplicating movie clips. This time around, though, we'll be animating from the top to bottom of the screen simulating what will appear to be a snowfall. The animation isn't going to be frame-based on the time line. Instead, it'll be code driven. Again, we'll use ActionScript and not tweens. As the snow falls to the ground, it will start to accumulate there. It's the perfect start to some much-needed holiday cheer!

Designing the animated wallpaper

First off, we're going to need two movie clips. One clip will be for our snowflake, called snowflake_mc. The other will be for the snow pile that will grow over time, which we call snow-pile_mc. For the purposes of this example, I'm going to give you the prebuilt assets snowpile_mc and snowflake_mc to save you some production time and allow you to simply get to the ActionScript that drives our snowfall effect. If you open \WallPaper\snowfall.fla (contained in the Chapter 7 source files) and look in the library, you can see them in there (see Figure 7-17).

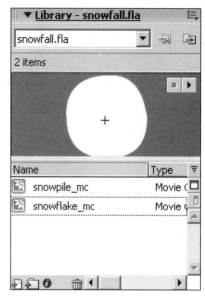

Figure 7-17. The animated snowfall wallpaper library

Next take a look at the stage, and you'll see the two clips in action. Look at Figure 7-18 to view our prebuilt stage with all its assets. The snow pile movie clip sits below the stage and moves up by increments as time progresses, simulating a pile of snow that is accumulating. Also notice our snowflake clip is merely a white dot. Again, we're keeping it simple here. You can customize the snowflake_mc any way you want after you complete this example's walkthrough, if you find your target device can handle something a bit more sophisticated.

Figure 7-18. Animated snowfall wallpaper

Next look at the time line, and you'll notice there are SnowFlakes, SnowPile, and Bg layers that contain all of our assets for this animated wallpaper (see Figure 7-19). You'll notice that the Bg layer is empty. You can put anything you want in there. I left it empty as an exercise for you; fill it in with additional animation or text. Go nuts! Make a snowman jump up and down, or add Santa to the skyline. If your device doesn't already display the date and time, you could even display that too (my device already does this, so I omitted it). You get the picture. Use your imagination. After all, it's the start to your own personalized wallpaper! Now back to the juicy bits of code to make our snowflakes fall.

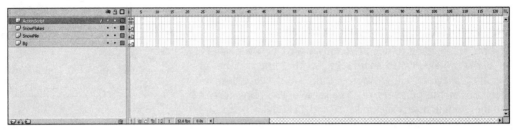

Figure 7-19. The animated snowfall wallpaper time line

Adding the code

Once again, the first step in the first frame is to expand the screen to fill up the whole stage. Start on the main time line, and add the following code to the ActionScript layer:

```
//-- this ActionScript sets your content to be full screen
fscommand2( "FullScreen", true );
```

Next, add the following code to frame 1. This is essentially the same ActionScript we used previously for our stars example, except we now move the snowflakes_mc to a random location above the stage, so they drift down slowly. Populating them on the stage should be a familiar concept to you from our previous wallpaper:

```
//-- total snowflakes
totalflakes = 50;

for ( i = 0; i < totalflakes; i++ ) {
  duplicateMovieClip( "snowflake_mc", "s" add i add "_mc", i );
  tellTarget( "s" add i add "_mc" ) {
    setProperty( eval( "s" add i add "_mc" ), _x, random( 220 ) );
    setProperty( eval( "s" add i add "_mc" ), _y, -0 - random( 100 ) );
    setProperty( eval( "s" add i add "_mc" ), _alpha, 50 + random( 50 ) );
  }
}
```

Now, for the fun part, we're going to be animating each of the snowflakes down the screen, simulating the falling snow effect. Open the snowflake_mc clip, and add the following ActionScript to frame 3; this will give each snowflake a random speed when drifting to the bottom on the screen into the snow pile:

```
_y = _y + random( 40 );
if ( _y > 225 ) { _y = -20; _x = random( 176 ) };
gotoAndPlay( "flake" );
```

Also label frame 1 of the snowflake_mc clip as flake in the Labels layer. Great! Now you should have a snowflake that, when duplicated, will run in its own time line, setting itself to random x and y values. It will move down the y axis at random speeds until it hits the bottom of the screen, simulating the accumulating snow. If you run the code now, it'll show what appears to be a snowfall or blizzard effect.

Adding the snow pile

Adding the snow pile is just a matter of adding the snowpile_mc clip and moving to a frame number greater than frame 12. We will use frame 22. Placing your ActionScript on a frame number greater than 22 will build up the snow pile slowly. Placing your ActionScript on a frame less than 12 will speed up the snow pile a bit. As you can see, it is easy to change the effect here if you find it too distracting. For the purposes of this exercise, I have sped it up a bit. Feel free to adjust the redraw delay in the time line as needed.

The following code moves the snow pile up after each frame iteration is completed; if the y value is ever less than 100, it restarts the snow pile again and resets back to its original value:

```
_y -= 1; //-- move the snowpile up

if ( _y < 100 ) {
    _y = 225; //-- if the snowpile covers a lot of ground then start over
}
```

As we did previously for our star field wallpaper, we want to verify the ActionScript code to make sure there are no syntax errors. Do this by pressing either Ctrl+T (Windows) or Option+T (Macintosh). Everything look good? Great! You shouldn't have any syntax errors now. We're finished! Not so surprisingly, that's all there is to generating our animated snowfall.

Deploying your second wallpaper

Once you are finished, it's time to test. First, give it a try in the mobile emulator. Did it work? If not, it's time to head back and make sure your code is correct. You can also check out \WallPaper\ snowfall_final.fla contained in the Chapter 7 source files for the final result. Once you are ready to deploy, it's just a matter of transferring the wallpaper to your phone and setting your wallpaper to the snowfall.swf animation. Again, these steps are device dependent. Check your documentation for details on this process.

How does the screen saver run once deployed on your target device? Is it too slow? Is it too fast? You may need to adjust the frame rate and tweak some of the settings with regard to the number of snowflakes, how fast they drift, and other parameters. A lot of this depends on your target device. After some modifications, you'll have something that works well for your device. See Figure 7-20 where we throttle our frame rate to 8 FPS for our k608i Flash Lite 1.1 phone.

You might be thinking this example might be the start of a nice screen saver too, which is, not so surprisingly, where we're heading to next.

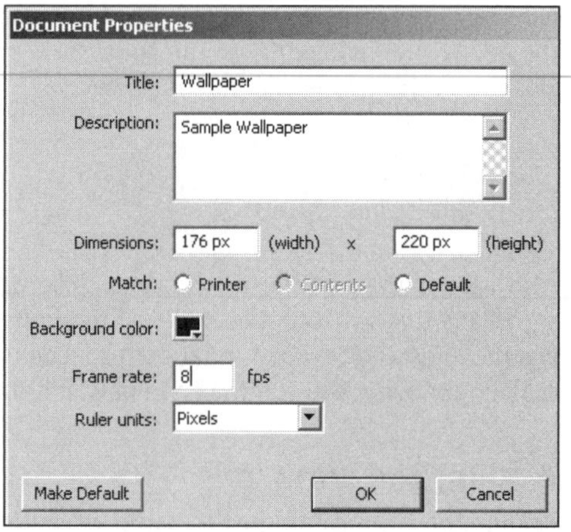

Figure 7-20. Adjusting the frame rate of the wallpaper for performance

Flash Lite screen savers

As we have just seen, wallpaper is quick and easy to build. We're now moving on to screen savers, another popular content type in the realm of mobile entertainment. If you thought wallpaper was fun, screen savers will be a blast too. Let's get right to work.

Creating a Flash Lite screen saver

Creating Flash Lite–enabled screen savers is very much the same process as creating wallpaper, except that you have a little more flexibility in the design, since it essentially runs as a stand-alone application. As a reminder, it's important to determine if the handset you are targeting actually supports screen saver mode. If not, you can just launch the content via browser or stand-alone mode. This will be a close approximation to what the screen saver will be like minus the "put to sleep" and "wake up" functionality that cannot be replicated without an actual physical device or emulator supplied by the manufacturer.

Matrix screen saver

We will be creating a Flash Lite 1.1 screen saver that is loosely based on *The Matrix*. If you have seen one of the movies in *The Matrix* trilogy, you have most likely seen the falling Kanji screen saver that is depicted in Figure 7-21. Our example here will show you how to create this for use as a Flash Lite–enabled screen saver.

Designing the Matrix screen saver

To save you some production time we have prebuilt the Flash library for you, so you can concentrate on assembling the movie clips for the animation. First, locate and open the source file called \ScreenSavers\matrix.fla.

Figure 7-21. Animated Matrix screen saver

Now, if you open the Flash library by pressing Ctrl+L (Windows) or Option+L (Macintosh), you'll notice there is a text_mc movie clip. Open this movie clip, and take a look at the three frames. Each frame contains a unique set of the characters that we want to scroll down the screen.

Next, open the line1_mc movie clip. Notice that there is a tween to move the text_mc clip we have just visited from top to bottom; see Figure 7-22. On the first frame, notice that there is an ActionScript layer that contains the following code:

```
if ( c != 1 ) {
//-- stream down for random amount of time (# of frames)
gotoAndPlay( random( _totalframes ) );
}
```

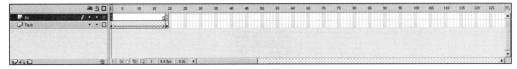

Figure 7-22. The animated Matrix screen saver time line for line1_mc

The ActionScript will jump to a random position in the tween after it is done. It will continue to repeat after reaching the last frame. If you scrub the time line or click any of the frames in the clip, you'll notice the effect we are going for here. Each line should also appear either in the foreground or background. To fake this, we're simply going to generate a random value from 25 to 150. With this value we will set the _xscale and _yscale of our line movie clip to the percentage given by the variable b. Again, this could be any value from 25 to 150.

The effect is that each line is resized to that percentage. At this point, you may be wondering why we didn't set the height and width properties. Remember, this is Flash Lite 1.1. _height and _width are, sadly, not properties of a movie clip. We have to resort to using the _xscale and _yscale properties to achieve this kind of effect. It's not ideal, but it works for us in the Flash Lite 1.1 framework.

This last bit of code merely sets the alpha of the movie clip to give it an appearance of being close or in the distance. This gives the appearance of depth for the falling text clips filled with Kanji character shapes:

```
//-- set the "distance" effect (set the alpha and also scale the kanji
//-- characters)
b = 25 + random( 126 );
setProperty( "", _xscale, b );
setProperty( "", _yscale, b );
setProperty( "", _alpha, ( b > 100 ) ? 100 : b );
```

Also note in this code that we are setting the property to an empty value of "". Well, not quite. In Flash Lite 1.1, this actually refers to the current time line. Think of it as a this statement, if you are familiar with ActionScript 1.0 or greater.

You're making good progress, but there's only one Kanji line right now, so what we want to do is duplicate this clip several times. Within the Flash library, right-click and duplicate the line1_mc. Duplicate four more movie clips. Assign each duplicated movie clip property names to line2_mc, line3_mc, line4_mc, and line5_mc respectively. After they are created, drag them onto the stage, and position them so that you have the layout pictured in Figure 7-23.

Give each movie clip its respective instance name of line1_mc, line2_mc, line3_mc, line4_mc, or line5_mc on the stage. Make an effort to position them as a step ladder (where one clip is higher than the next clip) in their respective y coordinates to offset the Kanji shapes for each line. This adds a bit to the overall effect we are trying to go for! Now you have the five line movie clips on the stage as the picture depicts in Figure 7-23.

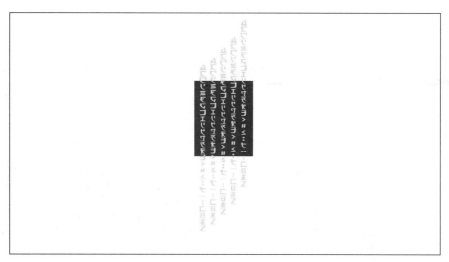

Figure 7-23. Animated Matrix screen saver

One last thing to note is that there is key catcher button on the UI layer offstage. You may be wondering what this is for. Well, it's just in case you are running this screen saver in stand-alone mode. The key catcher button allows you to easily exit the screen saver by just pressing any device key. Normally, screen savers don't require a key catcher to exit, as the device takes care of that functionality. This is just a precaution in case a user decides to run the screen saver as stand-alone content. Since the default behavior of a screen saver is to stop after a user event occurs, this doesn't cause any issues with the content.

Test your ActionScript, and run your movie in the Flash mobile emulator. If everything has gone according to plan, you'll see you have your very own Matrix screen saver! If not, no worries. Just open the \ScreenSavers\matrix_final.fla source file, and see where you went wrong.

Got it working now? Congratulations. Now, if you want to go one step further, you can modify the length of the individual time lines of the line clips, so that they differ in length (see Figure 7-24). This will lessen the repetition that could happen if clips pick the same random number while animating.

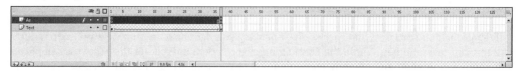

Figure 7-24. Modifying the animated Matrix screen saver's falling text time lines

Now if you run the Matrix movie, it should render the text lines much more randomly. Congratulations, you've just created your very first screen saver animation for Flash Lite. Now, you can take the Matrix wherever you go!

Deploying and testing the Matrix screen saver

Now that you have been through all the steps to create the screen saver, it's time to deploy and test it.

Once you are ready to deploy, transfer it to your phone, and set your screen saver to the matrix.swf file. Again, you may want to tweak the frame rate of the Matrix screen saver to adjust for CPU usage. You don't want to max out your CPU by having a frame rate that's too high, yet you do not want it too low either. It's all about finding that happy medium between performance and quality that leads to the best user experience. Depending on your handset, this will be 8–20 FPS. For my Matrix screen saver, I have defined the default frame rate to 8 FPS.

Now that you have completed a Flash Lite screen saver, we want to move on to briefly discuss animated ring tones, more commonly known as Chaku Flash.

Chaku Flash

Flash remains possibly the best tool in the marketplace today for vector-based animations. Of course, this is also true for mobile as well. When content on i-mode needed animation, Flash was one of best ways to deliver it. Flash Lite has the capability to deliver not only animated wallpaper and screen savers but also animated ring tones—Chaku Flash.

Chaku Flash remains an elusive feature here in the Western part of the world. However, it has become very popular feature found on handsets in Japan. With Chaku Flash, an incoming phone call is intercepted, and a Flash Lite animation is displayed onscreen. These custom animations can be highly personalized and interactive, as shown in Figure 7-25.

Chaku Flash and animated content in general are big business in the APAC region, and because of this, I think it is important to present a case study as it pertains to mobile entertainment. Other types of Chaku include Chaku-uta and Chaku-motion. These let you receive a call with songs of your favorite artists, using large-capacity movie clips with sound. However, Flash Lite is not yet supported for these types, so I won't cover them at all here.

Figure 7-25. An animated ring tone ("Chaku Flash")

Charajam: animated Flash Lite content

Since early 2003, a significant portion of i-mode–specific content in Japan has been animated. The animated content has matured from cutesy little animations (using Flash Lite 1.0) to sophisticated things like animated screen savers, backgrounds, ring tones, games, and other such entertainment services (using Flash Lite 1.1).

I don't think this chapter would be complete without talking about one real-world example in the marketplace of Flash Lite animations. Because of the existing and successful Flash Lite ecosystem in Japan, I feel it makes sense to talk about a company in that particular region. Don't get me wrong—there are numerous other case studies around the world. I just feel this one relates most specifically to the topic of this chapter, mobile entertainment.

Our case study is the product called Charajam, which is owned an operated by a company called Pikkle located in Tokyo. Charajam is focused on providing interactive and connected mobile content to Flash Lite–enabled consumers. The content currently consists of personalized screen savers and ring tones (Chaku Flash) as well as other Flash Lite animations. Check out Figure 7-26 for an example of Charajam.

Figure 7-26. Charajam

By using the Charajam product, a user can mix and match from an array of animated characters, background graphics, ring tones, functional items such as overlay calendars and clocks, as well as personalized photos and custom messages (see Figure 7-27). Charajam taps into a worldwide consortium of designers who create and maintain the available content such as FlashPalz. Users pay for the FlashPalz content by using a subscription-based model that is typical in Japan.

In Japan, the amount of Flash Lite entertainment content is growing every day. There are even discussions about Flash Lite content surpassing Java content in this market, so this is proof of the power and importance of Flash Lite in this area of mobile technology. Charajam is just one such company taking the charge in Flash Lite and mobile entertainment development.

For more information about Charajam, please visit www.pikkle.com or www.charajam.com.

Figure 7-27. A Charajam user interface

Summary

This chapter has discussed some of the basics of mobile entertainment as it pertains to Flash Lite. We practiced creating wallpaper and screen savers, two popular content types available in the global Flash Lite market. Despite the fact that many of the content types remain region specific, I hope that as Flash Lite becomes more pervasive across devices, it will offer new and more-interactive content types. As the worldwide mobile entertainment business continues to evolve, I hope that this type of Flash Lite content will find its niche there.

What are my thoughts on Flash Lite 2? Although Flash Lite 2 is not being leveraged as a format for entertainment-based content such as wallpaper and screen savers just yet, it is clear that it is only a matter of time before this happens. With the powerful capabilities found in Flash Lite 2, a new breed of interactive content types may be on its way. The announcement of Flash Lite for BREW on Verizon Wireless handsets offering screen saver support in the United States means that we could see this content in the marketplace sooner rather than later. All of this is quite exciting. I can't wait to see what types of content will be possible in the next iteration of Flash Lite on devices and handsets.

In the next chapter, we'll cover the intricacies of Flash Mobile sound. There we will cover both Flash Lite 1.1 as well as Flash Lite 2 sound. This includes capabilities, limitations, and considerations to make when working with sound on Flash Lite–enabled portable devices.

Chapter 8

FLASH MOBILE SOUND

Sound is, perhaps, one of the most-powerful rich-media features found in Flash. Even considering its animation prowess, there is little doubt that Flash would not be considered one of the greatest multimedia tools out there today without its accompanying sound capabilities. In fact, Flash content without sound would be very like television without audio—a much less impressive user experience!

Not surprisingly, then, sound is an important feature in the exciting world of Flash-enabled portable devices. Whether it's a handset, PMP, PDA, or other handheld device, finding a Flash-enabled device that does not support sound is extraordinarily rare these days! From the very humble beginnings of Pocket PC Flash on PDAs to Flash Lite on other handheld devices, sound continues to play a crucial role within the mobile application space in user interfaces, entertainment-based content (e.g., animation, music, ring tones), causal games, and much more.

This chapter will further explore the sound capabilities available in Flash Lite 1.1 and Flash Lite 2 that was applied to games in Chapter 6. I'll first highlight the differences between working with native and device sound. Next, I'll talk about some of the popular mobile sound formats available on devices today. From there, I'll examine the commonly used methods of sound playback in Flash Lite and walk through an example of a custom MP3 player built with Flash Lite 2. I'll conclude this chapter by discussing some of the considerations you should make when working with Flash Lite sound on portable devices.

I will not cover sound for the Pocket PC versions of Flash in this chapter. Because of the release of Flash Lite 2.1 for Windows Mobile 5, I feel strongly that it is only a matter of time before Flash Lite becomes the predominant Flash Player for this platform. For the purposes of this chapter, therefore, I'll stick to discussions surrounding Flash Lite.

Flash Lite sound

In Chapter 6, we applied embedded sound effects and music to some of the Flash Lite games we created. You learned a little about the process of using Flash Lite 1.1 to add sound to your games. In this section, I will discuss sound in greater depth, including methods of sound playback in both Flash Lite 1.1 and Flash Lite 2. Before we jump into these subjects, however, we need to talk about some fundamentals. We need to discuss one of the most important topics in regards to Flash Lite sound—the differences between native and device sound formats.

Device sound vs. native sound

The distinction between these two types of sound is, perhaps, the most-important item to note when developing Flash Lite content that has music, sound effects, or other types of audio. The differences can be briefly summed up as follows:

- **Native sound**: This refers to sound that is played back directly within the Flash Lite player. Native sound is essentially any sound that Flash recognizes, whether it is in a WAV, ADPCM, or other such file format. Playback occurs within the player as long as the sound format is supported during the publishing process. This is referred to as **digitized** or **recorded sound**, since the sound is passed directly to an analog-to-digital converter and then on to the speakers of the device for output.

- **Device sound**: This refers to sound played outside of the player, so the sound is passed from the player to the device's operating system. Some commonly used device sound formats are MFi, SMAF, and MIDI. These are often referred to as **synthetic sounds**. The device hardware interprets and plays the sounds contained inside data files using its own internal sound synthesizer components. From there, the sound reaches the speakers after a final digital-to-analog conversion process.

Native sounds

As I have said before, native sounds are sound file formats that Flash knows about and understands how to play without assistance. Native sounds in Flash can either be event-based or streamed over a time line. Event sounds play independently of the Flash time line, whereas streamed sound attempts to play in sync with the Flash time line. You should know a few things about native sounds in Flash Lite:

- **Limitations**: There are two limitations you should know about when working with native sounds in Flash Lite:

  - Flash Lite does not support native play of externally based MP3 files. However, if the target device supports MP3 playback, Flash can usually load in external MP3s for device sound playback.

  - Flash Lite does not support speech encoding (for voice-over audio). If you are looking to utilize speech compression, you must choose another supported format for the audio recording you intend to use.

- **8 kHz Conversion**: Prior to Flash Lite 2, if you played back on a device an audio file that was exported at 5 kHz, 11 kHz, 22 kHz, or 44 kHz, Flash Lite re-encoded the sound at the sampling speeds the target device was capable of providing, which was typically 8 kHz or 16 kHz. This re-encoding caused minor performance problems and additional memory usage. However, in Flash Professional 8, you can now export native audio at 8 kHz when publishing a Flash Lite SWF using an optional feature in the Sound Properties dialog. You can export each individual sound or globally export every sound in your Flash Lite application. Each sound's Sound Properties dialog (see Figure 8-1) now has a check box for this feature under the Compression settings. It is also located in the Sound Settings dialog shown in Figure 8-2, which is accessible under the File ➤ Publish Settings ➤ Flash tab.

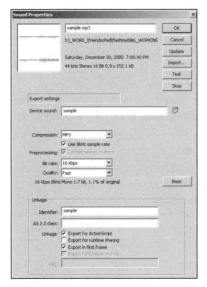

Figure 8-1. The Sound Properties dialog

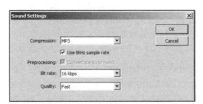

Figure 8-2. The Sound Settings dialog

Using this new feature prevents your application from using too much memory and limits CPU consumption when dealing with sound.

Device sounds

You have already worked with device sounds in some of the games in Chapter 6, but I want to recap a few things here. First, when working with device sounds, you can either bundle the sounds together with a SWF or dynamically load, or even attach, sound files from the device's local file system, a memory card, or over a network connection. Also, device sounds are almost always event based; this means that they play independently of the time line. You should also be aware that the sync, effect, and edit interface properties commonly used with native desktop sounds are not available when using device sounds for Flash Lite content—you can't use these properties during playback in Flash Lite. Here's another great tip: when embedding sound on the time line in Flash Lite, you can easily distinguish between the two formats by the color of the sound wave contained in the time line. Blue indicates native sounds, and green means that a proxy sound file targets a device sound. Proxy sounds are required to link device sound formats that are not supported in the Flash authoring environment to supported types on the target devices. Device sounds are typically a lot smaller than native sounds, since as we have previously discussed, they are synthesized sound formats. You'll see some examples of these in the next section.

Mobile sound formats

It's important to know what formats Flash Lite can handle when developing your content. Let's explore some of those. Flash Lite 1.1 and Flash Lite 2 support the popular MIDI, MFi, SMAF, WAV, and ADPCM sound file formats. When using device sounds, Flash Lite supports any sound format that the target device supports. For the purposes of this book, I will refer to the following commonly used sound formats:

Common device sounds:

- **MIDI**: Musical Instrument Digital Interface (MIDI) is a high-quality audio file format, and on mobile devices, it is used for playing back simple tracks of music and sound effects.

- **MFi**: The Melody Format for i-mode (MFi) proprietary sound format is common on NTT DoCoMo phones and found in Japan.

- **SMAF**: Synthetic Music Mobile Application Format (SMAF) is a data format specified by Yamaha that defines multimedia content for use on handheld portable devices. The most common use for the SMAF format is the creation of ring tones for mobile phones. However, the full specification defines support for graphics too. Yamaha sound chips feature in many of today's mobile phones; any device incorporating one of these chips is capable of playing SMAF sound files. This sound format is primarily found in Japan.

- **MP3**: I'd be surprised, since you are reading this book, if you don't know what an MP3 is. However, just in case, an MP3 is a digital audio compression algorithm that achieves a compression factor of about 12 while preserving sound quality. MP3 files can be played using software available for most operating systems and platforms, including some mobile devices. It is typically a native sound format used in desktop Flash applications. However, it's important to note that the MP3 sound format is usually treated as a device sound and not a native one in Flash Lite, though this is largely dependent on the target device and its capabilities.

- **AAC**: Because of its exceptional performance and quality, Advanced Audio Coding (AAC) is at the core of the MPEG-4 specification and is a preferred audio codec for Internet, wireless, and digital broadcast arenas. AAC provides audio encoding that compresses much more efficiently than earlier formats, such as MP3, yet delivers quality rivaling that of uncompressed CD audio.

Common native sounds:

- **WAV**: WAV, short for WAVE form audio format, is a Microsoft and IBM audio file format standard for storing audio on PCs. WAV is used in desktop Flash applications, typically under Microsoft Windows.

- **ADPCM**: Adaptive differential pulse-code modulation (ADPCM) is a technique for converting sound or analog information to binary information. It is sometimes used in desktop Flash applications.

When working with sound formats, you should remember that available formats differ from device to device, so while one device supports the MP3 format, another device very well may not. For instance, Flash Lite 2 can support MP3 natively provided System.capabilities.hasMP3 is true. Otherwise, only device audio is supported.

Sound Bundler tool

From the section on creating and using sounds and music in Chapter 6, you should be acquainted with the Flash Lite Sound Bundler (see Figure 8-3). To recap, this tool allows you to bundle multiple device sounds (MIDI, MFi, MP3, and other formats) into a single FLS file for deployment on your target devices. When playback of sound occurs on the device, only the supported device sounds will play, and the audio file that most closely matches the supported formats in the FLS file will be used. You should also note that the Sound Bundler tool is available only for Windows. The Sound Bundler tool is located in the same directory as Flash.exe in Windows, so by default, it should install to \Program Files\Macromedia\Flash 8\FlashLiteBundler.exe. Otherwise, it will be wherever you have installed your Flash 8 authoring environment.

Figure 8-3. The Flash Lite Sounder Bundler dialog (Windows only)

This is quite a powerful little tool to use when deploying sound across Flash Lite–enabled devices. I urge you to study the section in Chapter 6 that covers the Sound Bundler, if you have not already done so. If you are planning on deploying an application that contains device sound across a variety of target mobile devices, you'll want to refer to that section.

Flash Lite 1.1 sound

I covered sound in Chapter 6 when we talked about the Sound Bundler and walked through an example of creating sound using Flash Lite 1.1. I will briefly recap of some of functionality in Flash Lite 1.1 here and continue our discussion of sound as it relates to Flash Lite 2.

Remember that in the Flash Lite 1.1 specification, you have access to the properties listed in Table 8-1 through ActionScript. These properties are all accessible via the main _root movie clip of any Flash Lite application and act as "global" variables.

Table 8-1. Flash Lite 1.1 sound properties

Property	Description
_capCompoundSound	Indicates whether Flash Lite can process compound sound. If it can, Flash Lite will attempt to figure out what device sound to use from a sound bundle file (FLS file) based on a target device's sound capabilities. Sound bundle files can be created using the Flash Sound Bundler tool, as explained earlier. These bundles can contain various SMAF, MFi, or even MIDI file formats for the target devices that support them.
_capMFi	Indicates whether the device can play sound data in the MFi audio format.
_capMIDI	Indicates whether the device can play sound data in the MIDI audio format.
_capMP3	Indicates whether the device can play sound data in the MPEG Audio Layer 3 (MP3) audio format.
_capSMAF	Indicates whether the device can play multimedia files in the SMAF format.
_capStreamSound	Indicates whether the device can play streaming (synchronized) sound.

All of these properties can be used to determine if playback should occur for a sound present in a Flash Lite 1.1 application. A value of one (essentially meaning "true") indicates that the property is supported. The following example will play the MIDI file contained on the frame labeled playmidi if and only if the device is capable of device MIDI playback:

```
//-- if user has midi capabilities, jump to the frame where the midi
//-- sound is embedded
if ( _capMIDI ) {
 gotoAndPlay( "playmidi" );
}
```

In Flash Lite 1.1, this very primitive method of sound support detection is your only option.

Flash Lite 1.1 methods

Only one real method is present in Flash Lite 1.1 to control audio playback. That command is stopAllSounds(), and its usage is as follows:

```
//-- stop all sounds from playing
stopAllSounds();
```

stopAllSounds() essentially pauses all audio. It stops all sounds from playing without stopping the playhead. Sounds set to stream resume playing as the time line playhead moves over the frames again. Event sounds are stopped dead in their tracks. This function essentially can act as a "mute" feature.

Loading local file sound via the FSCommand Launch

In Chapter 6, you used the time line to play back audio placed on Flash layers. This type of embedded device sound is typically the best and most-controllable method of playing audio within Flash Lite 1.1. You typically use this method when constructing Flash Lite 1.1 that utilizes sound. However, there are a few other methods to play audio in Flash Lite 1.1. One such method is by using the FSCommand Launch command. The syntax for this method follows:

```
//-- launch the device audio player with a file specified (your path and
//-- application may vary!)
fscommand( "Launch", "Z:\\System\\Apps\\MediaPlayer\\MediaPlayer.app,➥
E:\\Videos\\sample.mp3" );
```

You need to specify the complete path to the audio player installed on your target device as well as the audio file name as an argument. Both of these paths vary from device to device; check your device documentation to figure out what external sound player your device supports and its specific location. This method of audio playback has a limiting factor: you must explicitly know the path to both the player and the audio file. Unless your target device is known beforehand, it has a good likelihood of failing. There is also no way to check error conditions in Flash Lite 1.1, so if it does fail, it will not be a pleasant sound experience for the user. Flash Lite also has no way to control the audio playback, because the target audio player takes care of that. The user must control the audio from the player once Flash Lite has launched the file.

Open /Sound/FL11_fscommand_launch.fla (shown in Figure 8-4) from this book's downloads to follow along with the code for playback using the FSCommand Launch. The code is attached to the key catcher button located off the main stage. Click the button, and view the ActionScript panel.

Determining the location of the audio player is the first step. Locating the path to the player may be tricky, so you want to use a device file manager (such as FExplorer on Symbian-based devices) to traverse the device and find the exact path to the audio player. Once the path is known, you can use the following FSCommand statement to launch it via Flash Lite. The Launch command attempts to start the audio player without a specified target audio file. I recommend that you first uncomment the following line from the sample file and use it to load the audio player without specifying a file, to verify that you are, in fact, loading the player:

Figure 8-4. Launching a sound using the FSCommand Launch command in Flash Lite 1.1

```
//-- run this test to find what path launches your music player (Use
//-- FEExplorer to determine this)
fscommand( "Launch", ➥
"Z:\\system\\apps\\MusicPlayer\\MusicPlayer.app" );
```

Once that is accomplished, you can insert the target device audio file to play. Remember that the sound format must be supported by the device. A playback error is likely to occur if you target a device that is not supported (or it may, in the worst case, fail silently).

Take a look at the following example: I have first found the path to the player and then used a second comment to add the target device sound for playback. Also note the various paths necessary to specify the locations of the player and sound file (your paths may and probably will vary greatly from what follows).

```
// this ActionScript sets your content to be full screen
fscommand2( "FullScreen", true );

//-- launch the audio player with a file specified (your path and
//-- application may vary!)
fscommand( "Launch", ➥
"Z:\\System\\Apps\\MusicPlayer\\MusicPlayer.app,➥
E:\\Sounds\\sample.mp3" );
```

When dealing with external sound files under Flash Lite 1.1, I recommend using getURL() instead of the FSCommand command we have just discussed. Although not perfect, getURL() does allow you to get around hard coding the path to the default audio player, as that path may be a bit elusive without some file exploration. I'll cover the getURL() method of sound playback next.

Loading local file sound via the getURL() command

Another option when dealing with external sound in Flash Lite 1.1 is to target the sound file with the getURL() command. This method only works if the target device has a default audio player installed and if the sound file targeted is a supported audio file type for the device. You can query the sound capability properties (e.g., the _capMP3 property) that we talked about earlier to find out if the file type is supported.

Open \Sound\FL11_getURL_local.fla in this chapter's downloads to see the following example:

```
// this ActionScript sets your content to be full screen
fscommand2( "FullScreen", true );

if ( _capMP3 ) {
  //-- using an absolute path to load a local sound
  //getURL( "file:///C:/Videos/sample1.mp3" );
  //-- absolute path to sound file

  //-- local path to sound file (must be in the same folder as the .swf)
  getURL( "sample.mp3" );
} else {
  trace( ".mp3 is not supported on this device!" );
}
```

In this example, shown in Figure 8-5, the audio file is played back within the default audio player. If no default player exists, getURL() fails. You may or may not receive an error notification, depending on your target device. If the device does not map the audio file type targeted, this may fail silently; therefore, using getURL() is not the most optimal way of playing audio in a Flash Lite 1.1 application. Besides, like the previous FSCommand, there is no way of controlling the audio once it has been loaded and played through the external player.

Figure 8-5. Launching a local sound via the getURL() command

Not only can you load in local sounds using getURL() but you can also load in remotely located external sounds for playback within the device's default audio player. Again, this is simply done through the getURL() command by specifying a URL pointing to the target audio clip to be played.

Loading external sound via the getURL() command

Yes, the getURL() method of loading sound also allows you to target an externally located audio file for playback by simply specifying the URL to the target file. This URL can be a path to a remotely located file as long as the target device has an open connection and nothing blocks the connection (such as a firewall or lack of an available signal). Open \Sound\FL11_getURL_http.fla, contained in the downloads for this chapter, to see the following example of this:

```
// this ActionScript sets your content to be full screen
fscommand2( "FullScreen", true );

if ( _capMP3 ) {
  //-- using an absolute URL to load a local sound
  getURL( "http://www.flashmobilebook.com/sound/sample.mp3" );
  //-- externally located audio clip via http
} else {
  trace( ".mp3 is not supported on this device!" );
}
```

This example, shown in Figure 8-6, checks to see if the target device plays MP3s and, if so, passes the file to the external audio player. There may or may not be a confirmation dialog for this operation depending on the target device. Playback begins immediately once the file has been downloaded. You are depending on the device for the playback of the audio, so you must specify a supported audio file format. Remember that you must also have an existing connection to the server for this to work, since there is no chance to check for these sorts of errors in Flash Lite 1.1 content!

Figure 8-6. Launching an external sound using the getURL() command and specifying a URL

Now that we have looked at embedded time line sound in Chapter 6 and the various methods of external sound playback in Flash Lite 1.1, including the getURL() method and the FSCommand Launch command, it's time to turn our attention to how Flash Lite 2 addresses mobile sound.

Flash Lite 2 sound

As you have seen thus far, dealing with sound under Flash Lite 1.1 is limited in some respects. Being unable to manipulate external audio files (without embedding them in a SWF) and the inability to control certain aspects of sound inside the time line are just two examples of the shortcomings with Flash Lite 1.1. However, with Flash Lite 2, the sound capabilities have been improved.

Sound in Flash Lite 2 is, in some respects, very much like Flash Lite 1.1, albeit with some much-needed improvements. All of the sound formats in Flash Lite 1.1 are also supported when developing Flash Lite 2 content. You can also bundle sounds in the same way; the Sound Bundler tool has not changed at all. The most notable difference in Flash Lite 2 is that you now have access to the Sound object using ActionScript 2. Therefore, sound can be manipulated through code, and you don't have to monkey around with frames on the time line containing embedded audio clips. Other than some other minor differences, dealing with sound in Flash Lite 2 is very like dealing with Flash sound on its counterpart, the desktop player.

You may recall from the previous Flash Lite 1.1 examples that importing audio files, setting proxy sounds, and embedding time line sound are the best ways to approach sound in Flash Lite 1.1, outside of the getURL() and FSCommand Launch command approaches spoken about earlier in this chapter. Flash Lite 1.1 audio is very much time-line based. In Flash Lite 2, you have the option of using sound controlled by ActionScript code. This is a very powerful tool at your disposal, since you're no longer reliant on time lines to hold your audio clips! Code reuse, manageable libraries of external audio files, and dynamically controlled sound can now be implemented without the hassle of time-line–based sound clips. This is a godsend if you're dealing with a significant amount of audio in your Flash Lite content. However, this does not mean that you must give up working with a Flash Lite 1.1 sound model. You'll have to make an evaluation based on your content and target devices to determine whether to stick to Flash Lite 1.1 or make the move to working with sounds under Flash Lite 2. There may even be a case for developing with a Flash Lite 1.1 sound model under Flash Lite 2. For instance, if you want to maintain portability across an application that straddles both Flash Lite 1.1 and 2.0, working with a Flash Lite 1.1 sound approach might make a whole lot of sense.

Before we talk about working with sound in Flash Lite 2, you'll want to determine exactly what audio formats your Flash Lite 2–enabled device supports. Recall that not all devices support the same set of features when it comes to audio. For instance, some phones support MFi and SMAF, while others support only MIDI and MP3. This is very device specific, so you'll need to verify all of this on your target devices before planning an application that contains audio content. To do this, check its sound capabilities. Checking sound capabilities and properties in Flash Lite 2 is different than in Flash Lite 1.1, as we discussed earlier in this chapter.

Testing Flash Lite 2 sound capabilities

Locate and open the /Sound/FL2_devicesound_capabilities.fla file located with the chapter downloads and depicted in Figure 8-7. Look at frame 1, and notice that we are dumping out all of the audio capabilities found on a particular target device that this application will run under. The System.capabilities object in Flash Lite 2 contains several properties regarding sound. Some of these properties are very similar to the Flash Lite 1.1 properties that we spoke of earlier. However, now they are more easily accessible with the Flash Lite 2 System.capabilities framework.

```
fscommand2( "FullScreen", true );

//-- config vars
var border_bool:Boolean = false;
var bordercolor_num:Number = 0xcccccc;
var textcolor_num:Number = 0xffffff;
var startingycoordinate_num:Number = 50;
var capabilitiessize_num:Number = 135;

capabilities_mc.createTextField( "prop_txt",➡
capabilities_mc.getNextHighestDepth(),➡
10, startingycoordinate_num, Stage.width-12, capabilitiessize_num );
with ( capabilities_mc.prop_txt ) {
  border = border_bool;
  borderColor = bordercolor_num;
```

```
    textColor = textcolor_num;
    multiline = true;
    wordWrap = true;
    text += "hasAudio = " + System.capabilities.hasAudio + "\n";
    text += "hasStreamingAudio = " +➥
      System.capabilities.hasStreamingAudio + "\n";
    text += "hasAudioEncoder = " +➥
      System.capabilities.hasAudioEncoder + "\n";
    text += "hasCompoundSound = " +
      System.capabilities.hasCompoundSound + "\n";
    text += "hasMIDI = " + System.capabilities.hasMIDI + "\n";
    text += "hasCMIDI = " + System.capabilities.hasCMIDI + "\n";
    text += "hasSMAF = " + System.capabilities.hasSMAF + "\n";
    text += "hasMFi = " + System.capabilities.hasMFi + "\n";
    text += "hasMP3 = " + System.capabilities.hasMP3 + "\n";
    text += "audio mime types = " + System.capabilities.audioMIMETypes;
  }

  var keyListener_obj:Object = new Object();
  Key.addListener( keyListener_obj );

  this.onEnterFrame = function() {
    if ( Key.isDown( Key.DOWN ) ) {
      _root.capabilities_mc.prop_txt.scroll++;
    } else if ( Key.isDown( Key.UP ) ) {
      _root.capabilities_mc.prop_txt.scroll--;
    }
  }
}

  stop();
```

Keep these properties in mind as you work through your own audio applications. They can aid you in creating more-robust applications that are able to display messages if sound is not supported on a target device, or even drive the logic needed to support the sound playback for multiple formats across more than one target device.

Run the compiled FL2_devicesound_capabilities.swf file on your target Flash Lite 2 device to display all the capabilities of the device via the System.capabilities object, as shown in Figure 8-7.

Figure 8-7. Sound capabilities (note that this code is running off the desktop, not a mobile device)

Always remember that some features vary from device to device—sound is no exception to this rule! Not every device supports the same sound features. A quick check of the capabilities determines what your device can or can't do. You just need to be consciously aware that not all devices support every single audio format. In addition, not all devices need the same amount of memory to play back sound. CPU usage can also be an issue! These are just some of the realities when working with device audio under Flash Lite.

Bundled device sound

I explained the process of working with embedded MIDI sound very briefly in the ActionScript primer earlier in this book. If you didn't cover that material, you may want to visit Chapter 3 now. The examples in this section draw heavily on your ActionScript knowledge. With that in mind, I'd like to revisit bundling sound for Flash Lite for just a bit. Don't worry—this is a recap of what you've already learned. I'll do a quick reintroduction to using sound in Flash Lite 2 before proceeding on to more-involved examples, such as the custom MP3 player later in this section.

Remember the MIDI example we did earlier in the book? Open \Sound\Midi\midi.fla, found in the Chapter 6 downloads. Right-click flourish.wav, and select Properties to bring up the Sound Properties dialog shown in Figure 8-8. Recall that you need to specify the target device sound in the Device Sound field under the Export Settings heading.

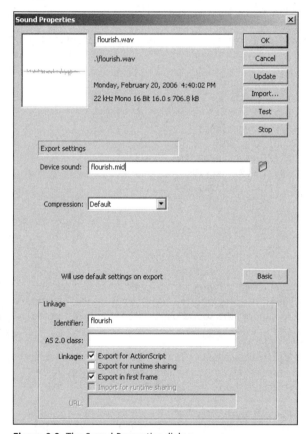

Figure 8-8. The Sound Properties dialog

Remember that the device sound specified in the dialog is the actual sound that is used when publishing. The imported sound is what is used during desktop and emulator testing. Whatever sound is imported acts as a proxy sound until you publish the Flash Lite content for deployment. At that time, the device sound is substituted and published into the compiled SWF.

You'll also notice the Linkage Identifier is set to flourish. This is very important in Flash Lite 2. It gives us a way to access the sound through ActionScript if it lives in the library. Typically with Flash Lite 2 development, you are going to pull in sounds at runtime or attach them directly from the Flash library. It's important to give your sounds unique and useful linkage identifiers (and instance names) in Flash Lite 2, so you can refer to them using ActionScript code quickly and easily.

Check out the following ActionScript code on frame 1 of the MIDI example you've opened:

```
// check if midi is supported
if(hasMIDI()) output_txt.text = "MIDI Supported";
else output_txt.text = "MIDI Not Supported";

// play sound on enter
var keyListener:Object = new Object();
keyListener.onKeyUp = function() {

  if (Key.getCode() == Key.ENTER)
  {
    // attempt to play midi anyway
    var snd = new Sound(_root);
    snd.attachSound("flourish");
    snd.start(0,0);
  }
}
Key.addListener(keyListener);

stop();


function hasMIDI()
{
  for(var i in System.capabilities["audioMIMETypes"])
    if(System.capabilities["audioMIMETypes"][i] == "audio/x-midi")
      return true;

  return false;
}
```

The essential parts of this example, which follow, are creating the Sound object via ActionScript 2 and attaching the sound from the library as well as playing it back in its entirety:

```
// attempt to play midi anyway
var snd = new Sound(_root);
snd.attachSound("flourish");
snd.start(0,0);
```

Checking for the MIDI MIME type was also something we touched on in the chapter on ActionScript. You can see that this is part of the System.capabilities object we talked about earlier in this section. You also can see that, in the following lines, we are merely checking whether the device supports the x-midi device sound format. If it does, the code returns true; otherwise, false:

```
if(System.capabilities["audioMIMETypes"][i] == "audio/x-midi")
    return true;
```

Are you still with me? Good, let's continue our discussion of sound. If you're not up to speed, I recommend you revisit the ActionScript primer. You can also refer to the section on game audio in Chapter 6 for a refresher as well. We are about to move into more ActionScript-heavy territory. Ready? Good; let's talk more about the Sound object in Flash Lite 2!

Mobile device sounds via the Sound object

The Sound object is a powerful tool that has made its way from the desktop Flash into Flash Lite 2. You've already seen it in action to some degree. In this section, we're going to explore it a bit further, as there is quite a bit of functionality to cover.

Just like any other ActionScript object, the Sound object has a unique set of properties and methods that you can use to query and even manipulate sound in Flash Lite 2. Although there are some innate limitations, you can use it to control your sound in your Flash Lite 2 content. Many of the limitations that existed with Flash Lite 1.1 sound no longer exist when working directly with the Flash Lite 2 Sound object. The first thing to note is that you can dynamically attach a sound from the Flash library by specifying its linkage name and assigning the loaded sound an instance name. Instead of embedding audio on the time line, as you do when developing Flash Lite 1.1 content, you can place the audio files within the library. This allows you to dynamically attach and play back dynamically loaded audio clips. Sound attached within a library is referred to as **locally bundled sound**. This is just one of the ways to use audio in Flash Lite 2 content.

Locally bundled sounds Creating a sound object to control the playback of a bundled sound file is straightforward, since everything is contained within the same Flash Lite application. For example, if you open the FL2_devicesound_library.fla file (shown in Figure 8-9), you find the following piece of code on frame 1. As with our previous MIDI example, this example simply attaches the audio directly from the library for playback:

Figure 8-9. Attaching and playing a sound from the library with Flash Lite 2

```
//-- create a sound instance dynamically from the flash
//-- library and attach it to the stage
var sample_snd:Sound = new Sound();
sample_snd.attachSound( "sample_id" );
```

It's important to note that the sample_snd instance is on the main time line. To control the clip, you must use _root.sample_snd, or simply sample_snd as in our example (since we are already on the main time line).

Notice that we're using the "sample_id" linkage name to pull the MP3 from the Flash library and assign it to the sample_snd Sound object by using the attachSound() method we covered in Chapter 6. This method is very much the same as the attachMovie() method that we have talked about previously, only it deals explicitly with sound. To begin playback, we merely call the start() method. Check out the key catcher button on stage for this code:

```
//-- play back the attached sound from the library!
sample_snd.start( 0, 0 );
```

Using the attachSound() method and bundled sounds has the benefit of not requiring any sounds to be embedded on the time line. Also, no sounds need to be external from the compiled SWF. If you want to avoid either of those issues, bundled sound might make sense for your application. You just have to be aware that storing bundled sounds bloats the resulting SWF. An added benefit is that the sound used is not exposed outside of the SWF. If protection is required for audio content, this limited security measure can aid you somewhat in that respect.

Loading local audio sounds Besides bundling audio inside a SWF, you can also dynamically load external audio files. This was not possible in Flash Lite 1.1 without embedding audio into SWFs or targeting an external sound player with a getURL() or FSCommand Launch (as we discussed earlier in this chapter).

Loading local audio files in Flash Lite 2 is very straightforward. The local files can be specified using either a relative or absolute file path. That path can be local, meaning residing on the device or memory card, or external, meaning located on a network and loaded in via HTTP or another protocol. We'll investigate loading external sound in a bit, but first, let's look at local audio clips.

Figure 8-10. Loading local sound in Flash Lite 2

If you open the /Sound/FL2_devicesound_local.fla file (shown in Figure 8-10) in the source downloads and take a peek at the code attached to the key catcher button, you'll see the following code:

```
//-- load up a sound file from the local file structure
var sample_snd:Sound = new Sound();

sample_snd.onLoad = function( success_bool:Boolean ):Void {
  if ( success_bool ) {
    sample_snd.start( 0, 0 ); //-- start playing the sound!
  } else {
    trace( "cannot load audio file! Is it in the correct location?");
  }
}

sample_snd.loadSound( "sample.mp3" );
//-- load from a local or "relative" path
//sample_snd.loadSound( "E:///Videos//sample.mp3" );
//-- load from an absolute path!
```

As you can see, the structure for loading locally defined audio clips is almost the same as for bundled clips, with a few notable exceptions. We use the loadSound() method to target the audio file instead of the attachSound() method we use for bundled device sound.

You'll also notice that we now have a callback event called onLoad( ) that is fired by the player after the loadSound( ) has completed. If the sound is loaded successfully, the audio starts from the beginning; otherwise, an error has occurred. Here we are just tracing out the error. However, in a real application, you would write your own error-handling mechanism, which might be a dialog or possibly even an instruction page. Later, we'll incorporate such a message into our MP3 player, when we build that.

One caveat worth mentioning is that you can't determine the specific error that occurs with sound. The return value for success_bool is a Boolean value; it can only be true or false. This is somewhat limiting, however, when dealing with sound loaded locally; it is usually a win-or-lose situation. On a Flash Lite–enabled mobile device, a losing situation usually means that a device error dialog appears. One such error is Bad sound format. Refer to Appendix A for other Flash Lite error codes.

Thus far, we have only talked about using sound that is located on the device itself. But what if our audio clip is externally located, say on a network? Let's address loading external sound in Flash Lite 2 next.

Loading external audio sounds Flash Lite 2 finally supports dynamically loading sound files across a network. Loading externally located sound files is shown in this section's example. Open the file FL2_devicesound_ http.fla (shown in Figure 8-11), which is among the downloads for this chapter. Select the key catcher button on the main stage, and open the ActionScript window to the code to load an externally loaded audio file from a network using the HTTP protocol. This, of course, assumes that the device supports loading sound over an HTTP connection (some networks may block this)! In addition, there must also be an active network connection with enough signal strength to pull down the sound. If all these conditions are met, loading external audio should not be a problem for your target Flash Lite 2–enabled device.

Figure 8-11. Loading an exernal sound via an HTTP network connection

Let's examine the following code:

```
//-- load up an external sound example from a remote location
var sample_snd:Sound = new Sound();

sample_snd.onLoad = function( success_bool:Boolean ):Void {
  if ( success_bool ) {
    sample_snd.start( 0, 0 ); //-- start playing the external sound!
  } else {
    trace( "cannot load audio file!" );
  }
}

//-- load up the sound via an absolute URL
sample_snd.loadSound("http://www.flashmobilebook.com/➥
/sound/sample.mp3" );
```

There are some important points to make about loading external sound; really, they are limitations. First, when externally loading audio files, the files are not streamed at all when the HTTP protocol is used. If you are familiar with the isStreaming parameter from desktop Flash, it will not function as intended. Flash Lite ignores this parameter, so loadSound("url", true); will not work. Flash Lite 2 does not have the capability to stream sound via HTTP. Sound is only event-based in this situation. The audio file is downloaded completely and then played back. It is an asynchronous operation. Flash Lite 2 differs from desktop Flash in that MP3 files are handled as device audio. The Flash Lite player passes the externally loaded audio data to get decoded by the device itself, so checking to see if the device supports the audio format is typically a good idea. You have already seen how to do this in our previous MIDI example. However, let's explore that now in more detail. This brings us to our next topic—detecting the sound capabilities for devices.

Detecting supported device capabilities

How can you check to see if a particular sound format is supported for a target device? In Flash Lite 1.1, you are stuck using a static property value, such as _capMFi (which checks for MFi capabilities), when checking for the supported sound formats. The limiting factor in this method is that only a set number of formats can be detected. Outside of those, you are out of luck. Refer to the previous section on Flash Lite 1.1 sound for a list of the sound capabilities available.

In Flash Lite 2, you now are able to check for sound capabilities more easily by using the audioMimeTypes array. The System.capabilities.audioMimeTypes array contains all the possible device sounds for a target device. This allows you to use it to check whether or not device sound should play. This approach is much more flexible in that the array dynamically changes based on the sound formats found, so where one device might support only five formats, another might support ten, and so forth.

For instance, say you want to check to see if a device supports the MP3 format in Flash Lite 2. This is how you would accomplish that:

```
//-- check to see if the MP3 device sound type is supported.
//-- If it is, then play back the sound!
if ( System.capabilities.audioMimeTypes[ "audio/MP3" ] ) {
  sample_snd.start();
}
```

The audioMimeTypes array contains all the supported types, so audioMimeTypes[0] may contain one format, audioMimeTypes[1] another, and so forth. The array is device dependent, and the order in which the formats are returned is not predictable. If the array is empty, the device supports no known audio formats. Check out FL2_devicesound_capabilities.swf in the /Sound directory of the chapter to run a quick capabilities check on your target Flash Lite 2 device. This returns the audioMimeTypes array containing all the sound formats that the device recognizes and understands.

One additional feature of the Sound object is that it can pull MP3 tag data. We will discuss this is in more detail in the next section, since we will use it in our custom MP3 player.

Working with ID3 tags

In the custom MP3 player we will build, we'll display ID3 tags corresponding to what's stored in the MP3s. ID3 tags refer to the metadata information stored within the MP3 itself and include such property strings as title and album name, as well as other information, such as the year of release, track number, and length of the song. Other custom tags are allowed as well, as long as they are defined in the MP3 and in the application. ID3 tags are specific to Flash Lite 2, since in Flash Lite 1.1, you do not have access to the Sound object.

The ID3 properties in Table 8-2 are accessible if they are set within the loaded MP3 file. Not all MP3 files have these properties though. There are multiple versions of the ID3 tag information (1.0, 1.1, 2.3, and 2.4, respectively). They differ slightly in implementation. Since Flash Lite 2 is based on the Flash 7 player, the Flash Lite 2.X ID3 properties are also supported.

For the purposes of the example in this chapter, I have used MP3 tagging software (iTunes) to assign the values shown in Figure 8-12 for use in the upcoming MP3 player example. Many software packages exist that allow you to easily modify the ID3 tags of MP3s. This metadata can be used for display purposes or even for functional purposes inside your sound application.

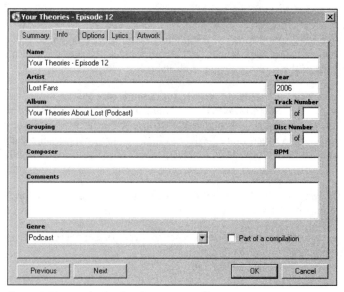

Figure 8-12. Sample ID3 data from an MP3 file

Table 8-2 lists some of the ID3 tags available that Flash Lite 2 content can handle. These are the same ID3 tags used by the Flash desktop player and many other MP3 players. Of course, in Flash, these are read-only values.

Table 8-2. ID3 tags available for use with Flash Lite 2

ID3 2.X tag	Information contained
TFLT	File type
TIME	Time
TIT1	Content group description
TIT2	Title, song name, or content description
TIT3	Subtitle or description refinement
TKEY	Initial key

ID3 2.X tag	Information contained
TLAN	Languages
TLEN	Length
TMED	Media type
TOAL	Original album, movie, or show title
TOFN	Original file name
TOLY	Original lyricists or text writers
TOPE	Original artists or performers
TORY	Original release year
TOWN	File owner or licensee
TPE1	Lead performers or soloists
TPE2	Band, orchestra, or accompanist
TPE3	Conductor or performer refinement
TPE4	Interpreted, remixed, or otherwise modified by
TPOS	Part of a set
TPUB	Publisher
TRCK	Track number or position in set
TRDA	Recording dates
TRSN	Internet radio station name
TRSO	Internet radio station owner
TSIZ	Size
TSRC	International standard recording code (ISRC)
TSSE	Software or hardware and settings used for encoding
TYER	Year
WXXX	URL link frame

Flash Lite 2 also supports ID3 2.X (specifically, 2.3 and 2.4) tags that are backward compatible with previous versions of ID3 (1.0 and 1.1). If an MP3 does not contain ID3 2.X information but does contain 1.X metadata, it is copied into the corresponding ID3 2.X properties. This ID3 tag mapping is listed in Table 8-3.

Table 8-3. ID3 2.X tags populated from an ID3 1.X–formatted MP3 file

ID3 2.X tag	ID3 1.X tag
COMM	Sound.id3.comment
TALB	Sound.id3.album
TCON	Sound.id3.genre
TIT2	Sound.id3.songname
TPE1	Sound.id3.artist
TRCK	Sound.id3.track
TYER	Sound.id3.year

To grab these properties from a loaded MP3, simply make a call to the properties of the loaded sound instance. For example, to get the file type of an MP3, use the syntax mysound_id.TFLT. Of course, the value must be set for this to work, and MP3 files are not required to have these values set.

The onID3() callback event for Sound objects is an event we will take advantage of with our MP3 player. By intercepting the onID3() call, we can trap the event and display the ID3 tag information as soon it is available with the sample_snd sound instance. In the /Sound/FL2_devicesound_id3.fla example provided in the downloads for this chapter (and shown in Figure 8-13), we have the code to pull the ID3 tag info; look at the code for frame 1 for an example of this:

```
//-- traces out all the id3 tags present for the specified MP3 file, and
//-- displays a few id3 tags on screen
sample_snd.onID3 = function(){
  //-- loop through and print out all the id tags that have been
  //-- encoded for the .mp3
  for ( var p in sample_snd.id3 ) {
    trace( p + " : "+ sample_snd.id3[ p ] );
  }

  //-- just display a few of the ID3 parameters in the MP3
  id3info_txt.text =  sample_snd.id3.track + ". Album: " +➥
    sample_snd.id3.album + "\n";
  id3info_txt.text += "Artist: " + sample_snd.id3.artist + "\n";
  id3info_txt.text += "Year: " + sample_snd.id3.year + "\n";
}
```

```
//-- load up the MP3
sample_snd.loadSound( "sample.mp3", false );
//-- load up the .mp3
```

In the preceding snippet, we are simply loading an MP3 and tracing its ID3 properties as soon as it has loaded and that data becomes available to the player. We also output the track number, album name, artist, and year within the text field in the application. Later, when we build the custom MP3 player, we'll use this same method to output the ID3 tags for three different loaded MP3 files. We'll get into that in a bit.

Figure 8-13. Retrieving ID3 parameters from a sound loaded in Flash Lite 2

Sound object functionality

Before we head into our first full-fledged Flash Lite 2 sound application, I want to inspect the nooks and crannies of the Sound object. Up until now, we have covered the essential methods of loading and playing audio in the Flash Lite 2. Let's now turn our attention to the other properties and methods of the object. Some of the functionality that I discuss will be useful in the next section, where I cover building a custom MP3 player in Flash Lite 2.

As you have seen, the Sound object in Flash Lite 2 is quite a welcome addition to working with Flash Lite sound, exposing a lot more functionality and features. But there's more! The Flash Lite 2 Sound object also has the following methods available for use:

- getVolume()
- setVolume()
- getPan()
- setPan()
- setTransform()
- getTransform()
- getBytesTotal()
- getBytesLoaded()
- start()
- stop()

Let's examine some of these methods in greater detail.

getVolume() This method returns the volume level for a native sound. It does not return the volume level if the sound is device audio. The return value is from 0 to 100, indicating the range between no sound (equivalent to mute) and the maximum sound level; this value is a percentage of the imported sound level.

```
//-- control the getVolume
var sample_snd:Sound = new Sound( _root );
sample_snd.attachSound( nativesound_id );
if ( sample_snd.getVolume() ) { //-- return the sound level value
  trace( "no sound!" );
}
```

setVolume() We can use the setVolume() command to adjust the sound level for native sounds in Flash Lite 2. The method takes in a number parameter in the range of 0 to 100; the number specifies the audio percentage level (0 means no sound):

```
//-- control sound level via setVolume()
var sample_snd:Sound = new Sound( _root );
sample_snd.attachSound( nativesound_id );
sample_snd.setVolume( 100 ); //-- set sound level to the maximum
```

getPan() Pan refers to the amount of sound level that winds up in the left and right channels. –100 means all sound is played back in the left channel; 0 means equal amounts of sound is played in both the right and left channels, and 100 indicates that all sound is played in the right channel.

The getPan() method returns the current pan setting, 0 by default. This feature is used for native sounds only and is not applicable to device sounds:

```
//-- What is the pan set to?
var sample_snd:Sound = new Sound( _root );
sample_snd.attachSound( nativesound_id );
trace( "Pan is currently set to " + sample_snd.getPan() );
```

setPan() Opposite to the getPan() command is setPan(). This allows you to set the amount of sound that is played in both the left and right speaker channels; again, this is for native sounds only, not device audio.

```
//-- Set the Pan to the left side only.
var sample_snd:Sound = new Sound( _root );
sample_snd.attachSound( nativesound_id );
//-- set the pan all the way to the left channel (no sound in
//-- the right channel)
sample_snd.setPan( -100 );
```

setTransform() **Sound transform** refers to the balance information that is maintained for each (native) Sound object. This is a more-sophisticated method than panning the sound.

By passing an object (the SoundTransformObject) into this function, you can more accurately set where a sound is played, in terms of the speakers available on a target device. Most devices support a mono configuration, but some devices support a stereo configuration. By passing a custom sound transform object, you can specify at what percentage of the sound's volume capacity and in what channel you want playback to occur.

The sound transform object contains these properties:

- ll: Percentage value specifying how much of the left input to play in the left speaker (0–100)
- lr: Percentage value specifying how much of the right input to play in the left speaker (0–100)
- rr: Percentage value specifying how much of the right input to play in the right speaker (0–100)
- rl: Percentage value specifying how much of the left input to play in the right speaker (0–100)

The net result of the parameters is represented by the following formula:

```
leftOutput = left_input ~ ll + right_input ~ lr
rightOutput = right_input ~ rr + left_input ~ rl
```

The values for `left_input` or `right_input` are determined by the type of sound (stereo or mono) in your SWF file. Stereo sounds divide the sound input evenly between the left and right speakers and have the following transform settings by default:

- `ll = 100`
- `lr = 0`
- `rr = 100`
- `rl = 0`

Mono sounds play all sound input in the left speaker and have the following transform settings by default:

- `ll = 100`
- `lr = 100`
- `rr = 0`
- `rl = 0`

The following example uses the transform on a Sound object in Flash Lite 2:

```
//-- example plays the left channel at half capacity and
//-- adds the rest of the left channel to the right channel
var sample_snd:Sound = new Sound( _root );
sample_snd.attachSound( nativesound_id );
var sampleTransformObjectHalf_obj:Object = new Object();
with (sampleTransformObjectHalf_obj) {
   ll = 50;
   lr = 0;
   rr = 100;
   rl = 50;
}

//-- var sampleTransformObjectHalf_obj:Object =
//--{ ll:50, lr:0, rr:100, rl:50 };
sample_snd.setTransform(sampleTransformObjectHalf_obj );
```

For more information about the transform capabilities, please consult the Flash Lite 2 documentation. Again, I will not cover a real example of transforming audio, because no target device supports it at the time of this writing.

getTransform() This method returns setTransformObject, as it has been set via the setTransform() method:

```
//-- get the transform info set from the previous example
var transforminfo_obj:Object =➡
  sample_snd.getTransform(sampleTransformObjectHalf_obj );
```

getBytesTotal() When loading a sound, you can use this method to get the total number of sound file bytes loaded into the player. When used in conjunction with a MovieLoaded loader and a sound, you can build basic preloading functionality.

```
//-- how many bytes total make up the loaded sound?
var totalbytes_num:Number = sample_snd.getBytesLoaded();
trace( "Total bytes loaded for the sound = " + totalbytes_num );
```

getBytesLoaded() Returns the number of bytes loaded for a sound that is currently loading. When used in conjunction with a MovieLoaded loader and a sound, you can build a basic preloader type functionality:

```
//-- how many bytes have been loaded for a sound?
var bytesloaded_num:Number = sample_snd.getBytesLoaded();
trace( "Bytes loaded this far for the sound = " + bytesloaded_num );
```

start() This method starts playing a loaded or attach sound. The first parameter refers to the number of seconds to offset the start in playing, and the second parameter instructs the Flash Player how many times to loop the sound.

```
//-- stop a sound from playing
var sample_snd:Sound = new Sound( _root );
sample_snd.attachSound( samplesound_id );
sample_snd.start( 2, 1 );
//-- start playing from 2 seconds into the sound clip and loop once
```

stop() This method either stops all sounds or stops the sound instance specified in the function's parameter:

```
//-- stop a sound from playing
var sample_snd:Sound = new Sound( _root );
sample_snd.attachSound( samplesound_id );
sample_snd.stop(); //-- on  later frame in the time line
//-- You can also specify the linkage id name: stop( "sample_snd" );
```

The Sound object in Flash Lite 2 also contains these specific properties:

- position
- duration

position The position property refers to the total milliseconds elapsed since a sound started playing. If a sound is looped via the start() method, the position value resets to 0. This is only good for native sounds, not for device audio.

```
//-- position refers to where the sound is at during playback
var sample_snd:Sound = new Sound( _root );
sample_snd.attachSound( samplesound_id );
sample_snd.start( 0, 1 );
this.onEnterFrame = function() {
  if ( _root.sample_snd.position > _root.sample_snd.duration/2 ) {
    trace( "We are half way through ..." );
  }
}
```

duration This property refers to the total duration of a sound (in milliseconds). The sound must be native and not a device sound for this to work.

```
//-- display the total length of a sound in milliseconds
var sample_snd:Sound = new Sound( _root );
sample_snd.attachSound( samplesound_id );
trace( "total length of second in milliseconds is " + sample_snd.duration );
```

The Sound object also exposes the onSoundComplete() event.

onSoundComplete() This event is called back when a loaded or attached sound finishes playing in its entirety. You can add custom code to this event to provide a replay action. It works for both native and device audio.

```
//-- replay an audio clip after it has finished playing
//-- through ("anonymous" function)
var sample_snd:Sound = new Sound( _root );
sample_snd.attachSound( samplesound_id );
sample_snd.start();
sample_snd.onSoundComplete = function() {
  _root.gotoAndPlay( "We finished playing the sound!" );
}

//-- replay an audio clip after it has finished playing
//-- through (named function)
var sample_snd:Sound = new Sound( _root );
sample_snd.attachSound( samplesound_id );
sample_snd.start();
sample_snd.onSoundComplete = weAreDonePlaying;
function weAreDonePlaying():Void {
  _root.gotoAndPlay( "We finished playing the sound!" );
}
```

Now that I have covered a lot of the Sound object, we'll move on to the MP3 player I have been talking about. The MP3 player requires a significant amount of ActionScript knowledge. If you haven't covered a lot of the basics, I recommend you revisit Chapter 6 and the ActionScript primer found starting in Chapter 3.

Creating a custom MP3 player with Flash Lite 2

Now we're going to step through creating an MP3 player using Flash Lite 2. It'll be cool, and you should have enough experience at this point with Flash Lite sound to tackle it. This example is a bit more involved than the sound samples you have seen thus far. To keep things as streamlined as possible, we are only going to focus on the ActionScript; the user interface is prebuilt for you to save you time.

After we step through this example, I encourage you to take what you have learned and apply it to extending the custom MP3 player that you build. Our MP3 player loads a few externally located MP3 files and plays them back within the player. It uses a lot of the sound features we have been talking about thus far including ID3 tag information, controlling sound playback, and MP3 audio MimeType detection.

Open `FL2_mp3player.fla` from the /Sound directory for this chapter. You'll notice that it's much less than 100KB. Wow! Yes, it's true. The player is that small, since all of the MP3s are separated from the application using externally loaded files. Virtually all of the ActionScript for this example is located one frame 1; the code is in a central place for your convenience. I know all this ActionScript looks a bit daunting at first, but this example will give you more practice with ActionScript 2 in Flash Lite 2. If you're ever stuck, or need some guidance, refer to the previous chapters on ActionScript in this book.

The MP3 player

With `FL2_mp3player.fla` open, locate the code on the ActionScript layer on the first frame of the main time line. The first thing you should notice is that the code imports the Tween class, which allows you to programmatically move objects rather than utilizing the Flash time line. We're going to use the Tween class later to move the navigation to give it a more of a fluid appearance. This makes for a user experience that's bit more interesting. We'll need to add the following code on the first frame:

```
//-- we'll be using the tween class to move the songtitle
//-- menu during navigation
import mx.transitions.Tween;
import mx.transitions.easing.Strong.easeInOut;
```

Next, we want our screen to go full-screen mode and disable _focusrect, as we have done many times previously in Flash Lite content. This is accomplished through the following statements:

```
//-- this ActionScript sets your content to be full screen
fscommand2( "FullScreen", true );
//-- turn off the focusrect (we will use our own selection method)
_focusrect = false;
```

We have quite a few configuration variables to define and for use later in the MP3 player. I won't talk about each one specifically, as they are documented within the code. However, notice that the MP3s we are playing are called electroplanktonA, electroplanktonB, and electroplanktonC.

We've hard coded these values. Though nothing stops you from putting these into an XML file to be read dynamically at runtime, for sake of simplicity, I have used static values for this example:

```
var mp3s_arr:Array = new Array( "electroplanktonA.mp3",➥
  "electroplanktonB.mp3", "electroplanktonC.mp3",➥
  "electroplanktonD.mp3" );
//-- for the purposes of this example, we are just hard coding the
//-- .mp3 values
var currentmp3index_num:Number = 0;
.
.
.
```

Next, we're going to create the ActionScript 2 objects, which we will use to control the sound in the MP3 player. clip_snd is the main Sound object; we will use it to load and control the MP3s. Our keyListener object will intercept the stop and play commands in our player:

```
//-- first, we are going to need a Sound object to play back our MP3s
var clip_snd:Sound = new Sound();

//-- we need to define our Key Listener for all our actions
var keyListener_obj:Object = new Object();

//-- used to tween the navigation
var tween_obj:Tween;
```

In the next code snippet, notice that the keys we just created have the ability to press Enter to play the currently selected MP3 or LEFT and RIGHT to move among our selection of MP3s. The controls for this exercise are very simple for demonstration purposes. However, you can see how relatively easy it would be to add more controls to this user interface to perform other functionality:

```
//-- listen for our events for this player
keyListener_obj.onKeyDown = function():Void {
  switch ( Key.getCode() ) {
    case Key.ENTER:
    if ( !cannotplay_bool) {
      //-- if user hits enter key, play the currently selected .mp3
      playmp3( currentmp3index_num );
    }
    break;
    case Key.LEFT:
      //-- move to left
      moveNav( "prev" );
      break;
    case Key.RIGHT:
      //-- move to right
      moveNav( "next" );
    break;
    default:
      //-- take care of other device keys pressed
    break;
  }
}
//-- listener for device keys
Key.addListener( keyListener_obj );
```

Our application wouldn't be complete without some custom functions to actually play the selected MP3 or navigate between our MP3 files. playmp3() is a function that loads a selected MP3 or toggles the playback of the currently loaded MP3:

```
//-- play the current mp3 selected in the menu
function playmp3( index_num:Number ):Void {
  currentlyloaded_str = mp3s_arr[ index_num ];
  if ( currentlyloaded_str != "" && currentlyloaded_str➡
    != undefined ) {
    if ( currentlyloaded_str != lastplayedfilename_str ) {
      id3info_mc.id3info_txt.text = "";
```

```
      //-- load up the file
      clip_snd.loadSound( currentlyloaded_str );
    } else {
      //-- just flip the state of the playback
      togglePlayBack();
    }
  }
}
```

togglePlayBack() very simply acts as a switch to toggle the player between its on and off states. If the onoff Boolean parameter is undefined, it flips the switch; otherwise, it sets the current state of the player to the value of the onoff parameter:

```
    //-- start playing back the clip
    function togglePlayBack( onoff_bool:Boolean ):Void {
      if ( onoff_bool == undefined ) {
        playpause_bool = !playpause_bool;
      } else {
        playpause_bool = onoff_bool;
      }
      ( playpause_bool ) ? clip_snd.start( 0, 0 ) : clip_snd.stop();

      _root.status_mc._visible = true;
      status_mc.gotoAndPlay( ( playpause_bool ) ? "playing": "stopped" );

      clearInterval( _global.TIMERID );
      if ( playpause_bool ) {
        _global.TIMERID = setInterval( function() { _root.➡
        status_mc._visible = false; clearInterval(_global.TIMERID ); },➡
        3000 );
      }
    }
```

moveNav() provides the navigation we need to select the MP3s; there is quite a bit of logic in this next code snippet. Essentially, when the application receives a LEFT or RIGHT keypress, it performs a tween on the songtitles_mc clip, sliding it to the left or right. Some time line animation easing is also applied to the slide to make the user interface a little more distinctive. This function allows you to select between the MP3s (there is some conditional logic to keep the selections between the valid start and end index ranges). Also note that after the tween completes and a new audio is selected, the player automatically loads the new MP3 using the playmp3() function we discussed previously.

```
    //-- navigate within the songtitles moveclip
    function moveNav( direction_str:String ):Void {
      togglePlayBack( false );

      if ( !moving_bool ) {
        if ( ( direction_str.toLowerCase() == "prev" )
        && ( currentmp3index_num > 0 ) ) {
          currentmp3index_num--;
          moveit_bool = true;
```

```
        //-- set x coordinate for song title
        xcoord1_num = lastxcoord_num;
        xcoord2_num = padding_num + lastxcoord_num;
    } else if ( ( direction_str.toLowerCase() == "next" )
    && ( currentmp3index_num < mp3s_arr.length-1 ) ) {
        currentmp3index_num++;
        moveit_bool = true;

        //-- set x coordinate for song title
        xcoord1_num = lastxcoord_num;
        xcoord2_num = lastxcoord_num - padding_num;
    }

    if (  moveit_bool ) {
        //-- set reset flags
         moving_bool = true;
         moveit_bool = false;

        tween_obj = new Tween( songtitles_mc,➥
         "_x", mx.transitions.easing.➥
        Strong.easeIn, Math.round( xcoord1_num ), Math.round( ➥
        xcoord2_num ), speedfps_num, false );
        tween_obj.onMotionFinished = function() {
        playmp3( currentmp3index_num );
          _root.lastxcoord_num = _root.songtitles_mc._x;
          _root.moving_bool = false;
        }
      }
    }
}
```

The next snippet provides the few core events that are part of this sample. These are all the methods we have discussed previously in this chapter including onLoad(), onSoundComplete(), and onID3(). The onLoad() event either makes a call to start playing the currently selected audio clip or bails out with an error message:

```
//-- event called when an .mp3 sound clip is loaded
clip_snd.onLoad = function( success_bool:Boolean ):Void {
  lastplayedfilename_str = currentlyloaded_str;
  if ( success_bool ) {
    cannotplay_bool = false;
    //-- start playing the example
    togglePlayBack( true );
  } else {
    cannotplay_bool = true;
    cannotplay_bool = true;
    id3info_mc.id3info_txt.text = "An error occurred playing➥
      the file: " + currentlyloaded_str + "!";
    trace( "An error occurred playing the .mp3!" );
  }
}
```

The onSoundComplete() event actually reinitializes the playback method once it's complete. It acts as a looping feature for the currently selected MP3:

```
//-- replay once a current .mp3 finishes playing
clip_snd.onSoundComplete = function():Void {
  //-- replay the sound clip?
  playmp3( currentmp3index_num );
}
```

The onID3() method event populates the text fields on the screen with some ID3 tag information that has been set in the audio files used (to view the ID3 properties, you can use a file explorer on your PC or Mac to explore them):

```
//-- take care of displaying the ID3 info
clip_snd.onID3 = function():Void {
  id3info_mc.id3info_txt.text = "";
  currentsongname_str = clip_snd.id3.songname;
  setSongName( currentmp3index_num );

  //-- now set id3 area with (artist, album, track, year, etc)
  id3info_mc.id3info_txt.text += "track: " + clip_snd.id3.track + "\n";
  id3info_mc.id3info_txt.text += "song: \"" +➥
    clip_snd.id3.songname + "\"\n";
  id3info_mc.id3info_txt.text += "artist: " +➥
    clip_snd.id3.artist + "\n";
  id3info_mc.id3info_txt.text += "album: " + clip_snd.id3.album + "\n";
  id3info_mc.id3info_txt.text += "year: " + clip_snd.id3.year + "\n";
}
```

The last pieces to the puzzle I want to talk about are the simulated equalizer, setting the song title, and detecting device capabilities for MP3 playback. I touched on the onEnterFrame() event earlier in this book. We use it here to assign random values to the equalizer movie clip. The equalizer doesn't really work, mind you. We are using it here to merely simulate the effect and as an indicator that playback is occurring. When the MP3 stops playing, the equalizer stops animating; otherwise, it randomly generates itself as an MP3 plays. Again, it should be noted the equalizer is not real; it's only simulated here for effect.

```
this.onEnterFrame = function():Void {
  if ( moveequalizer_bool ) {
    if ( _root.equalizer_mc._x < -240 ||➥
      _root.equalizer_mc._x >= 180 ) {
      flipit_bool = !flipit_bool;
    }
  }
.
.
.
```

We also have a function to set the current song name to whatever the currently played MP3 is; this occurs as soon as an MP3 clip is loaded:

```
//-- set the name of our song so it's displayed
function setSongName( index_num:Number ):Void {
  with ( songtitles_mc[ "songtitle" + index_num + "_txt" ] ) {
    text = currentsongname_str;
    textColor = 0xefef00;
  }
}
```

Lastly, we have some logic to detect whether the target device is capable of playing device audio MP3s. If it is, it starts playback at the initial MP3; otherwise, it throws an error.

```
//-- detect for .mp3 capabilities for our example
if ( !System.capabilities.hasMP3 ) {
  //-- can't play MP3s, no player for decoding
  id3info_mc.id3info_txt.text =➡
  "Sorry, we don't appear to be able to play MP3s➡
    on this target device!";
  cannotplay_bool = true;
} else {
  for ( var i:Number = 1; i <= 10; i++ ) {
    with ( _root.equalizer_mc[ "level" + i + "_mc" ] ) {
      _rotation = 180;
    }
  }

  //-- we can play MP3s, so allow user to select an mp3 to play
  playmp3( 0 );
}
```

That's it for the code necessary to drive the MP3 player. Figure 8-14 depicts the MP3 player in action. I encourage you to explore the other assets in the movie to get an idea of how the user interface is set up. You can find the final player and code in /Sound/FL2_mp3player.fla. Look at frame 1 of the ActionScript layer for the complete code listing for the MP3 player. It may seem like a lot to take in, but when it is broken down, the player itself is very straightforward. I recommend that you study each area and do some experimentation with the code. Extend the player, or create your own! Don't be shy about changing around the way it works. Remember, it's your very own MP3 player now.

Figure 8-14. The Flash Lite 2 custom MP3 player

As you can see, the Sound object is a powerful feature in Flash Lite 2. It's quite impressive that you can create a simple Flash Lite–based MP3 player in well under 1,000 lines of code! I'm sure you would agree that sound is a very powerful tool to use in Flash Lite indeed. The Sound object makes working with audio on mobile devices incredibly easy when compared to doing so for other available technologies. With the introduction of the sound features in Flash Lite 2, I see a clear indication that much of the desktop Flash player functionality is slowly creeping into mobile devices, and I can't wait for what comes next!

Now that you've completed the MP3 player, I'd like to move on to a few more advanced topics specific to dealing with sound in Flash Lite 2.

Synchronizing device sounds with animation

Flash Lite treats Flash device audio as event-based only, so you may be wondering if Flash Lite 2 can approximate a synchronized streaming effect with device audio. Well, yes, it can. This new feature was added in the latest player. The _forceframerate property instructs the Flash Lite Player 2 to drop frames as needed to keep up with the frame rate of the movie as it is played on a mobile device:

```
//-- force frame rate so that the current time line animations sync up
//-- to the audo being played
_forceframerate = true;
```

This newly added property is useful, for example, if you need to keep an animation synchronized with loaded sound (see Figure 8-15). Prior to Flash Lite 2, this feature was not available. When using this new property, as long as the sound's duration is the same length as your animation clip's, you should be good to go. However, you need to test on the actual device to see how well the content plays when using a particular device sound clip to make sure the CPU can keep up and limit the amount of frames dropped!

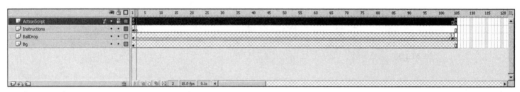

Figure 8-15. Sound synchronization on the Flash time line

Syncing device sound with time line animation

I have a sample for you (see Figure 8-16). We'll walk through setting up an animation to sync to the frame rate of the movie by using the _forceframerate property. Open FL2_forceframerate.fla, and look at frame 1.

```
fscommand2( "FullScreen", true );

//-- We have an .mp3 that is 7 seconds long. In order to sync it, we
//-- have to  have 105 frames because our frame rate is 15 fps. 15 * 7
//-- = 105 frames total.

//-- set the forceframerate property so our animation keeps in sync
//-- with our time line animation
_forceframerate = true;

var ballisDropping_bool:Boolean = false;
```

Figure 8-16. The syncing sound and animation example

```
var keyListener_obj:Object = new Object();
Key.addListener( keyListener_obj );

function ballDrop():Void {
  trace( "ballDrop()" );

  //-- start the ball falling
  falling_snd.start( 0, 0 );

  //-- start playing our animation
  play();
}

//-- load in our device sound
var falling_snd:Sound = new Sound();
falling_snd.loadSound( "falling.mp3" );

falling_snd.onLoad = function():Void {
  trace( "Ball ready to fall ..." );

  //-- ok, to show instructions now
  instructions_mc._alpha = 100;

  //-- if user hits any hit then drop the ball
  keyListener_obj.onKeyDown = function() {
    if ( !ballisDropping_bool ) {
      _root.ballDrop();
    }
  }
}

stop();
```

Notice that, on our time line, we have a simple animation that we want to sync to some audio. We first set the _forcefraterate property to true:

```
//-- set the forceframerate property so our animation➥
//-- keeps in sync with our time line animation
_forceframerate = true;
```

Next, we wait for a keypress from the user before beginning to drop the ball:

```
//-- if user hits any hit then drop the ball
keyListener_obj.onKeyDown = function() {
  if ( !ballisDropping_bool ) {
    _root.ballDrop();
  }
}
```

Once the key is pressed, the ball-drop animation starts playing on the main time line. At the same, we are also playing the main time line animation of the ball dropping into the background:

```
function ballDrop():Void {
  trace( "ballDrop()" );

  //-- start the ball falling
  falling_snd.start( 0, 0 );

  //-- start playing our animation
  play();
}
```

If all goes well, you should see the ball dropping from an overhead view into oblivion, as shown in Figure 8-17. As it drops, the sound should sync to the animation on the time line. This simple example demonstrates the power of this new feature, which designers and animators alike should take advantage of.

Media Playback API

One of the less well-known sample content pieces in the Flash Lite 2 CDK is the Media Playback API. I've held off on mentioning this until now, so that you have a better understanding of how to work with Flash Lite 1.1 and Flash Lite 2 sound before considering this example API. The Media Playback API provides some prebuilt sample assets that you can quickly integrate into your existing Flash Lite 2 applications, including sample class files and content. The Media Playback API is part of the Flash Lite 2 CDK install. It should be found in the following directories:

Figure 8-17. The sound syncing example on a mobile device

- **Windows**:

  ```
  \Program Files\Macromedia\Flash 8➥
  \Samples and Tutorials\Samples\Flash Lite 2.0\MediaPlaybackAPI
  ```

- **Mac**:

  ```
  \Applications\Macromedia Flash 8➥
  \Samples and Tutorials\Samples\Flash Lite 2.0\MediaPlaybackAPI
  ```

The API consists of a simple SoundPlayer class, and ImageViewer, VideoViewer, and MimeType checker classes. Figure 8-18 depicts the sample file provided with the FlashLite 2 CDK. I recommend that you investigate the SoundPlayer and MimeType checker classes further to see if these are appropriate to leverage in your future Flash Lite applications. If you are looking for a quick way to integrate simple sound detection and primitive playback control, this sample API might offer a good starting point for you.

Flash Lite sound considerations

In this section, I want to present you with some considerations for dealing with sound within your Flash Lite content. Unfortunately, device limitations can sometimes impede what you are trying to do. It is not completely uncommon to encounter memory errors or sound-quality issues when developing a mobile application for the first time. Preventing these boils down to being somewhat conservative with respect to audio usage. For instance, having a 10MB MP3 file play on a resource-constrained mobile device, such as a handset, is most likely going to be problematic. This is not necessarily a reflection on Flash Lite itself but on the hardware and platform the content is running on and the current state of affairs with portable devices. Always remember that you're dealing with constrained devices in terms of both memory and CPU!

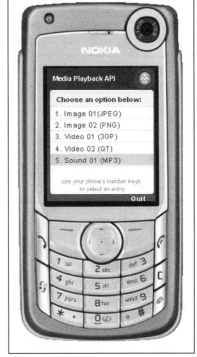

Figure 8-18. The Media Playback API sample

I'd like to focus on a few topics:

- File size, memory, and CPU limitations
- Sound quality
- Using 3GP audio

File size, memory, and CPU limitations

When you are dealing with large sound files in Flash Lite 2, such as large MP3 files, errors may occasionally occur. Typically, these are in the form of Bad sound format or Out of memory errors (refer to Appendix A for more information). The sizes of MP3 and other audio file formats is definitely a challenge when you are developing your Flash Lite applications. You may also experience a Stream not loading error or Bad sound data error when dealing with sound with Flash Lite. Often these errors refer to either file size or encoding problems. Always remember to double-check your sound files. Verify that the sound is in the correct target format, one that the device supports. Also, be conscientious about how large your audio files are. Decompressing large sound files can be both memory and CPU intensive!

Also note that, with device audio play, Flash Lite relies on the device hardware for sound playback. This means that device memory is consumed during playback. Therefore, not only is memory required for the actual file but some memory is also required when the sound is decompressed. I recommend keeping the file size for the MP3 files under 1 or 2MB (where possible). This is sometimes device specific, so you need to do some testing on your target device(s) to determine an acceptable limit. As a general rule of thumb, it's always a good idea to try to optimize sound as well as possible before using it or importing it into your Flash Lite application.

In addition to file size, a considerable amount of CPU usage is sometimes incurred while sound is being played. It is important not to go overboard with complex sounds, especially in mobile games where game play may be affected by a CPU taxed by excessive use of sound. Keep things simple, and avoid the temptation to add too many unnecessary sound effects or too much background music. Using device sound instead of native sound can also put less strain on the CPU (if the target device supports device sound).

Sound quality

Whether you use native or device sound in your application depends on what you are trying to accomplish. In general, device audio sounds better than native audio, because the target device handles the playback of the sound. This is not to say that device sound is inherently better to use, however. The target player is handed the audio file for playback, so there is some overhead in regards to memory usage and performance, as we have discussed previously. Needless to say, with sound capabilities in Flash Lite, you will spend some time figuring out the middle ground between using native and device audio in your content. It's better to sacrifice a bit of sound quality if performance or memory becomes an issue for your mobile game or application.

Using 3GP audio

A trick to higher-quality Flash Lite sound that consumes fewer resources is to use 3GP-encoded audio files. This is one possible way to avoid the memory and sound quality issues I mentioned previously. If a target device supports 3GP video, it should also support 3GP audio playback. By using this format, you can sometimes avoid some of the memory restrictions to using native and device sound. This is not to say that you should always use 3GP files—the effectiveness of 3GP depends on your target device capabilities as well as the particular sound files you are using. I mention it here merely as a useful tip in certain circumstances, such as when the target sound files are problematic and the device supports 3GP format.

Summary

This chapter covered many of the essentials of Flash Lite sound. I started things off with a discussion on the differences between native and device sound. I also outlined some of the most common mobile device sound formats you may encounter. From there, we quickly moved into the various methods of sound playback in Flash Lite 1.1 and spent some time discussing sound as it applies to Flash Lite 2, which included how to detect supported sound formats using the system capabilities object as well as working with the Flash Lite 2 Sound object. In the final sections, we walked through an example of a very basic MP3 player using Flash Lite 2 and briefly touched on both synchronized device sounds and the Media Playback API. Finally, I offered some advice on how to best use Flash Lite sound when dealing with the limitations found on portable devices today.

Despite the current limitations (because of hardware and platform constraints), sound is still a crucial element to many Flash Lite games, applications, user interfaces, and the like. It's always important to take sound into consideration when planning your next Flash Lite project. A more-successful mobile application or game can be created by thoughtful and effective use of sounds. Sound can make it or break it! Plan your content wisely, and use sound as sparingly as possible and where it makes the most logical sense.

It is also a good idea to test content as frequently as possible on physical devices throughout the development process. Although the mobile emulator can save precious development and testing time, it is important to always test and tweak your sound based on the *actual* user experiences gathered from the target devices you are working with.

Where to next? It's only natural to take one step forward. In the next chapter, I'll cover another exciting topic for mobile devices—video. To be more specific, I'll be talking about device video supported on certain Flash Lite 2–enabled devices.

Chapter 9

FLASH MOBILE VIDEO

If Flash has a "killer app" (i.e., an application that really stands out from the competition), Flash video is most likely it. Flash video is an amazing achievement that makes it possible to create more-engaging and more-interactive user experiences for the Web.

From its humble beginnings in Flash 6 to the more recent versions in Flash 8 and 9, video capability has come quite a long way. Today, Flash video has a tremendous impact on how video content on the Web is being designed, developed, and deployed. Whether it is progressive or streaming, Flash video is changing the way people interact with new media content on their desktops.

What about mobile devices? Yes, there too we are starting to see Flash video handsets, PDAs, PMPs, and other devices leveraging the power of Flash Mobile video. From Pocket PC Flash to Flash Lite 2, creating video content specifically designed for portable devices is now easier than ever. This book would just not be complete without discussing Flash Mobile video. In the coming years, it has the potential to revolutionize the mobile user experience, just as it has on the desktop!

In this chapter, we'll tackle the intricacies of Flash video on devices. First, I'll cover some tricks to playing video content within the Flash Lite 1.1 player. Next, I'll explain the most recent device video capabilities as well as the most commonly used features in Flash Lite 2. We'll also explore the differences between desktop and mobile device video and some of the innate limitations of video on portable devices today. Toward the end of this chapter, we'll walk through a basic Flash Lite 2–enabled video player. Finally, I'll wrap up with some thoughts on Flash Lite 2 device video.

299

This chapter is not intended to act as an introduction to video. The discussions from now on will assume you have at least a rudimentary understanding of how video works. In this chapter, I will concentrate on Flash Mobile video, and in particular, Flash Lite 2 device video. If you are seeking a more-general reference on the basics of video with Flash, I recommend reading Foundation Flash Video 8 *by Tom Green and Jordan Chilcott (Berkeley: friends of ED, 2006).*

Fundamentals of Flash Mobile video

Second to only sound, video is one of most-compelling examples of next-generation content for mobile devices today. Not only can you find stunning video capabilities on handsets but also across numerous portable media players, PDAs, and other such devices. For all intents and purposes, mobile video has arrived.

Device manufacturers are incorporating video capabilities into their products as we speak. Already, many content providers also deliver both on-demand and streaming video services to customers, including music and TV. In fact, video is rapidly gaining popularity within mobile entertainment communities around the world. In all likelihood, this trend will continue as bandwidth becomes more readily available across regions, new portable video devices come to market, and people learn to adopt this new medium in their mobile lives and daily routines.

There is no denying that video has a great deal of potential in the mobile landscape, but we are only beginning to see the implications of video across portable devices such as handsets. It is not a question of how but of at what point video will become mainstream. When will mobile video become a global phenomenon? All indicators point to sooner rather than later!

How does Flash tie into video on mobile devices? In this chapter, I'll answer that question. We'll take a look at how video has evolved on Flash-enabled mobile devices. As we have discussed previously, video is one the core strengths of Flash. Now that Flash Lite is beginning to introduce more video capabilities, we are just starting to reap the benefits on handsets. As Flash Lite and other versions of mobile Flash continue to evolve, grow, and mature, we are likely to see more video content leveraged across Flash-enabled devices.

Needless to say, I am quite excited about the future of Flash Mobile video and all the possibilities! But let's first turn our attention to the very humble beginnings of Flash video on mobile devices. Let's talk about video on Pocket PC Flash–enabled devices, a not-so-distant relative to today's Flash Lite device video.

Flash video on Pocket PC

Macromedia (now Adobe) began exploring the possibilities of Flash video on devices during the evolution of Pocket PC–based Flash as recently as version 6. Pocket PC Flash video was, and still is, being used to deliver video across PDAs. Everything from guided video tours to games, e-learning tools, and much more has found its way onto Flash-enabled Pocket PC–based PDAs.

However, for the intents and purposes of this book, I am going to concentrate much more heavily on Flash Lite device video than Pocket PC Flash video for one reason—it has the potential of becoming a mainstream mobile video format. This is evidenced by the sheer number of mobile handsets and consumer electronic devices that people own and use today.

That is not to say that Pocket PC–based Flash has gone away. On the contrary, at the time of this writing, Adobe has released the Pocket PC 7 SDK, which brings Pocket PC Flash up to par with Flash 7 functionality. Having said that, I think it is worth at least outlining Pocket PC Flash video before heading into Flash Lite device video. I'll concentrate on Pocket PC 6 Flash video in the next section, but these methods of playback can also be achieved with Flash 7 video on Pocket PC.

Pocket PC Flash 6 embedded video

The Pocket PC Flash 6–based player supports ActionScript 1.0 and much of the functionality of the desktop Flash 6 player. There are limitations, however. You should consult the Flash Pocket PC 6 IDK and CDK available from Adobe for more information on designing and developing for this platform.

With regard to video, Pocket PC 6 supports embedded Flash MX video on the time line (see Figure 9-1). However, this is not to say that you should import and embed significantly large video clips into your Pocket PC–based video applications! You should try to keep things simple and as small as possible when dealing with embedded video on Flash-enabled PDAs.

Video playback occurs through the Pocket Internet Explorer (PIE) or stand-alone Flash executable. Embedding large video clips often leads to a poor user experience because of performance limitations (in CPU and memory) found on most PDAs. Your mileage may vary depending on the target device and content. You should take this into consideration when attempting to work with embedded Flash video under Pocket PC Flash 6 and above.

One of the potential benefits of using this method is that the resulting SWF contains the embedded video content. If you are deploying and only want one file (containing both the SWF and embedded video) to exist, you might want to explore this avenue. Just remember the performance issues associated with using this method. Besides embedded video, there is a second method of dealing with video, which we'll discuss in the next section.

Figure 9-1. A Flash Pocket PC time line containing embedded video

Pocket PC Flash 6 external video

A far more-efficient solution to dealing with video under Pocket PC Flash is to save video clips as Microsoft Windows Media files (WMV) and let the Microsoft Windows Media Player deal with the actual video content outside of the Flash Player. This alleviates the undue stress that can be imposed by using video content that is not optimized or is unruly (excessively large clips), which requires significant amounts of CPU and memory.

Almost all PDA devices running the Microsoft Pocket PC 2002 OS or later will have the Windows Media Player preinstalled, so you can be virtually certain that the end users will have a more user-friendly experience than if you embed the video on the time line. The external player will take care of video natively, rather than depending on the Flash Player. The possible limitations that the Flash Player might impose on the video content are thus avoided altogether.

I have included an example using external video in the content folder found at \Video\ PPC6FlashVideo.fla in this chapter's downloads. Take peek at the application shown in Figure 9-2. First, notice that everything is in ActionScript 1.0. This is Pocket PC Flash based on Flash Player 6, so it's prototype-based ActionScript.

To play back a video, you need to use utilize the getURL() command, as shown in the following code snippet. This syntax uses an absolute file path to grab the video file for playback. The following code is attached to the Play button, called video_btn, found on the main stage; select the Play button, and open the ActionScript panel to view the code:

```
//-- remember, this is PocketPC Flash 6 so it's ActionScript 1.0 syntax
on ( press) {
  //-- absolute file path
  getURL( "file://My
Documents/PPCFlash6Video/video1.wmv" );
}

//-- second method uses a relative path
//-- to the video clip (must reside
//-- in the same directory as the .swf!)
on ( press) {
  //-- absolute file path
  getURL( "video1.wmv" );
}
```

When the button is pressed and the getURL() command is run, the WMV file is opened by the default Windows Media Player found on Pocket PC–enabled PDAs. The actual playback occurs outside of the Flash Player inside the Windows Media Player, which has more available resources to deal with the video clip.

Figure 9-2. A sample Pocket PC Flash 6 video application using an external getURL() call

External vs. embedded video in Pocket PC Flash

You have just seen two examples of how to deal with Flash video when working under Pocket PC Flash 6. There are pros and cons for each approach. In summary, some of the benefits of using the external getURL() method for video are as follows:

- The playback is smoother, because the Pocket PC Flash application leaves dealing with the video to the external media player.

- There can be one SWF for the user interface. You can externalize multiple video content clips, so you can swap out video without recompiling the entire SWF.

- There is no need to import and tweak video files for optimized playback, since an external player is leveraged.

- You can make changes to the user interface of the SWF player without interfering with the video content. This approach is even recommended by Adobe when circumstances arise where video playback performance is an issue. Testing with actual content will reveal whether you should take one approach over the other.

Let's continue our exploration with some of the mobile video formats you may encounter in the world of portable devices. I have already covered one, the Windows Media video format. Let's look at some more in the next section.

Mobile video formats

Up to this point, we have only been working with WMV files with Windows-based Pocket PC Flash. However, there are quite a number of mobile video formats available today. We'll discuss a few of them in this section. For the forthcoming examples dealing with Flash Lite content, I'll mostly stick with 3GP-encoded videos clips. However, MP4 is also becoming a popular video format for mobile devices. Some of the popular and commonly found mobile video formats follow:

- 3GP and 3GP2 (or 3GPP2)
- MPEG-4 (MP4)
- MOV
- AVI
- WMV

Support for each of these video formats varies from device to device. For the purposes of this section, I will mostly cover 3GP, which is supported on a lot of Flash Lite 2–enabled handsets. MP4, or MPEG-4, is perhaps the second most commonly found format on mobile devices. This is turning into the new standard because of significant advances in both device hardware and graphical capabilities. I anticipate MP4 becoming the new standard after 3GP. 3GP is a multimedia container format defined by 3GPP for use on 3G mobile phones; it is a simplified version of MPEG-4 (MP4).

3GP files typically have the file name extension .3gp. 3GP stores video streams as MPEG-4 or H.263 and audio streams as AMR-NB or AAC-LC format. 3GP also describes image sizes and bandwidth, so content is correctly sized for mobile display screens. 3GP files are viewable on a PC using QuickTime, MPlayer, VLC media player, Real Player, or other third-party applications.

For the sake of simplicity, I'll use exclusively the 3GP format for the Flash Lite 2 video examples presented in this chapter. This is the more-common format, though MP4 may be substituted if your target device supports that device video format.

Converting desktop video to mobile video

Mobile video content is quite different from desktop content. When dealing with Flash Mobile video, you almost always need tools to help you in the process of converting video from desktop to mobile format. This may sound a tad obvious, but it's an important point to make.

It is highly unlikely that you will be able to transfer a desktop video file onto a mobile device and expect it to work right off the bat. Compatible video format is one issue, and file size is another. What video formats does a device support? How big can video files be before the device, essentially, chokes because of memory constraints?

Naturally a conversion process is needed, and for that, you need software. Some of the tools available and used today follow:

- Apple QuickTime Pro (Version 7 and above)
- Nokia Multimedia Converter (2.0 and above)
- ImTOO 3GP Video Converter
- Total Video Converter
- Xilisoft 3GP Converter

These software tools enable you to take a desktop-encoded video file and convert it into a video file destined for device delivery. Often, the software includes options to optimize your video, edit it, and selectively export it to multiple format features. The software packages listed previously all support 3GP export. As we have discussed, this is the standard for mobile video on most portable devices. The software usually includes a step-by-step process to export (see Figure 9-3 for an example). In some instances, this process can even be automated.

The end result of running any one of these applications is a video file that is one step closer to running on a mobile device. Of course, some tweaking may be involved, but this will mainly be determined by how large the clip is and how much your target device can actually handle (without encountering CPU and memory restrictions).

Sometimes, it is necessary to make changes to the actual content before export. In this case, you need to make edits to the video. With regard to video-editing software, Adobe Premiere and Adobe After Effects are two products that allow you to do significantly more than just straight video conversion. They are

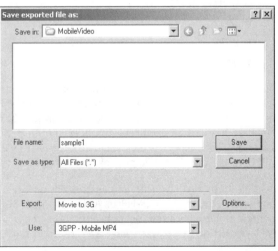

Figure 9-3. Exporting a video file to the 3GP video format

full-blown video editing packages that allow you to edit your video content before conversion. This includes using features such as time line changes (cutting, copying, pasting, and so on), adding effects and transitions, optimizing, and so on.

Some handsets actually come preinstalled with video editor software as well! Nokia, for example, has just started shipping models that have preloaded video-editing software. Others may soon follow.

For now, editing your video content on a device is only for the most primitive of tasks. Desktop software is recommended and often gives you the powerful features needed to make your video content a success when deployed across mobile devices.

Flash Lite video

There is little doubt that Flash Lite device video has to be one of the stunning achievements to be included in the release of Flash Lite 2. Prior to Flash Lite 2, the only way to do video on Flash Lite 1.1–enabled devices was to resort to using a series of sequential JPG images or launching an external video player. Prior to 1.1, there was no real way of providing video at all, only simulated animations in Flash Lite 1.0.

Before we jump into the Flash Lite 2 video that is the meat and potatoes of this chapter, it is important that you grasp what is possible in Flash Lite 1.1, because Flash Lite 1.1 is still prevalent and is preinstalled on a good deal of devices on the market today. As more Flash Lite 2–capable devices appear, however, the video features in Flash Lite 2 will be a viable option for designers and developers looking to take advantage of device video.

Flash Lite 1.1 simulated video

By using embedded video, the most you can hope for is a simulation of video, or "fake video," as I refer to it here. An example of this method follows. If you open /Video/FL_simulate_video.fla in the Chapter 9 downloads, you can see a simple example of this method of animating video in Flash Lite 1.1. Figure 9-4 shows the final output of the SWF.

Figure 9-4. Simulated video in Flash Lite 1.1

As you can see on the time line (see Figure 9-5), the video is just a series of JPG images strung together. This is why it's called "simulated video"! It's not the most ideal way of doing video, to say the least. But when dealing with Flash Lite 1.1 content, this is one option, despite its shortcomings.

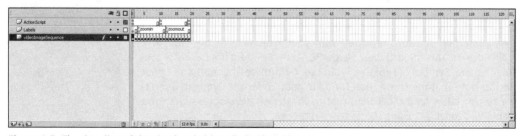

Figure 9-5. The time line of the simulated video clip in Flash Lite 1.1

305

There are numerous disadvantages to using this method, including performance, quality, and overall size. However, it also represents the only method of video in Flash Lite 1.1 that provides a substitute for video content directly inside of the Flash Lite Player; outside of the player is another matter. Let's talk about another method of launching video in a Flash Lite 1.1 application, by way of the FSCommand Launch and getURL() commands.

Flash Lite 1.1 launched video

The method we discussed previously has a lot of limitations. Most notably, these limitations are in video quality and performance. The second method for video playback in Flash Lite 1.1 is via the getURL() command. By making a local, or external, HTTP call to a video file, video playback is possible through an external video player.

When intercepting a getURL() command, the Flash Lite Player attempts to invoke an external video player on the device to play the specified video. During this process, it's important to note that the external device video application takes precedence over the Flash Lite application. The Flash Lite content suspends play until the video player in the foreground is closed, usually when the user closes the default video player that has been invoked by the getURL() command.

Some conditions must also hold true for video playback using this method. First, the device must support the device video format specified, and secondly, the device must have an external video player loaded (such as Real Player). Yet, a third condition is that the device must be smart enough to associate the video file name and extension with the default device video player. If all these conditions are met, then the getURL() command is a viable option for video playback under Flash Lite 1.1. Now that you understand how the whole process works for Flash Lite 1.1, let's take a look at some examples.

Local video with Flash Lite 1.1

The following examples (shown in Figure 9-6) demonstrate how to load video using a getURL() command. The first method uses a local file. This means that the video file must reside on the device itself and not somewhere external, like a web server. In the example I provide, the video file must also be located in the same directory as the SWF that calls it:

```
//-- local video playback from the same directory as the .swf
getURL( "sample1.3gp" );
```

If the location of the local file differs from the SWF, say it's on an external memory card, you must specify an absolute path to the video file:

```
//-- using an absolute path to load a local video
getURL( "file://C:/Videos/sample1.3gp" );
```

The hardest part is figuring out that path. To determine the path, use the synchronization software provided with your handheld. In the case of a Nokia device, this is exclusively Nokia PC Suite. By navigating using a tool such as the Symbian FExplorer, you can determine the paths on your device. Note that the convention for a file path under the Symbian operating system takes on a familiar format to most web developers—that of a web-based local URL using the file:// directive.

Figure 9-6. Flash Lite 1.1 video via local getURL()

In this example, we are targeting the sample1 video that is located in the C: drive of the device under the Videos folder. If you open \Video\FL11_getURL_local.fla in the Chapter 9 downloads and view the attached ActionScript for the key catcher button on the stage, you'll see the code for this example.

Try out the relative or local path first, but be aware that when running the example inside the inbox, certain security measures may apply. Playback of video using the relative path and getURL() is not guaranteed. The absolute path should work in every case, so long as the path is correct, the video file is valid, and there is an internal video player to use on the device.

Launching video via FSCommand

It is also possible to launch video via the FSCommand Launch command, but only if the device supports it (the video file format is mapped to the device video player). You need to check the documentation of your target device to verify if this possible. On some devices, you can run the following launch command to load your default device video player (the following example is depicted in Figure 9-7):

```
//-- run this test to find what path launches your media player (Use
//-- FExplorer to determine this)
fscommand( "Launch", "Z:\\system\\apps\\MediaPlayer\\➥
MediaPlayer.app" );
```

By specifying your video file in the second parameter, you can invoke its playback, assuming both the player and video exist, and your target video player has the following specified path:

```
//-- launch the device video player with a file specified (your path
//-- and application may vary!)
fscommand( "Launch", "Z:\\System\\Apps\\MediaPlayer\\➥
MediaPlayer.app,E:\\Videos\\sample1.3gp" );
```

This example expects the video to be located under the E: partition of your target device in the Videos folder. It also requires that you have the mobile Real Player installed under the Symbian OS in its default location. Your setup may vary. Some tweaking on your part may be needed, as this is a very device- and OS-specific way of launching video.

Figure 9-7. Flash Lite 1.1 video via the FSCommand Launch

If you open the file \Videos\FL11_fscommand_launch.fla located in the Chapter 9 downloads, you'll notice the code is attached to the key catcher button on the stage. You should first use the code to determine the path to launch your external player. Once you have completed that, you should proceed to launching the video with a file as a parameter. By proceeding in a stepwise manner by first locating the player and then specifying the file to play, you can minimize syntax and path errors you may introduce. Launching video this way is not very forgiving. One typographical or syntax error likely means it won't work!

External video (HTTP) with Flash Lite 1.1

Much like the local video we talked about previously, external video loading (shown in Figure 9-8) involves fetching a file from an external server. In most cases, the protocol used to download the video file is HTTP. The device makes an external HTTP call to download the file and passes it to the getURL() command. Next, getURL() passes the video to the external video player, which in turn, downloads the video and plays it back using its own interface. The line of code that invokes the playback is simply

```
//-- external HTTP video playback
getURL( "http://www.flashmobilebook.com/video/sample1.3gp" );
```

If you open \Videos\FL11_getURL_http.fla in the Chapter 9 downloads, you'll notice the ActionScript on the key catcher button on the stage.

Remember that you are dealing with the getURL() command, so you are limited to having only one instance of the command in the foreground at any given time. There must also be a network connection present, so that the video can be downloaded. Another consideration is that there must not be any file permissions or other security measures in place (such as a firewall). Yet another caveat to this approach is that an external video player is not always present on devices, and thus the getURL() command may not be able to pass off the video file for playback.

Figure 9-8. Flash Lite 1.1 video via HTTP and getURL()

Given all of these considerations, the getURL() approach is only recommended if you know the devices you are targeting for deployment and can afford to have this feature fail if the device is unable to handle the external video playback; otherwise, you should avoid its use.

Limitations of video in Flash Lite 1.1

As you have seen thus far, the methods of delivering video to Flash Lite 1.1–enabled devices are quite lacking, and we have already resorted to some tricks in prior sections. Unfortunately, since true internal video was not part of the original Flash Lite 1.1 specification, there is no prebuilt way to check to see if your target device supports video playback.

While it is possible to check for certain sound capabilities (e.g., _capMFi, _capMIDI, _capSMAF, or _capStreamSound), this is not the case for video at all! There is also no way to easily check if a file exists before playback, and there is no way to check for any errors that might occur. It's a one-shot deal—either the video will play back or it won't. Either the video will throw an error, or it will play back flawlessly. This is a fact of life with Flash Lite 1.1 video, as it was never meant as a core feature.

What does all this mean? It is important for you, the developer, to plan your application very carefully with regard to video playback with Flash Lite 1.1. Know your target devices and the video capabilities of those devices before you even suggest it as a feature of an application.

Let's now turn our attention to the powerful video capabilities found in Flash Lite 2. This is arguably one the best and most-useful rich media features found in the second version of Flash Lite. Video capabilities in Flash Lite 1.1 pale in comparison to what is available in Flash Lite 2 with the device video support added.

Flash Lite 2 device video

With the advent of Flash Lite 2, we have seen the first introduction to real video capabilities for Flash Lite content. For all intents and purposes, Flash Lite 2 is capable of the following four methods of video playback:

- Bundled device video (embedded video)
- Local file device video (file)
- External device video (HTTP)
- Streaming video (Real Time Streaming Protocol, or RTSP)

There are pros and cons to each of these three types of playback, and we will discuss each in some depth.

If you are wondering whether Flash Lite 2 can record video through the use of the digital recorder, this is not something inherently supported at this time. Flash Lite 2 device video is playback only. There is no support for recording video directly on devices (although this would be quite a cool and useful feature!).

What is device video?

Device video refers to the video formats or encodings that are natively supported by the target device that Flash Lite 2 is installed on. With Flash Lite 2, these are most commonly 3GP and MP4, both of which I have covered earlier in this chapter. Device video differs from its Flash desktop counterpart in that it is not the Flash video that the Flash 6 (or above) Player is capable of. There is no native FLV (Flash video file format) playback; there are no cue points that can be set; there are no Sorenson and on2 codecs; and streaming video via Flash Media Server is not supported at this time.

You may ask yourself, "Why?" Well, there are many reasons, but perhaps the most important is player size. By not embedding the desktop video player, space is conserved. The size of the player is an important consideration. Other considerations include memory and CPU usage. With the current state of devices and capabilities, it only made sense to go the route of device video for Flash Lite 2. Flash Lite device video provides a streamlined and realistic approach to delivering video across mobile devices.

How does it work? When the Flash Lite 2 player encounters a video for playback, it invokes the native video player on the device, which in turn, loads the designated video content for playback. It is much like the external video playback in Flash Lite 1.1 that we talked about earlier.

The video is played within the confines of Flash Lite content in a predefined video window at the specified height and width defined in the content. Device video provides seamless intercommunication between the video playback and Flash Lite 2. This allows you to communicate with the video content as if it were native video content.

The Flash Lite 2 device Video object

Although very similar to the desktop Flash Video object present in Flash 6 and above, there are a few key distinctions that pertain to the mobile Flash Lite 2 Video object. From the ActionScript 2.0 primer in this book, or your working knowledge of Flash, you should be familiar with how objects, movie clips, and movie clip instances work. I recommend you review that section if you have not already read

309

it. If you are skipping ahead to this section, visit that area in order to better understand the inner workings of the device Video object. For the remainder of this chapter, I'll be covering the Video object in Flash Lite 2 in quite some depth, which requires a good deal of knowledge about properties and methods.

How does device video differ from desktop video? I'll cover that next. Later, we'll take what you've learned thus far and apply it to building the custom video player I mentioned at the beginning of this chapter. Let's get into some of the supported features and limitations of Flash Lite 2.

Supported video features

The video found in Flash Lite 2 closely resembles that found in the desktop Flash 7 Player. Because of this, a lot of the properties, methods, and supported features are much the same. We'll discuss all of this functionality shortly. However, I'd first like to reference some of the specific video functionality that is supported in Flash Lite 2.

When dealing with device video in Flash Lite 2, keep the following information in mind:

- Video playback always occurs above any other content in the Flash Lite application.
- Flash Lite 2 supports embedded (or bundled), local, and streamed video (with restrictions we will discuss).
- Playback controls consist of play(), stop(), pause(), resume(), and close().
- The screen size, more specifically, the height and width, can be set.
- Scaling is possible.
- Motion tweening is allowed.
- Only one video may be played at a time.

These are some of the core features that you should be aware of when developing video applications under Flash Lite 2. A lot of this will come into play when you start to implement the custom video player later in this chapter.

Let's now turn our attention from the supported features to those that are unsupported in Flash Lite 2 video. No, Flash Lite 2 video is not perfect. There are some drawbacks to video on mobile devices that you also need to be aware of.

Unsupported video features

As I have previously stated, this implementation of video has been custom tailored to fit the restrictions and limitations of most mobile device profiles. It is different than both the Flash Pocket PC and desktop Flash Player video, and there are limitations to consider. Many of these are attributed to the CPU and memory restrictions imposed by most devices today.

For instance, some of the unsupported features in Flash device video under Flash Lite 2 follow:

- **Volume control**: There is no code-based volume control for video.
- **Rotation**: You cannot use set _rotation for video content.
- **Masking**: You cannot set masks on video.
- **Alpha**: No alpha values are allowed on video clips; they are all 100 percent alpha.

- **Setting cue points**: Cue points for video are not supported.
- **Checking available bandwidth**: You cannot check available bandwidth before video playback.

These are just some of the restrictions when dealing with Flash Lite 2 content video. However, as you will see, outside of these slight differences, the video capabilities are very similar to those found with Flash video on the desktop.

Much of the Video object from Flash 7 has found its way into the implementation of Video found in Flash Lite 2. Ready to explore the Flash Lite 2 Video object? OK—let's get to it.

Video object

Besides the few unsupported features we have spoken about thus far, the Video object works very much like its desktop counterpart. In this section, we'll explore some of the video API found in Flash Lite 2. We'll also discuss many of the core methods and properties that are available for use within your video-enabled Flash Lite 2 applications. It should be no big surprise, since Flash Lite 2 is based on Flash 7 and ActionScript 2.0, that a Video object now exists for developers to take advantage of. It allows for basic control of video content in Flash Lite 2 content.

As we move through the API in this section, I'll point out the basic elements you need to know to help create the custom video player we'll be assembling later in this chapter. Let's start off by exploring some of the prebuilt functions that are part of the Flash Lite 2 Video object. We'll dissect each one; later, we'll use these to build some very basic video applications.

With Flash Lite 2, the Video object's available methods are Video.play(), Video.stop(), Video.pause(), Video.resume(), and Video.close(). The Video.onStatus() method is also supported to some degree, as we'll discuss shortly. Let's look at each of these methods.

Video.play() Calling this method opens a video source and begins playback of a video. This method can also take in a relative, absolute, or URL path to an external video, for example:

```
//-- relative file playback
sample_vid.play( "sample.3gp" );
//-- from a folder
sample_vid.play( "videos/sample.3gp" );
//-- from an absolute filepath  (device must support file:// protocol)
sample_vid.play( "file://c:/videos/sample.3gp" );
//-- external URL (device must support it!)
sample_vid.play( "http://www.sample.com /sample.3gp" );
```

The return value for the play() method is true or false, depending on whether the target device supports video playback.

Video.stop() This method stops playback of the video and clears the video that is onscreen. Playback occurs at the beginning of clip when a play event is next received.

Video.pause() This method stops playback of the video and continues to render the current frame on the screen; the current frame is the one that is present at the time the pause() event is received.

Video.resume() Yes, you guessed it—calling this method resumes playback of the video.

As you can see, these methods—play(), stop(), pause(), and resume()—are self-explanatory. They act much like the controls on your DVD player.

> *In some special cases, other functionality, such as* pan, slow, *and* forward, *is possible through an undocumented* Video.seek() *command. These are not part of the original Flash Lite 2 specification and are custom to device manufacturers who choose to add these commands. See the undocumented commands section for more information.*

Video.close() The only notable exceptions to the typical video commands is existence of the close() method. When executed, this stops playback of the video, frees the memory associated with current Video object, and clears the onscreen video area.

onStatus() event You may be asking yourself how you go about catching errors thrown during playback or obtaining status information, such as when a video has completed playing. This is done through the onStatus() event. During playback, events, or messages, are fired within the Flash Lite Player to indicate that overall progress of a video clip during its existence. onStatus() is a callback handler that can be invoked by the device to indicate status or error conditions during playback.

It is important to note that these status and error conditions are device specific. A code or error description on one target device might be totally different on another. It's in your best interests to do significant testing on the actual target devices when using this event to trap errors and status codes to make sure your code acts as it is intended.

Here's the syntax of onStatus() callback event:

```
onStatus = function(infoObject:Object) { /* code to handle errors➥
    and status information */ }
```

The following example shows how to create a Video.onStatus() function that displays a status or error condition and how to handle it:

```
sample_vid.onStatus = function( o:Object ) {
  if ( o.level ) {
    trace( "Video Status Msg (" + o.level + "): " + o.code );
  } else {
    trace( "Video Status Error: " + o.code );
  }
}
```

The object passed into the onStatus() function contains two properties: a code property, which consists of the error or status condition string, and a level property, which is a number code. For example, if level is 0, an error has occurred. Nonzero values mean the status has returned successfully. These return values are highly device dependent, so unfortunately, I can't provide a lookup table for your benefit.

What good is the onStatus() event? We'll utilize the onStatus() event as part of the custom video player example later in this chapter to automatically loop a sound file. You'll have a better idea of how it can be used effectively in your video applications there.

Unavailable methods

There are some key points to note in device video regarding what is available through the Video object. If you are coming from a Flash video background, you may want to take a peek at the limitations, as they may aid you in the development of Flash device video applications.

Learning these limitations can also alleviate some serious head scratching when it comes to trying to figure out why certain desktop Flash video functionality is not working in Flash Lite 2!

The following methods are not currently supported within the Flash Lite 2 Video object:

- `Video.attachVideo()`
- `Video.clear()`
- `Video.deblocking`
- `Video.height`
- `Video.smoothing`
- `Video.width`
- `Video._visible`

We will not discuss these methods in any detail, since they are not supported. You should not be concerned about them when developing a Flash Lite 2 video application, except to note that they do not exist and should never be used.

Undocumented methods

Under certain implementations of Flash Lite 2, there are two additional methods available for use. However, you need to explicitly consult your particular target device manufacturer to see if these are, indeed, supported. These methods are

- `Video.mute()`
- `Video.seek( seconds )`

`seek()` allows you to create very simple fast-forward and rewind capabilities for video playback.

The `mute()` function toggles the sound on and off during video playback.

Again, these are not officially supported, so you'll have to do some discovery to see if your target devices actually support this unique set of functionality.

System.capabilities for video

In Flash Lite 1.1, there was no native method of determining if a device supports various video formats. Of course, this has changed with the release of Flash Lite 2 and its video capabilities. Video detection is now accessible through the `System.capabilities` object.

Since I have already covered the basics of the `System.capabilities` object in our ActionScript 2 primer, refer to Chapter 4 for details on its overall syntax and usage.

313

There are also several methods now available for use in for video. Some of the properties available for verification follow:

- System.capabilities.hasEmbeddedVideo
- System.capabilities.videoMIMETypes
- System.capabilities.hasStreamingVideo
- System.capabilities.hasVideoEncoder

I will briefly explain these properties as they apply to Flash Lite 2 device video.

.hasEmbeddedVideo This indicates library support for device video. It always returns true in Flash Lite 2, unless the Flash Lite 2 Player implementation specifically disallows video playback (this would be rare on new devices, however!).

.videoMIMETypes The System.capabilities.videoMIMETypes array contains all the possible video types that the target device supports. If the array is undefined, no device video types are available, and video playback cannot occur for the target device. Otherwise, all the entries in the array are valid video content types for device video playback.

To look up and verify that a particular video format exists, you specify it as a parameter in the array, such as in the following piece of ActionScript code:

```
if (System.capabilities.videoMIMETypes["video/3gpp"]) {
  sample_vid.play("sample1.3gp");
}
```

This simple example checks whether or not the Flash Lite 2 device supports 3GP video playback. You can then use this return value to determine whether or not to play a particular video file format for the targeted Flash Lite 2 device. The videoMIMETypes array is the recommended method of checking whether a device supports video.

.hasStreamingVideo This property cannot be used to determine whether a target device supports streaming video, as it refers to FLV videos. Flash video files are not supported under Flash Lite 2. It is only valid for Flash 7 on the desktop. It always returns false for Flash Lite 2 content, at the time of this writing.

.hasVideoEncoder System.capabilities.hasVideoEncoder always returns false. Unfortunately, there is no video encoding in Flash Lite 2 at this time.

That's it for parameters dealing with video contained in the System. capabilities object. I have included a video capabilities example in this chapter's downloads: \Video\FL2_video_capabilities.fla. This simple script reports to you what specific video capabilities your target device supports, as shown in Figure 9-9.

Be sure to run this to verify that your target device supports the 3GP video MIME type before proceeding! Otherwise, the examples I show next may not work as expected (however, feel free to tweak the code to allow for MP4 or another supported video format if need be).

Figure 9-9. Flash Lite 2 device video capabilites test (running from the desktop)

Bundled device video

The most convenient way of incorporating video clips into your latest Flash Lite creation is by bundling the video. Bundling device video is a similar concept to embedding video in desktop Flash. However, the bundling differs in that no actual time line frames are used to store the content. The video is just attached along with the Flash Lite application SWF as an internal object. Before we can even begin working with video content, you need to understand how to get that content into the Flash IDE environment; you need to know the steps for importing video files for bundled video. Let's begin by importing a simple video.

Importing a video file

The first step to working with device video is to import the video content into the Flash authoring environment. How does one do this? It's very straightforward, and the process is almost identical to the one used in importing videos in desktop Flash.

The first method is by right-clicking the library panel and selecting New Video. You are prompted to specify a file to import. This is the very first step. Flash asks for you to enter some properties, as depicted in Figure 9-10, which include the symbol name for the video.

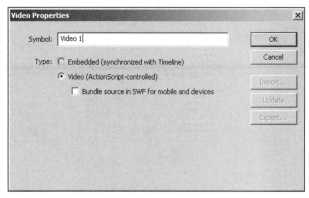

Figure 9-10. Importing a video in Flash Lite 2

Also note that this dialog has a check box labeled Bundle source in SWF for mobile and devices. When checked, this deploys your Flash Lite application with your video content in one convenient package (the SWF file)—hence, the term "bundled video." The video content is bundled inside the compiled SWF file. You'll notice a significant increase in the resulting SWF file size because of this bundling procedure. Go ahead and check the Bundle source in SWF for mobile and devices check box.

Now, the Export for ActionScript check box should be available, as shown in Figure 9-11. When checked, this option allows you to target the video playback and control it via play(), stop(), and other such commands. If you don't check it, your imported video is essentially inaccessible from ActionScript. It is usually a good idea to check this check box and assign a unique linkage identifier for later use.

The Import button is used to locate the video file and process it. When you select the Import button, you are prompted to locate your video content. Typically, this is a 3GP or MP4 file. You can select one of the test video files found in the \Video\ directory. Once the video content has been imported, you are good to go.

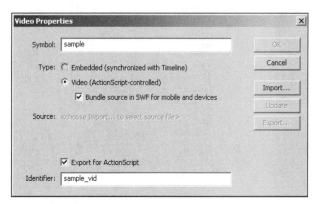

Figure 9-11. The Flash Lite 2 Video Properties dialog box

315

The next option is the Update button that appears after you have successfully imported a valid video file. During development, you may want to change or update the video without reimporting it. This allows you a quick way to do just that. The Export button allows you to export the currently selected video file once it has been imported.

An alternative method for importing video

You have seen the "right-click library" method of importing video into your application. However, there is a second way of importing video, using the Import Video wizard. Although the methods are essentially the same, this second one is a little more user friendly. Both methods provide the required functionality to import your video content. There are two steps to the import process using this method. To begin the process, go to File ➤ Import ➤ Import Video. Next, select the video to use, as shown in Figure 9-12.

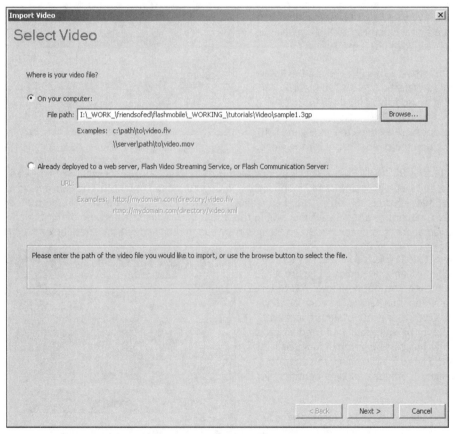

Figure 9-12. The Flash Lite 2 Import Video wizard Select Video dialog

Next, you are presented with the second step of importing video, shown in Figure 9-13. Here, the only deployment choice is the As mobile device video bundled in SWF radio button. Click the Finish button to complete the import process.

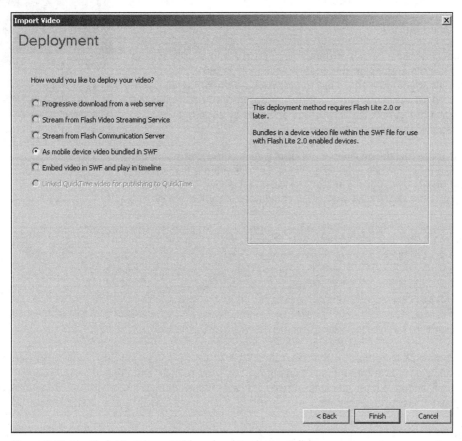

Figure 9-13. The Flash Lite 2 Import Video wizard Deployment dialog

After these steps are completed, you will have the video in your library. Right-clicking the video library item gets you into the Properties menu, so you can set properties as you did in the previous import. Now that you have seen both methods of importing video, you can proceed to the next step—actually working with the imported video.

Working with local device video

Congratulations! Now you have imported a video, and it is your library. You are one step closer to working with the video content in Flash Lite 2. Next, you need to use the video within some Flash Lite content. Right now, it resides in the library but not on the Flash stage. Not to worry, it's just a matter of placing it there. Drag it and drop it from the library to the stage.

You should now have a video representation of the object on stage (a box with crosshairs), as depicted in Figure 9-14. As with desktop Flash video, this is normal behavior. On the main Flash time line, there should now be a frame occupied by the onscreen device Video object. Typically, you'll place the video in its own separate layer on the time line as a best practice.

You should notice a couple of things. First, Flash automatically assigns default size dimensions on the imported video clip; 160×120 pixels is the default. If you want the video to play back on the full screen, you need to adjust the width and height properties in the Video Properties box, shown in Figure 9-15. This can be accessed by clicking the Stage video clip and selecting Properties.

Figure 9-14. A Flash Lite 2 Video object on screen

Second, the actual device video is not displayed, just the crosshair indicator. This is normal behavior, so don't worry. Your video is loaded and waiting to go. This is just a friendly feature that allows you to work alongside other content on your stage; think of it as a guide mode.

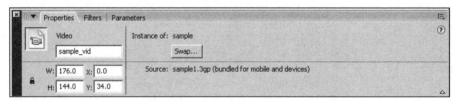

Figure 9-15. Flash Lite 2 video properties

An important point to make is that creating a Flash Video object dynamically using ActionScript and then loading a video at runtime is not an option. You must have at least created a Video object in your Flash library and have it on your stage. Creating a new instance of a Video object through ActionScript 2 is not valid in Flash Lite 2 content.

Testing and deploying the video

Now that you have the video on stage, the only remaining piece left to play the video clip is to add the ActionScript. By default, Flash does not automatically play device video. You need to tell it to do so explicitly by issuing a play() command as follows:

```
//-- start the video playback!
sample_vid.play();
```

If you add this command to frame 1 and recompile the FLA, you should now see the video play immediately after being published. The video plays back within the Mobile emulator. If video playback does not occur, there are two likely culprits.

One possibility is that you do not have the QuickTime plug-in installed on your development machine. This is a requirement. The Flash authoring environment depends on the existence of the QuickTime plug-in for Flash device video rendering within the Mobile emulator. Check to see if QuickTime is installed if you are not seeing the video play back.

Also, check to make sure the instance name of the video clip matches the one used in your ActionScript. In this case, the instance name sample_vid found under the video instance should match the ActionScript video object name used to initiate playback: sample_vid.

After troubleshooting, if all is well, you should be seeing Flash Lite 2 device video running within the Mobile emulator. Now for the fun part!

Deploying it to your Flash Lite 2–enabled, video-capable phone is the next step. Transfer the resulting SWF to the handset and run it. It's absolutely crucial that your device supports the device video format that was imported. To verify that it does, you need to consult the documentation that came with the device or run the System.capabilities application that I spoke of earlier. Either of these will tell you whether your device truly does support video. If your target device supports video, you should now be enjoying some video on your Flash Lite 2–enabled device.

If you are having trouble, there is a completed example of the bundled video method of delivering Flash Lite 2 video. Open the \Video\FL2_device_local.fla file in the Chapter 9 downloads if you had trouble getting the sample video to play. Attached to the key catcher button on the stage, you'll see the play() command initiated on an Enter key-press event. Take a peek at the final SWF to see where you went wrong.

When you think about it, it's pretty amazing that video is even possible on such low-processor and memory-deficient devices! This is quite a feat, to say the least. Flash Lite 2 has opened the possibilities to some great video-based content on mobile devices.

The "Error preparing video" dialog

Errors are, unfortunately, a fact of life in both hardware and software. This is also true in mobile applications, so Flash Lite device video is no exception to that rule. In fact, if you work long enough with Flash device video, sooner or later, you will receive an error message. But don't be too alarmed. There is usually good reason to get this dialog. The three most common reasons follow:

- Insufficient memory
- Video format errors
- Video player errors (outside of the Flash Lite Player)

Insufficient memory If the Flash Lite Player is unable to comply with a request to play back because of a significantly large video file or if the external player causes an error, a dialog showing an Error preparing video message is displayed.

The actual error may vary slightly, as error strings and codes vary between devices. It is important to remember that a good deal of both CPU and memory are required during video playback. You should take this into consideration when working with your video content. Keep an eye on the amount of memory and the size of the video content clips that are used.

There is no official limit to the size or amount of memory that I can state here. The optimal settings for video content are highly device specific and require a good amount of testing and tweaking on your part to determine. The best way to get these specific numbers is to use regression techniques on your content to find the best size-versus-quality tradeoffs for your video content.

Video format or video player errors The first thing to do, if you receive these errors, is to make sure that your video is in the correct format for the device. You should also check it within the default video player on the device to verify it does, in fact, play correctly.

Video player errors are perhaps the most difficult to track down. Since Flash Lite 2 does not specifically handle video playback, it relies on the device for this. If the device encounters any errors during video playback, the dialog appears.

Unfortunately, as with other Flash Lite 2 errors, there is no way of catching these errors and dealing with them in an elegant manner. Hopefully, this will be resolved in future versions of Flash Lite. For now, you must pay close attention to video content size.

As a rule, always keep your Flash Lite 2 videos as small and as optimized as possible to avoid memory issues.

Bundling multiple device videos

Up until this point, we have only been dealing with bundling one video. However, Flash Lite 2 actually allows multiple videos to be bundled together. This is useful if you are deploying several videos and just want to use a single Video object for playback. The syntax for playing back video in this case is by using the symbol keyword as a locator:

```
videoplaceholder.play( "symbol://video1_vid" );
```

This will load in the Video asset from the library with the instance name assigned, video1_vid, and play it back with the videoplaceholder object on the stage. For instance, if you had a second clip in the Flash library named video2_vid, you could target that clip using the linkage identifier name: video2_vid.

In many respects, bundling multiple device videos acts as a kind of library or repository if you have multiple video clips. By using the symbol:// command and associated linkage ID, you are able to pull multiple clips in from the library for playback.

One limitation to bundling multiple device video files into one SWF is size. The more bundled files you add, the bigger the SWF will be. File size limitations are based primarily on your target device. Generally speaking, your bundled SWF should not exceed 1MB. However, your mileage may vary. To be safe, the smaller you can get your video clips, the better off you will be. Otherwise, you may receive an Error preparing video message.

Both video optimization (trying to optimize before importing) and being realistic about how much video your application and target devices can handle (of course, a 10MB video file isn't going to work well!) are things you should consider when working with Flash Lite 2 video content. If you are planning on bundling multiple video files, preplanning and significant testing should be conducted throughout the development process to avoid any potential playback errors.

The following example is a simple library of video clips utilizing multiple bundled videos. A total of two clips are stored in the FLA; the clips have been optimized, in terms of quality and size, for playback. Open the /Video/FL2_device_bundlelibrary.fla file in the Chapter 9 downloads to follow along with the example, which is shown in Figure 9-16. Attached to frame 1 in the ActionScript layer you have the following code:

```
        fscommand2( "FullScreen", true );

        var currentvideoindex_num:Number = 0;
        status_txt.text = "";

        //-- listener for input keys: 1 or 2
        var keyListener_obj:Object = new Object();
        Key.addListener( keyListener_obj );

        keyListener_obj.onKeyDown = function() {
          playVideoFromLibrary( chr( Key.getCode() ) );
        }

        //-- depending on what key is pressed, playback the
        //-- corresponding video from the bundled videos
        function playVideoFromLibrary( i:Number ):Void {
          if ( !isNaN( i ) && ( i >= 1 && i <= 2 ) ) {
            currentvideoindex_num = i;
            _root.gotoAndPlay( "playing" );
          }
        }

        placeholder_vid.onStatus = function( status_obj:Object ):Void {
          placeholder_vid.clear();
          _root.gotoAndPlay( "init" );
        }

        stop();
```

Figure 9-16. Bundled library videos

This code very simply waits for a key press of 1 or 2. When these occur, the code travels to the playing state where the video is first stopped:

```
        //-- stop the current video playing
        placeholder_vid.stop();
```

From there, the bundled sound is pulled from the library and playback occurs. Notice that we are using a special syntax of symbol:// to pull the video instance from the library. This notation is custom to Flash Lite 2. The instance name must match what you have assigned in the library; otherwise, it will fail to open the correct clip.

```
        _root.status_txt.text = "Playing clip # " + currentvideoindex_num +➨
          " from library";

        //-- play the current video
        placeholder_vid.play( "symbol://video" + currentvideoindex_num➨
          + "_vid" );
```

That's it! If the user selects another video, the process is repeated. As you can see, working with multiple bundled videos is very easy. You just need to be careful about the size issues we discussed earlier.

Testing is also a crucial piece when using this technique with your Flash Lite 2 video projects. Remember to always test on the actual target device! Got all that? Great. Now that we have covered multiple bundled videos, it's time to move on to our next topic: loading local device video.

Local file device video

Local file device video differs from local bundled device video in one significant way: the video is not bundled with the SWF. It is kept as a separately located file from the SWF.

In some respects, one could think of this method of playback as the closest thing to desktop Flash video with FLV files. However, there is no native FLV playback with Flash Lite 2! Instead of FLV, the actual device video file format is used (3GP, MP4, or another supported type). This method of loading in external video files has the benefit of not only lessening the overall file size impact to the application, but it adds the flexibility of being able to interchange video content files without recompilation of the SWF.

Both of these benefits are extremely valuable, and the only drawback is that the video file is left exposed as an external file to the SWF application. If content protection is ever an issue, you'll need to investigate the digital rights management (DRM) methods for the device your content will live on. For this book, I'll forgo this, since our content does not need to be protected. For more information on DRM, you can check out http://en.wikipedia.org/wiki/Digital_Rights_Management.

In the examples that follow, we'll load a video based on a local relative path, where the SWF and video are in the same folder. We'll also load video using absolute file paths, where the SWF and video reside in different locations. Let's explore loading video using these two possibilities.

Relative video path Loading video files in Flash Lite 2 using the relative path is straightforward. You just need to target the video that is stored in the same folder as the SWF that makes the call to play it:

```
//-- load the locally specified video file, and then play it back
//--(must be in the same folder as the .swf)
sample_vid.play( "sample1.3gp" );
```

You can also specify a folder path as a parameter in the play() command. For example, if you wanted to store all your clips in a video folder, you would use the following syntax:

```
//-- load the locally specified video file, and then play it back
//--(must be in the videos folder)
sample_vid.play( "videos/sample1.3gp" );
```

Pretty easy, huh? Now, let's say we want to load off of a memory card or other location. For this we must use an absolute path, which we will discuss next.

Absolute file path Loading video files with an absolute path is required if your content resides on an external memory card, for instance. Here, you must target the video clip using a full path, as follows:

```
//-- local the sample video file from the E: MMC drive under
//-- the Videos folder
sample_vid.play( "file://E:/Videos/sample1.3gp" );
```

By using an absolute video file path, you can target an external memory card or location by giving the whole path. In my case, the memory card is E:\. However, because device configurations vary, this may differ in your setup.

If you open \Videos\FL2_device_file.fla in the Chapter 9 downloads, you can view an example of using device local video files. Look at the code attached to the key catcher button on the stage and try both relative and absolute file paths to videos. It takes a bit of testing to figure out where to place your videos and the path to use to access them.

If you encounter an error message during playback, an incorrect path is likely the cause. Try a relative path first and then determine an absolute path to a video file, such as sample1.3gp. Another important note to make is that the device you are using must support the file:// protocol for the absolute file path to work. Check your documentation to see if this is true, or run the SWF to get a trial-by-fire test execution on your target device(s).

Local file video vs. bundled video Local file device video definitely has some advantages over using bundled device video. However, for each application, the situation is different. You need to evaluate whether or not you want to expose your video file (are there security issues?) or whether you are worried about overall content size for your SWF. Testing both methods is highly recommended to determine your explicit needs for the devices you are targeting for deployment.

There is no rule that says you must use one method over the other. The choice is likely to come down to how you want to deliver your video content. Bundled video has the benefit of encapsulating everything, whereas using local video allows you to interchange videos more quickly. As we have discussed in this section, there are pros and cons to using both approaches.

Besides using local video, we also have external video. Let's explore using external video in Flash Lite 2.

External device video

One limitation of locally bundled and local file device video is that a device can only hold so much information. Storage is always a concern on a mobile device, particularly when it is a handset. Storing video files externally from the target device and then loading them is a more-flexible approach to multiple files.

However, this is not to say that external video is not without its potential limitations. One such problem is that certain carriers block network ports as well as file types. If they block your requests for some reason, you are out of luck. However, in some cases, port HTTP traffic is never blocked and is virtually unrestricted, to allow users to access web sites from their mobile web browsers. So loading video over HTTP is a worthy pursuit in some, but not all, cases.

For a simple example of loading external device video, check out the following example using a remote HTTP call to load in the external video. Open the /Videos/FL2_device_http.fla file in the Chapter 9 downloads, which is shown in Figure 9-17.

Figure 9-17. Flash Lite 2 video loading using HTTP

Attached to the key catcher code on the stage is the ActionScript we will be concerned about:

```
//-- download the video completely via HTTP (port 80), then start the
//-- video playback!
sample_vid.play( "http://www.flashmobilebook.com/➦
    /video/sample1.3gp" );
```

This simple example demonstrates loading an external device video file from a remote web server over HTTP. Depending on your device's capabilities and your carrier, this may or may not work.

If it does work, you will notice that there is some lag time while the video loads and plays back. The process of loading and playing a video is not at all progressive over HTTP. A request is made for the video file; it is downloaded and handed off to the video player; and then Flash Lite Player makes a call to render the video content. If this example throws an error, the most likely cause is that your device does not support HTTP video loads. It may, instead, support Real Time Streaming Protocol (RTSP).

Before we head into creating our custom video player, I want to acquaint you with the last type of Flash Lite 2 device video. We need to discuss streaming video using the RTSP protocol.

Streaming video

It is possible to stream video in Flash Lite 2. However, quite a few conditions need to be met for it to be successful. Streaming video is, perhaps, the most difficult aspect of video playback to replicate with Flash Lite 2. This is not so much a reflection on Flash Lite itself, but it is partly because of the limitations imposed on actual target devices. Not all devices support video, and the ones that do are not always guaranteed to support streaming video. You need to consult your device documentation or search online to verify this important requirement before even considering streaming video with Flash Lite 2 content.

If that isn't enough, some operators may impose a "walled garden" approach to their services; this means that it's not always possible to work freely within the confines of their data network infrastructures. Sometimes they will block ports, limit bandwidth, or generally make it difficult to access data services outside of what they offer. Therefore, though a streaming video may work on one Flash Lite 2–enabled device, it is not guaranteed to work on another. Significant preplanning, assessment of device capabilities, operator network considerations, and copious amounts of testing are all requirements before even recommending Flash Lite 2 video streaming for an application. Take careful note of this.

In addition to the Flash Lite 2 Player, there has to be a streaming server to deliver the video to the Flash Lite 2–enabled device. This can be essentially any server that can stream the 3GP format. For example, both the Helix Streaming Server (Real Networks) and the Darwin Streaming Server (Apple) support 3GP streaming video.

Streaming video with Flash Lite 2 Now that we have discussed some of the difficulties in Flash Lite 2 video streaming, it's time to turn our attention to some of the implementation specifics. We have already talked about how Flash Lite handles device video: it hands it off for the device video player to render. This is also true for streaming video files. Although in this case, instead of the specified video file, a Universal Resource Locator (URL) is passed to connect the player to the external streaming server via RTSP.

Here is an example of this; it assumes that there is a valid video window instance on the stage called sample_vid and that the external 3GP file is still accessible at the specified address:

```
//-- using the rtsp protocol to stream a 3gp video from a Streaming
//-- Media Server, provided all conditions are met: device supports
//-- video and streaming video, rtsp is supported, there are no
//-- firewall or carrier restrictions, and the bandwith is readily
//-- available!
sample_vid.play( "rtsp://68.251.168.13/zwih.3gp" );
```

The most critical factor is that the target device must inherently support streaming video. Not all devices support this. It is important to check the documentation for your target devices to verify this, or construct a quick proof of concept, such as the one found in the previous ActionScript code.

For instance, a Nokia Series 60 device, such as the Nokia 6620, does support streaming video and has been shown to stream video successfully using the RTSP protocol with Flash Lite 2, under the strictest of conditions.

Flash Lite 2 streaming video is known to work under all of the following specific conditions:

- Helix Streaming Server (Real Networks)
- Streaming a 3GP-encoded file-generated Real Helix Mobile Producer
- Nokia 6620 with Flash Lite 2 installed
- T-Mobile (a carrier) with an unlimited data plan

The following generic configuration requirements must be met:

- The target device must support streaming video (RTSP).
- An unhindered network connection must be present; RTSP ports must not be blocked (typically port 554 TCP/UDP is used for RTSP).
- The video clip to be streamed must be formatted and encoded for the target device video format.
- Bandwidth must be available to properly stream the video (or the user experience will suffer).
- The streaming server must be capable of RTSP (if that is the protocol to stream with on the device).

Because of the complexity of configuration and deployment of a streaming server, I am not able to document with 100 percent accuracy an example configuration that would work across all devices and networks. There are far too many variables.

Besides, you would need exactly the same requirements and conditions in order to get it to work properly. For this reason, I will not cover streaming video further in this text. As streaming video becomes a popular trend, and the bandwidth becomes more readily available, the community will discuss their configuration as well as troubleshooting tips in this gray area of Flash Lite 2 video.

For now, perhaps the most-optimal way of delivering external video to handsets is to embed bundled video inside of the external SWFs and load them on demand with a loadMovie command. By using this method, you can circumvent a lot of the shortcomings of streaming video that we have discussed in this section.

Flash Media Server If you are wondering whether or not Flash Media Server is supported in Flash Lite 2, it is not possible to integrate the two at this time. Hopefully, in the future, as device hardware and bandwidth become more readily available, it will be possible to leverage Flash Lite with Flash Media Server.

For now, we must rely on the other, third-party, commercial RTSP streaming servers available, such as the Helix Streaming Server or other low-cost (or free) alternatives, such as Apple's Streaming Media Server (Darwin).

Controlling Flash Lite 2 device video

Up until this point, we have been focusing on simply playing device video. That doesn't do you much good in and of itself. You need more control! You need to tie device video with a user interface that allows a user to interactively control the video as it plays. Some sort of custom video player is needed.

This is where the `Video.play()`, `Video.stop()`, `Video.pause()`, `Video.resume()`, and `Video.close()` methods come into play. These are the building blocks that we will now use. Let's get started walking through a complete Flash Lite 2 device video example. We'll create a custom video player in Flash Lite 2.

Device video example

Now that you have your feet wet with the basics of device video, it's time to move on to more-complicated video playback! In the following example, I will take you through the steps to create a custom video player in Flash Lite 2.

We will be using a significant amount of ActionScript 2 and the information we talked about previously in this chapter to construct a user interface and to control a video clip. The custom video player pictured in Figure 9-18 is what you will create in this section.

Figure 9-18. The custom video player

Capturing the video

The first step to working with mobile device video is to actually have the source video. This can come from a variety of sources. Actually, several high-end handset devices today come preinstalled with a custom video recorder. This is usually an additional device feature if it supports a camera, so if your target device has a camera it should (but may not always) also support video. You need to verify this on your target device. Typically, these recorders have a feature to record short clips of video. The supported recording format is usually 3GP or MP4.

Capturing video on an actual device is not your only option. Digital cameras, digital camcorders, and web cameras are all additional ways you can quickly and easily record video. You just need to make sure that the video captured can be converted down into a mobile format such as 3GP. In the case of our example, we'll just be using the onboard device video recorder to record short clips in 3GP format. You will find the video we are using for the example in \Video\.

However, feel free to shoot your own video or use your another 3GP video you may have found on the Web or elsewhere. An excellent place to search online for 3GP clips is www.google.com. For example, you can enter in the terms: filetype:3gp keyword, where keyword is the video subject you want to search on. There's not a massive amount of 3GP content being aggregated right now, but you may find a clip here or there in the search results. Just remember to be careful of infringing on any kind of digital content rights!

Converting the video

Once the captured video is attained, it's time to convert the video to mobile format. Since the video we have is already in 3GP format, we don't need to do much. However, if you are moving video from desktop to mobile, you need to run some of the conversion tools we discussed earlier in this chapter. You'll have to step through the conversion process and export to 3GP format.

For example, using QuickTime Pro is an easy and quick way to convert desktop video to 3GP mobile format. By using the Export feature and selecting Export to 3G, you can easily output your video content to the 3GP file format. Apple's *QuickTime User Guide* has an excellent walkthrough for this process and can be downloaded at http://images.apple.com/quicktime/pdf/QuickTime7_User_Guide.pdf.

Other tools have their own tutorials and documentation for how to export to 3GP format.

Setting up the movie and the user interface

Once you have your video content to use, you're ready to start working with the source files. First, open \Video\FL2_CustomVideoPlayer_start.fla in the Chapter 9 downloads. This will act as the main starting point of our custom video application. If you want to skip ahead and take a look at the final source, feel free to open \Video\FL2_CustomVideoPlayer_final.fla in the Chapter 9 downloads. The compiled SWF is the video player we will soon create.

Once \Video\FL2_CustomVideoPlayer_start.fla is open, take a look at the prebuilt time line, shown in Figure 9-19. I've saved you some time by creating the necessary time line layers, frame states, and user interface, so that you can concentrate on coding part of the custom video player, rather than the design and user interface. Since most of our discussion in this chapter has been about the Video object, we'll be concentrating on the ActionScript that drives and controls the actual video playback.

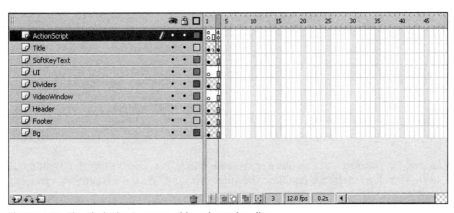

Figure 9-19. The Flash Lite 2 custom video player time line

If you open the library, you can also see that I have already made all of the assets for you. This will save you time as well. I want you to get familiar with core video functionality that we discussed earlier and not deal with creating a custom user interface from scratch.

Working with the Video Window layer

If you open the library, you'll notice that there is a movie clip in there called playerwindow_mc. This is what we will use to play back our video. Inside the playerwindow_mc movie clip is a video object called videowindow_vid.

Since it's not already on the stage, go ahead and drag and drop it in the Video Window layer on the time line. Position it so that it is centered both vertically and horizontally on the screen. It should fit nicely between the header and footer as shown in Figure 9-20.

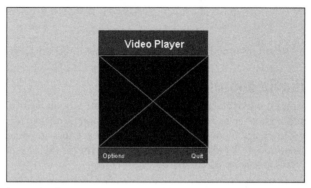

Figure 9-20. The custom player window

Next, open the properties of playerwindow_mc. You can leave the height and width alone, since the video fits in the area we have predefined without interfering with the interface. However, you need to give it an instance name. Name the clip playerwindow_mc, as shown in Figure 9-21.

Figure 9-21. The custom video object properties

Also notice that the bundled video we have specified is 0KB in size. Don't worry; I did this on purpose. We'll be using local file video, not bundling the video with the actual SWF (although you can if you want to later).

Now that we have our video player window on the stage and have assigned it an instance name, we can begin to apply the user interface controls.

Adding the player controls

Inside the library, you'll notice several player control buttons located in the buttons folder, including play_mc, stop_mc, and pause_mc, as shown in Figure 9-22. These three clips will allow us to control our movie playback.

Notice that I have used movie clips instead of buttons. For all intents and purposes, you can think of the movie clips as buttons for our example. Movie clips allow us to save the state of our buttons within the application.

For each control clip, there are enabled, disabled, and active modes. When playback is active, the play_mc switches to the frame labeled mode 2. When disabled, it is in mode 0, and when selected, it has a mode state of 1.

Take a look at the time line of the play_mc clip to get an idea of what this looks like (see in Figure 9-23).

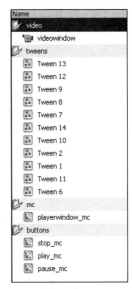

Figure 9-22. The custom video library

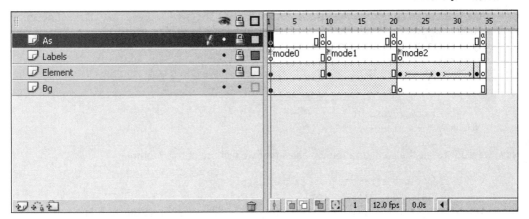

Figure 9-23. The custom video play_mc time line

Now that you've seen the control clips, it's time to add them to the stage. Drag and drop each of the buttons onto the stage, so they line up at the bottom of the screen.

Also, assign an instance name to each clip under the properties for each: pause_mc should have an identifier called pause_mc and so forth. This is important. We will want to target the movie clips and jump to different frame states during the execution of our video.

Once you have all the clips assembled on the stage, you should have something like the screen shown in Figure 9-24.

Figure 9-24. The stage for the custom video player

Now that all the control elements are on screen, we can start the best part—coding.

Adding the code

One of the first things you should note is that time line ends on frame 3. If you open the ActionScript layer on frame 3, you should see the following comment: /*** code for video player ***/. If you see this, you are in the right place to start adding code!

One the first things we want to do is turn off _focusrect. If we don't, we'll ruin the custom selection effect we have. Add the following code:

```
//-- turn off focusrect
_focusrect = false;
```

Now, we want to set the configuration variables that we will use in this example:

```
var currentvideo_str:String = "sample1.3gp";
//-- initial video file to load
var states_arr:Array = new Array( "play_mc", "pause_mc", "stop_mc" );
//-- the 3 different control states
var stateindex_num:Number = 0;
//-- the current state we are in (play, stop, pause)
var playstate_num:Number = 1;
//-- (1 means playing, 0 means stopped,and -1 means paused)
var lastcontrol_str:String = ""; //-- the last control used by the user
```

Next, we want to be able to handle the key events from the Play, Pause, and stop buttons.

In order to capture the events, we need to add a key catcher. Since we are using Flash Lite 2, we will take advantage of the new keyListener object:

```
//-- catch any keys that are pressed
var keyListener_obj:Object = new Object();
```

```
Key.addListener( keyListener_obj );

//-- listen for user interface commands
keyListener_obj.onKeyDown = function() {
  switch ( Key.getCode() ) {
    case Key.ENTER:
      processControl( lastcontrol_str, 2 );
    break;
    case Key.LEFT:
      if ( stateindex_num > 0 ) {
        stateindex_num--;
      } else {
        stateindex_num =  states_arr.length-1;
      }
      processControl( states_arr[ stateindex_num ], 1 );
    break;
    case Key.RIGHT:
      if ( stateindex_num < states_arr.length-1 ) {
        stateindex_num++;
      } else {
        stateindex_num = 0;
      }
      processControl( states_arr[ stateindex_num ], 1 );
    break;
  }
}
```

You'll notice a bunch of things happen in the key catcher. The Enter key is used to process the currently selected control. The left and right directional keys are used to cycle through the control clips you added to the stage. Left and right keys navigate between the different play states of video player.

Stateindex_num keeps track of the currently selected ID of the controls. It will be used later to look up the actual state clip selected when the user actually presses the Enter key to process the control.

Notice we're passing mode values of 1 and 2 to processControl(). Mode 1 sets the current clip to its stated state, and mode 2 actually runs the operation of the clip. When a user presses the Enter key the currently selected operator starts, whether that operator is play(), stop(), or pause().

What does the processControl() function do? We'll take a look at that next:

```
//-- process the control passed in, and set the mode as well
function processControl( whichcontrol_str:String,➥
  mode_num:Number ):Void {
//--  reset control states to their initial states ( mode0 = inactive )
resetControls();

//-- set current mode
this[ whichcontrol_str ].gotoAndPlay( "mode" +  mode_num );

//-- active mode, figure out what operation to call
```

```
if ( mode_num == 2 ) {
  switch ( whichcontrol_str ) {
    case "play_mc":
      if ( playstate_num == -1 ) {
        //-- if the player was paused, resume playback
        playerwindow_mc.videowindow_vid.resume();
        playstate_num = 1;
      playstate_num = 1;
      } else if ( playstate_num && lastcontrol_str ==➡
      whichcontrol_str ) {
        //-- if play is hit twice, then pause the player
        processControl( "pause_mc", 2 );
      } else {
        with ( playerwindow_mc ) {
          //-- stop any video currently playing first!
          videowindow_vid.stop();
          //-- start playing the video now
          videowindow_vid.play( currentvideo_str );
        }
      }
    break;
    case "stop_mc":
      if ( playstate_num == 0 && lastcontrol_str ==➡
      whichcontrol_str ) {
      whichcontrol_str = "pause_mc";
      playstate_num = 1;
        //-- call the play, since pause was hit twice
        processControl( "play_mc", 2 );
      } else {
        playstate_num = 0;
        //-- stop the player cold in its tracks
        playerwindow_mc.videowindow_vid.stop();
      }
    break;
    case "pause_mc":
      if ( playstate_num == -1 && lastcontrol_str ==➡
      whichcontrol_str ) {
        //-- start playing the clip again, as user hit the
        //-- pause command twice
        processControl( "play_mc", 2 );
      } else {
        //-- pause the playback
        playstate_num = -1;
        playerwindow_mc.videowindow_vid.pause();
      }
    break;
  }
}
```

```
    //-- set last control used
    lastcontrol_str = whichcontrol_str;
}
```

There's a quite a bit code here, so let me explain it.

First, the function takes in the name of the control and the mode it should be set to (0, 1, or 2 corresponding to the disabled, selected, and active states). The clip is then updated by calling a gotoAndPlay() and advancing to its mode number. If the mode is set to 2, the user has pressed the Enter key and is expecting the video player to start, stop, or pause playback of the video.

You'll also notice a lot of conditional logic. The conditional logic takes care of the various states possible within the three buttons. The default behavior of the player is to play and pause. If the user clicks the stop button, the video is stopped, and playback starts from the beginning again when the user presses Play. Spend a moment taking in all of the code.

One additional feature we want is to be able to tell the player to go to "stop mode" once the video has completed. To do this, we utilize the onStatus() method that we discussed earlier in this chapter. Once the video has completed playing, the onStatus() method fires an event, and the status code has a value of completed. We can then take the appropriate action. In our case, we'd like to set the control clip to stop mode. That's what the following code does:

```
    //-- handle the status of the video window
    playerwindow_mc.videowindow_vid.onStatus =➡
      function( status_obj:Object ) {
        if ( status_obj.level ) {
          trace( "Video Status Msg (" + status_obj.level + "):➡
            " + status_obj.code );
        if ( status_obj.code == "completed" ) {
          _root.playerwindow_mc.videowindow_vid.close();
          _root.playstate_num = 0;
          _root.processControl( "stop_mc", 1 );
        }
      } else {
        trace( "Video Status Error: " + status_obj.code );
      }
    }
```

It's important to note that the code and level properties of the status object depend on which target device you are working with. Not all return values for the code and levels are the same. You may have to modify these to correspond to your device.

The final piece of the puzzle is to start the video playback when the application is loaded. If you don't want the video player to start automatically, you could always remove this statement. It's really up to you what the expected behavior should be here:

```
    //-- autostart it!
    processControl( "play_mc", 2 );
```

Now that you have added all the code, you should run this on your Flash Lite 2–enabled device. When deploying, you need to make sure that the SWF and the video file reside in the same folder if you have used a relative path. If you want to move the video file, you only need to change the currentvideo_str configuration variable to a folder path, an absolute URL, or even an external video. If all is well, you should now have your very first custom video player.

Congratulations, you're well on your way to working with Flash Lite 2 device video!

Modifying the UI and design

Creating the player was fun, wasn't it? Flash Lite 2 makes it extraordinarily easy to generate these sorts of video applications.

Once you have re-created the custom video player shown in Figure 9-25, it's fairly simple to modify the look and feel of it. For the sake of simplicity, I have kept the time line very basic (only a few frames in length).

The assets can be replaced with your own custom graphics. You can change the background by changing the Bg layer found on the time line. The title is also its own layer, in case you want to customize the text. I also included a header and footer that you can customize to your liking. Changing the buttons as a simple as modifying the different graphics in the Element layer of each control clip: play_mc, stop_mc, pause_mc.

Figure 9-25. The custom Flash Lite 2 video player

I leave it as an exercise for you to make your very own design for the player. Have fun!

Media Playback API

As we discussed in the previous chapter on Flash Mobile sound, the current Flash Lite 2 CDK comes with the Media Playback API. Part of this API is a class to help streamline and abstract some of the development effort needed to work with Flash Lite 2 video.

You may wish to check out the VideoViewer class and MimeType checker class if you are seeking a quick way to start developing your own Flash Lite 2 device video API. Again, this sample API can be found in the following directories:

- **Windows**:

  ```
  \Program Files\Macromedia\Flash 8➥
  \Samples and Tutorials\Samples\Flash Lite 2.0\MediaPlaybackAPI
  ```

- **Mac**:

  ```
  \Applications\Macromedia Flash 8➥
  \Samples and Tutorials\Samples\Flash Lite 2.0\MediaPlaybackAPI
  ```

Thoughts on device video

In this chapter, we have looked at Flash device video as it relates to Flash Lite 2. From importing videos to creating simple video players, we have run the gamut. You also have walked through some more sophisticated examples of Flash Lite Video content. Let's now talk about the benefits, the limitations, and the future of Flash Lite device video.

Reaping the benefits of device video

Flash Lite 2 brings a very easy platform to design, develop, and create video applications. The authoring tool and Mobile emulator both provide the best means necessary to produce mobile video quickly, easily, and successfully.

Development and production time is streamlined, as you have the added benefit of not dealing with multiple tools; Flash is the only tool you need. Another benefit to using Flash device video is that you can very seamlessly incorporate your video directly into your Flash content. This avoids launching an external player interface and keeps the user experience consistent.

This is where Flash device video really shines. A well-designed and well-thought-out user experience is perhaps the most important part of any successful mobile application. Of course, with all of these great benefits, there are bound to be a few limitations, which we'll discuss next.

Avoiding the limitations of device video

Video, in general, is a tricky business on mobile devices, because you have to think about such things as device memory, content file size, screen size, and CPU usage.

What's more, you also have to make considerable tradeoffs when dealing with video, and Flash device video is no different from the other technologies out there. A critical point to the success of Flash Mobile video is keeping down the file size of video content. Of course, there is no set target size, because it will vary from device to device. But as a general rule, you should spend a significant amount of time figuring out how to best optimize the video content at hand without sacrificing too much video quality.

Testing both within the Mobile emulator and on the target devices is critical to avoiding file-size limitations. As discussed throughout this book, the emulator provides only a quick mechanism to design and develop content. It was never meant to replicate the entire mobile experience. This is particularly true with Flash video applications.

Always test your video content on the actual target devices.

The future of mobile Flash video

Flash device video has been a stunning achievement in the release of Flash Lite 2. But what does the future hold for Flash video for mobile devices?

It is clear that the ideal future will be one in which native Flash video found on the Flash desktop will make it into the Flash Lite Player. However, at this point in time, the native Flash video format supported in Flash 8 (and even 9) is somewhat of a lofty goal given the current state of affairs with mobile devices. For now, we must rely on Flash Lite device video to satisfy our appetite for video content on devices.

As mobile hardware and software continue to evolve, we can expect Flash Lite video and FLV capabilities to soon follow suit across newer and more-advanced devices. Flash Media Server integration may also be a possibility in future versions of Flash Lite, but we are not there quite yet! There is a long road ahead of us. If or when this does happen, it'll be an exciting time for those of us working with Flash Lite.

Summary

I hope that this chapter has enlightened you to the video capabilities of Flash Lite 2. Despite the current device limitations, video is still a powerful feature starting to take hold in the mobile world. Flash Lite 2 provides, perhaps, the easiest way to integrate simple video content into mobile applications today.

Just as Flash video has evolved on the desktop, it is almost inevitable that it will evolve on mobile devices at some point in the future. It will be exciting to see how Flash Lite video changes in the coming years.

In the next chapter, we'll talk about how to extend the current capabilities of Flash Lite. Chapter 10 will cover creating custom components for Flash Lite, as well as external methods for reading and writing text files in Flash Lite applications. We'll also discuss how to build demo-triggered content (content that expires after an extended period of usage). We'll complete the chapter with a look at creating Flash Lite applications that communicate with the Python scripting language.

Chapter 10

EXTENDING FLASH LITE

In the previous chapters, we talked in depth about how to develop useful and exciting Flash applications that take into account mobile device limitations, such as bandwidth and memory availability. In this chapter, we will look at how you can work around some of the limitations of the Flash Lite Player, such as the inability to write files for storing persistent data like the latest news articles, and how to access native functionality of mobile devices.

Limitations of Flash Lite

The limitations of Flash Lite are caused mainly by the host devices. These devices' lack of fast CPUs and limited memory mean that the Flash Player for desktop computers is heavily stripped down to make it perform nicely on mobile devices, such as phones or multimedia players like the iRiver U10. In the previous chapters, you have seen the kinds of wonderful things you can make with Flash Lite; in this chapter, you will learn to circumvent some of the previously mentioned limitations of Flash Lite.

As you may recall from Chapter 4, some of the classes and functionality of the desktop version of the Flash Player are missing from Flash Lite. In a nutshell, the following functionality isn't supported in Flash Lite:

- Socket communication using the XMLSocket class (supported in Flash Lite 2.1)
- Communication with Flash Media Server
- Remote shared objects (partially supported in Flash Lite 2.0)
- Native Flash video file (FLV) playback
- Use of the Flash Application Protocol (used by Flash Remoting)
- Cascading style sheet (CSS) formatting using text fields
- Masking using device fonts
- Inline text fields (supported in Flash Lite 2.1)
- Bitmap smoothing to render high-quality images

Now, let's look at a few of these points in more detail.

The XMLSocket class

It's sad that the XMLSocket class still isn't supported in Flash Lite 2.0, but the upcoming Flash Lite 2.1 will have support for the XMLSocket class. In the "Controlling iTunes with commands" section later in this chapter, you can find a simple example of how to use the XMLSocket class in a Flash Lite application.

> *Polling is requesting updates within a specific time constraint, for example, every three seconds. The Flash Lite application requests a specific URL through* loadVars *or* getURL *for new updates or content. These polling methods require a lot of bandwidth compared with an* XMLSocket *solution, which will receive a notification when updates are available.*

Video playback

The video playback in Flash Lite is limited to the supported video formats on the mobile devices. In other words, Flash Lite is only capable of playing video formats that are natively supported by the mobile device. Therefore, Flash video isn't supported, because its use would required a lot of time and memory and would increase the size of the Flash Lite Player.

Creating components for Flash Lite

Components are nothing more then special movie clips. If you know how to work with movie clips, you already know how to create your own components. Creating Flash Lite components is similar to creating components for SmartClips for Flash 5 (for Flash Lite 1.0/1.1) and Flash MX 2004 or later (for Flash Lite 2.0).

Before we start creating components, let's look at the benefits of using components in developing Flash Lite projects and the differences between version 1.X and 2.0 components. The benefits of using components in your Flash Lite projects follow:

- **Reusability**: Avoid reinventing the wheel for each project by reusing parts of code; simply drag and drop components on the stage.
- **Simplicity**: The components can easily be reused by other people by changing variables of the component through a simple user interface (Flash 2.0 only).
- **Self-containment**: The component bundles all of the assets and code.

> *The components approach is frequently used in other platforms or languages, such as the .NET Framework or Delphi, where creating and selling components is a big business. Delphi developers can download free and commercial components from sites such as* www.torry.ru. *For Flash, you should have a look at* www.flashcomponents.net.

Differences among Flash Lite 1.X and 2.0 components

Creating components in the two versions of Flash Lite is quite different, because Flash Lite 1.X lacks the support of ActionScript 2–style components, where the IDE of Flash MX 2004 and Flash 8 depend on ActionScript 2. An easy way to make your own component library full of Flash Lite 1.X components is by creating a new Flash Lite FLA file and putting all of the movie clips you want to reuse in the library. You can then import that FLA file in your project's FLA file using File ➤ Import ➤ Open External Library. Flash will open your FLA file and its library panel, so you can easily drag and drop the components you want to use into your movie.

Table 10-1 shows some of the differences among Flash Lite 1.X and 2.0 components.

Table 10-1. Functionality differences among Flash Lite 1.X and 2.0 components

Functionality	Flash Lite 1.X	Flash Lite 2.0
Use of ActionScript 2–based components	No	Yes
Use of the Components panel in Flash	No	Yes
Dragging and dropping components on to the stage	Yes	Yes
Changing properties via Flash's Property panel	No	Yes

As you can see, the features the Flash environment offers for using components are limited to using ActionScript 2 components. Because you can only use ActionScript 2 in Flash Lite 2.0 movies, you can only make use of the handy tools in these movies.

Building an inline text field for Flash Lite 2.0

In this example, we are going to make an inline text field for a Flash Lite 2.0 project. The purpose of this component is to enhance the user experience by improving how text fields are handled. Normally, when you use a text field in your Flash movie, Flash Lite shows its own Edit dialog box, where you can enter a value for the text field. The component we will build avoids the use of this dialog and clones the functionality of T9 (nonpredictive) text. In Figure 10-1, you can see the final component.

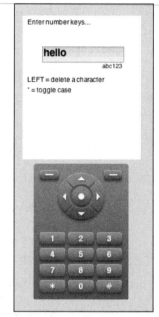

Figure 10-1. The final result of the inline text field component

What you need

Before we begin creating our inline text field, we should first examine functionality it should offer. If you look at the T9 functionality available on the Nokia 6681, you can see that it consists of the following functionality:

- Ability to switch between uppercase and lowercase letters
- Ability to remove a character by pressing the left arrow key
- Ability to insert a space by using the number sign (#) key
- Entering letters by pressing multiple times on one of the numeric keys (for example, pressing the 2 key will cycle through "a", "b", "c", and "2")

Enabling these functions requires creating the following elements:

- **Input indicator**: A text field that shows if the user is in the mode to insert uppercase or lowercase letters—abc123 for lowercase mode and ABC123 for uppercase mode
- **Blinking arrow cursor**: A marker that shows the user that it's OK to pick the next character
- **Dynamic text field**: A text field that includes the inserted letters

As you can see, we need three movie clips for the elements: two for the markers and one for the component itself.

> If you want to know more about how the component is created, download Chapter 10/InlineTextField.fla, which contains a commented version of the InlineTextField.as file.

Making the text field component

In this section, you will create the component from scratch. Follow the steps in this section to create your own, full-blown, inline text field:

1. Create a new blank document that publishes to a Flash Lite 2.0 document, and save the document as InlineTextField.fla.

2. Create a new movie clip symbol named InlineTextField. This will be the main component movie clip.

3. Open a new ActionScript file to write the ActionScript 2.0 for this component. If you are using Flash 8 Professional, you can make an ActionScript 2 file. If not, you should create a new text file in your favorite text editor.

4. Add the following code to the new ActionScript file:

```
/**
 * Simple inline TextField class
 * Foundation Flash Applications for Mobile Devices
 */
import mx.utils.Delegate;
class InlineTextField extends MovieClip {
  // alpha numeric keys A-Z etc.
  public static var ALPHA:String = "alpha";
  // numeric keys 0-9
  public static var NUMERIC:String = "numeric";
// all keys A-Za-z0-9
  public static var ALPHA_NUMERIC:String = "alphaNumeric";
  // character change timeout
  public static var CHAR_CHANGE_TIMEOUT:Number = 1500;

  public var inputMode:String = ALPHA_NUMERIC; // default input mode

  private var __labelField:TextField;
  private var __arrowMC:MovieClip;
  private var __inputModeMC:MovieClip;

  private var __hasFocus:Boolean = false;
  private var __charIndex:Number = 0;
  private var __enteringChar:Boolean = false;
  private var __upperCase:Boolean = false;
  private var __previousKey:String = "";
  private var __deleteKey:Number = Key.LEFT;
  private var __caseKey:Number = 42;  // * key
  private var __timeoutInterval:Number = null;
  private var __keys:Object = { _1:49, _2:50, _3:51, _4:52, _5:53,➡
    _6:54, _7:55, _8:56, _9:57, _0:48}; // key mapping

  // the list of available characters and ➡
  // how these can be accesed per key
  private var __chars:Object = { _1:[".",",","'","1"],➡
                                 _2:["a","b","c","2"],➡
                                 _3:["d","e","f","3"],➡
                                 _4:["g","h","i","4"],➡
                                 _5:["j","k","l","5"],➡
                                 _6:["m","n","o","6"],➡
                                 _7:["p","q","r","s","7"],➡
                                 _8:["t","u","v","8"],➡
                                 _9:["w","x","y","z","9"],➡
                                 _0:[" ","_","0"] };
```

343

```
public function set upperCase(toggleUpper:Boolean) {
  __upperCase = toggleUpper;
  if(__upperCase) __inputModeMC.gotoAndStop("alphaNumericUpper");
  else __inputModeMC.gotoAndStop("alphaNumeric");
}

public function get upperCase() : Boolean {
  return __upperCase;
}

public function InlineTextField () {
  var kl:Object = new Object();
  kl.onKeyDown = Delegate.create(this, onKeyPress);
  Key.addListener(kl);
}

public function setFocus (toggleFocus:Boolean) : Void {
  __hasFocus = toggleFocus;
}
public function setDeleteKey(keyCode:Number) : Void {
  __deleteKey = keyCode;
}

public function setCaseKey(keyCode:Number) : Void {
  __caseKey = keyCode;
}

private function onKeyPress () : Void {
  if(__hasFocus)
  {
    // Check to see if it is an upper case command
    if(Key.getAscii() == __caseKey)
      {
        upperCase = !upperCase;
      }
      else if(Key.getCode() == __deleteKey)
      {
          __labelField.text = __labelField.text.substr(0, ➥
__labelField.text.length -1);
      }
      else
      {
        processInput();
      }
    }
  }

  private function processInput() : Void
  {
    var str:String = __labelField.text;

    for(var key in __keys)
```

```
      {
        if(Key.getCode()==__keys[key])
        {
          if(__enteringChar && (key == __previousKey))
          {
            if(__charIndex < __chars[key].length-1) __charIndex++;
            else __charIndex = 0;
            str = str.substr(0, str.length-1);
          }
          else __charIndex = 0;

          clearInterval(__timeoutInterval);

          str += (__upperCase) ? __chars[key][__charIndex].➥
                   toUpperCase() : __chars[key][__charIndex];
          __enteringChar = true;
          __previousKey = key;
          __timeoutInterval = setInterval(this, "inputTimeout", ➥
CHAR_CHANGE_TIMEOUT);
        }
      }

    __labelField.text = str;
  }

  private function inputTimeout() : Void
  {
    __enteringChar = false;
    __arrowMC.play();
    clearInterval(__timeoutInterval);
  }
}
```

5. Save the ActionScript file as InlineTextField.as. You should save the file in the same directory as the Flash document that you created in the first step.

6. Return to InlineTextField.fla, and open the library (see Figure 10-2) by pressing F11 (Windows) or Apple+L (Mac).

7. Select the movie clip you made in step 2 in the library palette, named InlineTextField, and open the Linkage dialog from the right click menu (or ctrl click for Mac).

8. For the linkage identifier of the InlineTextField movie clip, enter the name InlineTextField in the Identifier text field of the Linkage dialog.

9. In the same dialog, enter the name InlineTextField in the AS 2.0 Class field.

10. Click the OK button on the Linkage Properties dialog box.

11. Drag the InlineTextField movie clip to the stage of the document, and give it the instance name itf.

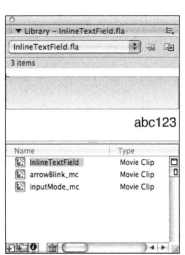

Figure 10-2. The contents of the library of InlineTextField.fla

12. Now add the following code to the first frame of the ActionScript layer. If this layer isn't yet available, you should make it yourself. The line `itf.setFocus( true )` gives the focus on the stage to our InlineTextField instance, so that the user can immediately start typing text.

```
fscommand2("FullScreen", true);
itf.setFocus( true );
```

Now, you have all the code to recreate the functionality of T9 text, so you need to add elements listed in the previous section. You currently have only one empty movie clip that is associated with the `InlineTextField` class. Next, you should create the assets required by your components. If you follow the next set of these steps, you should have your own working component!

13. Return to `InlineTextField.fla`, and open the library by pressing F11 (Windows) or Apple+L (Mac).

14. Create a new movie clip named `inputMode_mc`. This will be the indicator to show whether the user is entering uppercase or lowercase letters into the text field.

15. Double-click this newly created movie clip, and create three layers: ActionScript, labels, and text. The text layer will include a static text field to indicate the mode of the inline text field.

16. Add the code `stop()` to the first frame of the ActionScript layer.

17. Next, create three key frames in the labels layer, and assign the following labels: alphanumeric for frame 1, alphaNumericUpper for frame 2, and numeric for frame 3.

18. Add a new text field to the text layer of the movie clip, and change the text values for the three frames as follows: abc123, ABC123, and 123.

19. The time line of the movie clip should now look like the one shown in Figure 10-3.

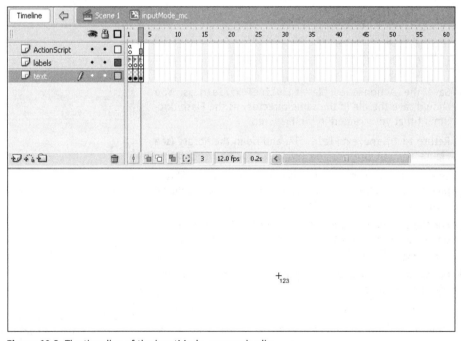

Figure 10-3. The time line of the inputMode_mc movie clip

Now that you have created the input mode indicator, you need to create the blinking arrow movie clip. This movie clip lets the user know he or she can pick the next character to insert. Let's use a simple animated triangle that will be played when the InlineTextField is ready for the user to pick the next character.

20. Again, return to InlineTextField.fla, and create a new movie clip named arrowBlink_mc.

21. Now, double-click this newly created movie clip, create one layer, and name it graphics.

22. Add the code stop() to the first frame of the graphics layer.

23. Add a new keyframe to the second frame of this layer by pressing F6 (Windows) or Insert ➤ Timeline ➤ Keyframe on the Mac.

24. Next, draw a simple triangle on this newly created keyframe (already available in InlineTextField.fla).

25. Once you have drawn the triangle, insert a new keyframe on frame 9.

26. To make the cursor appear to be blinking, add blank keyframes on frames 5 and 6 complete the blinking arrow animation movie clip for your control. The time line of this movie clip should now look like the one shown in Figure 10-4.

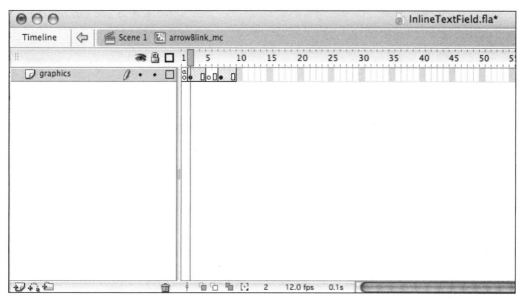

Figure 10-4. The time line of the arrowBlink_mc movie clip

Finally, you are finished creating the required movie clips for your component! Now, you only need to join all the elements in the InlineTextField movie clip, so that the associated ActionScript file can access the instances of the movie clips. Of course, you still need to add your dynamic text field; without this field, your inline text field would be missing is most important element. Let's begin the final steps for your component, by adding the movie clips we created previously in the InlineTextField movie clip. If you follow these steps, you should have fully working inline text field for your Flash Lite 2 projects.

27. Return to InlineTextField.fla, and double-click the InlineTextField movie clip in the library.

28. Drag the inputMode_mc movie clip from the library to the stage, and give it the instance name __inputModeMC.

29. Change the x position of this movie clip to 88.0, and the y position to 22. Now that you have correctly positioned the input mode indicator, you should add and reposition the blinking arrow movie clip.

30. Repeat steps 27–29 for the arrowBlink_mc movie clip, give this movie clip the instance name __arrowMC, and reposition the movie clip using the following coordinates: 0.1 for the x position, and 25 for the y position.

31. Next, drag an input field from the toolbox to the stage, name it __labelField, and change it into a dynamic field. By selecting Dynamic text field in the Properties panel. Make the text field fit nicely between the previously added movie clips (see Figure 10-5).

32. You should now make some minor changes to this text field to make it easy to read on the small screen. In the Properties panel, change the font size to 15, and the font name to _sans of the textfield.

33. If you want, you could add a background below this text field; see Figure 10-5 for a suggestion.

34. Test your component. You should see your inline text field instance. If so, you can add characters by pressing the numeric keys in the emulator.

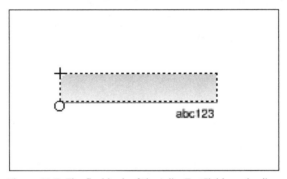

Figure 10-5. The final look of the InlineTextField movie clip

In this section, you have learned how to create your own custom components for Flash Lite. The InlineTextField component avoids the use of the Input dialog of Flash Lite and allows the user to enter text in way that's similar to T9 text input. In the next section, we will have a look writing text files on the mobile device.

Writing text files using Write2File

For security reasons, you will not be able to write data to text files in Flash Lite. If you want to write data to a text file, you need to use an application that's native to the mobile device. For most mobile phones, this means writing an application for Symbian.

In this section, you will write a program to write text files on the device. To make this program work, we need to dive into the wonderful world of Symbian and C++. J2ME doesn't allow you to write to the file system of the mobile device, so it's not the right choice for this job. Fortunately, the code we need for writing the files isn't too complex overall. The code can be found in many textbooks or C++ books. For this little utility, we are going to use the widely available Standard C library for input/output called STDLIB, which implements the methods you need to open and write to text files. After we have completed this section, you will be able to write text files anywhere you like using a small Symbian application.

In Chapter 8, we discussed how you can execute external programs using the FSCommand("launch", "application") command in ActionScript. This solution heavily depends on this functionality of Flash Lite to execute external programs; without this functionality, we would go nowhere. Go to the next section to find out what tools you need to get started!

> *If you would like to learn more about developing Symbian applications for your mobile devices, take a look at the following resources on the Internet:* www.symbian.com, www.symbian.com/developer/tech_papers/papers/cpp_gettingstarted.asp, *and* www.forum.nokia.com/main/resources/technologies/symbian/documentation/getting_started.html.

What you need

Now, you know that you need to write a Symbian application for the mobile phone, so you need the tools of the software developer. To write applications for Symbian-based mobile phones, you need to choose a platform. The platforms most-frequently used by phone manufactures follow:

- Nokia Series 60 (Nokia 6680, N70, N90)
- Nokia Series 80 (Nokia 3250, 9500)
- UIQ (Sony Ericsson P900)

In this section, we will use the most-commonly used Nokia Series 60. Today, most of the Nokia mobile phones are Series 60 phones and capable of using our application. Let's call it Write2File for now!

> *The application you are creating in this section has been successfully used on a Nokia 6681.*

Now that the platform is selected, you need the compiler that is included as part of the SDK available for Nokia Series 60. You can download the latest SDK at www.symbian.com/developer/sdks/sdks_series60.asp. Once you have installed the SDK (in this chapter, I will assume it's installed in the default directory), you will have a Symbian directory in your C: drive. This directory includes all the tools you need to compile the code in the following sections.

> *You should not install the Symbian SDK in a directory name that contains spaces. Names containing spaces aren't supported by most of the Symbian tools. Avoiding the use of spaces will save you from a lot of problems.*

After you have installed the Symbian SDK, you might need to install ActivePerl on your computer too. You can download ActivePerl on the www.activestate.com web site. The Symbian SDK depends heavily on Perl scripts, and these Perl scripts aren't supported by Windows out of the box.

The most important subdirectory is the Epco32 directory; it contains all the headers and libraries that are required to compile the Write2File application.

Before you can compile the Write2File application, you need to check if the Symbian SDK is correctly installed on your computer by executing the following command in a command prompt:

```
bldmake bldfiles
```

This command should trigger the following error:

```
BLDMAKE ERROR: Can't find "\BLD.INF"
```

If this happens, you can be assured that the Perl scripts used for compiling the Write2File will be available. Next, you will compile your Write2File application.

Compiling Write2File under Windows

The Write2File application source code consists of the following files:

- bldd.inf: The master project file contains a reference to the Write2File.mmp file.
- Write2File.mmp: The project makefile contains a list of all sources file and required libraries.
- Write2File.c: The actual source code does the heavy lifting.

> *The files required for compiling Write2File, our first Symbian application, can be found in the Chapter 10 downloads, in the* Chapter10\Write2File *directory.*

bld.inf

The bld.inf file is a simple text file that contains a list of makefiles that are part of the project. The Write2File project only contains a reference to the Write2File.mmp makefile. Use your favorite text editor to make a new text file, give it the name bld.inf, and add the following content:

```
// BLD.INF
// Component description file
//
// Foundation Flash Applications for Mobile Devices
// Write2File - Writing text files on the mobile device
//
// The list of make files for this project
PRJ_MMPFILES

Write2File.mmp
```

Write2File.mmp

Write2File.mmp is the project makefile, which contains the list of all source files and libraries that are part of the project. The file includes all the information the compiler needs to build your application. For this file, you should make a text file in your favorite text editor with the name Write2File.mmp, and add the following code:

```
// Writ2File.mmp
// Foundation Flash Applications for Mobile Devices
//
TARGET  Write2File.exe  // The name of the target/application
TARGETTYPE  exe  // The type of the target
UID  0  // The unique identifier of the application

SOURCEPATH  .
SOURCE  Write2File.c

// Path to the system include files (#include <filename>)
SYSTEMINCLUDE  \Epoc32\include\
SYSTEMINCLUDE  \Epoc32\include\libc

// List of libraries used by the application
LIBRARY  estlib.lib
LIBRARY  euser.lib

//
STATICLIBRARY  ecrt0.lib
```

> You might see that we are linking statically to the library ecrt0.lib, the library that includes an implementation of STDLIB for Symbian. Don't forget to include this line in your file; otherwise, the compilation will fail for sure!

Write2File.c

The actual application is the Write2File.c file; it includes the C code for writing to a text file using STDLIB. The most-important part of the STDLIB is the file pointer. A **file pointer** is a pointer to information that defines various things about the file, including its name or the current position within the file. The file pointer basically identifies a file on disk. A file pointer is defined as FILE in the stdio.h file:

```
#include<stdio.h>
#include<string.h>

int main ( int argc, char *argv[] ) {
  // argc = total given arguments
  // argv = array with the argument values

  FILE *fp;  // the file pointer
  char FILENAME[ 100 ];  // the filename
  char FILEDATA[ 255 ];  // the contents of the file
```

```
        strcpy( FILENAME, argv[1] );  // copy the value from args to FILENAME
        strcpy( FILEDATA, argv[2] );  // copy the value from args to FILEDATA
        // open the file with the given filename
        fp = fopen( FILENAME, "w" );
        // write the string to the file
        fputs( FILEDATA, fp );
        fclose( fp );  // close the file

        return 0;
    }
```

The Write2File application uses the following basic file functions: fopen(), fclose(), and fputs().

fopen() The fopen() function opens the file specified in the filename variable and returns a file pointer to this file:

```
        fp = fopen( FILENAME, "w" );
```

The preceding code opens a the file specified in the variable FILENAME; the second parameter, with the value "w", means that the file should be created or cleared when the file already exists and defines in which mode the file should be accessed.

fputs() The fputs() function writes a string to the current position within the given file:

```
        fputs( FILEDATA, fp );
```

The preceding code writes the contents of the variable FILEDATA to the given file pointer defined in the fp variable as obtained via the fopen() function earlier.

fclose() The fclose() function closes the file associated with given file pointer:

```
        fclose( fp );
```

Compiling Write2File

Now that you have prepared all of the files required to compile your Write2File application, we can start the compilation process. You won't need a fancy IDE to compile the application; some simple commands in a command prompt should do the job just fine. If you follow the instructions in this section, you will have your Write2File.exe file at the end of the process. You can open a command prompt window using Start ➤ Run ➤ cmd ➤ Enter.

Before you enter any commands in the DOS prompt, go to the directory where you have stored the files. For example, if you have stored your files in the directory Write2File on the C: drive, type in the following line to end up in that directory:

```
        cd \Write2File
```

Once you are in this directory, type the following command:

```
        bldmake bldfiles
```

This command creates a new file called ABLD.BAT in the current directory; this is the starting point for the Perl script that is used to compile the application. Now, you can compile your application for the mobile phone. Do so by typing in the following instructions:

```
abld build armi urel
```

After you enter this command, you will see some magic on the screen—that is the compilation process! Normally, this process should finish without problems. You can verify this by checking if the last lines of the output contain the text PETRAN (see Figure 10-6). If you see this text near the end of the output, you can be sure the compilation process was successful. The result, sadly, can't be found in the current directory but has been hidden away deep in the Symbian SDK directory.

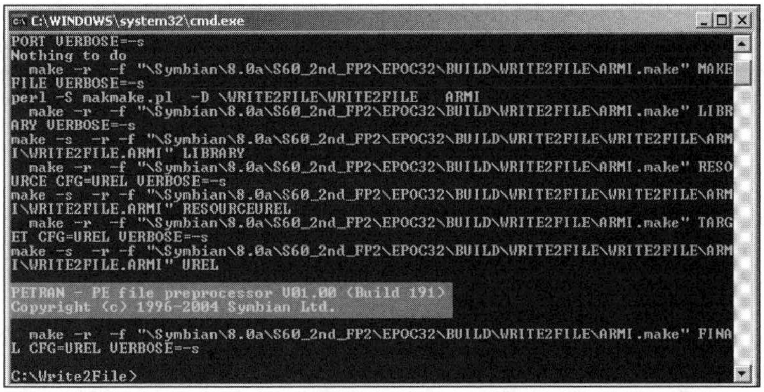

Figure 10-6. A successfully completed compilation process

You should be able to find the Write2File.exe file in the subdirectory Epoc32\Release\armi\UREL at the location where you have installed the Symbian SDK. Write2File.exe is the result of our first adventure in the world of Symbian, and it will let you write files on the mobile phones!

Now that you have seen how you can create your little application in Symbian C for writing text files for use with Flash Lite, it's time now to turn our attention on how to use Write2File in Flash Lite applications. In the section titled "Creating an evaluation version for Flash Lite applications," I'll show you how you can make an evaluation version of a game using Write2File.

Compiling Write2File under Mac OS X

If you want to compile Write2File on an Apple computer, you will encounter some problems. First of all, the Symbian SDK doesn't support Mac OS X as a platform (it doesn't support Linux either). This means you have to depend on solutions built by third parties. For Mac OS X, you can use the wonderful Xcode Plugin for Symbian OS written by Tom Sutcliffe. You can download this plug-in at www.tomsci.com/xcodeplugin. This plug-in adds Symbian OS support to Apple Xcode, which is a free development environment created by Apple for developing applications for Mac OS X.

> *Please note that the Xcode Plugin for Symbian OS doesn't support the Series 60 3.X SDK. The main reason for this is that the Xcode Plugin would require fully rewriting or porting the utilities used to Mac OS X. Let's hope Series 60 3.X SDK will be supported at some later date.*

What you need

Before you are able to start developing Symbian OS applications under Mac OS X, you need to download and install the following applications:

- Apple Xcode 2.1 or later
- Symbian OS Series 60 or Series 80 SDK, or UIQ SDK
- Xcode Plugin for Symbian OS

Most of the time, you will already have Apple Xcode installed on your Mac; normally, you can find it in Macintosh HD/Developer/Applications. If not, you can find Xcode on your Mac OS X installation CDs, or you can download the latest version of Xcode at http://developer.apple.com after completing a free registration. The web site also includes useful materials explaining how to develop using Xcode. Once Apple Xcode is installed, install the Xcode Plugin for Symbian OS by clicking the xCode Plugin for SymbianOS.mpkg file. This will start the installer for the plug-in; just follow the instructions shown. After you have installed the plug-in, you should prepare the Symbian SDK.

Getting the Symbian SDK

Before you start developing Symbian applications with Xcode, you need to prepare the Symbian SDK, so that it can be used by the Xcode plug-in; it needs several utilities and header files that accompany the SDK for Windows. Luckily, the plug-in comes with a utility called InstallSDK, which will assist you in unpacking the Symbian SDK installer. In Figure 10-7, you can see the InstallSDK in action. After the utility is finished unpacking, you should have a directory with the contents of the Symbian SDK installer.

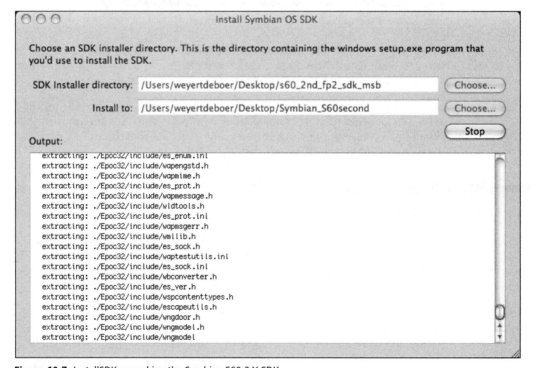

Figure 10-7. InstallSDK unpacking the Symbian S60 2.X SDK

Compiling the Write2File project

Now that you are all set to start compiling the Write2File project in Xcode, you should open Xcode. Go to File ➤ Import Project. After you have selected this option, you will see the Import Project Assistant dialog, shown in Figure 10-8. In this dialog, you should select Import Symbian OS MMP file. This option will assist you in setting up the XCode project and make compiling it possible. Before this Xcode project gets created, you will encounter the Import Project Settings dialog, shown in Figure 10-9. In this dialog, you need to specify which MMP file and EPOCROOT directory you would like to use. For the EPOCROOT directory, specify the directory where you copied the result of the InstallSDK utility. Click the Next button to create a new XCode project, as shown in Figure 10-10. You should now be able to compile this application by clicking the Build button of the Project window shown in Figure 10-10.

Figure 10-8. The Import Project Assistant dialog

Figure 10-9. The Import Project Settings dialog

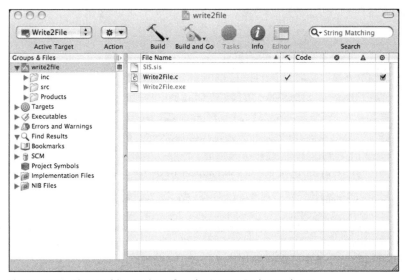

Figure 10-10. The resulting project after the Import Project assistant

355

Creating an evaluation version for Flash Lite applications

After you have finished your Flash Lite application, you may wish to sell it. It's important to offer an evaluation version of your creation to your future customers. Convincing users that your application is useful is hard without letting them try it out. It's easy to make your own evaluation version of your Flash Lite application.

You have a few options to consider for making your application into an evaluation version:

- Time out after a few minutes
- Time out after a specified period of time and never run again
- Lose functionality after a certain period of time

In the examples in this section, I will explain how you can implement these three options in the Mad Bomber Flash game from Chapter 6.

Converting your game into a date-based evaluation version

Creating an evaluation version of a Flash Lite game isn't a difficult task. Begin by opening the Mad Bomber game in the Chapter 10 folder, MadBomber/MadBomber.fla, and rename it to demo_MadBomber.fla. One of the very first things you must take into account is the need to add an extra screen to the game to inform the user that this is an evaluation version and to explain how to obtain the real version. You need to need to add this new screen to the main time line of the game.

In your UI layer, make space for the start screen, which should appear before of the menu. Move the appropriate frames in such a way that your time line looks like Figure 10-11.

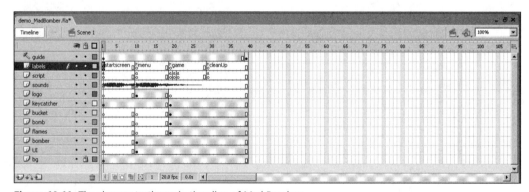

Figure 10-11. The changes to the main time line of Mad Bomber

At this stage, you'll notice that the screen doesn't appear to be right. You need to remove and add several elements from to the start screen to make it look like Figure 10-12. You may need to add a text field, such as the second text field shown in Figure 10-12, to inform the user how many days of fun are left.

Next, we're going to adjust the ActionScript that was broken by adding the start screen. You need to move the ActionScript code from frame 10 in the script layer to frame 1. You should add a single stop() command to the now-empty frame 10.

We need to add the evaluation functionality to the game next. For this, you could use local shared objects (a Flash Lite 2–only feature) to store the information. Instead, in this example, you will use your own Write2File application to store the information to a plain text file in its own directory called config. You will put Write2File.exe, which you created earlier in this chapter, into this directory. The directory also includes a file called config.dat, which contains the following text:

```
expiryDate=20061119
```

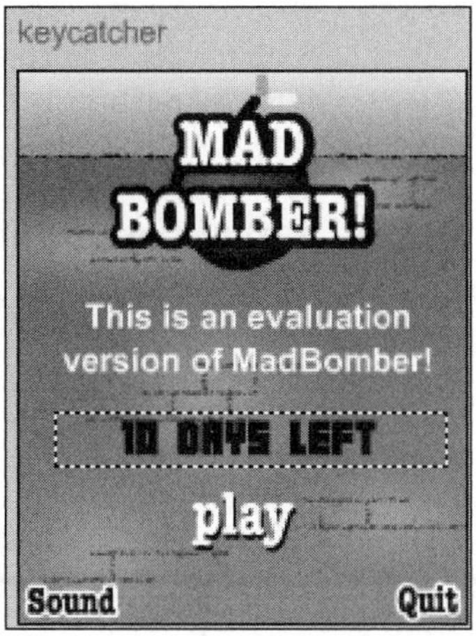

The expiryDate variable in the text file describes on which date the game should stop functioning; after that date, the user won't be able run the game anymore. The most important step is the implementation of the evaluation functionality itself. We will create a new movie clip called EvaluationMaker. Edit the movie clip, and type the following code on frame 1:

Figure 10-12. The evaluation version start screen

```
_level0.expiryDate = -1;
loadVariablesNum("config/config.dat", 0 );
```

The code in frame 1 loads the value from the config.dat file. The real validation code is executed in frame 5, but first, you need to add some code (in frame 2) to check that the expiryDate value has been loaded:

```
if ( _level0.expiryDate != -1 ) {
  gotoAndStop(5); // go to frame 5 to validate the date
} else {
  // the value hasn't been loaded keep waiting
  gotoAndStop(2);
}
```

The following code checks whether the current date is after the expiryDate value. As long as this condition is valid, the user should be able to play the game. You need the following code in frame 5:

```
// returns the current day (1-31)
day = fscommand2( "GetDateDay" );
// returns the  current month (1-12)
month = fscommand2( "GetDateMonth" );
// returns the current year (2006)
year = fscommand2( "GetDateYear" );

// appends the above strings, results in 11052006
currentDate = int(year)*10000 + int(month)*100 + int(day);
expiryDate = int( _level0.expiryDate );
if ( currentDate > expiryDate )
{
  // stop the application when the current date passed expiry date
 trace("quit");

}
stop();
```

357

If the expiration date is after the current date when this code compares the expiration date stored in the text file with the current date, the Flash game will be stopped using the Quit command. It's very simple—if you put this movie clip in a layer on the first frame, the application will quit when the user is out of days!

Making a play-based version

Great! We now have a Mad Bomber game that will stop working after 11 May 2006. But what if you want the user to play a specific number of times before the game stops working? This isn't difficult either; you only need to change the code in the EvaluationMaker movie clip, so that it keeps track of the number of times the game is played. But first, you need to change the config.dat file stored in the config directory. Replace the existing content with the following text:

    uses=295

You might think that it's strange to set the number of uses to 295 to start, but this is because we are piping this number through a simple formula to figure out the real number:

$$value = 300 - (3n^2 + 5)$$

The *n* is equal to the number of uses so far. This is a simple way to obfuscate the real number of uses to make it a bit harder for the user to expand the number of uses left. If you store the real number, the user could just change the value and have the full amount of fun left again. Let's look at some of the values generated by this formula in Table 10-2.

Table 10-2. List of the number of uses and storage value mapping

Number of Uses	Value to Store
0	295
1	292
2	283
3	268
4	247
5	220
6	287
7	148
8	103
9	52

Now that you are able to hide the real number of uses, update the code in the EvaluationMaker code to make use of this formula. This code isn't much different from the previous code for frame 1:

```
// load in number of uses from config file
_level0.uses = -1;
loadVariablesNum("config/config_uses.dat", 0 );
```

You basically only had to the change the variable names used in frame 1; the code for the other two frames in the movie clip is a bit longer. The code in frame 2 will convert the value stored in the text file to the real number using the preceding formula. The code for frame 2 is as follows:

```
// loop until number of uses has loaded
if ( _level0.uses != -1 ) {
    // convert the value from the text file to the real number of uses
    numUses = 300 - _level0.uses;
    numUses = ( numUses - 5 ) / 3;
    numUses = ( numUses == 0 ) ? 0 : int( Math.sqrt( numUses ) );
    gotoAndPlay( 5 );
} else {
    gotoAndStop( 2 );
}
```

Now that you know the current number of uses of the game, you should check whether the current number of uses exceeds the maximum allowed number of uses. This check will be done in frame 5 of the movie clip. When this condition isn't met, the number of uses in the text file will be increased by one. The code that you need for frame 5 follows:

```
// check if the player hasn't played more then nine times
if ( numUses >= 9 ) {
    // the demo version is expired we should quit the game
    fscommand2( "Quit" );
}
// update and calculate the new uses value
numUses++;
uses = 300 - ( ( numUses * numUses ) * 3 + 5 );

// update the number of uses in the text file
app = "c:/documents/flash/write2file.exe";
path = "c:/documents/flash/config.dat";
data = "uses=" add uses;

// write the contents to the file
argument = app add ", " add path add "," add data
fscommand( "Launch", argument );
```

As you see in the preceding code, you finally make use of the Write2File application—to update your text file. The special FSCommand command Launch is used to execute Write2File in the background. For more information about the FSCommand method, please see Chapter 8. After it has been executed, the file will be updated with the number-of-uses value of the game.

Making a functionality-based evaluation version

The only other evaluation option that is left is the one where you lose functionality when the evaluation version has expired. For this option, you need to update frame 5 to store a new variable that will be true only when the evaluation period is over. The code you would need to change in the previous example is the line fscommand2("Quit"). Instead of having the Flash game quit when the period is over, you only want it to lose functionality. You will use a Boolean variable called evalExpired to specify if this evaluation period is over. The code you need to use follows:

```
if ( numUses >= 9 ) {
    evalExpired = true;
}
```

You can now use this variable within your Flash Lite movie to check if it needs to lose some functionality, because the evaluation period is over. For example, you could give the user only one life instead of the normal three lives.

> *The evaluation-version solutions presented in this chapter have some pitfalls. Because of the nature of Flash, the protections themselves are very weak. It's possible to obtain the protections' code by using utilities such as ASV, which makes it possible to decompile your SWF file to its original FLA file. It's hard to write a cracker-proof protection using Flash because of this possibility. Hopefully, Flash Lite will someday support the digital rights management (DRM) that becomes increasingly standard on modern mobile phones. The use of DRM would probably be the safest way to make an evaluation version of your Flash Lite application. Sadly, as long as Flash Lite doesn't support DRM, we still have to use weak protections. If the Flash Lite applications you sell are inexpensive enough, people will probably buy them anyway. Look at the ring tones for your phone; these files aren't protected by DRM either, and still, the ring-tones business is huge. More information about DRM can be found at http:// en.wikipedia.org/wiki/Digital_Rights_Management.*

Native Functionality

Flash is really limited in the amount of control you have of the mobile device it runs on. You won't be able to use technologies such as Bluetooth or GPS on the mobile device; such native functionality of the mobile device can't be accessed from within Flash, but there are ways to work around this limitation. You might be aware of solutions such as Screenweaver (for more information, see http://screenweaver.com) for stand-alone Flash projects on desktop computers. These solutions build on the availability of the function FSCommand to forward instructions to the host. You can use such solutions on some mobile devices too. The Flash player for the Pocket PC supports forwarding instructions to the host program by using FSCommand. Sadly, this functionality of FSCommand isn't available for mobile devices like the mobile phone. But we can work around this by launching an application similar to Write2File or using a local web server instead. Because I already showed you how you can launch and use applications such as Write2File, I will now give you an example of how to access native functionality on the Pocket PC and mobile phone by using a local web server.

Accessing native functionality on the Pocket PC

In this example, we will write a solution for accessing native functionality available on a Pocket PC. The solution is similar to the one used by Screenweaver for stand-alone projects on desktop PCs. The Flash Player available for the Pocket PC is less limited than the Flash Lite Player. For example, the Flash Player for the Pocket PC supports the use of FSCommand commands for communicating with the host program, so we are now able to write a simple application for the Pocket PC using the .NET Framework that will host the SWF file. This way we can keep track of all of the FSCommand commands sent to the host application from within the SWF file. In this section, we create a simple solution to access native functionality of the Pocket PC based on a simple Microsoft .NET Compact Framework application.

The idea is that the Flash movie hosted by the application uses FSCommand to send commands to the host application, which will then execute the given command on behalf of the Flash movie. If you would like to write to a text file you can use the writefile command. The application can easily be extended with new commands. The nice thing is that the .NET Framework comes with a wide variety of standard functionality for writing and encrypting files, drawing images, and accessing databases. All the functionality that the .NET Framework offers on the mobile device can, in theory, be accessed from within the Flash movie as long as you implement commands to access this .NET Framework functionality. In Figure 10-13, you can see the application flow of our solution.

At the end of this section, you will be able to compile the application for the Pocket PC, and you will know how to extend the available commands to use the ones you prefer.

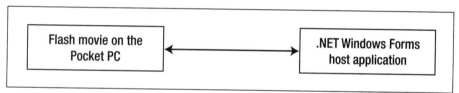

Figure 10-13. Application flow of the solution

What you need

To access native functionality on the Pocket PC, you need to have several extra applications running on it:

- Flash Player 6 for the Pocket PC
- Microsoft .NET Compact Framework 2.0

Flash Player 6 for the Pocket PC Of course, I don't need to explain to you that you need to have a Flash Player installed on the Pocket PC to view SWF files. Our solution depends heavily on the Flash Player plug-in for PIE, the Pocket PC version of Internet Explorer. You can download the Flash Player for the Pocket PC on the Adobe web site: www.adobe.com/products/flashplayer_pocketpc/downloads/player.html.

Next, you should transfer the file to your device from your computer using ActiveSync. To do so, open ActiveSync, and click the Explore button in the toolbar (see Figure 10-14). A new Windows Explorer window called Mobile Device will be opened showing the contents of your devices; you should drag-and-drop the CAB file to this window (see Figure 10-15). Now, look up the CAB file on your device, and double-click it to initiate the installation.

Figure 10-14. The ActiveSync dialog with Explore button

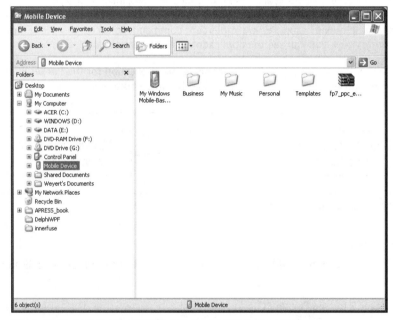

Figure 10-15. Dragging the CAB file into the Mobile Devices window

Please note that you need a Windows Mobile 5 or Pocket PC 2003 device to be able to install the Flash Player for the Pocket PC.

Microsoft .NET Compact Framework Microsoft .NET Compact Framework brings the powerful programming environment of the Microsoft .NET Framework to the Pocket PC. The Microsoft .NET Compact Framework is exclusively designed for mobile devices, and it takes the limitations of such devices into account. The .NET Framework itself allows you to quickly write applications in the language of your choice. For this application, we will use C#, because it is closely related to ActionScript 2.0 and should be easy to understand if you have experience with ActionScript 2.0.

The reason that we are specifically are using version 2.0 of the Microsoft .NET Compact Framework is that this version enables you to host ActiveX controls easier than the earlier version. If you want to use version 1.0, you should use a third-party library called CFCOMM instead, which makes hosting the Flash Player ActiveX control a lot easier.

Now that you know what you need for creating your application on the Pocket PC, you need the real deal for the software developers—you need an IDE to write .NET Compact Framework applications. In this example, we will use the Microsoft IDE Microsoft Visual Studio 2005. Once you have installed this IDE, you can start creating the .NET Framework application itself.

> *You can't use the Flash Player for the Pocket PC in the Pocket PC emulator, so you need to test the final application on the device itself.*

Compiling Flash on the Pocket PC

Once you have installed Microsoft Visual Studio 2005, start Visual Studio 2005, and open the FlashOnPocketPC2003SE.csproj project file. The project file can be found in Chapter 10/ FlashOnPocketPC. Figure 10-16 is a screenshot of the project open in Visual Studio.

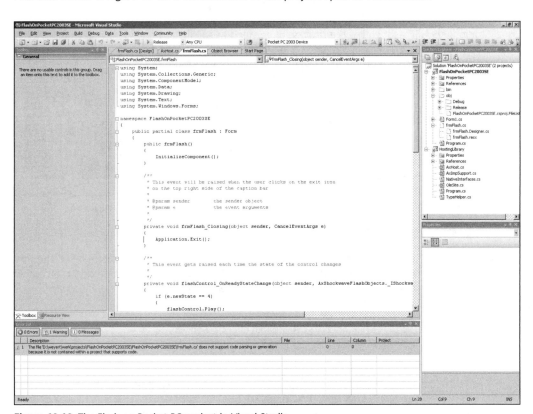

Figure 10-16. The Flash on Pocket PC project in Visual Studio

After you have opened the project, you should be able to compile this project by pressing F5; compiling shouldn't take long. When the compilation process has been completed you will be asked, if you want to test the application in the emulator or on the real device (see Figure 10-17). You should choose to test the application on the real device, because, again, the Flash Player for Pocket PC can't be installed in the emulator.

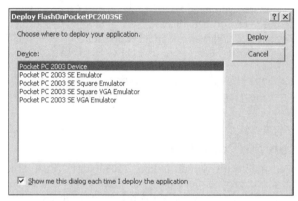

Figure 10-17. Select the deploy device

Visual Studio 2005 will assist you in the process of getting the application on your Pocket PC; it will automatically send the application via ActiveSync to your Pocket PC. The application on the Pocket PC should look like the one shown in Figure 10-18.

On the bottom of the screen, select File ➤ Open to open the File dialog, which enables you to select the Flash movie you want to open. You should be able to open any SWF movie that is published for Flash 6.0. In Figure 10-18, you can see the flash movie TestForPocketPC.swf opened in our application.

This version of the application only supports one simple command FileOpen. This command will return the value Return result of the FileOpen command when you use the following ActionScript code:

Figure 10-18. The application running on an Acer n30

```
fscommand( "FileOpen" );
```

If you want to add more commands that should be supported in the application, edit the file frmFlash.cs, the source file where all the magic happens. The most important method in this file is flashControl_FSCommand(), which is the method raised when a Flash movie uses the FSCommand function:

```
private void flashControl_FSCommand(object sender,
    AxShockwaveFlashObjects._IShockwaveFlashEvents➥
    _FSCommandEvent e)
{
    // The triggered FSCommand() in the Flash Movie
    string sCommand = e.command;
    switch (sCommand) {
```

```
                    case "FileOpen":
                        flashControl.SetVariable("$FSD", ➥
                            "Return result of the FileOpen command" );
                        break;

                    default:
                        flashControl.SetVariable("$FSD", "-1");
                        break;
                }
            }
```

As you see in the code snippet of the function, the application set a new variable in the Flash movie called $FSD. This is the variable that will be used to exchange any data between the Flash movie and the host application. You might be asking yourself, "How can I add a new command to write a text file on my Pocket PC?"

This can be quite easy; you would need to update the flashControl_FSCommand() method, so that the application is aware of the newly added command. For now, call the method WriteFile; the purpose of the method is to write a string to a text file. Add the following code above the default: line:

```
case "WriteFile":
    this.writeFile( e.command, e.args );
    break;
```

This little code snippet adds the support for your new command. When a Flash movie uses the code fscommand("WriteFile", "mystring"), the code snippet forwards this request to a new method called writeFile. This method does the actual work of writing the string to a text file. Because FSCommand calls are limited to only one parameter, you need to include all of the required information in a single string. An example of the parameter string for the WriteFile follows:

```
filename=test.txt&content=Hello, World!
```

This parameter string specifies that you need to write the text Hello, World! to a file with the name test.txt. The parameter string will be analyzed by the WriteFile method in your .NET application. The first line in the next code snippet analyzes the parameter string by splitting the string by every semicolon (;) character. Each occurrence will appear in a new array. The Split() method returns an array of strings with each element in the array corresponding to the value between the specified delimiters (the semicolons). The second and third lines define the requested file name and the contents of this file.

```
string[] params__ = parameters.Split( new  char[] {'&'} );
string filename = params__[ 0 ].Split( new  char[] {'='} )[ 1];
string content = params__[ 1].Split( new  char[] {'='} )[ 1];
```

Now, you only need to have the real code for writing a string to a text file, and the .NET Framework supplies standard functionality for this in the File class. The following method should be added to the frmFlash class; this method writes the values of the variables filename and content to a text file:

```
private void writeFile( String parameters ) {
  string[] params__= parameters.Split(new char[] { '&' });
  string filename = params__[0].Split(new char[] { '=' })[1];
```

```
    string content = params__[1].Split(new char[] { '=' })[1];
    using (StreamWriter sw = new StreamWriter(filename))
    sw.Write(content);
}
```

Let's examine the code to see what it's doing:

1. Create an instance of the StreamWriter class; this is the class that will write the text to the file.

2. Write the text to the file, using the Write() method of the StreamWriter class.

3. The StreamWriter class includes an overload that brings support for the file name; meaning you won't need to create a FileStream class first. The Write() method also automatically closes the file.

Using this example of writing text to a text file, I have shown you how you can expand the functionality of the Flash for Pocket PC application (note that this is your application, not to be confused with the Flash Player for Pocket PC) using standard functionality of the .NET Framework. If you wish, you can write functionality to show the system file dialogs for opening and saving files. In the next section, we will look at how to do the same thing for Flash Lite on a mobile phone.

Writing a web server in Python

In the previous section, we looked at how you can use a .NET application on the Pocket PC to give Flash access to the native functionality of mobile devices. This solution works like charm on Pocket PCs, but the Pocket PC centralization won't help when you want to access native functionality on your mobile phone.

Earlier in the chapter, I mentioned that you can't use FSCommand to send instructions to the host application on mobile phones. But the Flash Lite Player has support for reading text files and opening of URLs using the getURL() or loadVariables() functionality. We are going to use this functionality to access some of the native functionality of the mobile phone; the idea is to use a local web server on the mobile phone to access the functionality.

You might ask, "Why don't we use J2ME instead of making a local web server?" The problem with J2ME is that it doesn't have full access to the functionality of the mobile phone; the J2ME sandbox limits which functionality can be accessed. We will use Python for the local web server instead, because it doesn't come with these same limitations. Also, you can extend Python by writing libraries in Symbian and by writing modules in C++—a functionality that is not possible with J2ME.

What's Python?

Python is a popular, object-oriented, functional programming language that has been designed for quality, productivity, and integration. The open source Python language has been invented and developed by Guido van Rossum and is available for all kinds of platforms including Windows, Mac OS X, and since January 2006, for the Symbian Series 60. The language is named after the British television show, *Monty Python's Flying Circus*.

Among the main goals of the Python developers are to make Python fun to use and to make it a highly readable language. It uses English keywords, where other languages such as C or Java would use punctuation. In other languages, you need to use opening and closing brackets ({ and }) or keywords such as begin or end, as in Delphi. Python doesn't use such syntax; it depends heavily on the indentation of code to define the blocks of code.

Python for Symbian Series 60 mobile phones enables you to access native functionality, including the following:

- Bluetooth technology
- GPRS networking
- SMS messages
- Address books

This makes it a perfect language to extend your Flash Lite application. You can use it to make a little server application that uses Bluetooth to send instructions to the outside world.

> *You might want to read a book written specially about Python to learn more about the language and how to program using it. I recommend* Beginning Python *by Magnus Lie Hetland (Berkeley: Apress, 2005), for the total beginner, and* Dive Into Python *by Mark Pilgrim (Berkeley: Apress, 2004), for the more experienced programmer wanting a fast-paced introduction.*

Installing Python on your computer

Developing Python scripts requires that you have the Python interpreter installed on your computer. Happily, Python is available for a wide range of systems. Most Linux distributions come with Python preinstalled. Also, Mac OS X 10.2 (or later) already comes with a command-line version of Python, though you probably want to install a Python version that includes a graphical user interface. Microsoft Windows doesn't come with any version of Python installed, but easy-to-use installers are available for this platform to install Python.

Python for Windows For Windows, you have two options available. Your first option is to use ActivePython available from ActiveState, famous for ActivePerl. This is an installer for Python, but it includes extras such as a full-blown IDE and some other Windows-based extension for accessing Windows-specific services, such as the Windows registry. However, since ActivePython is not downloadable for free, we will be using the second option: the Windows version of Python offered by the developer responsible for Python. This version of Python for Windows is even open source, which isn't true for ActivePython.

The instructions for installing Python on Windows follow:

1. Download the latest Python Windows installer by going to www.python.org/download. This page lists the current production-ready versions available. At the time of this writing, the latest version available is Python 2.5 with the filename python-2.5.msi.

2. Double-click the installer you just downloaded from the web site.

3. Go through all of the steps of the installer.

After the installation is finished, you can close the installer and select Start ➤ Programs ➤ Python 2.5 ➤ IDLE (Python GUI). IDLE is a simple development environment for Windows that enables you to easily try out Python code and includes simple debugging functionality. You can see the IDLE application in Figure 10-19.

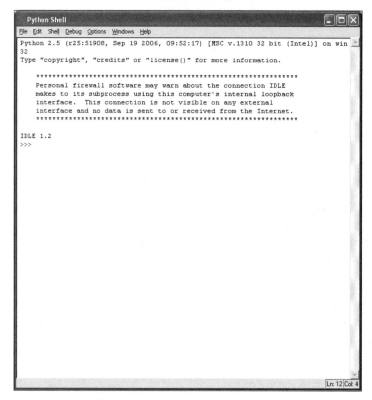

Figure 10-19. Python IDLE on Windows

Python for Mac OS X On Mac OS X, you have also two options: you can use the preinstalled Python, or you can install your own version of Python available from the Python developers. Because Mac OS X 10.2 comes with a command-line version of Python preinstalled, you can use this version without a problem. But if you want to use the latest version of Python, you need to download it on your own. The following steps to install the newest version of Python on your Mac:

1. Download the latest Python Mac OS X disk image by going to www.python.org/download/mac. This page lists the current, production-ready version available for Mac OS X. I downloaded this version for Mac OS X 10.4 at http://www.python.org/ftp/python/2.5/python-2.5-macosx.dmg.

2. If your browser hasn't yet opened the disk image, you need to double-click the file to mount the disk image.

3. Double-click the installer MacPython-OSX.pkg.

4. Go through all of the steps of the installer (see Figure 10-20).

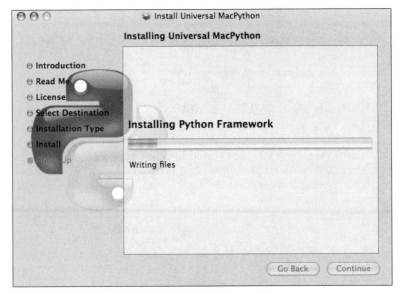

Figure 10-20. Python for Mac OS X installation in progress

After the installation, you can close the installer. You now have a new folder in your Applications folder called MacPython-2.5 If you double-click IDLE, you will have the Mac variant of the IDE. You should see the application shown in Figure 10-21.

Figure 10-21. Python IDLE on Mac OS X 10.4

> *You should check the Python web site to see if you need to install any extra utilities to make this new version of Python coexist peacefully with the preinstalled version of Python.*

Installing Python on your mobile phone

If you have a Symbian Series 60 mobile phone, you can easily use the available installer to install Python on your mobile phone. You can download the installer for Python 1.2 or later for Series 60 at www.forum.nokia.com/python. Once you have downloaded the file, send the PythonForSeries60.SIS file included in the zip file to your mobile phone. Open this file on your mobile phone to start the installation process for Python. If the installation is successful, an icon for Python will occur in the phone menu (as shown in Figure 10-22).

Figure 10-22. Python installed on a Nokia 6681

If you select the Python icon, the Python interpreter is launched. If you press the left softkey on your mobile phone, a pop-up menu appears with the option Run Script. This function will open and execute a Python script on the phone.

You now have a version of Python installed on your desktop computer and Python for Series 60 on your mobile phone. You should be able to type in python at the command line, which should give results similar to the following:

```
Python 2.5 (r25:51918, Sep 19 2006, 08:49:13)
[GCC 4.0.1 (Apple Computer, Inc. build 5341)] on darwin
Type "help", "copyright", "credits" or "license" for more information.
>>> The local web server in Python
```

Normally, writing a web server in Python can be done quite easily by using the SimpleHTTPServer module, which is part of the standard Python library. The module implements the server side of the HTTP protocol. The code you need to make your own web server using this module follows:

```
import BaseHTTPServer
import cgi
class myRequestHandler( BaseHTTPServer.BaseHTTPRequestHandler ):
  def do_GET(self):
    length = int( self.headers.getheader('content-length'))
    requestData  = cgi.parse_qs( self.rfile.read(length), ➥
      keep_blank_values='true' )

    # the query string includes the action parameter
    action = requestData[ 'action'][0]
    print "ACTION " + action + "\n"
    # send response code 200 meaning the request
  # has been successfully handled
    self.send_response( 200 )
server = BaseHTTPServer.HTTPServer( ('localhost', 8082), ➥
            myRequestHandler )
server.serve_forever()
```

The preceding code runs a web server on port 8082, which handles GET requests. Each time the server receives a GET request, the server will send a message to the control that tells what action has been requested. You can try this example by executing the Python script from the command line using something like the following: python simplewebserver.py.

You can now use some simple ActionScript code to make a connection to this server:

```
var _response = new LoadVars();
var _result = new LoadVars();
_response.action = "write2File";
_response.sendAndLoad("http://127.0.0.1:8082", _result,"GET");
stop();
```

If you try this code, you can see the following output in the command line where the web server is running:

```
ACTION write2File
localhost - - [14/Apr/2006 11:08:54] "GET / HTTP/1.1" 200 -
```

This output means that the POST request to the local web server has been successful. You can also see that we have requested the write2File command. If you now send this Python script to your mobile device, you can see that the preceding script won't be running. The Python script uses several modules available in the standard Python library that aren't available for the Symbian Series 60 version of Python, so you need to write your own web-server implementation that works for this version of Python. The following code snippet shows working code that acts similar to the previous example:

```
import socket
import string
import mimetools
```

```
import httplib
import time

# change this part if you want to connect to a diff. port
HTTP_PORT = 8082
# end of line marker for the http protocol
EOL = '\r\n'
_headers = ''
# the type of request i.e. GET or POST (only GET supported)
_command = ''
# request command/path
_path = ''
# the version of the received htptp request
_request_version = ''

# send the feedback through the server
def send_message( client_socket, message):
    message_len = len( message )
    client_socket.send('HTTP/1.1 200 OK\n')
    client_socket.send('Content-type: text/html\n')

    contentLength = 'Content-length: %d\n' % ( message_len )
    client_socket.send( contentLength )
    client_socket.send('Connection: close\n\n')
    client_socket.send( message )

# send the error message to the console
def send_error(code, message):
    print code, message

# parse and analyze the incoming http request
def parse_request(headers):
    request_version = version = "HTTP/0.9"
    requestline = headers[0]

    if requestline[-2:] == '\r\n':
        requestline = requestline[:-2]
    elif requestline[-1:] == '\n':
        requestline = requestline[:-1]

    words = requestline.split()
    if len(words) == 3:
        [command, path, version] = words
        if version[:5] != 'HTTP/':
            send_error(400, "bad request version")
            return 0
    elif len(words) == 2:
        [command, path] = words
        if command != 'GET':
```

```
            send_error(400, "bad request type (HTTP/0.9)")
            return 0
    else:
        send_error(400, "bad request syntax")
        return 0

    _path, _command, _request_version = command, path, version
    return _command

def translate_path(path):
    print "path:",path
    words = path.split('/')
    words = filter(None, words)
    return words

def handle_request(client_socket, command_name, params):
    # list of available command and the associated method
    print "ACTION ", command_name
    commands = {'write2file':cmd_writefile}
    commands[command_name]( client_socket, params )
    return True

def cmd_writefile(client_socket ,params):
    send_message(client_socket ,"writing a text file" )

serv = socket.socket(socket.AF_INET, socket.SOCK_STREAM)
serv.bind(('127.0.0.1', HTTP_PORT))
serv.listen(5)
while True:
    print u"Waiting for connection at port ", HTTP_PORT
    (cs,addr) = serv.accept()

    print u"Connection opened with ", addr
    temp = cs.recv(1024)
    headers = string.split(temp, '\r\n')
    _command = parse_request(headers)

    # convert the requested url to a valid command name
    # by removing / etc.
    commandName = translate_path(_command)
    commandName = commandName[0]

    # handle the command
    handle_request(  cs, commandName, '' )

    cs.close()
```

You can test this script by sending the Python script to your mobile phone via Bluetooth. You will receive a message asking you how you want to install the Python script. You should install it as Python Script. Next, start the Python interpreter on your phone, and select Options ➤ Run script. You will see a dialog box where you can select your Python script from a file list.

The preceding code basically opens a socket on the mobile device on port 8082 and keeps listening for any incoming request. The incoming request is output to the console of the Python interpreter, so you can see that the request arrives at your simple web server. The function handleRequest() handles the incoming requests; currently, it shows only the incoming request.

The function handleRequest has an array called commands that contains the list of commands supported by the web server. Every command is handled in one dedicated function unique to the command name, to make the script comprehensible. Look at the current array:

```
commands={'write2file':cmd_writefile}
```

This means that when the command write2file is called, the function cmd_writefile will be executed. This function includes code that will write a string to a text file. For now, the function will only show a message in the console. Change the current code of the cmd_writefile function to the following code, so it will write a text file to a hard-coded location:

```
def cmd_writefile(client_socket ,params):
    filelocation = 'C:\\documents\\flash\textfile.txt'
    file = open( filelocation,'w' )
    file.write( 'Hello, world!' )
    file.close()
```

> As you might have noticed already, the code to write a text file in Python is nearly exactly the same as the code we used in Write2File to write text files in Symbian!

Of course, you can extend the commands array with your own commands—just don't forget to make the function in the Python script too! You can copy the example of cmd_write(), and just change the function name to the one you prefer. You'll be on your own writing the code for the command. You might also want to play with using the Bluetooth support of Python.

You now can use the following code to connect to the local web server, and let it execute your commands:

```
var result_lv:LoadVars = new LoadVars();
result_lv.onLoad = function(success:Boolean) {
    if (success) {
        debug_txt.text = "Success! " + result_lv.welcomeMessage;
    } else {
        debug_txt.text = "Error connecting to server.";
    }
};

var send_lv:LoadVars = new LoadVars();
```

```
send_lv.action = "writefile";
send_lv.sendAndLoad("http://127.0.0.1:8082", result_lv, "GET" );
stop();
```

After you have sent the SWF to the phone using Bluetooth, you should start the local web server in the Python server first. Next, switch to Flash without exiting Python, and open your SWF file. If you switch back to the running Python instance, you should see the string ACTION writefile received.

As you see, you can now use the Python web server to access native functionality that you normally wouldn't have access to from within Flash Lite.

Using the XMLSocket class in Flash Lite 2.1

The latest version of Flash Lite brings support for the class, which makes it possible to expand the world of Flash Lite. Now, you can make multiuser mobile games easily, without needing to poll servers (polling is used in multiuser games; examples of such games in Flash can be found at www.dinkywars.com and http://moock.org/unity/uclientflash). As mentioned earlier, polling allows you to ask the server for updates every once in a while; with XMLSocket, polling is not needed anymore. The Flash Lite application can now receive updates from the server without asking for them.

In this section of the chapter, we will look at how a Flash Lite 2.1 application can become the user interface for a simple, mobile application for controlling iTunes on your computer. This example will make use of the XMLSocket class. It consists of the Flash Lite user interface on the mobile phone and a simple XML socket server that will handle all the requests from the Flash Lite user interface and forward them to the iTunes application. In Figure 10-23, you can see how the iTunes remote control will be built.

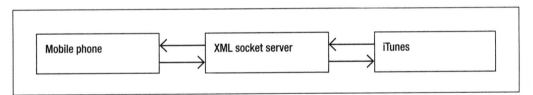

Figure 10-23. The structure of the application

> *Don't know what XML sockets are or how they work? Please refer to any of the good resources about the internal workings of the XMLSocket protocol. I recommend* Flash and Director: Designing Mulituser Web Sites *(Blaha, Thomas et al., Berkeley: friends of ED, 2002).*

What you need

Before you can start writing your iTunes remote control, you first need to prepare your system with the required software. Because the XML socket server will be written in Java, you need to have the Java developer kit installed on our computer. You can check if you have Java installed on your computer by entering the following command in the command prompt:

```
java -version
```

If you already have Java installed on your system something similar to Figure 10-24 will be shown in the command prompt.

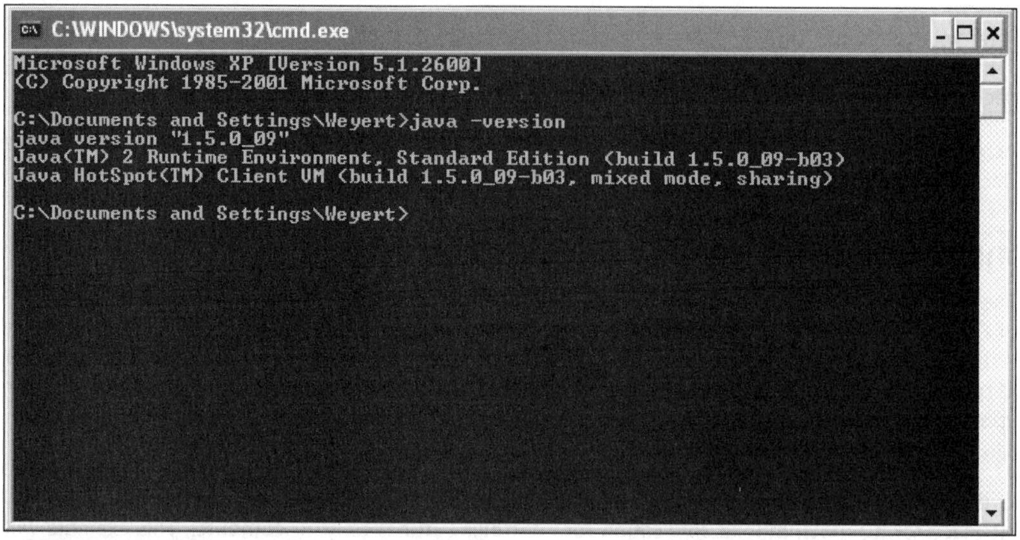

Figure 10-24. The results of calling java -version

However, if you haven't already installed Java on your computer, the command prompt will return the following message:

```
'java' is not recognized as an internal or extenal command,
operable program or batch file.
```

You can download and install the latest Java developer kit from http://java.sun.com. Also download the Java Development Kit (JDK). If you are sure you have installed the JDK and you continue to get the previous error, please make sure the bin directory of the JDK directory on your computer is in the PATH system variable of your computer.

> You might want to install an application that specializes in developing Java applications, such as Eclipse. More information about Eclipse can be found at www.eclipse.org.

Writing the XML socket server

Earlier in the chapter, you wrote a simple local web server in Python for the mobile phone. This time, you are going to write a simple XML socket server for your desktop computer, and you will write the server in Java instead of Python. You will see that the basics will be the same.

The XML socket server will listen to a predefined port number for simple textual instructions received from the mobile phone. The XML socket server will then talk with the iTunes application installed on your computer. The commands listed in Table 10-3 will be supported by the XML socket server.

Table 10-3. Available commands for the iTunes server

Command	Description
play	Play the currently selected track in iTunes
pause	Pause the currently playing track
stop	Stop the currently playing track
next	Play the next track in the play list
previous	Play the previous track in the play list
info	Receive track information, such as the artist and title of the track
tracklist	Receive a list of the tracks available in iTunes

How does the server work?

The iTunes XML socket server will be written in Java and will only work under Microsoft Windows. The reason that this example only works under Microsoft Windows, and *not* under Mac OS X, is that Windows offers a very easy way to communicate with an iTunes instance. You can control iTunes by code or scripts; this technology is called the Component Object Model (COM), and it's basically the same technology that enables you to automate Word or Excel.

> *If you want to have more information on how you can write scripts or automate Apple iTunes on your Windows computer, you can download the iTunes SDK at* http://developer.apple.com/sdk.

Apple iTunes comes with a COM object—the iTunes 1.X Type Library. This object enables you to obtain the play lists available in iTunes and to play and stop tracks. For example, if you want to list all the tracks in the main play list, you can use the following code by saving it as a text file with the file name listPlaylist.js in your favorite text editor, for example, UltraEdit:

```
var iTunesApp = WScript.CreateObject("iTunes.Application");
var mainLibrary = iTunesApp.LibraryPlaylist;
var tracksInList = mainLibrary.Tracks;

for (i = 1; i <= tracksInList.Count; i++)
{
  var currTrack = tracksInList.Item( i );
  WScript.Echo( currTrack.Name + " by " + currTrack.Artist );
}
```

After you have saved the code to a text file, you can run this code in the Windows Script Host, by entering the following command at the command prompt:

```
cscript listPlaylist.js
```

The `cscript` application outputs the result of the `listPlaylist.js` script in the console. You can use `wscript`, if you want to use message boxes instead. For an example of the output in the console, please see Figure 10-25.

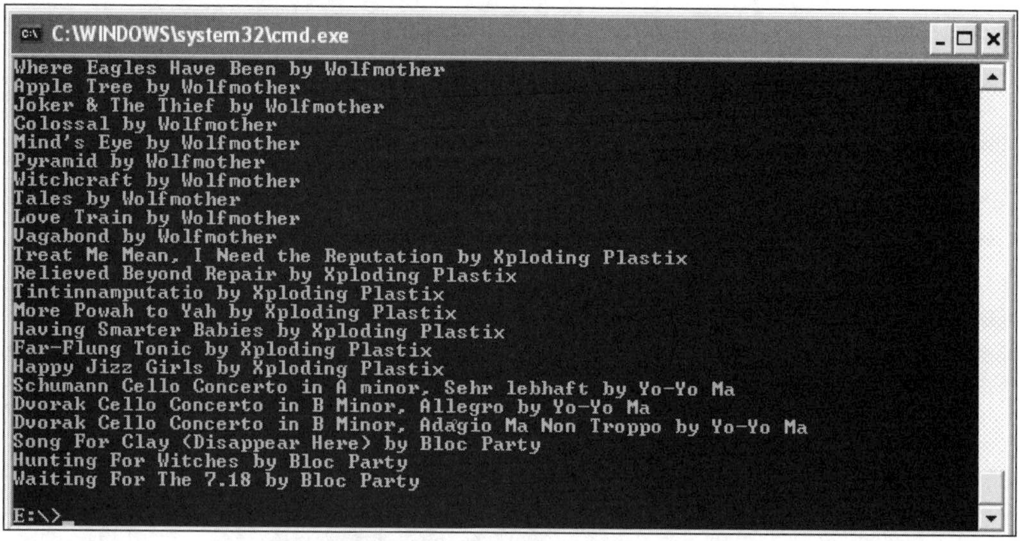

Figure 10-25. The output of the listPlaylist.js script

Of course, you can write more-advanced scripts to fill the play list with tracks of a specific genre or with all tracks without cover art, for example. The same technique used in the previous script will be used by our server to communicate with iTunes only not through script files but directly.

Writing the basic XML socket server

The server supports several commands, listed in Table 10-3, that are made available by iTunes through the COM object. Each time the XML socket server receives a message, it verifies if it received a known command to which it should respond. Each time the server recognizes a command, it forwards this command to iTunes using iTunesController, which we will make later on. The supported commands are simple keywords, such as PLAY, STOP, and NEXT. But before the server can handle these commands, you need to have the server listening for incoming messages!

Making an XML socket server in Java is easy. The server basically opens a port and keeps looking for incoming connections from clients. Each time a client tries to connect to the server, the server will accept the connection and listen to the connected client. The following Java code opens a port and keeps listening until someone tries to connect:

```
import java.io.*;
import java.net.*;
```

```
public class SocketServerSimple
{

    public SocketServerSimple( int port ) {
        ServerSocket server;

        try
        {
            server = new ServerSocket( port );
            System.out.println( "Server running on port: " + port );

            while( true )
            {
                Socket socket = server.accept();
                System.out.println( "Connection established." );
            }
        }
        catch(IOException ioe)
        {
            System.out.println( "Server error:" + ioe.getMessage() );
        }
    }

    public static void main( String args[] )
    {
        SocketServerSimple server = new SocketServerSimple( 8888 );
    }
}
```

Save the preceding code as a text file with the name SocketServerSimple.java. After that, you can compile and run the server by entering the following commands at the command prompt:

```
javac SocketServerSimple.java
java SocketServerSimple
```

> Please note that later in the chapter, you will be adding more Java files, and each of the Java files you use needs to be compiled using javac before you can run the server. You can find an accompanying Eclipse project and all of the Java files in the chapter10\ITunes folder.

The first command compiles the Java application, and the second command runs the server application. You can use telnet to connect to 127.0.0.1 at port 8888 by using the command telnet 127.0.0.1 8888. If everything goes well, you will see a Connection established message in the window where the SocketServerSimple application is running. The next step in the creation of the iTunes server is to separate the code that handles the incoming message from the code that listens for incoming connections. The easiest way to do this is by using the Thread class, which lets you run code in separate threads.

Before you start separating the code, first make a copy of the Java file, and name it iTunesServerApp.java. This will be the main file for your server and will be enhanced with more functionality later in this chapter. Now, open the newly created text file, and add the following code after line 18:

```
ITunesClientThread client = new ITunesClientThread ( this, socket );
client.start();
```

Before you can try out these changes, you need to create the new ITunesClientThread class by copying the following code in a text file named ITunesClientThread.java; the file includes methods that aren't yet used by the code, but these will be added later on:

```
import java.io.*;
import java.net.*;

public class ITunesClientThread extends Thread
{
  private BufferedReader input;
  private PrintWriter output;
  private char EOF = (char)0x00;
  private ITunesServerApp server;
  public ITunesClientThread ( ITunesServerApp server,  Socket socket )
  {
    this.server = server;

    try
    {
      output = new PrintWriter( socket.getOutputStream(), true );
      input = new BufferedReader( new InputStreamReader( ➥
          socket.getInputStream() ) );
    }
    catch (IOException ioe)
    {
      try
      {
        System.out.println( "Server closing due to error: "➥
                                    + ioe.getMessage() );
        socket.close();
      }
      catch (IOException e)
      {
        System.out.println("Server unable to close:" + e.getMessage());
      }
    }
  }

  public void sendMessage( String message ) {
  System.out.println( "OUT: " + message );
  output.println( message + EOF );
  }
```

```java
public void handleCommand( String message ) {
  System.out.println( "Incoming message: " + message );
  this.sendMessage( "PONG!" );
}

public void run()
{
  char buffer[] = new char[1];

  try
  {
    while( input.read(buffer, 0, 1) != -1 )
    {
      String incomingMessage = "";

      while( buffer[0] != '\0' )
      {
        incomingMessage += buffer[0];
        input.read( buffer, 0, 1 );
      }

      // handle the received message
      handleCommand( incomingMessage );
    }
  }
  catch ( IOException ioe )
  {
    System.out.println("Error: Socket disconnected.");
  }
}
}
```

The preceding code can be considered a client connected to the server. Each client gets its own instance of the ITunesClientThread class. The class digs up the incoming message from the client and redirects it to the handleCommand() method. This class is a fully working XML socket server that already handles one simple command—the PING-PONG command. If the client sends the PING command, the server will answer this request with PONG. Before we continue, we are going to test your XML socket server using a simple Flash movie, which will connect to your XML socket server and send the PING command. When everything goes well, you will see a PONG! message in the Output panel of Flash.

Recompile the server, create a new Flash movie with the publish settings set to version 6.0 or above, insert the following ActionScript code, and test the movie:

```actionscript
stop();

socket = new XMLSocket();
socket.connect( "127.0.0.1", 8888 );
socket.onConnect = function() {
  trace("Connected.");
  socket.send( "PING" );
```

```
    }

    socket.onData = function( data ) {
      trace("INCOMING: " + data );
    }
```

You should now have your own XML socket server and client, which we will extend later on. Nice!

Controlling iTunes with commands

Now that you have your own XML socket server running, you need to extend the functionality, so that it will recognize the predefined set of commands. You will add support for these commands by altering the handleCommand() method in the iTunesClientThread class. This method will compare the incoming message with the predefined set of commands, and when a command has been recognized, it will forward the request to the newly made ITunesController class. Before you extend the method, let's make a dummy ITunesController class for testing purposes.

The class consists of the methods listed in Table 10-4.

Table 10-4. Methods in the ITunesController class

Method	Command	Description
nextTrack()	next	Plays the next track in the main play list
previousTrack()	previous	Plays the previous track in the main play list
playTrack()	play	Plays the currently selected track in the main play list
pauseTrack()	pause	Pauses or resumes play of the currently active track
stopTrack()	stop	Stops the currently playing track
getTrackInfo()	info	Returns the current track information (such as the artist and title)
getPlaylist()	playlist	Returns the names of the tracks in the main play list

The ITunesController class has the following responsibilities:

- Starting iTunes
- Mapping incoming commands to their appropriate iTunes versions
- Relaying iTunes playback events to the client

Once again, start by creating a new text file and renaming it ITunesController.java. For now, create dummy methods for the methods listed in Table 10-4 for testing purposes, so that you can be sure the ITunesController class is working correctly without the cluttering code for communication with the iTunes COM object.

The dummy methods are basically the methods in Table 10-4 with a simple System.out.println() command, which outputs the name of the method in the console. You create the class using the following skeleton:

```
import java.util.*;
public void ITunesController {
  private ITunesServerApp server;
  private String message;
  public ITunesController( ITunesServerApp server)
  {
    this.server = server;
    initiateITunes();
  }
  public void initiateITunes()
  {
    // create the com object
  }
  // dummy method should come here
}
```

As you might have noticed by now, Java is very similar to ActionScript 2. To finish the ITunesController class, you need to create the dummy methods. You should copy the following lines of code for all the methods listed in Table 10-4 and replace [methodName] with the appropriate method name:

```
public void [methodName]()
{
    System.out.println( "[methodName]()" );
}
```

After you have finished the creation of this class, modify your existing classes, so that the received commands are forwarded to the ITunesController class. Let's start with the ITunesClientsThread class. Earlier, you changed this class, so that it sends reference of the ITunesServerApp class. You are going to use this reference to send the received commands to ITunesController via the ITunesServerApp class. Before you can use the reference, you need to update the handleCommand() method in ITunesClientThread; this method is responsible for analyzing and forwarding the commands to the server class.

The new code for handleCommand() forwards the request for analyzing the incoming messages to the server class, which then transfers it to the final destination, the ITunesController class:

```
public void handleCommand( String message )
{
  if ( server != null )
  {
    server.doAction( message );
  }
}
```

Now that you have modified the handleCommand() method in the client thread class, you only need to add the real analyzing code in the server class. Open the ITunesServerApp.java file, and add the following doAction() method, which as you see, refers to an instance of the ITunesController class. This means the requests get forwarded to the ITunesController, which again relays the request to iTunes and the ITunesController class that will do the heavy lifting.

```
public void doAction( String message )
{
  controller.handleCommand( message );
}
```

Leveraging iTunes

Now we are going to look at how we can communicate with COM objects, such as the one available for iTunes from Java. Java doesn't support this kind of communication out of the box, but it supports interoperation with native applications, such as DLLs. This framework is well known under the Java Native Interface (JNI). For your iTunes server application, you will use the open source library Jacob, which adds this support for communicating with COM objects from within in Java application. The required library is available for download at http://sourceforge.net/projects/jacob-project.

Once you have the required library, the first thing you need to do is import the definitions of the iTunes COM object, which are available through a type library. The type library definition is included within the iTunes executable. The Jacob library comes with the utility jacobgen to create the classes required to access the COM object. You can create these classes by executing the jacobgen command in the following way:

```
jacobgen -p com.apple.itunes -o com.apple.itunes [path to itunes.exe]
```

jacobgen generates a stack of files in the com.apple.itunes directory. These class files are automatically generated based on the iTunes type library and shouldn't be changed. Copy the generated directory together with jacob.jar and jacob.dll to the root directory where you stored the other Java files.

Your ITunesController class will make use of these classes for the following activites:

- Starting Apple iTunes
- Receiving events from iTunes when tracks get changed within iTunes
- Issuing commands for iTunes

Once again, begin by opening the existing ITunesController.java file, which you will update, so that it makes use of the iTunes jacob classes. The first thing you need to do is import the classes you generated earlier by adding the following lines of code below the first import statement:

```
import com.jacob.activeX.ActiveXComponent;
import com.jacob.com.*;
import com.apple.itunes.*;
```

> *Now that you are using the Jacob library, you need to change the way you compile your Java application. You need to specify where the* Jacob.jar *file can be found by using the class path parameter:* –cp.
>
> *This means the new lines are* javac -cp ./jacob.jar; [java file] *and* java -cp ./jacob.jar;. ITunesServerApp.

After you have added the three lines that import the Jacob library and the iTunes classes, you will add the code that initiates an instance of iTunes using a COM object. The initiateITunes() method will be used to do this job:

```
public void initiateITunes()
{
  ComThread.InitMTA( true );
  ActiveXComponent iTunesCom = new ActiveXComponent(
      "iTunes.Application" );
  Dispatch iTunesController = iTunesCom.getObject();

  iTunes = new IiTunes(iTunesController);

  //Dispatch events.
  new DispatchEvents(iTunes, new ITunesEvents());
}
```

The preceding code uses a private class called ITunesEvents to receive events from iTunes when a user changes songs in the iTunes instance itself. The implementation of the ITunesEvents class is quite easy. It will trigger the method fireEvent() in the container class. The implementation of the ITunesEvent class is a subclass of the ITunesController class:

```
public class ITunesEvents
{
  public void OnPlayerPlayEvent(Variant[] args)
  {
    fireEvent();
  }
}
```

The fireEvent() method is used to get a signal when a track begins to play in iTunes, so that you are able to send the updated track information to the client. The fireEvent() constructs an XML string in the following format: <track artist="artistname">songtitle</track>. That string gets sent to the connected client, so that it can update the track information on the screen. This is the same result that you get when you issue the info command from the client side.

385

The most important code in this class is the code in the handleCommand() method, because this is the place where you tell iTunes what to do:

```java
public void handleCommand( String command )
{
  if ( command.equals( "play" ) )
  {
    iTunes.play();
  }
  else if ( command.equals( "stop" ) )
  {
    iTunes.stop();
  }
  else if ( command.equals( "pause" ) )
  {
    iTunes.playPause();
  }
  else if ( command.equals( "next" ) )
  {
    iTunes.nextTrack();
  }
  else if ( command.equals( "previous" ) )
  {
  iTunes.backTrack();
  }
  else if ( command.equals( "info" ) )
  {
    fireEvent();
  }
}
```

After all of this code the server is finally ready, and you have a working XML socket server that can control your iTunes instance. The final source code of the XML socket server can be found in the subdirectory test of the Chapter 10/itunes/server folder. This folder also includes an Eclipse project for your convenience. In the next section, we will look at the client application, which uses the new XMLSocket support of Flash Lite 2.1.

Writing the Flash Lite user interface

The Flash Lite application for the iTunes remote controller basically has to do the following things:

- Connect to the XML socket server
- Receive and handle commands

The Flash Lite application is basically a nice skin around the functionality of your iTunes XML socket server. You only need code that connects to the XML socket server and code that sends and receives commands to this server. The code for connecting to the XML socket server can be found in Chapter 10/itunes/client/itunes.fla, which adds the code to send the messages to the XML socket server.

To send a message to the server, you can use the send() method of the XMLSocket class instance. For example, if you want to send the command to play the next song you only need the following line:

```
xmlsocket.send( "next" );
```

This little code snippet sends the command next to the server, which lets iTunes play the next song. Now, to make your iTunes Flash client, you only need to add some buttons to control iTunes from your mobile phone. In the Chapter 10/itunes/client folder you can find the file itunes_final.fla, which is my version of the Flash Lite client for the server. It shows the currently playing track in iTunes and even gets updated when someone changes tracks in iTunes.

Testing the controller

After you have completed your XML socket server and Flash Lite application, you can start testing your application in real life. Start the XML socket server by executing the following line at the command prompt:

```
java ITunesServerApp [portnumber]
```

If everything went well, Apple iTunes should start on your computer, and you can try out the Flash Lite application on your mobile phone. If you are unable to connect to the XML socket server you might want to make sure that you have a signal and that you can access the XML socket server from a different location.

You can test whether you can connect to your XML socket server using a telnet connection with it, as shown earlier in the section titled "Writing the basic XML socket server." If the client gets connected, you will see that the server outputs a message similar to the following:

```
Connected with client 192.168.100.13 established.
```

If not, you might want to open your firewall, or ask your network administrator to help you. Once you can connect to the server from different locations, you can try out the Flash Lite application on your mobile phone. Keep in mind that you have updated the HOSTNAME and PORT_NUMBER variables in the Flash Lite movie according to your local situation. In Figure 10-26, you can see the server and Flash Lite application running on my mobile phone and computer.

> *If you are using a firewall, you need to open the port number with which you have started the server. You may even need to forward the port to the correct computer in your network to make the XML socket server fully accessible to the outside world.*

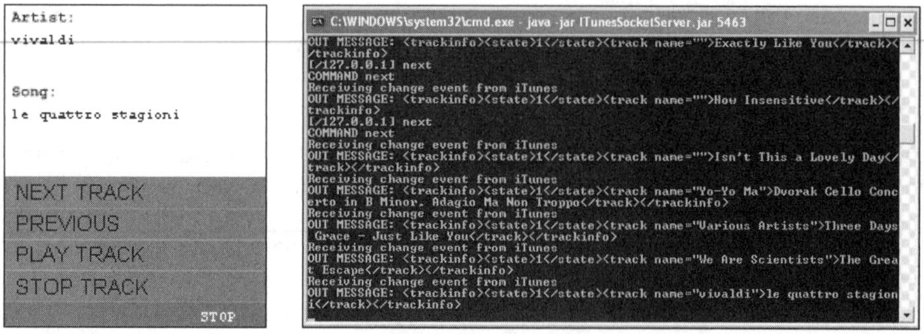

Figure 10-26. The iTunes controller in real life

Now that you have finished the iTunes remote control, you have learned how to write your own XML socket server in Java and how to communicate with COM objects available under Windows. You might want to write a similar project that will control Windows Media Player or the lights in your house. If you want to control your lights, you might want to have look at X10, which enables you to control lights and appliances using a Java interface.

Summary

You can work around limitations of Flash Lite by using one of the solutions presented in this chapter. Of course, the functionality of Write2File can be integrated in the local HTTP server, but why would you want to run a local web server only to write text files on the mobile phone? For that purpose, I think the Write2File application will do just fine, but when you want to access native functionality of the phone, the use of a local HTTP server might help. The XMLSocket support in Flash Lite 2.1 is a nice addition; the class avoids the polling requirement, which is still around when using a local HTTP server. While parts of this chapter may have been difficult to grasp, I hope it gave you ideas about how to extend the basic functionality of Flash on the mobile device of your choice. As you can see, Flash Lite gives you the opportunity to create compelling user experiences on the mobile phone.

In the next chapter, we will look at how you can deploy and distribute your creations to customers around the world.

## Part Three

THE POST-DEVELOPMENT STAGE

Chapter 11

DISTRIBUTION AND DEPLOYMENT

In the previous chapters, we talked in depth about how to develop useful and exciting Flash applications that take into account mobile devices' limitations, for example, bandwidth and memory availability.

This chapter will help you through the process of distributing and deploying your Flash applications to your customers for their various mobile devices. My goal is to present you with all of the information you need to make this happen, including the pitfalls you should watch out for. The topics I will cover include:

- The Web (WML and XHTML Mobile Profile)
- Making installers
- Existing content providers
- Service providers

The Web (WML and XHTML Mobile Profile)

In this section, we will explore the Extensible Hypertext Markup Language (XHTML) and how to develop web sites for mobile devices. You will be able to create web sites that host Flash Lite applications that are accessible from the Internet, and you will learn advantages and disadvantages of using XHTML in this context. For example, the rich web sites loaded with images and animation that we have become accustomed to of late won't fit on the small screens of mobile devices. Besides the small screens, the available memory and bandwidth on the mobile devices won't allow users to view these rich web sites with the same quality they experience on desktop computers.

The currently existing markup languages follow:

- **Hypertext Markup Language (HTML)**: This markup language is used on the Internet.
- **Extensible Markup Language (XML)**: This is the markup language used to describe data.
- **Wireless Markup Language (WML)**: This markup language is for mobile devices. Now that an increasing number of mobile phones seem to support XHTML Mobile Profile, WML will be phased out, so it can be considered deprecated.
- **XHTML**: XHTML uses the definitions of HTML 4.0 but requires proper XML syntax.
- **XHTML Basic**: This simpler version of XHTML can be used for mobile devices.
- **XHTML Mobile Profile (XHTML MP)**: This language is based on XHTML Basic but has enhanced functionality, including additional presentation elements and support for internal style sheets.
- **Ajax on Mobile:** Brings Asynchronous JavaScript and XML (Ajax) and the Web 2.0 principles to the mobile phone offered by Opera.

XHTML Mobile Profile

XHTML MP 1.0 is the official markup language of Wireless Application Protocol (WAP) 2.0. WAP 2.0 is the most-recent mobile-services specification created by the Open Mobile Alliance (OMA), formerly known as the WAP Forum. The goal of this specification is to merge the markup languages for mobile devices into one used for the Web. XHTML MP is a subset of XHTML, which is a stricter version of HTML. An important part of the WAP 2.0 specification is WAP Cascading Style Sheets (WAP CSS), a close companion of XHTML MP.

The goal of XHTML MP is to bring together the mobile Internet browsing technologies and the technologies for the World Wide Web. XHTML is very accessible to web developers, as they won't need to learn any new tags to get going. For more information about web development for mobile devices, have a look at the World Wide Web Consortium (W3C) Mobile Best Practices page at www.w3.org/TR/mobile-bp.

A well-formed XHTML MP document must adhere to the following rules:

- The document must contain a root element (in our case, <html> for XHTML MP).
- All other elements are children of this root element.
- All elements begin with < and end with >.
- All end elements begin with </ and end with >.
- All start elements should have an end element.

Every XHTML MP file must begin with a standard prologue, including an XML header and a document-definition tag:

```
<!DOCTYPE html PUBLIC "-WAPFORUMDTD XHTML Mobile 1.0EN" ➡
  "http:www.wapforum.org/DTD/xhtml-mobile10.dtd">
<html xmlns="http://www.w3.org/1999/xhtml">
```

The rest of the code must be surrounded by <html> and </html> tags. Skeleton code for an XHTML MP page follows:

```
<!DOCTYPE html PUBLIC "-WAPFORUMDTD XHTML Mobile 1.0EN"
"http:www.wapforum.org/DTD/xhtml-mobile10.dtd">
<html xmlns="http://www.w3.org/1999/xhtml">
<head>
  <meta http-equiv="Content-Type"
   content="text/html; charset=iso-8859-1" />
  <title>Document Title</title>
</head>
<body>
Content of the document
</body>
</html>
```

XHTML MP basics

The best way to learn how to use XHTML MP is by example. I'd like to go through the process of developing a simple web page where users can download the game installer (created later in the "Making installers" section of this chapter) or click through to a direct link to the Flash SWF file. Most Flash Lite–capable phones should be able to handle such pages without problems. In the first example, we will create a simple page to download a Flash Lite game directly to the mobile phone. In the second example, we will embed the Flash Lite game in the page itself.

Creating a download page

Creating a download page so that customers can download your Flash content over the Internet is very simple. You basically need to store the files you want to make available somewhere on a web server and make a link to these files. You can make links in a web page by using the <a> tag. If you want to put the link to the file in the same folder as your web page, you can use the following line:

```
<a href="myfilenamehere">My description of
the file here</a>
```

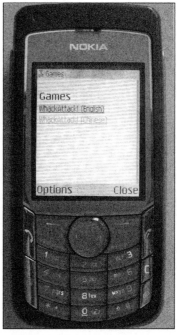

Figure 11-1. The download page on a Nokia 6681

For example, to make a list of downloadable games, you can use something like the following; the result is shown in Figure 11-1:

```
<!DOCTYPE html PUBLIC "-WAPFORUMDTD XHTML Mobile 1.0EN"
   "http:www.wapforum.org/DTD/xhtml-mobile10.dtd">
<html xmlns="http://www.w3.org/1999/xhtml">
<head>
<meta http-equiv="Content-Type" content="text/html;
        charset=iso-8859-1" />
```

393

```
      <title>Games</title>
    </head>
    <body>
      <h1>Games</h1>
      <a href="whackattack_en.sis">WhackAttack! (English)</a><br />
      <a href="whackattack_ch.sis">WhackAttack! (Chinese)</a><br />
    </body>
  </html>
```

> *Before you are able to download SIS packages from a web server, you need to associate the MIME type* application/vnd.symbian.install *(for second-edition Symbian phones) or* x-epoc/x-sisx-app *(for third-edition Symbian phones) with the* .sis *file extension. You can find more information about how to make these changes at* http://httpd.apache.org/docs/1.3/mod/mod_mime.html.

Creating an embedded Flash page

Embedding Flash in a web page for mobile phones isn't much different from doing the same thing for a web page on the Internet, but you need to be aware that not all mobile phones will recognize the Flash content in a browser. Web pages with embedded Flash content will only work when the phone's embedded browser supports Flash Lite. This means that such pages won't work with the stand-alone version of the Flash Lite player for Symbian phones. In Figure 11-2, you can see what Flash Lite looks like in the embedded browser.

Figure 11-2. Embedded Flash on a Nokia N80

Based on the web page skeleton presented earlier, you would only need to add the following code between the <body> and </body> tags to create the Flash Lite image shown in Figure 11-2. This code adds the Flash content into the page using the <object> object, similar to the way it's handled in browsers such as Firefox or Safari:

```
<object data="myflashmovie.swf" type="application/➥
x-shockwave-flash" width="325" height="385">
  <param name="bgcolor" value="#FFFFFF" />
  <param name="loop" value="on" />
  <param name="quality" value="high" />
</object>
```

As you can see, it's easy to make web pages that are accessible by the browser of the mobile phone. Using web pages like this makes it easier to access or download Flash Lite content from the Internet.

Making installers

Once you have made your Flash application, you also want to distribute your application to the clients in the most user-friendly way—using an installer that assists in the process of installing the application on the mobile device. In this section, we will look at how you can make installers for mobile devices, such as mobile phones and Pocket PCs.

This section requires you to have the Symbian SDK installed (you learned how to install the Symbian SDK in Chapter 9). Please refer to the "Compiling write2file under Windows" section of Chapter 10 to learn more about how to compile Symbian applications.

Again, mobile phone installers are used to install software on the mobile phone, and there are two ways to distribute your content to the mobile phones of your customers. The first way is to give the customer a link to the Flash movie or web page, as shown earlier in the download page example. However, the second option is the most-frequently used solution—using the standardized SIS packages on Symbian-enabled mobile phones.

For information about the deployment of mobile applications on mobile devices that don't support Symbian SIS packages, such as the Nokia Series 40 phones, please refer to the section "Deploying by pushing" later in this chapter.

Understanding SIS packages

SIS packages provide a standardized and convenient way to distribute software for Symbian mobile phones. They make it easier for end users to install software on their mobile phones. The main reasons to make use of SIS packages on mobile phones are as follows:

- End users can install/uninstall a SIS package through PC connectivity or from other mobiles phones.

- SIS packages come with versioning mechanisms for easy upgrading.

After the end user receives a SIS file on the mobile phone, the file can be automatically recognized because of the known file extension. The Symbian operating system executes its installer software to start the installation process of the application using the content stored within the SIS file. In Figure 11-3, you can see an installation in progress. In the following sections, we will look at how such a SIS file is made and how you can add menu icons to the mobile phone for your Flash movie.

Figure 11-3. Installation software on a Symbian phone

Distributing content with SIS packages using SWF2SIS

SWF2SIS is a wizard for the Symbian SDK made by the British company BlueskyNorth. The application makes it easy to create installers and will add icons to the phone menus. In the next section, we will explore what SWF2SIS is doing in the background. But first, I will show you how to make menu icons for your application using this wizard-style application. More information about SWF2SIS can be found at the following web site: www.blueskynorth.com/swf2sis. Please note that SWF2SIS is currently not compatible with third-edition Symbian mobile phones.

The installation process of SWF2SIS is easy; you should only need to unpack the obtained ZIP file, which includes the SWF2SIS.exe application. You can start SWF2SIS by clicking the application's icon. Each time you start SWF2SIS, the application searches the computer for installed Symbian SDKs. If you have any of the supported SDKs installed, the main screen will appear (see Figure 11-4).

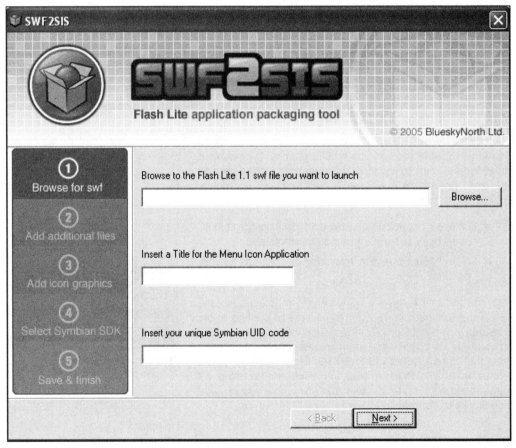

Figure 11-4. The main screen of SWF2SIS, "Browse for swf"

As you can see in Figure 11-4, SWF2SIS consists of the following steps:

1. Selecting the Flash movie to be installed on the mobile phone
2. Adding additional files, such as text files
3. Selecting the menu icons
4. Selecting one of the available Symbian SDKs
5. Saving and finishing

In the first text field on the first screen, you need to select the Flash Lite movie that you want to launch when the user selects the menu item for this movie. In the second text field, you need to specify the title you want to see below the icon associated with your application. The third text field asks you to insert a Symbian UID code; this is a unique number for your application. On the www.symbiansigned.com web site, you can request a set of unique numbers that will be associated with you from now on. Click the Next button to go to the second step of the process (see Figure 11-5).

Figure 11-5. The second page of the SWF2SIS wizard, "Add additional files"

As the screen in Figure 11-5 shows, you can add more files that you want to distribute. If your Flash movie uses external assets, such as extra Flash movies, you must add these in the text box. In the second text field, you are able to specify the name of the subfolder where these additional files should be stored. Click the Next button to move on to the third screen of the wizard (see Figure 11-6).

Figure 11-6. The third page of the wizard, "Add icon graphics"

In the third screen, shown in Figure 11-6, you can select the icon that should appear in the menu of the mobile phone. In the first text field, enter the file path to the image you want to appear for your application in the menu. In the second text field, enter the application mask, the picture that's used to make the icon transparent. The black pixels of the icon mask represent the pixels that should be replaced with transparency in the application icon selected in the first box. Figure 11-7 shows the third page of the wizard with the text fields filled in. Please note that SWF2SIS comes with a "read me" file (or see www.blueskynorth.com/swf2sis/read_me.pdf), which explains how to make application icons and masks images.

Figure 11-7. The third page of the wizard with the application icon and application mask file paths specified

Click the Next button to move to the fourth screen of SWF2SIS (see Figure 11-8), where you can select the Symbian SDK you want to use for creating the menu icon from a list of all Symbian SDKs installed on your computer. You should select the SDK that matches the Symbian version of your target mobile phone.

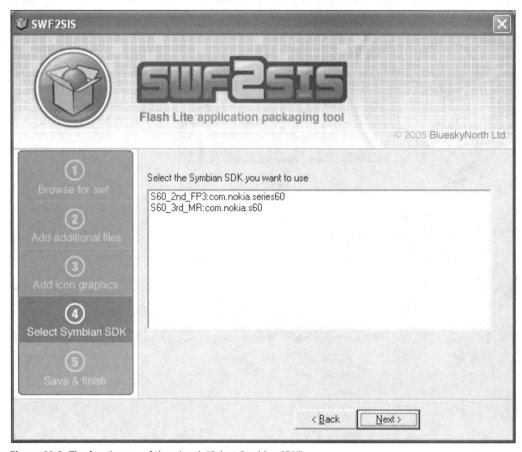

Figure 11-8. The fourth page of the wizard, "Select Symbian SDK"

In the last step of the SWF2SIS wizard, you have to specify the name of the final SIS file and its location on your computer. After you have specified this, as shown in Figure 11-9, you can click the Finish button to create the SIS file.

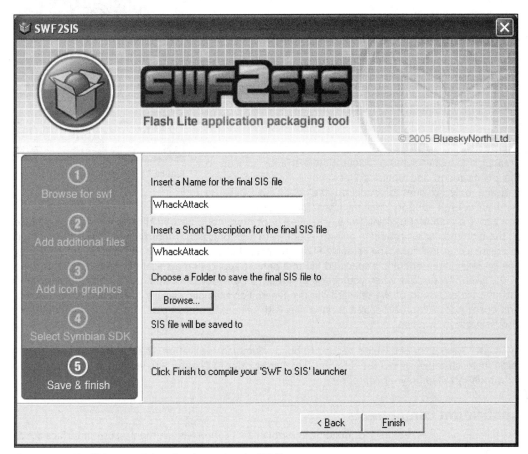

Figure 11-9. The fifth page of the wizard, creating the SIS file

Once SWF2SIS is finished creating the SIS file, you can send the resulting file to your mobile device using Bluetooth or in some other way. In Figure 11-10, you can see the final result on a real device.

Creating installers the hard way

Of course, you can use tools such as SWF2SIS to create your installer packages for distributing your Flash applications to the client's phone. But what if you want to make your own installers without using the wizard? In this section, we will look at how you can make installers using the tools available through the Symbian SDK.

Figure 11-10. SWF2SIS icon on a Nokia 6681

Creating a launcher Symbian application that adds an icon to the phone menu and opens a Flash movie isn't hard to do. Basically, only six lines of code do the real work. Because Symbian doesn't support creating icons for applications that don't have a graphical user interface, you need a lot more code beyond those six lines, to introduce all the required classes to create an application with a graphical user interface—we won't be using it to create a user interface. The reusable Flash launcher that we will build in this section will have only one responsibility—opening a specified file in a default application associated with the file extension of the given file. Just like when you click a desktop icon on your computer, the application associated with the file extension of the selected file is opened. For example, clicking files with the .psd extension opens Adobe Photoshop, and clicking files with .fla extensions opens Flash. This functionality is also available in Symbian.

In Chapter 9, we discussed what's needed to build a Symbian application. The requirements are no different here, although we will use different files. Please refer to Chapter 9 to verify that you have all the right tools installed on your computer.

Application components

The minimum classes required for building a Symbian application with a graphical user interface are as follows:

- **Application View**: The class is the main view and implements the main window of the application, similar to the stage of a Flash movie.
- **Application UI**: This class creates an instance of the Application View class.
- **Application Document**: This class handles all nongraphic aspects of the application.
- **Application**: This is the main entry class; it starts the application by creating an instance of the Application Document class.

For our Flash launcher, we will only be using the Application and Application Document classes. Because we won't make use of any graphical user interface, we won't need to implement anything else. Of course, these classes still have to be in our application, only they won't do anything but exist.

Creating the application

The Flash launcher project is organized using the advised Symbian directory structure. You can download these files from this book's page at www.friendsofed.com if you get sick of typing! The directory structure follows:

- \aif
  - FlashLauncherAif.rss
- \inc
  - FlashLauncher.h
- \src
  - FlashLauncherApp.cpp
  - FlashLauncherAppUI.cpp
  - FlashLauncherDocument.cpp
  - main.cpp
- \group
  - bld.inf
  - FlashLauncher.mmp
- \data
  - flashlauncher.rss
  - flashlauncher_caption.rss
- \sis
  - FlashLauncher.pkg

To create the Flash launcher application, you need to perform the following steps:

1. Create the application header (.h) file.
2. Create the resource (.rss).
3. Create the source code for the application classes declared in the header (.cpp).
4. Create project definition (.mmp and .bld.inf) files.
5. Build and run the example on the PC-based emulator.
6. Create the target package definition (.pkg) file.
7. Generate the SIS package (.sis), and install it on the phone.

Creating the header file

Use your favorite text editor to make a new text file, give it the name FlashLauncher.h, and store it in the inc directory:

```
#ifndef __FLASHLAUNCHER_H__
#define __FLASHLAUNCHER_H__

// INCLUDES
#include <aknapp.h>
#include <aknappui.h>
#include <akndoc.h>
#include <apgcli.h>

// CLASS DECLARATION
class CFlashLauncherApp : public CAknApplication
    {
    public:
        TUid AppDllUid() const;

    protected:
        CApaDocument* CreateDocumentL();
    };

// CLASS DECLARATION
class CFlashLauncherAppUi : public CAknAppUi {
    public:
        void ConstructL();

        CFlashLauncherAppUi();

        virtual ~CFlashLauncherAppUi();
    public:
    private:
    };

// FORWARD DECLARATIONS
class CEikApplication;

// CLASS DECLARATION
class CFlashLauncherDocument : public CAknDocument
    {
    public:
        static CFlashLauncherDocument* NewL( CEikApplication& aApp );

        static CFlashLauncherDocument* NewLC( CEikApplication& aApp );

        virtual ~CFlashLauncherDocument();

    public:
```

```
        CEikAppUi* CreateAppUiL();

    private:
        void ConstructL();

        CFlashLauncherDocument( CEikApplication& aApp );
    };

    #endif // end of __FLASHLAUNCHER_H__
```

Creating the resource files

Use your favorite text editor to make a new text file, give it the name FlashLauncher.rss, and store it in the data directory:

```
// RESOURCE IDENTIFIER
NAME FLEX

// INCLUDES
#include <eikon.rh>
#include <avkon.rh>
#include <avkon.rsg>

RESOURCE RSS_SIGNATURE {
}
```

Use your favorite text editor to make a new text file, give it the name FlashLauncher_caption.rss, and store it in the data directory:

```
// INCLUDES
#include <apcaptionfile.rh>

// RESOURCE DEFINITIONS
RESOURCE CAPTION_DATA {
    caption      = "FlashLauncher";
    shortcaption = "FlashLauncher";
}

// End of File
```

Use your favorite text editor to make a new text file, give it the name FlashLauncherAif.rss, and store it in the aif directory:

```
#include <aiftool.rh>

RESOURCE AIF_DATA {
    app_uid = 0x10005B91;
    num_icons = 1;
    embeddability = KAppNotEmbeddable;
    newfile = KAppDoesNotSupportNewFile;
}
```

Creating the source files

Use your favorite text editor to create the following text files, and store them in the src directory:

FlashLauncherApp.cpp
```cpp
// INCLUDE FILES
#include "FlashLauncher.h"

// UID for the application;
const TUid KUidFlashLauncher = { 0x10005B91 };

CApaDocument* CFlashLauncherApp::CreateDocumentL() {
    // Create an FlashLauncherApp document, and return a pointer to it
    return (static_cast<CApaDocument*>
                    ( CFlashLauncherDocument::NewL( *this ) ) );
}

TUid CFlashLauncherApp::AppDllUid() const {
    // Return the UID for the FlashLauncherApp application
    return KUidFlashLauncher;
}
```

FlashLauncherAppUI.cpp
```cpp
// INCLUDE FILES
#include <aknapp.h>
#include <aknappui.h>
#include <akndoc.h>
#include <apgcli.h>

#include "FlashLauncher.h"

// the relative path to the file has to be opened
// with the default application
_LIT( KBootstrapFileName, "\\documents\\flash\\myFlashFile.swf" );

void CFlashLauncherAppUi::ConstructL() {
  // session of the application server architecture
  RApaLsSession currSession;
  TThreadId currThreadId;  // the threadid of the default application
  TFileName appPath;  // get the application name and the path
  TFileName bootstrapFileName;  // the actual bootstrap file

  CleanupClosePushL( currSession );

  // connect this client to the app arch. server
  User::LeaveIfError( currSession.Connect() );

  // get the drive letter from the application location
  appPath = Application()->AppFullName();
  bootstrapFileName = TParsePtrC( appPath ).Drive();
```

```
    // add the drive letter to the location of the bootstrap file
    bootstrapFileName.Append( KBootstrapFileName );

    // open the file using the default application associated with
    // the mimetype of the bootstrap file
    //
    // when this command fails our application will be closed silently
    User::LeaveIfError( currSession.StartDocument(
            bootstrapFileName, currThreadId ) );

    // close the connection of this client with the app arch. server
    currSession.Close();
}

/**
 * Constructor
 */
CFlashLauncherAppUi::CFlashLauncherAppUi() {
}

/**
 * Destructor
 */
CFlashLauncherAppUi::~CFlashLauncherAppUi() {
}
```

FlashLauncherDocument.cpp
```
// INCLUDE FILES
#include "FlashLauncher.h"

CFlashLauncherDocument* CFlashLauncherDocument::NewL( CEikApplication& aApp ) {
    CFlashLauncherDocument* self = NewLC( aApp );
    CleanupStack::Pop( self );
    return self;
}

CFlashLauncherDocument* CFlashLauncherDocument::NewLC( CEikApplication& aApp ) {
    CFlashLauncherDocument* self =
        new ( ELeave ) CFlashLauncherDocument( aApp );

    CleanupStack::PushL( self );
    self->ConstructL();
    return self;
}

void CFlashLauncherDocument::ConstructL() {
    // No implementation required
}
```

```
CFlashLauncherDocument::CFlashLauncherDocument( ➥
    CEikApplication& aApp ) : CAknDocument( aApp ) {
    // No implementation required
}

CFlashLauncherDocument::~CFlashLauncherDocument() {
    // No implementation required
}

CEikAppUi* CFlashLauncherDocument::CreateAppUiL() {
    // Create the application user interface, and return a pointer to it;
    // the framework takes ownership of this object
    return ( static_cast <CEikAppUi*> ( new ( ELeave )
                                        CFlashLauncherAppUi ) );
}
```

```
main.cpp
// INCLUDE FILES
#include "FlashLauncher.h"

// Entry point function for Symbian Apps.
GLDEF_C TInt E32Dll( TDllReason /*aReason*/ ) {
    // DLL entry point, return that everything is ok
    return KErrNone;
}

// Create an application, and return a pointer to it
EXPORT_C CApaApplication* NewApplication() {
    return ( static_cast<CApaApplication*> ( new CFlashLauncherApp ) );
}
// End of File
```

You now have all the source files, so let's create the project files we need to build the application.

Creating the project files

Use your favorite text editor to create the following text files, and store them in the group directory:

```
FlashLauncher.mmp
TARGET          FlashLauncher.app
TARGETTYPE      app

// Change the second number here to change the UID for this
 application
UID             0x100039CE              0x10005B91
TARGETPATH      \system\apps\FlashLauncher

SOURCEPATH      ..\src
SOURCE          main.cpp
SOURCE          FlashLauncherApp.cpp
```

```
SOURCE          FlashLauncherAppui.cpp
SOURCE          FlashLauncherDocument.cpp


SOURCEPATH      ..\data
RESOURCE        FlashLauncher.rss
RESOURCE        FlashLauncher_caption.rss

USERINCLUDE     ..\inc

SYSTEMINCLUDE   \epoc32\include

LIBRARY         euser.lib
LIBRARY         apparc.lib
LIBRARY         cone.lib
LIBRARY         eikcore.lib
LIBRARY         avkon.lib
LIBRARY         apgrfx.lib
LIBRARY         efsrv.lib

LANG            SC


AIF FlashLauncher.aif ..\aif FlashLauncherAif.rss c12 ➥
    menu_icon_color.bmp menu_icon_mask.bmp

// End of File
```

abld.inf
```
PRJ_MMPFILES
FlashLauncher.mmp
```

Now you are finished creating all of the files you need to build the application. Most of the files for the FlashLauncher project are required to place an icon in the menu of the mobile phone, because you can only get an icon in the menu of the mobile phone when you have an application with a graphical interface. In the preceding project file code, you can find the common code used to create an application with a graphical user interface. The only code you need to add to that application is the code you find in the ConstructL method of the CFlashLauncherAppUI class. The code you need to add follows:

```
// session of the application server architecture
RApaLsSession currSession;
TThreadId currThreadId;  // the threadid of the default application
TFileName appPath;  // get the application name and the path
TFileName bootstrapFileName;  // the actual bootstrap file

CleanupClosePushL( currSession );

// connect this client to the app arch. server
User::LeaveIfError( currSession.Connect() );
```

409

```
// get the drive letter from the application location
appPath = Application()->AppFullName();
bootstrapFileName = TParsePtrC( appPath ).Drive();

// add the drive letter to the location of the bootstrap file
bootstrapFileName.Append( KBootstrapFileName );

// open the file using the default application associated with
// the mimetype of the bootstrap file
//
// when this command fails our application will be closed silently
User::LeaveIfError( currSession.StartDocument( ➥
bootstrapFileName, currThreadId ) );

// close the connection of this client with the app arch. server
currSession.Close();
```

The preceding code performs the following steps:

1. Get the drive letter based on the location of the launcher application.

2. Append the drive letter to the KBootstrapFileName variable.

3. Open the file specified in KBootstrapFileName in the default application associated with the MIME type or file extension of the file.

The preceding code tries to open myFlashFile.swf in the \\Documents\Flash directory, the same drive that the launcher application has been stored in. If you want to open a different Flash file, for example, a Flash movie called snake.swf, you should update the path specified in the KBootstrapFileName variable at line 3 of FlashLauncherAppUI.cpp.

Building the application

Go to the directory where you have stored the source files created in the previous steps. In this folder, you created the group directory earlier; this group directory is the place to be. Before you build the application, don't forget to put the icon bitmaps in the aif folder. Otherwise, you won't have your own customized menu icons. The following bitmaps are required: menu_icon_color.bmp and menu_icon_mask.bmp.

To build the application, you need to type the following commands at the command prompt:

```
bldmake bldfiles
abld build wins
```

After the compilation completes, use the epoc command in the command prompt to start the emulator. Once the emulator is running, you will see the icon of your choice in the menu. If you try to run this application by clicking the icon now, you will get a system error, because the Flash Lite player isn't available in the emulator. But you can still use the emulator to verify that your icons are displayed correctly!

If you are happy with your Flash launcher, you can build the application again—this time not for the emulator but for mobile phones. Instead of using abld build wins, you should use the following command:

```
abld build thumb urel
```

After you have successfully built the application, you should create the PKG file that will be used to create the SIS package file. The PKG file includes the instructions for which files should be wrapped into the SIS file and what should happen with these files on the mobile phone. The contents of the FlashLauncher.pkg file follow:

```
; FlashExecutor
;
;Language - standard language definitions
&EN

; standard SIS file header
#{"FlashLauncher"},          (0x10005B91),   2,  0,  0, TYPE=SISAPP

;Supports Series 60  v2.0
(0x101F7960), 0, 0, 0, {"Series60ProductID"}

;
"\Symbian\8.0a\S60_2nd_FP2\Epoc32\release\thumb\urel\FlashLauncher.➡
app" -"!:\system\apps\FlashLauncher\FlashLauncher.app"

"\Symbian\8.0a\S60_2nd_FP2\Epoc32\data\Z\system\APPS\FlashLauncher\➡
FlashLauncher.rsc" - "!:\system\apps\FlashLauncher\FlashLauncher.rsc"

"\Symbian\8.0a\S60_2nd_FP2\Epoc32\data\Z\system\APPS\FlashLauncher\➡
FlashLauncher_caption.rsc" -➡
"!:\system\apps\FlashLauncher\FlashLauncher_caption.rsc"➡

"\Symbian\8.0a\S60_2nd_FP2\Epoc32\data\Z\system\APPS\FlashLauncher\➡
FlashLauncher.aif"-"!:\system\apps\FlashLauncher\FlashLauncher.aif"➡

"myFlashFile.swf" - "!:\documents\flash\myFlashFile.swf"
```

After you have created this file, don't forget to copy the file(s) you want to install, which is only myFlashFile.swf in this example, to the same location as FlashLauncher.pkg. After you have done this, you can create the SIS file by typing the following command at the command line:

```
makesis FlashLauncher.pkg
```

Now you should have a SIS package file that adds a menu icon to your mobile phone and tries to open the myFlashFile.swf file when you select this icon.

Deploying by pushing

There are several ways to get content to mobile users. Users can go to a web site to download the content, which means that the user **pulls** the content from the server. But, you can also use the popular SMS and MMS technology to **push** the content from the server to the user. The companies who sell ring tones and wallpaper frequently use this method.

The push method is probably the easiest way for the user to obtain content, because it causes the least amount of hassle for the users.

Earlier you sent SIS packages via Bluetooth to your mobile phone. You can also use Bluetooth as a way of pushing content to your mobile phone, but you should keep in mind that when you want to use the push method, you need server solutions that can send SMS or MMS messages.

Existing content providers

Once you have packaged your mobile content, you also need to sell your goods. Content providers can assist in selling your mobile content to customers. They allow you to place your content in a catalog that can be accessed by interested customers or operators using the network, so you have access to millions of potential customers.

Nokia Preminet

Nokia Preminet is a marketplace that makes it possible for developers to sell their creations. Because Preminet allows developers to submit their content for addition in the Preminet Content Catalog, the content will be globally available by operators that are part of Preminet.

Developers, like you, can submit their content through a simple web interface. This interface allows developers to specify details about their applications, such as supported devices, genres, and descriptions. Once Preminet has accepted the content, the content will be available through the following methods:

- **SMS store**: Access the store via simple SMS messages.
- **WAP interface**: Browse the catalog using simple web pages.
- **Internet store**: Browse the catalog via the World Wide Web.
- **Preminet purchasing client**: This client can branded in the house style of the operator.

In Figure 11-11, you can see examples of the purchasing client and the web interface of Preminet.

Nokia Preminet offers the try-buy solution, where the end user can preview or try interesting content before buying it. This solution avoids end users' irritation at buying "bad" content, that is, content that isn't what they expected. Preminet is not only useful from the end user's point-of-view; it can help operators setting up services with ready-made, quality content.

Figure 11-11. Screenshots of interfaces of Nokia Preminet

Handango

Handango, another leading mobile content provider, offers developers a platform where their content can be delivered to the end user. The Handango web site (www.handango.com) serves millions of interesting content for all kind of platforms from mobile phones and smart phones to palmtops.

Through the Handango Content Partner Program, Handango offers developers direct access to millions of potential customers using Handango's multichannel network. Handango helps content providers market and deliver their content to these customers. The Handango multichannel network includes the following channels:

- **Consumer through Web**: The Handango web site provides customers with a pool of rich content.

- **Handset manufacturers**: Handango has been chosen by manufacturers such as Nokia and Samsung as the preferred content provider.

- **Mobile operators**: Operators, such as Verizon and Vodafone, use Handango's network to provide their users with Handango content.

The Handango Content Partner Program comes with a nice web site where content developers can administer the content that they want to sell through the Handango channels. Handango offers one full-featured web site for managing products as well as the marketing and sale of your products (see Figure 11-12). This makes it easy for independent content providers to tap into the world of mobile entertainment.

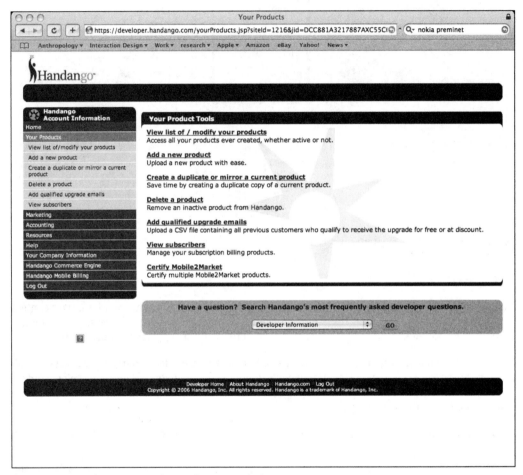

Figure 11-12. Handango Content Partner Program web site

Adding Flash content to Handango

As of November 2006, the Handango web site accepts Flash content for Symbian Series 60 and Series 40 devices. If you become a content partner member (see http://developer.handango.com), you are able to add content and mark it as Flash content. All the Flash content you would like to supply to Handango needs to be wrapped into SIS packages, as mentioned previously. To add content, choose Add a new product from the menu on the web site. This will bring you to a web page were you can specify on which platform your Flash content works; normally, this platform will be Symbian OS or Windows Mobile. After you have selected the platform, you will get the Product Detail Information page, shown in Figure 11-13, where you can specify if your content is Flash content. The rest of the process for adding content is related to defining information, such as support contact details. Once you have completed the form, you have to upload the product itself and specify more information for product registration.

As you can see, selling Flash content through the Handango platform is easy. Figure 11-13 shows the previously created Snake game being added to the web site, and Figure 11-14 shows the products overview page.

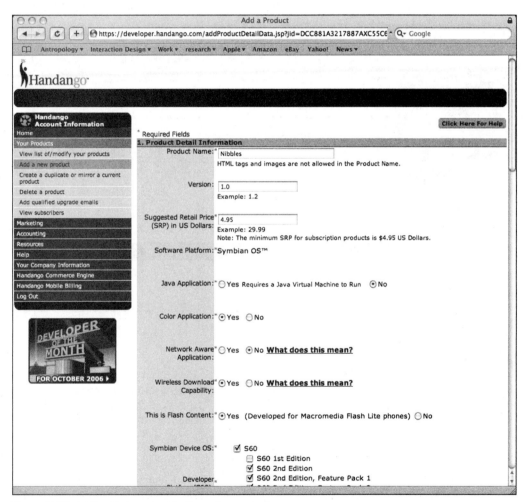

Figure 11-13. Adding Flash content to the partner web site

Figure 11-14. The products overview page of the partner web site

Service providers

In the mobile world, a **service provider** provides subscriptions or services to businesses or individuals. The service can be Internet access or mobile content to subscribers. In this section of the chapter, I will discuss service providers and how they provide their mobile content to subscribers.

FlashCast

Until this point, we have talked about Flash Lite as it relates to the creation of applications, games, wallpapers, screensavers, and other such content. You may have wondered, "Are there any Flash Lite–enabled products out there?"

Yes, in fact, FlashCast (www.adobe.com/products/flashcast) is a product that has been around for quite some time in the Flash mobile world (since Flash Lite 1.1). For the most part, FlashCast has been kept tightly under wraps by Adobe. Unfortunately, it remains a closed technology available only to operators and content providers, not to the public developer community.

Despite this limiting fact, FlashCast is a serious tool for the delivery and distribution of Flash Lite entertainment-based content, which is one the many reasons why I mention it here. In some respects, FlashCast acts as a specialized aggregator for Flash Lite content.

What is FlashCast?

FlashCast is a system developed by Adobe that was introduced early in the days of Flash Lite 1.1. It is an end-to-end, client-server solution that is designed to effectively create, deliver, and consume rich data services. In many respects, it straddles the boundaries between service, system, and product. It has evolved to become a successful tool for delivering mobile data services and content to devices.

Today, FlashCast is in use in several regions around the world. In Japan, it is utilized as part of the NTT DoCoMo i-Channel News and Information portal. Several other operators may be using it at the time that you are reading this book.

The Adobe FlashCast system consists of both a FlashCast runtime client as well as a proprietary FlashCast server on the back end. Scheduled content is delivered, or pushed, to devices over an operator's network. FlashCast utilizes an occasionally connected and persistent data model to move content and data from the server to the FlashCast-enabled clients.

The diagram shown in Figure 11-15 shows that there are several parts of the FlashCast system, including the following:

- FlashCast client
- FlashCast feed server(s)
- FlashCast data source server(s)
- Content aggregators and content providers

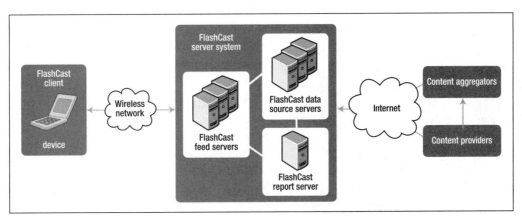

Figure 11-15. FlashCast architecture, from the Adobe whitepaper "The Macromedia FlashCast Solution" (2007)

For the sake of brevity, I will not cover all of these pieces of the FlashCast system in this book and will concentrate on the front end: the FlashCast client and FlashCast server.

What is a channel?

The FlashCast system provides channels that subscribers can "tune into." A **channel**, much like a channel on your TV, is an entity that contains content. FlashCast uses Flash Lite as the content contained within channels. The subscribers, in this case, are the individuals who are downloading the channels via their mobile devices.

The number and types of subscriber channels available depends on what the FlashCast service is set up to deliver and could be anything from data-feed information, such as news, weather, horoscopes, or sports scores, to entertainment applications, including games, ring tones, wallpapers, and screensavers. The possibilities are limitless.

Figure 11-16. Subscribing to a FlashCast channel

You can imagine a channel as being a bit like a slot in a vending machine. You have all these entertaining goodies (channels) that you can buy (subscribe to) from the vending machine (FlashCast server). Figures 11-16 through 11-18 illustrate some typical Flash Cast channels you may encounter in the marketplace.

Figure 11-16 shows the screen where you can subscribe to a FlashCast channel. Figure 11-17 shows the home screen, with a list of subscribed channels.

Figure 11-17. The home screen with subscribed channels

Figure 11-18. Example channel front page

Figure 11-18 shows the front page of a channel.

Each operator and content provider may choose to distribute specific channels to their subscriber bases. Data services and entertainment are probably the best examples of marketable channels. Online animated comics, games, ring tones, sports scores, and horoscopes are all examples of the types of channels that exist today for subscribers lucky enough to have the service.

FlashCast client

The FlashCast client is a mobile device application that uses Flash Lite as the primary interface. By leveraging the Flash Lite Player, a much richer user experience is possible. The FlashCast client is responsible for caching and rendering channel content delivered to the device. An integrated menu system allows subscribers to navigate among the various channels offered. The client is also responsible for user interaction, memory, security, and content channel updates delivered from the FlashCast server at scheduled intervals.

At the time of this writing, the FlashCast client is approximately 550KB in size and requires a minimum of 128KB of memory to run. The client has implementations available in both Symbian OS and BREW platforms.

FlashCast server

The FlashCast service is managed and delivered by a carrier-grade server hosted by mobile operators. It is built on a J2EE-compliant component architecture that separates content aggregation from content delivery. The server manages subscriber accounts, aggregates information, delivers channel updates to subscribers, and processes billing transactions. It sends only incremental updates of channels used in the service for each subscriber of the system.

The overall server architecture (see Figure 11-19) is made up of a database data source server, feed server, and reporting server:

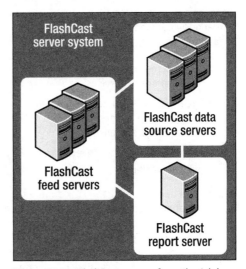

- **Data source server(s)**: The data source server downloads and collects channel content from the web servers of content aggregators and content providers. It passes this content to the feed server, which churns it out to the various FlashCast clients.

- **Feed server(s)**: It's the job of the feed server to deliver content and updates to the FlashCast clients. It also does quite a bit to manage bandwidth consumption, access control, billing for premium channels, and content discovery.

- **Reporting server**: The reporting server generates logs from the feed and data source server activities; it also allows for report generation.

Figure 11-19. FlashCast servers, from the Adobe whitepaper "The Macromedia FlashCast Solution" (2007)

The inner workings of these servers are quite complex, so I leave this subject for another mobile book dedicated to FlashCast, and the technology would have to be much more open for such a book to be feasible!

Mobile entertainment via FlashCast

Up until this point, we have been discussing how FlashCast plays an important role in the distribution of Flash Lite content. Although FlashCast is currently targeted toward information-retrieval channels, such as news and stock quotes, it is also being used to deliver interactive applications including polls, surveys, and blogs. The recent i-channel deployment targets these specific areas to their customer bases.

As the technology improves and more operators adopt FlashCast, we should see a lot more mobile entertainment available including games, downloadable ring tones, and other such media. It'll be exciting to see what kinds of channels appear and how the FlashCast technology evolves to suit the needs of the next generation of mobile users.

BREW

Recall from Chapter 2 that "BREW" stands for Binary Runtime Environment for Wireless, and it's made by Qualcomm. The BREW platform enables application developers to distribute their applications on BREW-enabled mobile phones, and it comes with an interesting marketplace for selling your creations. Qualcomm has three types of marketplaces where developers can sell their rich applications to clients:

- marketOne provides easy content delivery for fast deployment of services.

- uiOne allows you to easily offer content such as themes or ring tones (Figure 11-20 shows the uiOne home screen).

- deliveryOne offers developers a unified way to deliver content.

Today, users in more than 31 countries utilize BREW-enabled mobile phones for accessing content and services. Since July 2006, mobile operators have been able to distribute their BREW phones with Flash Lite for BREW. Of course, the decision to distribute Flash Lite rests totally with the mobile operators. Verizon is one of the major mobile operators that uses BREW in the United States.

The Flash Lite for BREW extension will be automatically downloaded over the air when the mobile phone user downloads the Flash Lite BREW application. This extension avoids the requirement to have Flash Lite already installed on your mobile phone.

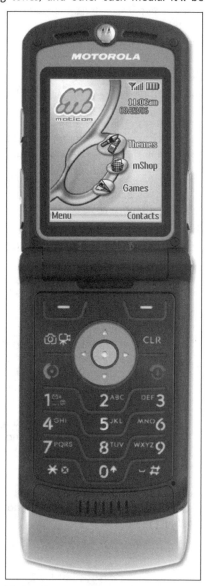

Figure 11-20. A BREW-enabled handset displaying the uiOneTM home screen

> *The Flash Lite for BREW extension supports only BREW version 2.1.3 or later.*

BREW and Flash Lite

Flash Lite for BREW makes the distribution of content easy, because Adobe has made a plug-in available for Flash 8 Professional that converts Flash movies to the native BREW application format for easy testing on a BREW device. Once your Flash movie works on a BREW device, you only need to be certified by Qualcomm to get your application in the pool of available content that can be leveraged by the mobile operators or aggregators.

If you want to test your Flash movie, you must be aware that the BREW-enabled mobile phone needs to be ready for development. More information on how to get your phone ready for development can be found at

```
http://brew.qualcomm.com/brew/en/developer/➥
resources/ds/business_faq.html#B15
```

> *Please note that Adobe has released Flash Lite 2.1 for BREW, as well as an accompanying update for the Flash 8 IDE to add support to create Flash Lite content for BREW-enabled devices. You can download this update at http://labs.adobe.com/technologies/flashlite_brew.*

i-mode

No chapter on distribution or deployment would be complete without discussing i-mode, Japan's premier mobile Internet service. As we discussed earlier in this book, Flash Lite has made a huge impact on the mobile economy in the Asian-Pacific region and continues to thrive, grow, and evolve at a rapid pace. Much of this content is provided through i-mode.

In this section, I hope to reveal how Flash Lite has played a part in the success of i-mode.

What is i-mode?

In 1999, NTT DoCoMo, a major operator in Japan, launched its data-centric Internet service—i-mode. Prior to that, the majority of the traffic was voice-centric. There was a need for more data-centric mobile applications and content.

Today, over 45 million i-mode subscribers are accessing content to conduct business transactions, check and send e-mail, play games, and even to perform such actions as booking train tickets and scheduling flights (see Figure 11-21).

NTT DoCoMo stared shipping Flash Lite 1.0 on i-mode–capable handsets in early 2003. Today, all new NTT DoCoMo i-mode–capable phones have at least Flash Lite 1.0 prein-stalled, if not Flash Lite 1.1. Surely, 2.0 will follow.

On the hardware front, with mobile phones transforming into multipurpose devices, such as music players, video players, cameras, and payment instruments, Flash Lite has an important responsibility to provide a richer and more user-friendly mobile experience for subscribers. Mobile graphical user interfaces designed, developed, and deployed using Flash Lite and FlashCast provide that much-needed experience!

> More information about i-mode can be found at www.nttdocomo.com/services/imode/index.html.

Figure 11-21. Sample i-mode content (animations and games)

The i-mode ecosystem in Japan

There is no question that the mobile economy in Japan is booming. Mobile commerce vendors made $9.6 billion in 2004 and an estimated $11.4 billion in 2005 (according to the Yankee Group). More than 20 million NTT DoCoMo subscribers have Flash Lite, including almost all 3G users. Among 3G users, more than 90 percent have Flash. There has also been a shift to 3G services in NTT DoCoMo phones that are enabled for Freedom of Mobile Multimedia Access (FOMA).

NTT DoCoMo and its competitor KDDI have enhanced their capabilities by adding additional services such as Flash Lite. With Flash Lite, as you have seen throughout this book, developing dynamic, cus-tomizable user experiences is both quick and easy. Creating engaging experiences, such as animated user interfaces, provides for content that is more quickly consumed.

More than 25 percent of i-mode users have received entertainment services; 24 percent of that con-tent has been made up of ring tones and image downloads, and games and horoscopes make up about 22 percent (Yankee Group Research 2005). About half of all content is entertainment related. It is an important part of the i-mode ecosystem.

NTT DoCoMo and Flash Lite

NTT DoCoMo was the first operator to realize the power of Flash Lite and incorporate it into its serv-ices. Today, the company heavily utilizes both Java and Flash Lite for a vast majority of its phones. As of the time of this writing, approximately 51 phone models are Flash Lite–enabled, and over 20 million subscribers have those phones. We can expect these numbers to increase as the market continues to evolve and expand. Although NTT DoCoMo remains the dominant player, there is a healthy competitor in the market who has taken an interest in Flash Lite as well: KDDI.

KDDI and Flash Lite

KIDDI released its first Flash-enabled phones in 2004 and has since been on a path similar to NTT DoCoMo's in its initial stages of deployment.

KDDI has differed from NTT DoCoMo in that they have provided a Flash Lite user interface in some of their initial models by utilizing Flash Lite 1.1 instead of Flash Lite 1.0, as NTT DoCoMo did with their rollout. Today, both rely on Flash Lite as a user interface instrument.

NTT DoCoMo and KDDI form the base of a Flash Lite–enabled mobile ecosystem for i-mode content in entertainment and other areas.

i-mode Flash Lite content

Flash Lite's first vital role in i-mode innovation was in informational services. This role has been steadily evolving to include other content areas such as databases, transactions, ring tones, stand-by screens, games, and other entertainment.

The breakdown of content available in 2005 follows:

- **Databases**: 5 percent
- **Transactions**: 9 percent
- **Ring tones and stand-by screens**: 24 percent
- **Information**: 12 percent
- **Games**: 24 percent
- **Other entertainment**: 26 percent

Animated ring tones (Chaku Flash) or personalized stand-by screens make up a significant portion of the Japanese mobile content available today. Flash Lite games are also gaining momentum as Flash Lite evolves. With the deployment of Flash Lite 1.1 (and 2.0 sometime in the future), it is likely games will become an even greater component of the mobile ecosystem in Japan. Currently, there are thousands of official Flash Lite–enabled i-mode sites accessible through the imenu (see Figure 11-22) on NTT DoCoMo phones. There are many more unofficial sites that serve Flash Lite content.

Clearly, Flash Lite has made an impact on the popularity of content served through i-mode. One such recently available content server is i-channel.

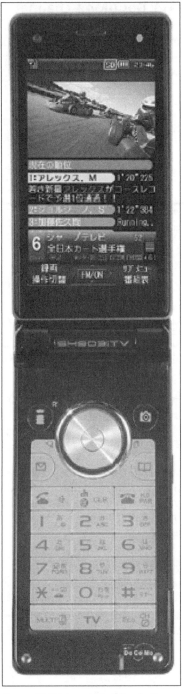

Figure 11-22. i-mode mobile phone with imenu

423

NTT DoCoMo i-channel

I mentioned i-channel in our discussion of FlashCast; this informational service was added by DoCoMo to try to attract late adopters to its mobile data services. It allows i-mode users to readily and easily attain information. Today, more than 2 millions users access i-channel. The amount of entertainment-based content will likely surpass the amount of information services as i-channel becomes mainstream.

Figure 11-23 shows an example of an i-mode i-channel.

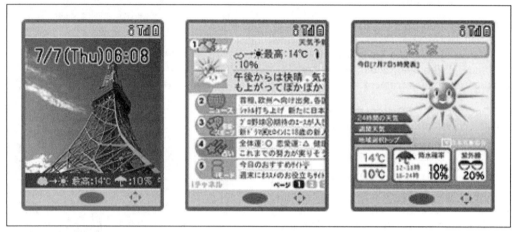

Figure 11-23. NTT DoCoMo i-mode channels

i-mode Flash Lite development

As we have been talking about throughout this book, Flash Lite 1.1 and 2.0 offer a great number of possibilities when it comes to building new, exciting, and entertaining pieces of content. This also applies to i-mode, but some limitations apply.

With Flash Lite 1.0, a file size of approximately 20KB was introduced because of restrictions outside of the player. Now with the Flash Lite 1.1 and beyond, that file size has increased to 100KB per content piece. The once-impossible task of creating a game or application is now a reality. As discussed previously, Flash Lite–enabled ring tones, stand-by modes, and games are a huge part of the success of i-mode content.

Flash Lite i-mode CDKs

I will not go into details about the Flash Lite CDKs for i-mode; I leave it for you to explore on your own. For the most part, content generation on the Flash Lite side of things is similar to that found outside of i-mode. If you are interested in developing for i-mode, I suggest you pick up a text dedicated to i-mode.

Flash Lite and the future of i-mode

For now, i-mode remains a Japanese market in regards to rich-media Flash Lite content. However, in the future, I hope that the services and technology available through i-mode, such as animated ring tones, i-channel, and other topics discussed in this section, will make their way into the global market. Already, this is happening to some degree in entertainment content (e.g., mobile TV and mobile music). We'll talk more about that in our last chapter.

Summary

In this chapter, you learned how you can make user-friendly installers for the clients of your mobile content. You learned to create a menu icon for your Flash content on Symbian mobile phones using the SFW2SIS wizard-style application and by compiling your own Symbian application (doing it the hard way). After that, we discussed several content-distribution options, such as Nokia Preminet and Handango, through which you can offer your content to a wide audience of potential buyers. Finally, I presented some information about the successful i-mode technology in Japan.

In the next chapter, we will discuss what Flash on mobile devices has brought us already, and what it can bring us in the future.

Chapter 12

THE FUTURE OF FLASH
IN THE MOBILE WORLD

Over the last few years, Flash Mobile has evolved significantly. From the first introduction of Pocket PC Flash on PDAs, to the more recent versions of Flash Lite on
other portable devices such as handsets and portable media players, Flash has had an
extraordinary impact on the current mobile landscape. This is true in several key
areas, most notably casual games, user interfaces, mobile applications, and entertainment. A lot of this we have already discussed in this book. All of these areas have
been met with great enthusiasm by both Flash users and other mobile professionals
around the globe.

But where is it all headed? What exactly *is* the future of Flash Mobile?

These are excellent questions. We will try to address them as best we can in the pages
that follow. Unfortunately, we can't make any guarantees or promises on
the thoughts given in this chapter. Perhaps some of our predictions will pan out;
others may not. The future is never an easy thing to predict, especially within the ever-
changing world of mobile technology! We do, nevertheless, provide some insight based
on our own experiences and observations, and the existing trends we find today.

Our personal feelings are that Flash Mobile is helping to revolutionize the way things
get done in the landscape of portable devices. But that's just our opinion—as you
read this chapter, you're likely to have your own thoughts on the future of Flash on
mobile devices. Now that you've nearly completed this book, try to draw upon your
personal experiences to form your own conclusions on what the future of Flash
Mobile might hold.

The evolution of Flash on mobile technologies

Over the past few years, Flash has grown from its humble beginnings as a vector-based desktop animation tool to the multimedia and application development tool it is today. With each successive release of both the authoring environment and desktop player, we have seen a commitment to new and innovative features, such as those found in Flash 8 and the soon-to-be-released Flash 9. As we discussed in Chapter 1, the evolution of Flash on the desktop has been a long and prolific journey.

But as the desktop Flash Player has continued to evolve, so too have its mobile counterparts: Pocket PC Flash, Flash Lite, Flash Lite for BREW, and even Flash Lite for Windows Mobile (see Figure 12-1)!

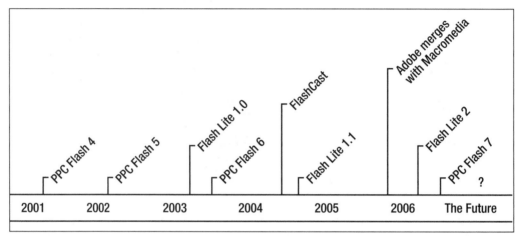

Figure 12-1. The Flash Mobile timeline

Having first started in the mobile PDA market with Pocket PC Flash applications (which we refer to as the "first generation" of Flash Mobile), Flash Lite has now found its way into mass market mobile devices including phones, personal media players, game consoles, and much more. With Flash Lite rapidly gaining ground on other existing mobile technologies, we have seen an enormous amount of effort by device manufacturers, operators, mobile developers, and other parties in leveraging Flash technology to make the mobile space a much more interactive, useful, and entertaining place.

One popular trend to come from these efforts is mobile entertainment, which we talked about in Chapter 7. This is especially true in Japan, the first epicenter of Flash Lite content. Today, this type of content is starting to proliferate around the world in several key geographical areas, including the United States and Europe. Casual games, screensavers, wallpapers, and animated ring tones are all being created with Flash Lite.

Another important trend is Flash Lite content distributed via FlashCast channels. The Japanese i-channel service is an excellent example of how this is being leveraged by millions of users (see Chapter 11) to interact with news, weather, and other types of information.

Flash Lite 2.X as a mobile application development tool (see Chapter 5) is yet another area that is quickly growing in popularity due to its advantages over existing mobile development tools such as J2ME and other platforms. As we have discussed throughout this book, mobile application development with Flash Lite is perhaps the easiest and quickest way to start developing content for mobile devices today.

Now that the Flash Mobile players are maturing, we are experiencing a second generation of Flash Mobile applications. The perception of Flash Mobile is evolving from merely a mobile entertainment tool to a powerful mobile applications platform.

The Flash platform and mobile technologies

With all of the Flash-based product innovation that has been happening over the past few years, it was only a matter of time before Flash was referred to as a platform. Products such as Flex, Adobe Acrobat Connect (formerly known as Breeze), and Flash Media Server (FMS) are just some of the tools that have enabled users around the globe to create and deliver Flash-based experiences in unique and highly interactive ways. The Flash platform is both a powerful and versatile one. All of these products and tools are used to create stunning and highly compelling user experiences.

It only makes sense that with the recent explosion of mobile technologies, the Flash platform now embraces the next era of technology: Flash on mobile devices. In fact, to be successful in the future, Flash Mobile needs to be part of this all-encompassing platform. Mobile applications and other content are quickly gaining popularity, and Flash offers a highly robust and interactive platform in which ideas can be built more quickly and easily than other products competing in this market space.

Also, let's think that a platform that allows desktop and mobile applications to more easily collaborate together is a powerful instrument in defining the mobile landscape of tomorrow. The notion of an "always connected" or "always mobile" world is a compelling one. I'm sure you can imagine a scenario where your desktop music, videos, and other content is always with you, *even* while mobile. This mobile framework is just one of the very promising ideas that the Flash Mobile platform has to potentially offer down the road.

But is this the future? We are not sure yet. There is much work to be done. We are only now just seeing the very first steps of this with services such as FlashCast. FlashCast provides a compelling example of how distributed content can impact mobile users in their daily lives (as discussed in Chapter 11). FlashCast offers a unique solution to delivering seemingly real-time content to thousands, if not millions, of subscriber handsets. Adobe is no doubt thinking about how the next iteration of FlashCast can reach even more people with even better features.

Also, let us not also forget the upcoming Adobe product code named "Apollo" slated to be released soon. Apollo will offer rich Internet applications the ability to run within a cross-platform runtime engine on supported desktop computers. What does this have to do with Flash Mobile? At some point in the future, it may make sense for mobile applications to communicate with Apollo applications on the desktop. Although this is not something that has been widely commented on, it is interesting to give some thought to how these two technologies might work together in the not-so-distant future.

Current Flash Mobile products and services

With Flash Mobile as part of the official Flash platform, we are starting to see the emergence of more products, services, and applications destined not only for the desktop, but for mobile devices as well. An important part of any established and healthy platform is that it has products and services. The existence and success of these two items is a clear indication that the technology is proving itself formidable in the marketplace.

We have already spoken of two of the Flash Mobile products and services, FlashCast and i-channel, in Chapter 11 and the Charajam in Chapter 7 of this book. Let's do a brief recap of these.

FlashCast

FlashCast is on its way to becoming an essential tool for delivering rich Flash Lite content to mobile users through its channels. With the impressive results and recent numbers (over two million subscribers) of the NTT DoCoMo (`www.nttdocomo.co.jp/english`) i-channel service (see Chapter 11), it is now apparent that companies such as NTT DoCoMo have found a more effective way of delivering their interactive and informational content to mobile customers. A better mobile user experience was needed, and companies are leveraging FlashCast as a means to get it to them. The mobile "push technology" that FlashCast empowers is likely to become one of the next-generation delivery mechanisms for interactive Flash Lite content. FlashCast offers a more controlled delivery solution in which Flash Lite content can thrive, grow, and mature.

Flash Mobile services

We have already talked about how Flash Mobile is making an impact on business. Small companies such as Charajam (`www.charajam.com`) and larger companies such as NTT DoCoMo are two such examples (see Chapters 7 and 11). There are many other such service and product companies in operation today. These are an indication that there is revenue to be generated by utilizing Flash Mobile technologies to provide services to mobile users. Speaking of which, the whole notion of return on investment (ROI) is an important one in the mobile service industry. We will discuss this further in the upcoming "Flash Mobile ecosystem" section. There is no doubt a clear demand for the Flash experience on mobile devices in the entertainment field, and more importantly, in Flash Mobile applications.

Mobile entertainment to mobile applications

We have seen a steady increase in the number of applications being created in Flash Mobile. With the introduction of the Flash Lite 1.1 and 2.X players (not to mention the Pocket PC 6 and 7 players), we have seen more practical and enterprise-focused Flash Mobile applications being created and deployed throughout the world. It's not just about entertainment and games; business applications and other enterprise tools are also important.

Flash Lite in particular is starting to evolve from its roots in animation and entertainment-focused content (Flash Lite 1.0 and Flash Lite 1.1) to more fully featured mobile applications (Flash Lite 2.X). As the marketplace demands more user-friendly applications and mobile experiences, the platform will adapt and evolve with tools and products to fit these needs.

Adoption of Flash Mobile applications in the marketplace is only a matter of time. Corporate businesses are already seriously looking into Flash Lite as their next strategy to tackling more mobile enterprise-type applications. With the generation of more Flash Mobile content and applications worldwide, ROI has become an increasingly important factor in the success and future of Flash Mobile.

The Flash Mobile ecosystem

Creating Flash Mobile ecosystems is yet another important task at hand. Adobe recognizes the importance of this and is taking steps to enable third-party companies to start aggregating and selling Flash Lite content online. They are working with these companies to define the ecosystems that will allow revenue generation from Flash Lite contents.

For example, Verizon Wireless, Smashing Ideas, Shockwave.com/Atom Entertainment, FunMobility, and the Moket Content Network are all currently aiming to aggregate and sell Flash Lite content through their own online services and catalogs. But where do these companies fall into the mobile ecosystem?

Apart from traditional client-server desktop computing, the mobile ecology is an interesting one. There are seemingly hundreds, if not thousands, of different entities in this ecosystem—from content providers, services, device manufacturers, and infrastructures, to enabling technologies such as Flash Mobile. The interaction between all these mobile "organisms" is a complicated and dynamic relationship. But where does Flash fit into this? What does the Flash Mobile ecosystem look like? What will it look like in the future?

From the very humble beginnings of Flash Lite 1.0 (as we talked about in Chapters 7 and 11), Japan's i-mode service has represented the epicenter of second-generation Flash Mobile technology—particularly Flash Lite. This area also represents the most successful ecosystem for Flash Lite content to date. That is changing as Flash Mobile sweeps across the globe into other regions. Flash Mobile has now penetrated into Europe and is slowly making its way into the United States. It was only a matter of time, energy, and money (arguably the most important factor) before this happened.

In order for the Flash Mobile platform to succeed, we're going to need successful ecosystems for Flash to thrive within the mobile space. These are systems in which profit can be generated, taken, and shared between all participants. As we see it, today's Flash Mobile ecosystem can be broken up into a set of layered, tiered entities, including the following:

- Operators
- Content aggregators
- Content providers
- Device manufacturers
- Content consumers

These five key entities represent what will need to grow and mature if a global or region-specific Flash Mobile ecosystem is to take hold and survive. The pieces of these complex ecosystems are already in the works as Adobe looks to license Flash Lite to operators and device manufacturers to stimulate the development of rich mobile user experiences through the use of Flash.

Next, we'll discuss some of the important pieces of information about each of these entities and their respective places in the Flash Mobile ecosystem food chain (see Figure 12-2).

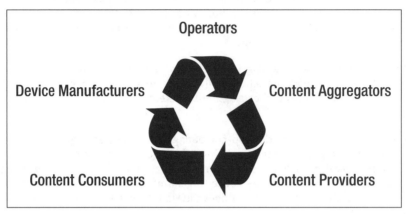

Figure 12-2. The Flash Mobile ecosystem food chain

Operators

The operators right now (such as NTT DoCoMo, KDDI, Verizon, and others) are the big fish in the pond. They are dictating in large part how Flash Lite content is being disseminated in various regions around the world. In Japan, Flash is a popular consumer-driven commodity. However, the rest of the world is just now catching up. For instance, Verizon already has Flash Lite content available to customers' handsets in the United States. Other operators around the world are likely to follow suit as Flash becomes a standard for smart phones and other type devices, and Flash content becomes more readily available to mobile users.

Content aggregators

Another important piece of the ecosystem puzzle is the existence of content aggregators—companies that specialize in cataloging, marketing, and selling mobile content. As these aggregators continue to build momentum and make it possible for money to be made, we should see more content produced for the ecosystem. Current aggregators of Flash Lite content include Nokia, Handango, Symbian One, Smashing Content, FunMobility, and Shockwave.com/Atom Entertainment.

Content providers and producers

On the middle tier of the food chain are the content providers, who range from companies specializing in Flash Lite to individual mobile developers. As creators of the content, these entities play a vital role for all within the Flash Mobile ecosystem. This tier is where you are likely to come into play—it's all about creating rich and compelling content for users, and managing the relationship between yourself and the content providers, aggregators, or operators.

Device manufacturers

Without the actual devices to run the Flash content, of course, the whole ecosystem falls apart. Device manufacturers are an important part of keeping the system healthy. With Flash Lite 1.1, we have already seen several encouraging deals made within the last year or so between device manufacturers and those with a vested interest in Flash technology.

Today, device manufacturers are now preinstalling Flash Lite 1.1 as well as 2.X onto handsets that are shipping throughout the world. Some of these current device manufacturers include Nokia, Samsung, Motorola, LG, iRiver, Fujitsu, Hitachi, Kyocera, Mitsubishi, NEC, Panasonic, Sanyo, Sendo, Sharp, Siemens, Sony Ericsson, and Toshiba.

Content consumers

These are the bottom feeders—the mobile users who want all this great content. They want a rich user experience on mobile, and they want it now. Without these consumers, the ecosystem wouldn't even exist. It is imperative that content providers seek to fill the needs of this group.

As you can tell from our discussion, the future of Flash Mobile is heavily dependent on the health of an ecosystem as we have described it here. However, each region will be different. Culture will play an important role in how these systems operate and thrive. As Flash Mobile technology evolves, so will these ecosystems.

The Flash Player roadmap for mobile devices

We have seen an amazing amount of innovation put into the Flash Lite technology, from its seemingly humble beginnings with animation and simple application content in 1.0 and 1.1, to the more sophisticated capabilities found in Flash Lite 2—such as video, sound, text, and OOP (ActionScript 2). We have also seen a push of the Flash Player 7 for Pocket PC and Flash Lite 2.1 for Windows Mobile 5.0 as of late. But what future does Flash Lite hold for mobile devices?

Surely more versions are slated for release in years to come—but is it likely for desktop Flash to meet up with mobile? While that remains to be seen, one thing is for sure: as mobile devices converge, and features and hardware become more sophisticated, Flash Player will continue to get faster, leaner, and more feature-packed to take advantage of all this device capability.

At some point down the road, the task will be making the functionality and feature sets of Flash seamless across all hardware. For now, though, it remains to be seen whether we will see the same exact player capabilities on both desktop and mobile anytime in the near future. Much more realistically, we can safely assume that Flash Lite will be around at least until devices and capabilities mature a bit.

We should expect to see Flash Mobile players to continue to evolve to provide the much-needed interactive and rich user experience that people are coming to expect of next-generation mobile content.

The Flash Mobile user experience

We believe that the success of the Flash Mobile platform hinges on the mobile user experience. It is clear that in large part, the mission of the Flash platform is to enable the much sought after "rich user experience." If there is one thing that Flash is great at, it's delivering an increasingly graphical and interactive way of presenting content to users. From custom Flash-based user interfaces, to content such as games and ring tones, to technologies such as FlashCast, the road is being paved.

Many device and handset manufacturers (including Sony, Samsung, iRiver, and Yukyung Technologies) are already using Flash Lite as their core means of navigation within devices, because it's cheap and easy to build, and provides the best user experience. Others in the consumer electronics market are also leveraging custom Flash players (most notably Leapfrog, Leapster, Kodak, and PSP). There is little doubt that the entertainment and user interface spaces have embraced Flash Mobile.

Also, the Pocket PC Flash marketplace is still very much alive and well. We are hopeful that the introduction of the Pocket PC 7 Player and Flash Lite 2.1 for Windows Mobile will bring a new era of exciting applications to the realm of Flash-enabled PDAs.

As these kinds of trends continue, we are likely to see more penetration of Flash Mobile into the marketplace, particularly with Flash Lite. The end goal, of course, is to have Flash on every mobile device screen possible, or simply to make Flash ubiquitous in the mobile world.

Potential obstacles ahead

With all good things, there are surely some hurdles to get past. We can expect this. After all, this second generation of Flash Mobile technology has only been around since early 2003. In many respects, it is still a new and emerging technology. Because of this fact, there are a few core obstacles that we are faced with.

Two important potential obstacles that need mentioning are the Flash Lite player penetration rate and the Flash Mobile ecosystem. If these can be addressed in thoughtful and innovative ways, the future of Flash Mobile appears to be a bright one. Adobe is hard at work addressing these potential roadblocks, and the Flash Mobile community is concurrently doing their part to set the stage for the next generation of Flash Mobile content.

Flash Lite Player penetration rate

The number one obstacle is probably the worldwide proliferation of the Flash Lite player, which is being thoroughly addressed by all the major device manufacturers. It's exciting to see devices outside of Japan finally come preinstalled with Flash Lite. For the foreseeable feature, we can expect more such devices sold and distributed across the worldwide markets.

Needless to say, having Flash Lite preinstalled is perhaps the cure for this particular problem, and everyone involved is making sure that it happens as quickly as possible. As we see it, this obstacle can be avoided if Adobe works diligently with the device manufacturers and operators. In many respects, this is happening now and will likely continue in the foreseeable future.

Many device manufacturers want to have Flash on their devices. Whether it is an added feature on the device itself or a core subsystem of the device (such as a Flash-based user interface), it is clear that the majority understand that the inclusion of Flash will make their devices better for their end customers.

A more ideal solution is to install the Flash Lite player via OTA (which is what Verizon has recently done with their service and content catalog). Instead of preinstalling the player on a device, you can download it along with an application or game.

Establishing the ecosystems

Clearly, the success of Flash Lite in Japan, Korea, and the rest of the Asian Pacific region has signaled many others in the world of mobile to take notice. Flash Lite now needs to go global. In many respects, this is happening as we speak. This is evidenced by the recent Verizon deal with Adobe to provide Flash to its customers, as well as the many announcements made with device manufacturers and other operators.

The creation of new content aggregators and providers is also a vital piece of this global ecosystem. Things are being ironed out, and meanwhile companies are figuring out how to incorporate their ideas and concepts into this new Flash Mobile ecosystem. Many are taking the "build it and they will come" approach, while those who have existing ecosystems are exploring new avenues for retaining existing customers and expanding to find new ones.

We are now just starting to see companies sell their Flash Lite content online, which is quite exciting. We are at the early stages of what appears to be a global ecosystem for the Flash Mobile platform.

Flash Mobile vs. the competition

No product or service exists by itself, and Flash Mobile is no exception. Throughout this book, we have made comparisons between Flash Mobile and other mobile technologies such as J2ME, C++, Python, Brew, and .NET. Deciding which tool is the best depends on the job, the requirements, and what you are trying to do.

The Flash Mobile platform is an attractive one for several reasons. Most notable are its speed to generate content, its rich feature set, and the level of interaction it provides in mobile content. Throughout this book we have touched on each of these areas. With all that you have seen in this book, I'm sure you'll agree that Flash Mobile is a powerful competitor in the mobile application development space.

Current and future trends

There is little doubt that Flash will continue to play an important part in the mobile entertainment space, particularly in the Asian Pacific region where it has become an essential part of the mobile ecosystem. But what will the second and third generations of mobile technology bring? What does the landscape of mobile Flash look like in a few years?

We believe that Flash Mobile (and in particular, Flash Lite) will be successful in a few trends that exist today, including the following:

- Flash Lite user interfaces
- Games and other forms of mobile entertainment
- Informational services (FlashCast)
- Rich media services (video and sound) and streaming services
- Rapid prototyping
- Mobile enterprise applications (for financial, government, medical, and science companies)

Surely there will be other new and exciting trends, including LBS (location-based services). Many of those will depend on how mobile technology evolves within each specific region. Culture of course plays a significant role in trends as well. Not all mobile users are a like. Each region has its own particular tastes for goods, services, and mobile practices.

Because of all these factors, it's anyone's guess as to how Flash Mobile will eventually pan out. Needless to say, we are very excited about the prospects of all these potential areas for Flash Mobile.

The Flash Mobile community

The most important part of any software platform is that a community surrounds and protects it. Flash is no different. For years, the Flash platform has survived due to the many efforts of designers and developers who believe in its capabilities and the future of Flash Player. The Flash community is truly an amazing one.

The Flash Mobile community has seen an explosion in the level of interest as Flash Lite has steadily become more advanced and powerful. Both designers and developers are finding new and exciting ways to change the mobile landscape using Flash Mobile technology. Other mobile developer converts are also finding Flash Lite a powerful tool in their daily mobile arsenal. Together, these two groups represent a powerful force.

As the Flash Mobile platform continues to mature and the ecosystem further develops, we're likely to see more folks join this community. This will fuel innovation in Flash Mobile technologies and further spark the essential mobile ecosystems.

For more information about the Flash mobile community, we recommend you check out the Flash Lite Yahoo user group at http://tech.groups.yahoo.com/group/FlashLite—it's one of the most active groups out there. Also recommended are the Adobe Flash Mobile user group of Boston at www.flashmobilegroup.org and the Flash Mobile Forum at www.flashmobileforum.org.

Of course, the Adobe Mobile Center is also a resource that should not be missed. Check it out at http://mobile.macromedia.com. These are all sites that play an important role in the growth and development of Flash Mobile.

If you're not already, it's time to get involved! As part of the Flash Mobile community, it is important that you participate. After reading this book, now is the perfect time to get actively involved and start creating your own unique and innovative applications, games, and other mobile content using the Flash Mobile tools available today.

Summary

In this chapter, we have laid out where Flash has been, where it is likely headed, and some of the potential obstacles it may face in the future. These are exciting times as Flash Mobile evolves, matures, and adapts to the needs of mobile professionals around the world.

From all that we have discussed in this book, the Flash Mobile future looks bright. The ideas are flowing and there is a very active and growing community. Companies are being established and ecosystems are being forged.

All in all, we can't wait to see how Flash will change the mobile world as we play a part in its continued success.

Part Four

APPENDIXES

Appendix A

ERROR CODES

This appendix lists the error codes and error messages for the various versions of Flash Lite. Table A-1 shows the error codes for errors that can occur in Flash Lite versions 1.0 and 1.1, and Table A-2 shows the error codes for versions 2.0 and later. (In the later versions, the missing error code numbers 5 and 9 are by design, probably because the engineers of Flash Lite see them as unlucky numbers.)

Table A-1. Error codes for Flash Lite 1.0 and 1.1

Error code	Error message
1	Out of memory.
2	Stack limit reached.
3	Corrupt SWF data.
4	ActionScript stuck. This error can occur if the code doesn't run within the preset time limits (normally meaning that the CPU of the device is too slow).
5	Infinite AS loop.
6	Bad JPEG data.
7	Bad sound data.
8	Cannot find host.
9	ActionScript error.
10	URL too long.

Table A-2. Error codes for Flash Lite 2.0 and later

Error code	Error message
1	Out of memory.
2	Stack limit reached.
3	Corrupt SWF data.
4	ActionScript stuck. This error can occur if the code doesn't run within the preset time limits (normally meaning that the CPU of the device is too slow).
6	Bad image data; corrupt or unsupported image file.
7	Bad sound data; corrupt or unsupported sound file.
8	Root movie unloaded.
10	URL too long.
11	Insufficient memory to decode image.
12	Corrupt SVG data.
13	Insufficient memory to load URL.

Appendix B

FSCOMMAND2 COMMANDS

This appendix gives a list of available FSCommand2 commands available in the different versions of the Flash Lite Player. Commands that are used by specific mobile devices won't be listed. Please refer to the development documentation of these devices to get an insight into the available commands.

> *Most of the FSCommand2 commands return a numeric value. If the command is not supported on the mobile device it will return -1, instead of the success value, 0 or higher.*

The two tables at the end of this appendix are for quick reference—print them out, and keep them at hand when you are developing your Flash Lite applications!

We use the word "deprecated" in certain commands' support information to indicate that although the command is still supported, there are other ways of accessing the given functionality. One example of this is is with the GetLocaleLongDate command. In Flash Lite 2 we can use the Date object instead, but you are still able to use the FSCommand2 command if you wish.

Launch

The Launch command enables you to launch another application on the mobile device. The command is only able to launch applications in the stand-alone Flash Lite Player. The supported parameter of this command is application-path, arg1, arg2, . . . , argn, with the name of the application being started and then followed with parameters separated by commas. The length of this parameter is limited, so verify that it works successfully on the mobile device of your choice.

Please note that this is an fscommand() command, and the support of this is dependent on the operating system of the device.

Support

Stand-alone Flash Lite Player only

Example of usage

```
appName = "z:\\system\\apps\\browser\\browser.app";
parameters = "http://www.flashmobilebook.com";
status = fscommand( "Launch", appName add "," add parameters );
```

Quit

The Quit command stops playback and exits the Flash Lite stand-alone player.

Support

Stand-alone Flash Lite Player only

Example of usage

```
status = fscommand2( "Quit" );
```

Escape

The Escape command encodes the given string to a format safe for network transfers; it returns the converted string in the given encoded variable.

Support

Flash Lite 1.1; Flash Lite 2.X (deprecated)

Example of usage

```
original_string = "My Original String";
status = fscommand2( "Escape", original_string, "encoded_string" );
trace( "Encoded String: " add encoded_string );
// outputs: Encoded String: My%20Original%20String
```

Unescape

The Unescape command decodes a given string encoded by the Escape command to its normal form; it returns the decoded string in the given encoded variable.

Support

Flash Lite 1.1; Flash Lite 2.X (deprecated)

Example of usage

```
original = "My%20Original%20String";
status = fscommand2( "Unescape", original, "encoded" );
trace( "Decoded String: " add encoded );
// outputs: Decoded String: My Original String
```

FullScreen

The FullScreen command shows the Flash content using the full display area of the mobile device. This command is only supported in the stand-alone Flash Lite Player, not in the embedded browser.

Support

Stand-alone Flash Lite Player only

Example of usage

```
status = fscommand2( "FullScreen", true );
if ( status != 0 ) {
  trace( "no fullscreen support" );
}
```

GetLocaleLongDate

The GetLocaleLongDate command sets a specified variable to the long format of the current date in the currently defined locale of the mobile device. For example, it returns a format like Wednesday, May 11, 2007.

Support

Flash Lite 1.1; Flash Lite 2.X (deprecated)

Example of usage

```
status = fscommand2( "GetLocaleLongDate", "current_date" );
trace( "The current date is: " add current_date );
// outputs: The current date is: Sunday, November 19, 2006
```

447

GetLocaleShortDate

The GetLocaleShortDate command sets a specified variable to the short format of the current date in the currently defined locale of the mobile device. For example, it returns a format like 11-05-2007 or 05/11/2007.

Support

Flash Lite 1.1; Flash Lite 2.X (deprecated)

Example of usage

```
status = fscommand2( "GetLocaleShortDate", "current_date" );
trace( "The current date is: " add current_date );
// The current date is: 19-11-2006
```

GetLocaleTime

The GetLocaleTime command sets a specified variable to the current time in the currently defined locale of the mobile device. For example, it returns a format like 22:56:39 or 11:56:39 PM.

Support

Flash Lite 1.1; Flash Lite 2.X (deprecated)

Example of usage

```
status = fscommand2( "GetLocaleTime", "current_time" );
trace( "The current time is: " add current_time );
// outputs: The current time is: 21:27:02
```

GetDateDay

The GetDateDay command returns the day of the current date; this is a numeric value between 1 and 31, without a leading zero.

Support

Flash Lite 1.1; Flash Lite 2.X (deprecated)

Example of usage

```
current_day = fscommand2( "GetDateDay" );
trace( "The day: " add current_day );
//outputs: The day: 19
```

GetDateMonth

The GetDateMonth command returns the day of the current date; this is a numeric value between 1 and 12, without a leading zero.

Support

Flash Lite 1.1; Flash Lite 2.X (deprecated)

Example of usage

```
current_month = fscommand2( "GetDateMonth" );
trace( "The Month: " add current_month );
// outputs: The Month: 11
```

GetDateYear

The GetDateYear command returns the day of the current date, this is a numeric value between 0 and 9999.

Support

Flash Lite 1.1; Flash Lite 2.X (deprecated)

Example of usage

```
current_year = fscommand2( "GetDateYear" );
trace( "The Year: " add current_year );
// outputs: The Year: 2007
```

GetDateWeekday

The GetDateWeekday command returns the number of the current weekday; this is a numeric value between 0 and 6, where 0 is Sunday, and 6 is Saturday. Table B-1 lists all the possible values.

Table B-1. The possible values of the weekday

Value	Description
0	Sunday
1	Monday
2	Tuesday
3	Wednesday
4	Thursday
5	Friday
6	Saturday

Support

Flash Lite 1.1; Flash Lite 2.X (deprecated)

Example of usage

```
current_weekday = fscommand2( "GetDateWeekday" );
trace( "The Weekday: " add current_weekday );
// outputs: The Weekday: 0
```

GetTimeHours

The GetTimeHours command returns the hour of the current time; this is a numeric value between 0 and 23. The hour is returned in 24-hour, or military, time.

Support

Flash Lite 1.1; Flash Lite 2.X (deprecated)

Example of usage

```
current_hour = fscommand2( "GetTimeHours" );
trace( "The Current Hour: " add current_hour );
// outputs: The Current Hour: 21
```

GetTimeMinutes

The GetTimeMinutes command returns the minutes of the current time; this is a numeric value between 0 and 59.

Support

Flash Lite 1.1; Flash Lite 2.X (deprecated)

Example of usage

```
current_minutes = fscommand2( "GetTimeMinutes" );
trace( "The Current Minutes: " add current_minutes );
// outputs: The Current Minutes: 29
```

GetTimeSeconds

The GetTimeSeconds command returns the seconds of the current time; this is a numeric value between 0 and 59.

Support

Flash Lite 1.1; Flash Lite 2.X (deprecated)

Example of usage

```
current_seconds = fscommand2( "GetTimeSeconds" );
trace( "The Current Seconds: " add current_seconds );
// outputs: The Current Seconds: 38
```

GetTimeZoneOffset

The GetTimeZoneOffset command returns the number of minutes between the current time zone and the universal time (UTC) in the specified variable. This numeric value can be both positive as well as negative; for example, -60 minutes is the value for European time (the Netherlands).

Support

Flash Lite 1.1; Flash Lite 2.X (deprecated)

Example of usage

```
status = fscommand2( "GetTimeZoneOffset", "timezone_offset" );
trace( "Timezone offset: " add timezone_offset );
// outputs: Timezone offset: -60
```

GetDeviceID

The GetDeviceID command returns the unique identifier of the mobile device (i.e., the IMEI number of the device in the specified variable). The command can sometimes cause a pop-up dialog on the mobile device as a security measure.

Support

Flash Lite 1.1; Flash Lite 2.X

Example of usage

```
status = fscommand2( "GetDeviceID", "device_id" );
trace( "Unique DeviceID: " add device_id );
// outputs: Unique DeviceID: 1234-5678-9012-345
```

GetDevice

The GetDevice command returns the identifier of the mobile device; normally this will return the model name of the device.

Support

Flash Lite 1.1; Flash Lite 2.X

Example of usage

```
status = fscommand2( "GetDevice", "device_model" );
switch ( device_model ) {
  case "Nokia 6681":
    trace( "The device is a Nokia 6681" );
    break;
  default:
    trace( "This device is: " add device_model );
    break;
}
```

GetFreePlayerMemory

The GetFreePlayerMemory command returns the amount of free heap memory, in kilobytes, available to the Flash Lite Player.

Support

Flash Lite 1.1; Flash Lite 2.X

Example of usage

```
free_memory = fscommand2( "GetFreePlayerMemory" );
trace( "Free player memory: " add free_memory );
```

GetTotalPlayerMemory

The GetTotalPlayerMemory command returns the total amount of heap memory, in kilobytes, allocated to the Flash Lite Player.

Support

Flash Lite 1.1; Flash Lite 2.X

Example of usage

```
total_memory = fscommand2( "GetTotalPlayerMemory" );
trace( "Total player memory: " add total_memory );
```

GetLanguage

The GetLanguage command returns the currently used language by the device. Table B-2 lists all the available language codes.

Table B-2. The available language codes

Value	Description
cs	Czech
da	Danish
de	German
en-UK	UK (or international) English
en-US	US English
es	Spanish
fi	Finnish
fr	French
hu	Hungarian
nl	Dutch
no	Norwegian
pl	Polish
pt	Portuguese
ru	Russian
sv	Swedish
tr	Turkish
xu	An undetermined language
zh-CN	Simplified Chinese
zh-TW	Traditional Chinese

Support

Flash Lite 1.1; Flash Lite 2.X (deprecated)

Example of usage

```
status = fscommand2( "GetLanguage", "language" );
switch ( language) {
  case "en-UK":
    trace( "The used language is International English" );
    break;
  default:
    trace( "The language is: " add language );
    break;
}
```

GetBatteryLevel

The GetBatteryLevel command returns the current battery level; this is a numeric value between 0 and the value returned by fscommand2("GetMaxBatteryLevel").

Support

Flash Lite 1.1; Flash Lite 2.X, no BREW support

Example of usage

```
battery_level = fscommand2( "GetBatteryLevel" );
trace( "The battery level: " add battery_level );
```

GetMaxBatteryLevel

The GetMaxBatteryLevel command returns the maximum battery level of the device for use with the GetBatteryLevel command; this is a numeric value greater than 0.

Support

Flash Lite 1.1; Flash Lite 2.X, no BREW support

Example of usage

```
battery_maxlevel = fscommand2( "GetMaxBatteryLevel" );
trace( "Maximum Battery Level: " add battery_maxlevel );
```

GetSignalLevel

The GetSignalLevel command returns the current signal level of the device, ranging from 0 to the value returned by fscommand2("GetMaxSignalLevel").

Support

Flash Lite 1.1; Flash Lite 2.X, no BREW support

Example of usage

```
signal_level = fscommand2( "GetSignalLevel" );
trace( "Signal Level: " add signal_level );
```

GetMaxSignalLevel

The GetMaxSignalLevel command returns the maximum signal strength level of the device for use with the GetSignalLevel command; this is a numeric value greater than 0.

Support

Flash Lite 1.1; Flash Lite 2.X, no BREW support

Example of usage

```
signal_maxlevel = fscommand2( "GetMaxSignalLevel" );
trace( "Maximum Signal Level: " add signal_maxlevel );
```

GetVolumeLevel

The GetVolumeLevel command returns the current volume level of the device, ranging from 0 to the value returned by fscommand2("GetMaxVolumeLevel").

Support

Flash Lite 1.1; Flash Lite 2.X

Example of usage

```
volume_level = fscommand2( "GetVolumeLevel" );
trace( "Volume Level: " add volume_level );
```

GetMaxVolumeLevel

The GetMaxVolumeLevel command returns the maximum sound level of the device for use with the GetVolumeLevel command; this is a numeric value greater than 0.

Support

Flash Lite 1.1; Flash Lite 2.X

Example of usage

```
volume_maxlevel = fscommand2( "GetMaxVolumeLevel" );
trace( "Maximum Sound Level: " add volume_maxlevel );
```

GetNetworkName

The GetNetworkName command returns the current network name. Table B-3 lists all the possible return values of the command.

Table B-3. The possible return values of the GetNetworkName command

Value	Description
0	No network is registered.
1	A network is registered, but the network name is not known.
2	A network is registered, and the network name is known.

Support

Flash Lite 1.1; Flash Lite 2.X, no BREW support

Example of usage

```
status = fscommand2( "GetNetworkName", "network_name" );
trace( "We are connected via: " add network_name );
```

GetNetworkStatus

The GetNetworkStatus command returns the current network status. Table B-4 lists all the possible network status values.

Table B-4. The possible network status values

Value	Description
0	No network registered
1	Connected to home network
2	Connected to extended home network
3	Roaming, not connected to home network

Support

Flash Lite 1.1; Flash Lite 2.X

Example of usage

```
network_status = fscommand2( "GetNetworkStatus" );
trace( "Network status: " add network_status );
```

GetNetworkConnectionName

The GetNetworkConnectionName command returns the name of the default or active network connection. Table B-5 lists all the possible return values of the command.

Table B-5. The possible network connection values

Value	Description
0	Successful, returns the active network connection name
1	Successful, returns the default network connection name
2	Unable to retrieve the connection name

Support

Flash Lite 2.0 or later, no BREW support

Example of usage

```
status = fscommand2( "GetNetworkConnectionName", "network_connection_name" );
trace( "Network Connection Name: " add network_connection_name );
```

GetNetworkConnectStatus

The GetNetworkConnectStatus command returns the current network connection status. Table B-6 lists all the possible network connection status values.

Table B-6. The possible network connection status values

Value	Description
0	Active network connection
1	Attempting to connect to the network
2	No active network connection
3	Network connection suspended
4	Network connection status cannot be determined

Support

Flash Lite 1.1; Flash Lite 2.X, no BREW support

Example of usage

```
network_connstatus = fscommand2( "GetNetworkConnectStatus" );
trace( "Network Connection Status: " add network_connstatus );
```

GetNetworkGeneration

The GetNetworkGeneration command returns the generation of the current mobile wireless network, for example, second generation (2G) or third generation (3G). Table B-7 lists all the available network generations.

Table B-7. Network generations

Value	Description
0	Unknown network generation
1	Second network generation (2G)
2	Two-and-half network generation (2.5G)
3	Third network generation (3G)

Support

Flash Lite 2.0 or later

Example of usage

```
network_generation = fscommand2( "GetNetworkGeneration" );
trace( "Network generation: " add network_generation );
```

GetNetworkRequestStatus

The GetNetworkRequestStatus command returns the status of the last HTTP request. The possible HTTP request status values are specified in Table B-8.

Table B-8. The possible HTTP request status values

Value	Description
0	Pending request: the network connection is established, the server's hostname is resolved, and the connection to the server has been made.
1	Pending request: the network connection is being established.
2	Pending request: the network connection hasn't been established yet.
3	Pending request: the network connection is established, and the server's hostname is being resolved.
4	The request failed because of a network error.
5	The request failed because of a failure in connecting to the server.
6	The server has returned an HTTP error (such as a 404 error).
7	The request failed while resolving the server name.
8	The request has been successfully made.
9	The request failed because of a timeout.
10	The request has not yet been made.

Support

Flash Lite 1.1; Flash Lite 2.X, no BREW support

Example of usage

```
netrequest_status = fscommand2( "GetNetworkRequestStatus" );
trace( "Network request Status: " add netrequest_status );
```

GetPlatform

The GetPlatform command returns the current platform of the mobile device; normally, this describes the class of the devices, for example, a FOMA1 or Symbian 8.0 phone.

Support

Flash Lite 1.1; Flash Lite 2.X

Example of usage

```
status = fscommand2( "GetPlatform", "device_platform" );
switch ( device_platform ) {
  case "FOMA1":
    trace( "The device is a FOMA1 mobile phone" );
    break;
  default:
    trace( "This platform is: " add device_platform );
    break;
}
```

GetPowerSource

The GetPowerSource command returns a numeric value, where 0 is a device running on battery power, and 1 is a device running on an external power source.

Support

Flash Lite 1.1; Flash Lite 2.X, no BREW support

Example of usage

```
powersource = fscommand2( "GetPowerSource" );
trace( "Powersource: " add powersource );
```

SetSoftKeys

The SetSoftKeys command enables you to remap the soft keys on the mobile device, if the command is supported. After the command is executed, the left soft key will generate a PageUp keypress event, and the right soft key will generate a PageDown keypress event. This command is only supported in the stand-alone Flash Lite Player, not in the embedded browser.

Support

Stand-alone Flash Lite Player only

Example of usage

```
status = fscommand2( "SetSoftKeys", "previous", "next" );
```

> Note that multiple soft keys are supported under Flash Lite 2.

GetSoftKeyLocation

The GetSoftKeyLocation command returns the current soft key location; this is a numeric value. The possible values are listed in Table B-9. The operating system of the device notifies the Flash Lite Player by sending an Insert key event—you need to implement a key listener to return the location to you, as shown in the example.

Table B-9. The possible values representing the soft key location

Value	Description
0	The top of the device screen
1	The left of the device screen
2	The bottom of the device screen
3	The right of the device screen

Support

Flash Lite 1.1; Flash Lite 2.X

Example of usage

```
on ( keyPress "<Insert>" ) {
    softkey_location = fscommand2( "GetSoftKeyLocation" );
    trace( "The softkey location: " add softkey_location );
}
```

ResetSoftKeys

The ResetSoftKeys command resets the soft keys to their original settings.

Support

Stand-alone Flash Lite Player only

Example of usage

```
status = fscommand2( "ResetSoftKeys" );
```

SetInputTextType

The SetInputTextType command enables you to set the input mode of the specified text field. Please note that not all mobile devices support all the possible input modes. If the input mode of the text field is successful, the command results in 1; otherwise, the value is 0. Table B-10 lists all the possible input modes.

461

Table B-10. The available input modes

Input Mode	Description
Numeric	Numbers only (0 to 9)
Alpha	Alphabetic characters only (A to Z, and a to z)
AlphaNumeric	Alphanumeric characters only (A to Z, a to z, and 0 to 9)
Latin	Latin characters only (Alphanumeric characters and punctuation)
NonLatin	Non-Latin characters only (such as Japanese)
NoRestriction	Default mode

Support

Flash Lite 1.1; Flash Lite 2.X

Example of usage

```
status = fscommand2( "SetInputTextType", "textfieldVarName", "Numeric" );
```

SetQuality

The SetQuality command enables us to set the quality of the rendering of animations. The possible values for the quality parameter are low, medium, and high.

Support

Flash Lite 1.1; Flash Lite 2.X (deprecated)

Example of usage

```
status = fscommand2( "SetQuality", "high" );
```

StartVibrate

The StartVibrate command starts the vibration mode of the mobile device; the command takes three parameters:

- The first one is the time_on parameter—the amount of time (in milliseconds) for which the vibration is turned on.
- The second one is the time_off parameter—the amount of time for which the vibration is off.
- The third one is the repeat parameter—the number of times the vibration should repeat (maximum is three).

The vibration will be stopped when the playback is stopped or paused and when the player quits.

Support

Flash Lite 1.1; Flash Lite 2.X

Example of usage

```
status = fscommand2( "StartVibrate", 3000, 1500, 3 );
```

StopVibrate

The StopVibrate command stops the current vibration of the mobile device.

Support

Flash Lite 1.1; Flash Lite 2.X

Example of usage

```
status = fscommand2( "StopVibrate" );
```

ExtendBacklightDuration

The ExtendBacklightDuration command extends the duration of the backlight for the specified time. The duration is given in seconds. If the time elapses without an additional call to this command, the backlight behavior reverts to the default duration. If duration is zero, the backlight behavior immediately reverts to the default behavior.

Support

Flash Lite 2.0 or later (device dependent), no BREW support

Example of usage

```
status = fscommand2( "ExtendBacklightDuration", 30 );
```

SetFocusRectColor

The SetFocusRectColor command sets the color of the focus rectangle to the specified color. The default color of the focus rectangle is yellow. The command takes red, blue, green parameters with numeric values between 0 and 255.

Support

Flash Lite 2.0 or later

Example of usage

```
status = fscommand2( "SetFocusRectColor", 255, 0, 255 );
```

FSCommand2 commands available in Flash Lite 1.1 or later

Command	Description
Quit	Stops playback and exits the Flash Lite Player
SetSoftKeys	Allows remapping of the multiple soft keys on the mobile device
ExtendBacklightDuration	Extends the duration of the backlight for the given amount of time (when supported)
FullScreen	Shows the content in full screen mode when run in the stand-alone player
GetLocaleLongDate	Returns the current date in long form, based on the currently defined locale
GetLocaleShortDate	Returns the current date in short form, based on the currently defined locale
GetLocaleTime	Returns the current time, based on the currently defined locale
GetDateDay	Returns the day number of the current date, for example, 28
GetDateMonth	Returns the month number of the current date, for example, 11
GetDateYear	Returns the year of the current date, for example, 2007
GetDateWeekday	Returns the numeric value of the name of the current day
GetTimeHours	Returns the hours of the current time in two digit form, for example, 7 or 21
GetTimeMinutes	Returns the minutes of the current time
GetTimeSeconds	Returns the seconds of the current time
GetTimeZoneOffset	Returns the number of minutes between locale time zone and universal time (UTC)
GetDeviceID	Returns the unique identifier of the mobile device, that is, the serial number
GetDevice	Identifies the mobile device, normally the model name of the mobile device
GetFreePlayerMemory	Returns the amount of free heap memory, in kilobytes, available to the Flash Lite Player
GetTotalPlayerMemory	Returns the total amount of heap memory, in kilobytes, allocated to the Flash Lite Player
GetLanguage	Returns the language currently used by the mobile device
GetBatteryLevel	Returns the current battery level of the mobile device
GetMaxBatteryLevel	Returns the maximum battery level of the mobile device
GetMaxSignalLevel	Returns the maximum signal level of the mobile device
GetMaxVolumeLevel	Returns the maximum volume level of the mobile device
GetNetworkName	Returns the network name currently used by the mobile device
GetNetworkStatus	Returns the status of the network

Command	Description
GetNetworkGeneration	Returns the generation of the network
GetNetworkConnectStatus	Returns the current network connection status
GetNetworkRequestStatus	Returns the status of the most recent HTTP request
GetPlatform	Returns the current platform and describes the class of the mobile device
GetPowerSource	Indicates whether the power source is a battery or external power source
GetSignalLevel	Returns the current signal level of the mobile device
GetVolumeLevel	Returns the current volume level of the mobile device
GetSoftKeyLocation	Returns the current soft key locations
ResetSoftKeys	Resets the soft key mappings to the default settings
SetInputTextType	Enables you to specify the mode of text entry
SetFocusRectColor	Sets the color of the focus rectangle
SetQuality	Sets the quality of the rendering of animations (high, medium, or low)
StartVibrate	Starts the phone's vibration feature
StopVibrate	Stops the phone's vibration feature

Commands deprecated in Flash Lite 2.0 or later

Deprecated Command	Flash Lite 2.X Description
Escape	escape() global function
GetDateDay	getDate() method of Date object
GetDateMonth	getMonth() method of Date object
GetDateWeekday	getDay() method of Date object
GetDateYear	getYear() method of Date object
GetLanguage	System.capabilities.language property
GetLocaleLongDate	getLocaleLongDate() method of Date object
GetLocaleShortDate	getLocaleShortDate() method of Date object
GetLocaleTime	getLocaleTime() method of Date object
GetTimeHours	getHours() method of Date object
GetTimeMinutes	getMinutes() method of Date object
GetTimeSeconds	getSeconds() method of Date object
GetTimeZoneOffset	getTimeZoneOffset() method of Date object
SetQuality	MovieClip._quality
Unescape	unescape() global function

Appendix C

GLOSSARY OF TERMS

AAC

Short for Advanced Audio Coding, a standardized lossy digital audio compression algorithm. Some see it as the successor of MP3.

ADPCM

Short for adaptive differential pulse-code modulation, a compression algorithm for digital audio.

AMF

Short for ActionScript Message Format. This is the data format used in Flash Remoting and by Flash Media Server. AMF is a binary format that is able to be rapidly transmitted over the Internet.

ANSI

Short for American National Standards Institute, a group that defines US standards for the information processing industry. ANSI is also known for the ANSI character set, which includes the ASCII character set and includes a further 128 characters.

APAC

Short for Asian-Pacific region. Countries in the APAC region include China, Taiwan, Korea, Malaysia, and Japan. The APAC region is commonly regarded as the most advanced in terms of mobile technology.

Apollo

A cross-platform runtime engine for Flash applications on desktop personal computers. Apollo allows for the inclusion of SWF and PDF files as well as HTML content in the same application. For more details, go to labs.adobe.com/wiki/index.php/Apollo.

API

Short for application programming interface, a set of interface definitions (functions, subroutines, data structures, or class descriptions) that together provide a convenient interface to the functions of an application and/or subsystem.

ASCII

Short for American Standard Code for Information Interchange. This standard describes the most commonly used set of characters in the English language as well as some special characters.

ASP.NET

ASP.NET is a web-development platform that can be used to build web applications and XML web services using Microsoft technologies, such as C# and VB.NET. Navigate to asp.net for more details.

AVI

A sound and (primarily) video file format on Windows systems.

BREW

Short for Binary Runtime Environment for Wireless. BREW is an application development platform by QUALCOMM for mobile phones; it's available in the United States and some parts of Europe and APAC. See brew.qualcomm.com/brew/en for more details.

bytecode

When code is compiled, it is converted into bytecode, which resides in the SWF file. The Flash Player knows how to read bytecode and executes the instructions contained within it to perform the logic inside your application.

CDC

Short for Connected Device Configuration. CDC is a device configuration for J2ME MIDlets. CDC devices include set-top boxes and have a little more processing power than their cell phone counterparts.

A device configuration is a set of criteria that a device must meet before being classified as CDC/CLDC. See also set-top box and CLDC.

CDK

Short for content development kit. A CDK is a collection of example files and documentation to get you started with creating content for a particular platform. You can find a CDK for both Flash Lite 1.X and 2.X at the Adobe web site (www.adobe.com/devnet/devices/development_kits.html).

CDMA

Short for Code-Division Multiple Access. CDMA is similar to GSM but optimized to use network bandwidth more efficiently. Therefore, it is good for long-distance transmission. See also GSM, EDGE, and 3G.

Chaku Flash

Animated ring tones popular on i-mode–based mobile devices in Japan. Chaku Flash has yet to reach areas outside of the APAC region.

class

A class is a collection of functions and properties. You can use classes to model an object in code, for example, a car. A car class might have properties like mass and topSpeed and functions or methods such as beepHorn and drive. Classes help to separate code into reusable elements. Classes can also be linked to library symbols to provide them with certain behaviors.

CLDC

Short for Connected Limited Device Configuration, a device configuration for J2ME MIDlets. At the time of this writing, most mobile devices qualify as CLDC devices. A CLDC device has very limited processing power and not a lot of RAM. However, there are cell phones being released now with more power, which qualify as CDC devices. See also CDC.

collision/collision detection

In gaming terms, a collision occurs when two sprites or movie clips intersect each other. Collision detection is the process of finding out when this happens and running some action as a result (see Chapter 6 for more about collision detection).

COM

Short for Component Object Model. COM is a standard developed by Microsoft for communication between applications; it was later extended with OLE and ActiveX. An example of this in action is when you copy data from a spreadsheet application and paste it into a word-processor document while keeping any formatting intact.

compile time

Compile time is the time when the Flash IDE or external compiler is examining all of your code and library assets, building the SWF file by evaluating the code you have written, and compressing the assets into a single SWF file.

CRM

Short for customer relationship management. CRM refers to the process of learning about and storing information on a customer base for the benefit of improving the sales or quality of a product or service.

DAO

Short for data access object. In computing terms, a DAO is an object that provides access to a storage mechanism, such as a database or hard disk. For more information, see http://java.sun.com/ blueprints/corej2eepatterns/Patterns/DataAccessObject.html. DAO also counts as a design pattern. See also design pattern.

design pattern

A standard set of code of functionality that solves a standard problem, thereby making it much easier to handle every time it crops up. For example, you could count Flash components as design patterns.

device sound

Flash Lite sounds that are played using a device's internal sound synthesizer components. MFi, SMAF, and MIDI are typical sound formats supported. See also MFi, SMAF, and MIDI.

device video

A 3GP or MP4 video that is played using a device's default mobile video player but can also be manipulated to some degree by Flash Lite via ActionScript commands.

design time

You are in design time when you are working inside the FLA or writing code. Nothing is running at this point—you may be adding things to the stage such as movie clips, and you may later choose to test the movie or compile the file.

DoCoMo

DoCoMo (meaning "anywhere" in Japanese) is Japan's biggest mobile service provider, with over 31 million subscribers. DoCoMo's i-mode is one of the few networks in the world that now provides subscribers with continuous access to the Internet via cell phone. The service lets users send and receive e-mail, exchange photographs, shop and bank online, download personalized ring melodies for their phones, and navigate among the more than 7,000 specially formatted web sites.

DOM

Short for Document Object Model, a representation of the structure of a markup document, such as an HTML web page. You can think of the DOM as a tree of objects, from the single trunk (the root element) right down to the individual elements on a page (the leaves.)

DRM

Short for digital rights management. DRM is a technology used to protect the interests of copyright owners; it's frequently used in the music and film businesses to discourage piracy. A file with DRM will often only run on a device that has been registered to the owner of the content, or it may be set to stop functioning after a specified time.

ECMA/ECMAScript

ECMA is short for European Computer Manufacturers Association. ECMAScript 262 is the standardized scripting language specification that both modern JavaScript and ActionScript 2 are based on. ActionScript 3 has also taken this same language as a basis—ActionScript 3 is actually the reference implementation for ECMAScript edition 4.

EDGE

Short for enhanced data rates for global evolution, an enhanced version of GSM or GPRS that allows for increased data transmission rate that's popular in the United States. See also GSM, CDMA, and 3G.

embedded Flash video

Flash video that is imported and used internally inside a Flash movie. The video resides on the Flash time line and is synched to the default FPS rate during playback.

EMEA region

Short for Europe, Middle East and Africa. Countries in the EMEA region include the countries of Europe such as the United Kingdom, Germany, and Spain; the countries of Africa such as Kenya, Niger, and Angola; and the Middle Eastern countries including Egypt, Saudi Arabia, and Turkey.

event

An event, in code terms, is a notification to a listening object that something the object was listening for has happened. You may dispatch events, meaning you broadcast a notification in the form of an event object. The event object contains information on what type of event has just occurred (e.g., a mouse click) the source of the event (known as the event target) and any other information you wish to include. In Flash, we use the EventDispatcher class to give an object the ability to manage listener objects, as well as dispatch events to them.

FlashCast

FlashCast is a flexible, client-server solution that effectively delivers rich, intuitive, branded mobile data experiences using Flash Lite. See www.adobe.com/products/flashcast for more details.

FLV

A Flash video file. FLVs are an increasingly popular video file format used by Adobe products; FLVs are not supported in Flash Lite 1.X or 2.X at the time of this writing.

FLS

A Flash Lite sound bundler file. An FLS file is required by the Flash Lite sound bundler to store information on which WAV/MP3 files to replace with mobile-specific sound files in the Flash Lite SWF currently being compiled.

FMS

Short for Flash Media Server. FMS is an Adobe product that offers video streaming capabilities. See www.adobe.com/products/flashmediaserver for more details.

FPS

Short for frames per second, the number of frames in an animation sequence shown in one second.

Short for first-person shooter. FPS can also mean first-person shooter; it refers to a genre of game in which you see out of the eyes of the character you are playing and have to rampage around battling enemies. Examples are Doom and Quake.

function

A function is a block of code that you can call upon to execute some logic over and over again when required. Dividing a program up into functions makes your code more efficient (you only need to write the code once, as opposed to every time you want to use it) and easier to follow (your code is more structured as a result), and the function's name lets someone know what that code does (as long as you've named it sensibly!).

GPRS

Short for General Packet Radio Service, a protocol for transmitting data over an operator's cell network (sometimes referred to as 2.5G). See also CDMA and 3G.

GPS

Short for Global Positioning System, a system that enables a device to triangulate its geographical position via satellites.

GSM

Short for Global System for Mobile Communications, a popular standard all over the world that allows cell phones to subscribe to networks operated by various operators for digital voice and data communications. See also CDMA, EDGE, and 3G.

handheld console

Any device for which the primary function is to play video games, for example, the Sony PSP, Nintendo Gameboy, or Nintendo DS Lite.

HCI

Short for human-computer interaction. HCI describes the process of any human being communicating with a computer system via a hardware or software interface.

HTML

Short for Hypertext Markup Language. HTML is the most widespread language found on the web. It's used for displaying text, images, and embedded rich content on web pages.

HTTPS

Short for Hypertext Transfer Protocol Secure, the standard protocol for delivering web content across the Internet securely using encryption.

ID3

ID3 is a tagging system that allows you to put music information into your audio files, for example, artist, song title, album title, lyrics, and so on. ID3 is commonly found in MP3 files.

IMEI

Short for International Mobile Equipment Identity, a 15-digit unique identifier associated with each modern mobile phone built.

i-mode

A popular Internet service found in Japan that allows i-mode compatible handsets and other mobile devices to connect to the Internet.

inheritance

Described in detail in Chapter 4, inheritance describes the relationship between classes when one class extends the functionality of another. For example, a Dog class extends an Animal class, and inherits its methods, such as eat and breathe, as well as having its own specialized methods, such as wag tail and bark. The parent class provides a base level of functionality, and the descendent class specializes and adds to that behavior.

JNI

Short for Java Native Interface. Java is designed to run on any supporting system without modification. The JNI allows platform-specific code to be executed using a common methodology.

JVM

Short for Java virtual machine. The JVM interprets the bytecode inside a compiled Java program and runs the program.

JSP

Short for JavaServer Pages. JSPs compile down to Java Servlets and provide a rapid way of developing dynamic web pages using the Java programming language.

J2EE

Short for Java 2 Platform, Enterprise Edition. J2EE is a platform from Sun that enables web developers to create large-scale web applications using the Java programming language. See java.sun.com for more information on this and other Java-related terms.

J2ME/JME

Short for Java 2 Micro Edition, a specialized version of Java used for developing applications for mobile devices. Programs written for J2ME are often referred to as MIDlets.

LBS

Short for location-based services. These are used to provide services to subscribers based on their current geographical position.

MAPI

Short for Messaging API, an interface developed by Microsoft that allows programs to send e-mails over the Internet.

MBCS

Short for multibyte character set. MBCS is an extended set of characters that allows for larger character sets to be used in applications, such as Hiragana, which is used in Japan. Each character is typically 2 bytes in memory, as opposed to 1 byte for ASCII characters.

method

Another word for a function, method is the term given to a function inside a class.

MFi

Short for Melody Format for i-mode, a popular format for storing sound information on i-mode mobile devices.

MIDI

Short for Musical Instrument Digital Interface, a standardized protocol for communication between electronic music devices and among computers and music devices.

MIDP

Short for Mobile Information Device Profile. At the time of this writing, this is either MIDP 1.0 or MIDP 2.0, a profile used to separate versions of J2ME programs written for mobile devices. A MIDP dictates that a certain level of software functionality is available to the host program.

MMI

Short for man-machine interface. An MMI is an interface or device that enables interaction between human beings and machines, for example, a computer mouse and keyboard or the steering wheel of a car.

MMS

Short for Multimedia Message Service. Often described as "picture messaging," MMS messages can include sounds and pictures as well as text.

MOV

Basically, a shortening of the Apple QuickTime Movie file format, and a popular video file format.

MP3

Short for MPEG Audio Layer 3. MP3 is a popular digital audio compression format. High compression rates make this good for music and sound effects equally, as it gives a good balance between low file size and reasonable quality.

MP4

Short for MPEG-4, a technology for compressing voice, video, and related control data. MP4 is the major rival to 3GP for mobile video files, as it can deal with much higher-quality files and includes more functionality for features like text overlays. On the downside, using MP4 can result in larger file sizes.

MSO/LSO

Short for mobile shared objects/local shared object. This is an object stored on the device's persistent memory (like the memory card or EEPROM.) You can use MSOs to store things like high scores, progress in a game, or cached data to save a call to the server.

MVNO

Short for Mobile Virtual Network Operator. MVNO refers to a company that provides mobile telephone services to its customers by buying network capacity from a network operator such as Orange or Cingular.

MXP

Macromedia extension format, a file format used by Macromedia (now Adobe) to package files that add functionality to existing products.

native sound

Sound played within the context of a Flash Player without hardware assistance, such as MP3 or WAV.

Nokia PC Suite

Nokia PC Suite software connects your Nokia phone to your Windows PC for fast file transfer and smooth synchronization (see http://europe.nokia.com/A4144903 for more details).

OMA

Short for Open Mobile Alliance. OMA is an organization that exists to oversee and govern mobile-specific standards. The OMA has subsumed several other committees, such as the WAP Forum and the SyncML initiative. See www.openmobilealliance.org for more details.

OOP

Short for object-oriented programming. OOP is a well-known programming paradigm that promotes the encapsulation of logic into different objects, or modules, for easier maintenance of the code and less code duplication. See also class and method.

operator

An operator is a company that offers a network infrastructure via which mobile devices can communicate with other mobile devices (for example, by voice, by text message, or over the Internet). Operators are also known as service providers. Examples include Verizon and Vodafone.

OTA

Short for over the air. OTA refers to any wireless networking technology commonly used to distribute applications through existing network infrastructure and over the Internet.

PPC

Short for Pocket PC, a PDA device that runs the Windows CE operating system. Flash 6 and Flash Lite 2 are available for certain versions of these devices.

PDA

Short for personal digital assistant, a handheld device that acts as a personal organizer. An example of this is a Pocket PC.

PHP

Short for PHP Hypertext Preprocessor, an open source programming language allowing web developers to create dynamic web applications that can interact with databases.

PIE

Short for Pocket Internet Explorer, the Internet browser that comes with Microsoft's Windows Mobile operating system.

PIM

Short for personal information management. PIM refers to the management of information pertaining to people, such as names, telephone numbers, and postal addresses.

PMP

Short for Portable Media Player. Such devices tend to have large storage capacity and can play back a variety of video and audio formats.

precalculation

This is the process of working out (ahead of runtime) mathematical values that will be used in your application. By doing this, you save valuable CPU cycles, which can be put to better use, for example, speeding up the overall execution of the application.

PSP

Short for Sony PlayStation Portable. Sony's flagship portable game console, the PSP includes the Flash 7 Player in a firmware update and was made available in the fall of 2006.

QCIF

Short for Quarter Common Intermediate Format, a standardized video format used for video conferences with a resolution of 176×144 pixels.

RDF

Short for Resource Description Framework. RDF is a framework that allows for the description of any Web location using metadata. The aim is to provide better interoperability between the disparate technologies used online.

registration point

Represented as a cross in the Flash IDE, this is the center point for any rotations, translations (movement), and scaling performed on a MovieClip.

RMS

Short for Record Management System. The RMS is the persistent data store, or database, available to your application, for example, J2ME MIDlets.

RIA

Short for rich Internet application. RIA is commonly used to describe web applications written using Adobe Flash because of their rich-media nature. Also see www.adobe.com/resources/business/ rich_internet_apps.

ROI

Short for return on investment. This is the amount you gain (in monetary and other terms) for the amount you originally invested. This term is used often when referring to advertising campaigns, for example.

RSS

Short for Rich Site Summary or Really Simple Syndication. RSS is an XML-based format for delivering summaries of news stories or blog postings over the Internet (with links to full stories or articles). RSS usually operates under a subscription-based model where users can subscribe to an RSS feed to retrieve updates whenever the feed is updated.

RTSP

Short for Real Time Streaming Protocol. RTSP is a client/server protocol that simplifies the distribution of multimedia content on the Internet; it's used in Adobe's Flash Media Server to distribute audio and video among clients and servers.

runtime

The runtime is the time when your application is running, for example, when the SWF is displaying in the Flash Player. You cannot edit the code within your application at this time.

SOAP

Short for Simple Object Access Protocol. An XML-based format for the consumption of web services, SOAP enables the standardized description of web services parameters and return values and deals with the serialization of said values to enable cross-platform, cross-language communication.

scope

In ActionScript, scope refers to the object block the code is running in. For more on scope, see http://livedocs.macromedia.com/flash/8/main/00001220.html.

SDK

Short for software development kit. An SDK is a collection of files that provide you with documentation, examples, and code relating to a particular platform or system, like Flash Lite. SDKs also include required tools for developing content for the platform in question.

set-top box

A set-top box is a device that plugs into a TV and provides access to digital and cable TV networks. These devices have a computer chip inside them, so they can run certain types of computer programs, like games.

shell

A shell is usually described as a command-line interface through which users can issue text-based commands to tell an operating system to execute specific functionality, such as copying files or listing directory contents. One example is DOS. With modern operating systems like Mac OS X or Windows Vista, users don't need to have as much exposure to the shell. However, for developers, having knowledge of how to use it is often useful for the compilation of programs and automation of tasks.

SIS

SIS files are software installation packages for Symbian-enabled mobile phones. This highly compressed file format acts as an installation file for Symbian software. It can include a custom icon and security certificate as well as the program itself.

SMAF

Short for Synthetic Music Mobile Application Format. This is an audio format often supported by mobile devices.

SMIL

Short for Synchronized Multimedia Integration Language. SMIL is markup language used to integrate video, text, and sound using timed sequences when delivering multimedia content. Also see MMS.

SMS

Short for Short Message Service. A system that allows text messages to be sent from one device to another. SMS messages are usually 160 characters in length, although multipart messages of up to three times that length are now available.

socket

A socket is a computing term for a connection provided by a computer or device through which another computer can communicate with it over an agreed protocol. In Chapter 6, we set up an XML socket on port 2048 through which a Flash Lite application can communicate with another program written in Java. Sockets can also be used to push data to the other computer, because the connection is kept open, unlike HTTP. With HTTP, the connection is closed until a request is made, so the computer has to request information every time you wish an update to occur, for example, when you navigate to a new web page.

soft key

A soft key is one of several keys on a device (usually directly under the screen) whose functionality changes based on context. Typically, they are used as the primary input for Yes/Confirm/Continue or No/Back/Cancel operations in user interfaces.

stage

The stage is the canvas that forms the visual base onto which all graphics are drawn in Flash.

Symbian FExplorer

A free and full-featured file explorer for the Series 60 platform (see www.gosymbian.com/fexplorer_new.php for more details).

synthetic sounds

Synthetic sounds are device sounds such as MFi, SMAF, and MIDI that use hardware components to render audio playback. You can think of these files as mathematical descriptions of sounds. This makes them akin to vector graphics in that they are usually very tiny in file size. See also MFi, SMAF, and MIDI.

text field

A text field is a visual entity that has the ability to display text characters on screen in Flash movies or HTML forms, for example. Some text fields can also be used to receive text input from the user. In Flash, text fields are instances of the TextField class.

time line

In the Flash IDE, you will see the time line as a series of small rectangles in a panel above the stage. The time line denotes the passage of time, broken down into frames of animation. You can place items such as animations and events at various points on a time line, and as time passes, those items will come into being or be triggered. The same applies for code placed in frames on a time line. Every movie clip in Flash has its own, independent time line for you to use.

3G

3G is also known as third-generation mobile technology. This standard is faster than GPRS and CDMA and enables both voice and data to be transmitted simultaneously at high speeds to a mobile device.

3GP and 3GP2 (or 3GPP2)

3GP is a very common and highly compressed file format used in mobile phones to store video. This file format is a simpler version of ISO 14496-1 Media Format and is similar to MOV files (used by QuickTime). This format can only carry video encoded as MPEG-4 or H.263. Audio is stored in AMR-NB or AAC-LC formats.

URL

Short for Uniform Resource Locator, a standard way of describing the location of a file or service on the Internet, for example www.flashmobilebook.com.

WAP

Short for Wireless Application Protocol, a standard that is used to transmit simple web pages to mobile devices. This is increasingly being overtaken by the standard HTML/XHTML found on the web as devices become more powerful and can now handle it.

WAV

A waveform audio file. A common audio format created by Microsoft, WAV has become one of the standard ways to store sounds on a computer because of the wide range of compression options available and high-quality reproduction of digitized sound.

web service

A web service is nothing more than some server-side functionality exposed via the Internet, so that it may be invoked on another computer, such as a mobile device. The Flash Player can consume services to pass values to and retrieve data from web services. An example of this can be found in Chapter 5.

WiFi

WiFi is a technology and protocol that enables computers to connect to the Internet wirelessly through an existing personal or corporate network. Some newer devices have WiFi abilities built in. You might be using WiFi when you browse the Internet on a laptop in a coffee shop without plugging in any wires.

WML

Short for Wireless Markup Language, the tag-based markup language used to create WAP pages. Also see WAP.

WMV

Short for Windows Media Video, a proprietary streaming video format created by Microsoft.

W3C

Short for World Wide Web Consortium, the body that governs creation of the major web standards such as HTML and CSS. See www.w3c.org for more information.

XHTML

Short for Extensible Hypertext Markup Language. XHTML is a web standard similar to HTML but designed to be stricter in how it is written, and as such, more easily processed by computers and software. XHTML is basically a reformulation of HTML in XML. See also HTML and XML.

XHTML MP

Short for Extensible Hypertext Markup Language Mobile Profile, a subset of the XHTML specification designed for creating web pages for mobile devices.

XML

Short for Extensible Markup Language. XML is a markup language based on SGML, but it's more specific to web-based languages. XML basically allows you to create your own custom markup languages for different purposes. Examples of custom markup languages based on XML are XHTML and MathML. You can find out more about XML at www.w3.org/XML.

XPath

Short for XML Path Language. XPath is a language used to query XML data and return specific nodes or values contained within it. You can find out more about XPath in Chapter 5.

INDEX

P